CHILDREN OF THE SOIL

Children of the Soil

THE POWER OF BUILT FORM
IN URBAN MADAGASCAR

Tasha Rijke-Epstein

DUKE UNIVERSITY PRESS
Durham and London
2023

Project Editor: Lisa Lawley
Designed by A. Mattson Gallagher
Typeset in Minion Pro by Copperline Book Services

Library of Congress Cataloging-in-Publication Data
Names: Rijke-Epstein, Tasha, [date] author.
Title: Children of the soil : the power of built form in urban
Madagascar / Tasha Rijke-Epstein.
Description: Durham : Duke University Press, 2023. | Includes
bibliographical references and index.
Identifiers: LCCN 2023008652 (print)
LCCN 2023008653 (ebook)
ISBN 9781478025290 (paperback)
ISBN 9781478020486 (hardcover)
ISBN 9781478027409 (ebook)
Subjects: LCSH: Architecture and society—Madagascar—
Mahajanga—History. | Sociology, Urban—Madagascar—Maha-
janga—History. | City planning—Madagascar—Mahajanga—
History. | Mahajanga (Madagascar)—Social conditions. |
Mahajanga (Madagascar)—History. | BISAC: HISTORY / Africa /
East | ARCHITECTURE / General
Classification: LCC NA2543.S6 R5525 2023 (print) |
LCC NA2543.S6 (ebook) | DDC 720.1/03—dc23/eng/20230602
LC record available at https://lccn.loc.gov/2023008652
LC ebook record available at https://lccn.loc.gov/2023008653

Cover art: Comorian sailors in Mahajanga, Madagascar,
ca. 1886–89. Courtesy of Archives du Ministère de l'Europe
et des Affaires étrangères—La Courneuve, Série P-Afrique,
A009210. Photographer: Albert Pinard.

For David, for everything and more

And in cherished memory of Pier Larson and Mama Agnes
Ireo izay tsy nisalasala nonoro lalana ahy

CONTENTS

For much of Madagascar's history, toponyms have been key vectors through which competing, successive groups framed their relationships to land, articulated conceptions of authority, and laid claims to territory. During French colonial times (1896–1960), administrators Frenchified urban toponyms, changing Antananarivo to Tananarive, Toamasina to Tamatave, and so on. Following the socialist revolution under President Didier Ratsiraka, the Malagasy national government renamed most of the island's urban centers as part of a broader project of Malgachization designed to efface the French colonial and linguistic influence. For all cities other than Mahajanga, I use the colonial names when referring to the period of 1896–1960 and the current place names for all other times.

Mahajanga is the exception to this. Throughout this book, I have chosen to use the contemporary name Mahajanga. The city's name, like other toponyms and key terms differentiating social groups, has been highly sensitive to political-economic transformations in the settlement's long polylinguistic history. In chapter 1, I explain the particular origin stories that are tied to each of the city's early, distinctive toponyms (Moudzangayeh, Moudzangaie, Mouzangaye, Mazangaya). These competing founding narratives and associated toponyms reflect the contested claims over how, and especially *by whom*, the city was established. In their nineteenth-century written correspondence, Merina administrators referred to the city as "Mojanga." At the dawn of French colonial rule in 1896, officials condensed the multiple iterations of the city's name into "Majunga," which postindependence officials subsequently changed to "Mahajanga" in an effort to return urban toponyms to their precolonial appellations after 1960.

I retain Mahajanga not to disavow that other Malagasy toponyms have their own contested histories but for purposes of clarity and to avoid privileging one particular version of the city's name and founding narrative over another.

This book was born through the collective labor and nurturance of so many people, and my debts are multiple, vast, and profound.

My greatest debt is to those in Mahajanga with whom I was privileged to collaborate, conduct interviews, and spend time. Words cannot fully express my deep gratitude to Battouli Benti, Ben Houssen and family, Mama Moana and Natascha, Mama Agnes, Roland and family, and the many residents of Mahabibo who generously opened their lives and shared their stories. Ben Taoaby provided invaluable research assistance and helped me understand the nuances of Malagasy dialect in Mahajanga. He and his parents—formidable intellectuals and historians in their own right—understood this project, debated the ideas within, and ushered it forward through endless conversations and introductions to so many individuals and families. They advised me with candor, took my family as kin, and never held back. Mama and Papa Taoaby, *lasa ray aman-dreninay amin-ny fo.*

Many others in Mahajanga generously offered insight and encouragement, and guided the research in important ways, including Bachir, Tsiavono, Said Hassan, Papa Khaled, Maître Youssef, Pastor Tovo, Valentin Razafindrakoto, Moussa, Marie-Rose, Mama and Papa Naby, Beben'i Elio, Mama Be, El Had, Twawilo, Ibrahim Amana, Djamila, Herman, Ishmael, Mama and Papa Rokiya, Jeanne, Farida, and Pauline. I was privileged to have met Hasandrama toward the end of my fieldwork, and his grace and wisdom were remarkable. The women of the Manga *fikambanana* welcomed me graciously into their fold: Dadi'Antra, Mama Zala, Mama Nyaam, Mama Tamida, Mama Bonhomme, Maolida, Tombo, Mama Abdou, Mama Farida, and so many others . . . *misaotra indrindra!* A chance meeting with Fatima at the University of Mahajanga led to friendship and shared sisterhood with her family. Thank you to Amida, Mama Kama, and Jeannot. Casimir, Chanael, Johnson, Steward, Patrick, Larissa, Raisa, Tahiry, Warda, Eriky, Florencinet, Grace, Taratra, and Philemon shared their honest thoughts, their worries, and their inspiring, heartfelt desires to explore new terrains. Our neighbors in Amborovy-Petite Plage brought conviviality and friendship, bestowing on us what we will never be able to fully reciprocate. I thank especially Rasoa, Berna, and Mama and Papa Saondra and their whole family for early morning *mokari*, raw *tantely*, long talks at the seaside, and so many celebrations. Mama and Papa Pauline, Mama and Papa Tatamo, and Rafotsy and her mother brought fullness and care to our lives. I thank Mama Elio and Mama Toky for patiently teaching me Malagasy, for nurturing our home and family, and for their tireless labor and support, which enabled the fruition of the research for this book.

Colleagues at the Mozea Akiva, including Herimalala Raveloson, Hortensia Rasolofondraibe, Hervé Randrianantenaina, Nirina, and Evariste, opened space for collaboration on an exhibit and primed my understanding of Mahajanga's complex, multiconfessional landscape. Daily conversations with my office mate, Anrifi, stirred my interest in the *rotaka* of 1976–77; I thank him for facilitating an early and pivotal interview. Miray and Nandriana, the Shattenbergs, Florian Winckler and Yolanda Fernandez, and Anna and Patrice Patanna shared friendship, delicious meals, and lazy conversations during our time in Madagascar. In Antananarivo, Ramilisonina, his daughter Olga, and their family welcomed us heartily, aided us during preliminary research, and provided invaluable help on every level—logistically, emotionally, and intellectually—to our family during an uncertain and difficult transition.

I thank the skillful and generous staff at the many archives consulted in the course of this book's life. In Madagascar, I am grateful for the patient assistance of the staff at the National Archives of the République Démocratique de Madagascar (ANRDM) under the able-handed direction of Directrice Sahondra Andrimihanina-Ravoniharoson; the Foiben-Taosarintanin'i Madagagasikara (Geographical and Hydrographic Institute of Madagascar; FTM); Willy Rahetilahy at the Malagasy Bibliothèque National; the Bibliothèque de Musée d'Art et d'Archéologie; Academie Malgache; Bibliothèque et Archives Universitaires at the Université d'Antananarivo; and Lalaina Ramamonjisoa at Société d'Équipment Immobilier de Madagascar (SEIMAD). In Mahajanga, several families shared generously with me their private photograph collections, including the Tourabaly family, the Yakoubaly family, and the family of Abdallah El Had Ben Ali Mohamed. Fathers Bernard Guichard and Jean-Claude Randrianirina at Maison Lieberman opened access to the private papers of the late Fr. Roland Barq in the Spiritan Catholic Congregation Archives, and nourished me with wonderful meals and lively conversation. Verson Heriniaina went above and beyond the call of duty to help me navigate records at the Service de la Topographie et des Domaines, and the staff at the Commune of Mahajanga and the Fokontany of Abattoir patiently tolerated my presence as I sifted through their photographs and records. Beyond Madagascar, I thank the staff at the Archives Nationales d'Outre-Mer (ANOM) in France; the London Missionary Service Archives, School for Oriental and African Studies (SOAS), and the British Library in the United Kingdom; and the Cleveland (Ohio) Public Library (East India Collection) in the United States.

The work on this book began with a dissertation at the University of Michigan's Program in Anthropology and History, where I was privileged to learn in the rigorous intellectual communities in Anthro-History, African History and Anthropology Workshop, and Science and Technology Studies. One would be hard pressed to find a better set of mentors. As a paragon of generous mentorship, Gillian Feeley-Harnik has taught me everything I know about striving for authenticity in writing, finding delight in serendipity, and honoring the humanity of the dead and the living, in every realm of scholarly life. She has continued to be a thoughtful, encouraging mentor whose willingness to read multiple chapters improved this book. Gabrielle Hecht, through her own extraordinary example, shone light on possible paths of undisciplined and profoundly principled scholarship, and provided uncompromising rigor. Her unwavering support pushed forward not only this project but also my intellectual path in innumerable ways. Both Gillian and Gabrielle saw the possibilities and forms of this project long before I could. Derek Peterson modeled meticulous scholarship, offered generous feedback, and gave supportive advice that shaped the course of this book. David William Cohen, Will Glover, Paul Johnson, Mamadou Diouf, Alaina Lemon, and Ruth Behar were important influences who pushed me to think creatively and ethically about writing and thinking about the rich relationships between past and present. Fellow graduate students offered conviviality, read chapters of the book, and generously shared their commentary. Special thanks are owed to Robyn D'Avignon, Luciana Aenasoiae, Tara Dosumu Diener, Dan Birchok, Zehra Hashmi, Steven Sparks, Nafisa Sheik, Edgar Taylor, Davide Orsini, Brady G'Sell, Emma Park, Benedito Machava, and Sara Katz. Pedro Monaville, with his warm friendship, brought me back to center too many times to count.

I met Pier Larson early on in this project, and it was indelibly shaped by his intellectual influence, tireless fine-grained readings of the chapters, and steadfast belief in its importance. He was a mentor par excellence, even braving the ten-hour taxi-brousse trip from Tana to Mahajanga to give me much-needed guidance and encouragement at a tenuous, early moment of my research. Through his mentorship and scholarship, he taught me how to tread in the past with highest caliber of ethical exactitude and profound sensitivity to the predicaments of our historical actors. His sudden passing, in the midst of revising this book, left me at once bereft and immensely grateful for the gift of his inspiring scholarship.

Scholars working on Madagascar are fortunate to enjoy a vibrant, growing collegial community, and I am grateful to Samuel Sanchez, Seth Palmer, Patrick Desplat, Kristina Douglass, Zoë Crossland, Sarah Fee, Sarah Gould, Chantal Radimilahy, Solofo Randrianja, Genese Sodikoff, Dominique Somda, Brian Klein, Andrew Walsh, Henry Wright, Klara Boyer-Rossol, Wendy Wilson-Fall, and participants in the Madagascar Workshop who offered feedback on parts of the book. I am especially indebted to Jennifer Cole and Michael Lambek. Jennifer counseled me on the pragmatics of fieldwork with children, engaged heartily and critically with my work, and supported my academic path. Michael generously facilitated relationships with families in the city during my research, posed consequential questions, and brought his deep knowledge to bear on several chapters of the book. Their continual support and insistence on the book's importance sustained me, and their rigorous, fine-grained commentary guided revisions.

At Vanderbilt University, I have been fortunate to find a community of colleagues who have generously shared their intellectual gifts with me and helped curate this project into a book. My colleagues in the History Department were especially supportive of this project, offering incisive ideas, reading chapters, and encouraging me at every juncture. I am grateful to Moses Ochonu for his thoughtful mentorship, untiring support, and resolute commitment to African history. I extend a very big thank you to Moses, Ruth Rogaski, and Leor Halevi for reading the entire manuscript and offering crucial feedback that guided revisions. Many colleagues directly contributed to the ideas in this book and read chapters, including Emily Greble and Arleen Tuchman, who provided critical feedback on the introduction, as well as Ari Bryen, Kim Welch, and Joel Harrington. Ari Joskowicz leapt in to help me think through maps in the final stretch. So many other colleagues in and beyond the department offered words of spirited encouragement, exchanged ideas, and weighed in with advice at key moments, including Celso Castilho, Lauren Clay, Samira Sheik, Paul Kramer, Michael Bess, Sarah Igo, Jane Landers, Tom Schwartz, Helmut Smith, Eddie Wright-Rios, Ashley Carse, Rebecca Van Diver, and Betsey Robinson.

The writing of this book was sustained by the fellowship and solidarity of my writing group partners: Aimi Hamraie and Sara Safransky. They read multiple chapters and taught me much about the art of generous critique, celebrated the joys of staying with the process, and expanded my purview on cities. The Vanderbilt University College of Arts and Sciences provided a Dean's Manuscript Studio Grant that enabled Kate de Luna, Laura Fair, and Brodwyn Fischer to review and comment on the entire manuscript, and their feedback was key in the development of this book. Beyond Vanderbilt, I am grateful to Sara Newland, Liz Bendycki, and Kristie Buckland, who offered accountability, encouragement, and camaraderie during our collective sojourn through academia.

Over the years, I presented parts of this book's chapters and ideas at a number of institutions, including Emory University, Michigan State University, the Mellon Workshop on Technology Studies in Africa, and the Technologies-in-Use Workshop held at the Max Planck Institute and Oxford University, as well as at numerous meetings of the African Studies Association, the Society for the History of Technology, and the Urban History Association. The feedback I received animated the revisions of the book, and for their insightful commentary I thank Joshua Grace, Clifton Crais, Adriana Chira, Benjamin Twagira, Lissa Roberts, and Stephan Miescher. A special thanks to Lissa Roberts for her continued support and incisive engagement with parts of chapter 6. Several colleagues read chapters with great care, offered generous input, and provided much-needed encouragement, including Jane Hooper, Zoë Crossland, and Pedro Monaville. Ned Alpers, Thomas Vernet, Samuel Sanchez, and Sophie Blanchy responded to many questions without hesitation. Betsy Schmidt nurtured my interest in African history as an undergraduate, has been a mentor in the years that followed, and generously offered ideas on chapters of the book. Kim Greenwell and Matt Somoroff brought sharp editorial lenses to the manuscript revisions. I thank all those named and unnamed who offered kindness and substantial feedback, and whose work shaped this book. The shortcomings and errors in the book are mine alone.

The field and archival research so central to this book were supported by a Fulbright-Hays Doctoral Dissertation Research Award and by generous support from the Rackham Graduate School, Center for Afroamerican and African Studies, and the Museum Studies Program at the University of Michigan. During the research period, I was fortunate to have an institutional affiliation with the Musée d'Art et d'Archéologie at the Université d'Antananarivo, through which I benefitted from the intellectual acumen and thoughtful insights of Chantal Radimilahy and Jean-Aimé Rakotoari-soa. At Vanderbilt University, the College of Arts and Sciences generously supported summer research trips, teaching leave, and a Subvention Grant for the development of maps and images. Without a fellowship from National Endowment for the Humanities that provided year-long support for the revision and completion of this manuscript, this book would not have been possible.

At Duke University Press, I am exceptionally grateful to Elizabeth Ault, who engaged heartily with this book from our earliest conversations and who pushed me in productive directions. Jennifer Cole and an anonymous reader provided incredibly constructive, thoughtful responses that helped reshape the book in critical ways. Ben Kossak and Lisa Lawley carefully shepherded this book through the production process. Tim Stallmann offered his deft hand, patiently collaborating with me to render complex historical processes into the maps lying within the book.

Many people have traversed the long journey of this book with me, all of whom offered abiding moral sustenance. Monica Patterson extended a treasured friendship that stretched across continents and life chapters, supported me in the gullies, and inspired me with her brilliance. Longtime friends Elinor Gingerich, Kathy Brewer, and Ashley Zwick have been there through it all, offering encouragement, keen insights, and parenting wisdom. The Baudriller, Delbende, and Salmon-Ortiz families enriched our time in France through hearty companionship, delicious meals, and joyful moral support that will not be forgotten. Julia Cohen's friendship and grounded advice at pivotal, uncertain moments made this a better book. Laura Stark welcomed me to Vanderbilt, taught me strength in vulnerability, and gave me inspiration for writing. Joshua and Jess Kullock have offered spiritual sustenance and taught me much about the transformative capacities of showing up. Our family has been sustained and nurtured by the profound friendship of the Cheng family—Jenny and Ed and their lovely boys—who read and listened to ideas within the book, shared walks in the woods, and scooped up our children when I needed protected writing time. The Epstein family has given much encouragement over the years, and I thank you for your love and support.

The seeds of this book were planted by my father, Robert Rijke, who opened the world to me through his stories and who bequeathed a restless pursuit of knowledge. Over many years, the braided ancestries and peripatetic global trajectories of the extended Rijke-Parmentier-Servaye family nourished the embryonic curiosities that led to this book in far-reaching ways. My mother, Diana Conte, guided me toward things unseen, fostered an intuitive sense of the world, and courageously modeled living an examined life. The book would not have existed without her nurturance of our family—caring for our children, helping to keep our household running, and anchoring me when I became unmoored. My relationship to the world has been most deeply shaped by my sister, Kelly Shaw, who envisioned promise and possibilities in the tributaries of our lives long before I could. She gave warm nurturance through the darkest passages, enduring support, and infinite love and anchored me with her sage, generative questions and deep-hearted humanity. I thank her and Dave for buoying my spirits with laughter, levity, and delightful diversions.

My deepest gratitude is to David Epstein, without whom this book would not have been possible. Over three years in Madagascar, he traversed the muddy, red-ochre roads, built an expansive network of friends for our family in Mahajanga through his vivacious sociality, and perfected the art of cooking *ravitoto amin'voanio*. Over a thousand journeys and across continents, he brought laughter, pushed me ahead, sustained our family, and protected space and time that enabled the writing of this book. He has taught me more about boundless generosity and graced me with more love than I ever knew possible. I dedicate this book to him. Together, we've shared the greatest joys of life in our children, each of them gifts that transformed our understanding of the world. Micah, River, and Zara: you fill our lives with light, joy, and love beyond measure. You've lived your entire lives with this book, and this book was crafted in the crevices of our lives together. Thank you for grounding me in what matters most and for bringing me back to the present, over and again—to things buried and soaring; to the vulnerable, vibrant beauty that abounds; and to the promises that await.

To all, I say:

Ity kely, fa ny foko mameno azy.

What I offer is small, but it is given with a full heart.

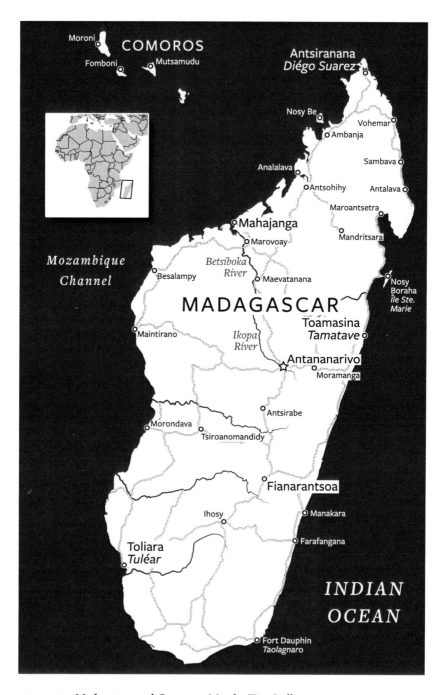

MAP FM.1 Madagascar and Comoros. Map by Tim Stallmann.

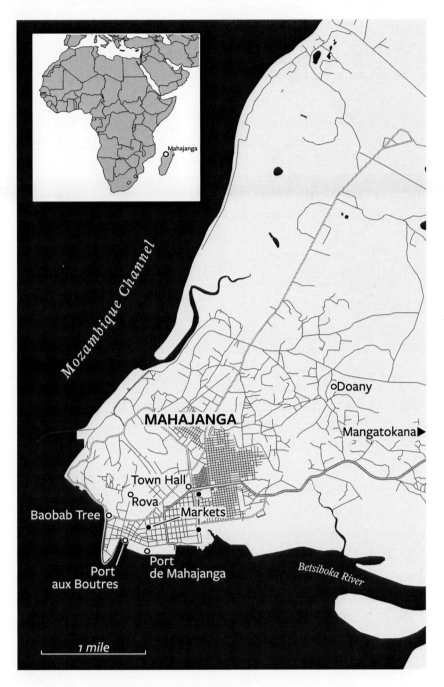

MAP FM.2 Mahajanga. Map by Tim Stallmann.

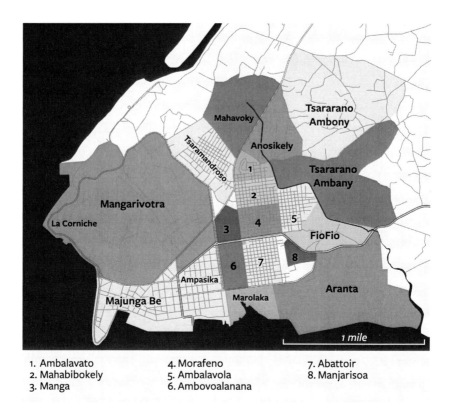

1. Ambalavato
2. Mahabibokely
3. Manga
4. Morafeno
5. Ambalavola
6. Ambovoalanana
7. Abattoir
8. Manjarisoa

MAP FM.3 Neighborhoods of Mahajanga. Map by Tim Stallmann.

MAP FM.4 Mahajanga (Majunga) during French Colonial Rule, 1896–1960.
Map by Tim Stallmann.

FIGURE FM.1
Mahajanga [Majunga
Ville] 1934.
Courtesy of Foiben-
Taosarintanin'I
Madagasikara.

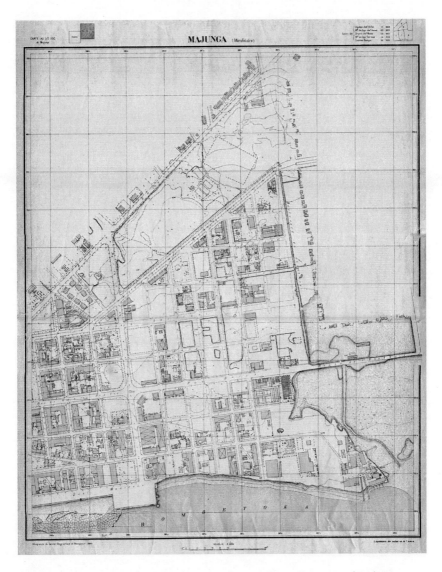

FIGURE FM.2 Mahajanga (Majunga Marofototra), 1934. Courtesy of Foiben-Taosarintanin'I Madagasikara.

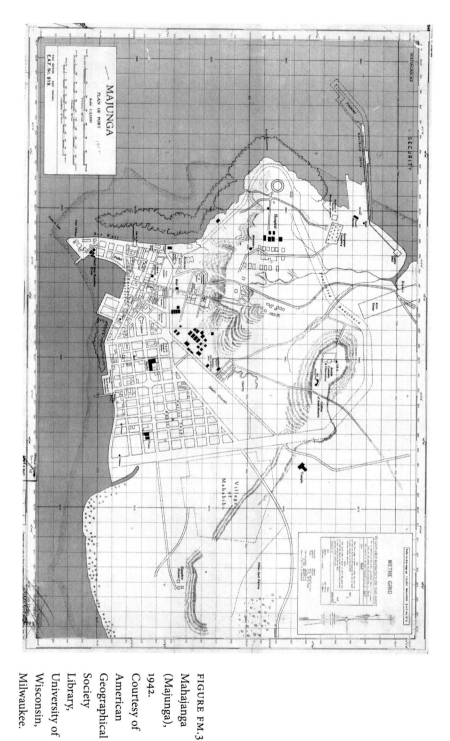

FIGURE FM.3 Mahajanga (Majunga), 1942. Courtesy of American Geographical Society Library, University of Wisconsin, Milwaukee.

Introduction

Material Histories

On a heat-saturated late September morning in 2012, the local neighborhood women's association (*fikambanana*) gathered to cook for a funerary ritual event honoring a deceased elderly neighbor in Mahajanga, a port city of some 300,000 people on the northwestern coast of Madagascar. Over cast-iron cauldrons steaming with *vary* (rice) and *girigitzi* (beef with coconut and tomato sauce), women of various ages traded stories and relayed jokes. Mama Nasra, one of the major leaders of the fikambanana, began to emphatically tell a story.[1] All eyes of the women nestled on the cool, concrete veranda, turned to her. "Listen closely," Mama Jaki whispered in my ear, "she's saying something important." When I finally caught the winding narrative, I gathered that Mama Nasra was describing a recent encounter with a newcomer in town. The migrant had questioned whether Mama Nasra was "really" Malagasy. Noticing her head and shoulder covering (*kisaly*) and flowing cloth wrap (*salovana*), the man had asked whether she was not in fact from the nearby Comoros, an island archipelago with a predominantly Muslim population. Muslims are a religious minority within Madagascar, but historically not so within Mahajanga, where they have comprised a significant portion of the town's population for centuries. Mama Nasra scoffed at the newcomer's ignorance and adamantly refuted his wrongheaded intimation that she might not be authentically Malagasy. "I told him," she passionately exclaimed, "my grandparents got this land, and they built their house of wood, and my parents rebuilt the house of corrugated steel! Ô! And now we've rebuilt the house of stone (*vato*)! You see this house, this stone house? This is proof that we've been here longer than you can imagine! We're children of the soil (*zanatany*)!"[2]

In the weeks and months to come, I would repeatedly hear similar stories. It became clear that Mama Nasra's account exemplified how people's senses of belonging to the city were intertwined with their spatial worlds. Although assertions to belonging have historically hinged on naturalized claims to land, the way Mama Nasra described the *texture* and *material substance* of her home was striking. By signaling the increased durability of her house, Mama Nasra indexed her family's investment in the city and their vested intentions to remain there, but she also forcefully affirmed their status as "children of the soil." What, I began to wonder, was the broader context of the city in which the accrued hardness of her home carried weight, and what kind of political import and imaginaries did durability offer? What did it mean to be a "child of the soil," and how did this category of belonging emerge and become linked to the material substance of her home? And how had the political, symbolic, and emotive valence of urban forms and building materials shifted from the foundation of the city and through its turbulent history under Merina conquest, French colonial occupation, and the postcolonial era? I came to gradually understand that for Mama Nasra and many others, one's home was a material artifact of their family's enduring continuity amid the convulsions of history and an evidentiary link among entangled lives, things, and places—past and present. Like other built forms, homes stood as archival sources, unfurled over a moral topography animated by the living and the dead, and ever mediated by asymmetrical political forces, ecological habitats, and tentatively held anticipations of the future.

Children of the Soil probes the significance of the material world in historical struggles to constitute power—over land, over people, and to define conceptions of belonging—in the Indian Ocean port town of Mahajanga, from its founding in the mid-eighteenth century through the cusp of independence in 1960. Drawing on archival and ethnographic research, this book explores how buildings in Mahajanga have served as politically charged inscriptions through which competing groups sought to rewrite the past, manage the indeterminacies of the present, and establish new conditions of possibility for aspired futures. As a history of city-making, this book chronicles how successive groups—Sakalava royal monarchs, highland Merina conquerors, Indian merchants, Comorian seafarers, and French colonizers—entwined ideas about power over people with specific building materials and designs, as they built their presence into the landscape. I argue that, in so doing, they transformed political debates about the relative value of lives, shifted the ethics of communal life, and determined the viability of social collectivities into dynamic building processes. At the same time, these negotiations and accruing architectural forms were indelibly informed by the more-than-human world—an uncertain domain of spirits, ancestral presences, trees, vital fluids, stubborn stones—in which they arose. In the chapters to come, I offer biographies of key human-constructed sites to illuminate how different groups labored and deliberated with one another and with the nonhuman realm through material assemblages, during shifting conditions associated with the expansion of global racial capitalism and imperial encroachment of the eighteenth and nineteenth centuries.[3]

Taking the lives of built spaces—in addition to written words, texts, images, and interviews—as its entry point, this book traces labor and materials to understand how agency operates through the deliberate and accidental efforts of people enmeshed in disparate political systems, with widely varying access to capital, ecological bounty, and otherworldly forces. Buildings occupy a mediating space between agency and structuring forces. As scholars have shown, buildings are both the outcome of overlapping human actions and ecological bequeathment and forces themselves that bear upon the possibilities of social interaction.[4] Built forms are ongoing processes through which people reflect broader sociopolitical hierarchies and relations, yet they also embody politics through distinctive material properties and arrangements that order socialities, channel mobilities, and enable collective imaginaries.[5] Yet it is through human action that buildings become meaningful and powerful things able to reorient historical trajectories. As a city of migrants, Mahajanga offers a vantage point from which to address more broadly how overlapping, densely clustered groups navigate the affordances and responsibilities of the city in their attempts to enmesh themselves in its social fabric. While the details are specific to Mahajanga, the challenges residents faced to negotiate their political possibilities, and the material strategies they employed, are characteristic of many African cities.

Recent scholarship has expanded the bounds of the archive, drawing on progressively more diverse sources, including images, archaeological remains, court records, novels, and song, to evince the experiential textures of everyday life and discernable agential acts of those who have left few, if any, written records. Over the past several decades, historians have developed increasingly nuanced methods for recuperating buried voices by combing through the documentary archive, churning it over, and reading suspiciously "against the grain" for counter-histories.[6] Yet African building dreams and urban designs have largely floated beneath the scholar's gaze. Historians and anthropologists of contemporary Africa have yet to fully explore built forms as lasting evidentiary sources, as epigraphs crafted by families and individuals who left few other written records, yet who inscribed buildings with memories, knowledge, and aspiration. Buildings are epistemic repositories that enfold historical narratives and unscripted imaginaries; as with any historical sources, our access to them is always mediated by layered histories of power.

Historians have often overlooked material forms, perhaps owing to their sheer omnipresence, which defies easy interpretation and challenges our confidence in fully grasping the capaciousness of history. Post-structuralist influences led scholars of Africa in particular to privilege interpretation of language, symbol, and ritual over material forms, and discursive notions of identity over embodied, technical expressive projects.[7] This need not be the case. Given the paucity of records for many communities across the African continent, the constraints of colonially composed archives, and the ever-more apparent need for decolonizing historical practice, I am convinced that buildings can and ought to be taken as evidentiary sources that reveal the experiences and aspirations of those who left few written traces.[8] Built sites exceed the written record; as archaeologist Lynn Meskell puts it, they are "material witnesses" that transcend generations and "instantiate the past in the present in a way that no textual account can fully achieve."[9] At the same time, Michel-Rolph Trouillot astutely reminds us that, like other forms of historical evidence, the material heft of buildings "hides secrets so deep that no revelation may fully dissipate their silences."[10] *Children of the Soil* contends that buildings—secrets and all—exhort us to explore the silenced and forgotten pasts that have been etched, sedimented, and compressed within and through them.

Attending to the histories embedded in materiality and ephemerality, commemoration and silence, also requires attending to the shifting role of the more-than-human world, which, no less than its earthly counterpart, has shaped the contours, temporalities, and designs of architectural forms across the city's history. Foundational to understanding power in many African contexts is the distributed nature of authority, in which ancestral spirits have not only been fundamental to political sovereignties but have also been capable of exerting force on sociopolitical and material conditions of life. Substantial scholarship in African studies has shown how topographies are laden with ancestral presences, spirits of the dead, and land- and water-dwelling spirits that impose themselves and wield power over human actors in authoritative, prohibitive, and concrete ways.[11] In Madagascar's historical context, active cohabitation between the living and the dead has palpably informed everyday life, and the living must continuously negotiate spirits and ancestral presences as they are entangled in the material world.[12] Spirits and ancestral presences are important figures in this material history, whether in determining appropriate conditions for building construction, forcibly "taking" living persons out of angry offence, or demanding offerings to rejoin a kin-based community. The particular tempos, demands, and contours of relations between the living and the dead are locally situated, but this general orientation has stretched across the diverse conceptual frameworks and broad expanses of time on the island.

Accordingly, *Children of the Soil* eschews the relatively discrete periods that organize most studies of early, colonial, or postcolonial building, casting its view across the broader expanse of time. Anchored in a two-century span, this book decenters colonial textuality and orality as the primary loci of historical knowledge production by foregrounding the forms people built, the materials they selected, and the activities they undertook in urban spaces from the city's earliest times, ever shaped by the political, economic, and ecological conditions at hand.[13] Rendering visible the (dis)continuities of emplacement and material expressions of citizenship across precolonial and colonial urbanisms, this study pushes against the reproduction of these as clear-cut chronological periods. Broadening the temporal frame also shows how early building processes took shape, and how subsequent rulers, builders, and everyday inhabitants grappled with *left-behind* architectural structures and remnants. Given the expansive breadth of time addressed, *Children of the Soil* does not attempt a comprehensive historical account of the city, but rather works through select sites that reveal broader dynamics of placemaking at key moments in time.

Chapter 1 offers a deep history of Mahajanga, describing how its founding and transformation in the mid-to-late eighteenth century emerged from major ecological, political, and migratory shifts in the region. Architectural tactics informed the regulation of communal life and the opening of new political possibilities during early Sakalava monarchal rule in the late eighteenth century. Chapter 2 charts the biography of a key site—the hilltop *rova* (governor's palace and fort)—and explores how Merina administrators in the mid-1800s drew on the knowledge and labor of competing groups to build themselves into power. Their authority was constructed and contested through the selective use of materials and architectural forms through which they intended to magnify their presence in the city and beyond. Chapter 3 examines how, following the French military conquest, colonial planners' visions to amplify their presence through built forms collided with the obstinate stone structures long established by Indian and Antalaotra traders. Indians in particular harnessed the architectural inertia of their homes and mosques to contest and negotiate colonial encroachment, but outbreaks of the bubonic plague in 1902 and 1907 stemming from the arrival of newly recruited workers from China and India brought unforeseen challenges to their efforts to retain autonomy.

The second half of the book considers what happened in the early to middle decades of the 1900s, when large numbers of Comorian migrants established households, drew on building acts to stake politically potent claims of autochthony, and positioned themselves as rightful heirs to the city. Chapter 4 excavates how burgeoning Comorian communities prioritized mosque construction as foundational means to root their attachments, even as they grappled with internal discord and intensifying colonial regulations. Enterprising leaders and everyday experts in these migrant groups creatively exploited the malleability of property regulations and erected gleaming limestone mosques that enunciated their ties to their adopted city, imprinted an Islamic presence on urban spaces, and invigorated their historic connections to the Muslim *umma* that spanned the Indian Ocean. Chapter 5 focuses on how mixed Malagasy-Comorian families established households and harnessed their homes to transform themselves, in contrast to new migrants from elsewhere on the island, from *vahiny* (outsiders) to *zanatany* (insiders)—the latter constituting a key idiom of inclusion, inflected by ideas of indigeneity and predicated on acknowledgment of the reciprocal relationships between the living and the already-present spirits dwelling in and around the city. By the 1960s, this generation of mixed progeny developed new expressive practices rooted in the street—a zanatany urbanism—that both reinvigorated and challenged long-standing moral norms around fraternal sociality, gendered spatial practices, and ancestral obligations. Comorian-Malagasy laborers played an important role in infrastructural work, and chapter 6 considers the city's waste and water systems as a lens through which to chart the political contours and affective dimensions of colonial-era infrastructure over the twentieth century. By flipping the script to show how particular people are worked into built forms, the chapter documents the continuous forms of harm spanning the life and afterlife of the colonial-era waste system. A brief epilogue connects Mahajanga's history of contested presence(s) to a critical, violent event in 1976–77 known as the *rotaka*, which revealed the perils of zanatany belonging and the unfinished work of decolonization.

Madagascar In and Beyond: The Port Town of Mahajanga

Far from a mythical, isolated "world apart," Madagascar has been central in the nexus of Indian Ocean, African, and Asian movements and migrations for centuries.[14] Settled at least 2,000 years ago by migrants coming from Indonesia and coastal East Africa, Madagascar's genetic and linguistic composition reflects these intertwined Asian and African influences. Archaeological evidence reveals how early migrants introduced technical knowledge in ceramics, metallurgy, and ironworking; plants, animals, and varieties of rice (which would become the island's staple); and divination and time-keeping systems.[15] In recent decades, scholars have documented the vital but overlooked role of Madagascar in African and Indian Ocean historical economies as a crucial site of provisioning that "tied together various regions of the world."[16] Within Madagascar, Mahajanga has a distinctive history of linguistic and cultural influences from Comoros, parts of East Africa, and beyond. Unlike its Swahili-coast counterparts, which emerged in the first millennium AD, Mahajanga was founded significantly later in the mid-1700s. Nourished by the lucrative trade in food provisions, cattle, and enslaved persons, it grew into what historian Sebouh Aslanian has termed a "nodal center" within southwestern Indian Ocean trade routes.[17] Nestled on a peninsula jutting into the Mozambique Channel and abutting the mouth of the Betsiboka River, the city benefited from its abundant limestone deposits, mangrove forests, and palm-studded grasslands as well as from the ample rice fields in its hinterlands. Culling from the earth's archive of stone, sand, and wood, compressed over decades and centuries, successive waves of migrants labored away, incrementally calcifying much of the city over generations. The correlation between durability and longevity was not always straightforward, however. Rather than following a simple teleology of soft to hard, ephemeral to obdurate, or thatch to stone, the becoming of Mahajanga witnessed the tangled coexistence of multiple materials with overlapping temporalities and distinctive meanings.

Profound historical transformations from the eighteenth century— including increased demand for enslaved workers in the French Mascarenes, Omani and European encroachment in the Indian Ocean trade region, and competition between island monarchies in Madagascar—brought an array of aspiring migrants and rulers to the city, each with distinctive ambitions and repertoires of expertise. Among the city's founders were Antalaotra seafaring merchants (akin to Swahili traders), whose Islamic ancestors hailed from parts of Arabia, East Africa, and Comoros and who, since the eleventh century, had traded along the shores of northwest Madagascar.[18] They forged coalitions with reigning leaders from the Sakalava Zafimbolamena dynastic state who had governed large swaths of the northwest in overlapping monarchies since the late seventeenth century. Traders and indentured workers from India (commonly referred today as *Karana*) arrived in the eighteenth and (in larger numbers) mid-nineteenth centuries, and many of them shared a common Islamic faith, but their Muslim ritual practices were by and large different from local iterations.[19] Those identified as Makoa (also known as Masombika), who came initially as captives through the trans-Mozambican channel slave trade in late eighteenth and mid-nineteenth centuries, adopted many of the Islamic customs of their Antalaotra, Comorian, and Karana slaving families.[20] Modest numbers of migrants from across Madagascar joined this polyglot community throughout the eighteenth and early nineteenth centuries.

Ruling over this vibrant trading port from the mid-1700s until 1824, Sakalava dynastic rulers faced challenges common to many precolonial African leaders. They needed to secure the allegiance of highly mobile political subjects of diverse origins, negotiate degrees of engagement with strangers, and navigate the ancestral presences through which they derived their power. Royal monarchs in and around Mahajanga built political community by pulling together people with different kinds of knowledge—technical, ritual, pastoral, and commercial.[21] They allied with Antalaotra traders who possessed commercial acumen, which afforded control over trade and access to lucrative tributes, enslaved captives, and imported goods like cloth and guns. They harnessed these prestige commodities into staged encounters with European traders, which almost always took place in royal architectural buildings. Royal compounds were constitutive to Sakalava political strategies of "extraversion," through which leaders cultivated ties to outsiders and selectively wielded foreign material objects to exert power in situ.[22]

Sakalava dynastic rulers combined these outward-facing strategies with tactics of architectural governance that linked them to their constituencies in reciprocal relationships of responsibility. Ritual prescriptions and prohibitions over building materials was a key way living royal rulers enacted hierarchies and called forth political communities through labor. In Madagascar, prohibitions on actions (*fady*) have historically been the means through which ancestral presences impose themselves and ruling elites demonstrate their authority over the living.[23] Many fady were rooted in specific places, designated the bounds of acceptable activity in a given locale, and were expected to be observed by all people dwelling in the city, not only those of Sakalava descent. Among these was a ban on constructing homes in durable materials that endured well into the eighteenth century. Hardened substances, especially limestone, were the preserve of the dead, material expressions of coldness and rigidity. By exclusively enforcing vegetative construction, Sakalava royal rulers (*mpanjaka*) sought to build their presence into the urban landscape.

Yet like any cultural practice, fady were and are dynamic processes that shift and change. By the 1780s, reigning monarchal leader Ravahiny (1780–1808) lifted this particular prohibition, making it possible for influential Islamic traders to solidify their political and economic connections.[24] Antalaotra masons and Makoa laborers brought well-honed stone-working techniques, which they used to erect double-storied, limestone homes near the port. In so doing, they drew on regional aesthetic and technical traditions that stretched from Mocha to Lamu and Mutsamudu.[25] These enduring stone houses became defining landmarks in the city, and their owners later drew on them as devices of architectural refusal to disrupt French planning initiatives.

During the early 1800s, the port city quickly became a key theater of contestation between two competing indigenous monarchies (*fanjakana*): the Merina kingdom in the highlands and the Sakalava monarchies on the northwest coast.[26] By the 1820s, Mahajanga had grown to between ten thousand and twelve thousand inhabitants who continued to claim wide-ranging origins: Antalaotra, Sakalava, Makoa, Hadrami Arab, Indian, Comorian, and migrants from across Madagascar.[27] Building on long-standing aspirations to dominate the island and with substantial British support, Merina monarch Radama I invaded the northwest region and took hold of its crown jewel, Mahajanga, in 1824–25. The conquest was violent, much of the city burned, and the reigning Sakalava ruler, Andriantsoly, together with part of the population, fled the region.[28] Merina administrators immediately occupied the Saribengo hilltop and rapidly constructed a military fort and governor's palace, informed by concepts of altitudinal power that equated elevation and access to air with political authority.[29] To efface the memories of the violent takeover and inaugurate a new era in the city's political path, Merina authorities ordered that a new shrine (*zomba*) be constructed within the fort's enclosure to encase the Sakalava royal relics (which Merina soldiers forcibly took from the existing shrine some 60 kilometers [40 miles] away), thus positioning Saribengo Hill as the ritual node of the region. By eviscerating the living presence of the Sakalava fanjakana in the urban landscape, Merina rulers foisted their dominating presence on the city. With this change, Mahajanga moved from relative resemblance to its Swahili coastal counterparts, with its mosques and stone houses, to a multi-confessional town in which Islamic religious structures were tightly juxtaposed with the town's Sakalava ritual shrine through the nineteenth century and joined by a wide array of churches in the early twentieth century.[30]

From 1825 until the 1880s, Merina rulers occupied the city. Despite the long-standing economic link between Mahajanga and the highlands, Merina authorities found themselves outsiders, unfamiliar with the city's distinctive Islamic and Sakalava political presence and cultural ambiance.[31] Nonetheless, eager to reap lucrative revenues from the city's trade flows, rulers imposed steep levies on arriving ships and incoming goods.[32] Beyond construction on the customs house and repair of the governor's residence, state-sponsored building projects lagged. Resentment mounted among inhabitants against the predatory state practices of local military officers who exploited their privileged positions to enrich themselves in the name of the Merina monarch. As English sailor J. S. Leigh journaled during his visit to the city in 1836, "the property of all inhabitants of Madagascar is at the queen's disposal, and she frequently makes use of it to pay her debts."[33] This policy of imperial plunder stretched into the 1830s and '40s and generated trade revenues that were critical for executing the monarchy's ambitious island-wide plans.[34]

Much of this hinged on unfree labor, a category encompassing both enslaved workers and obligatory labor required of all free men (*fanompoa*). Merina officials relied increasingly on the latter as French demands for slave labor in the Mascarene plantations depleted access to captives within the island; but for much of the nineteenth century, Madagascar's role within Indian Ocean slave trade was one of simultaneously demanding, supplying, *and* retaining enslaved persons.[35] Although scholars continue to debate the precise volume of enslaved persons transported through northwest Madagascar, and Merina official correspondence is silent on these figures, enslaved communities were an important presence in the city. Visiting Mahajanga in 1869, Alfred Grandidier observed that "the slaves were *more numerous* than the free; there were more than 1500."[36] These enslaved individuals were hardly a homogenous community; they derived from different origins within the region stretching between Malindi in the north and southward to the mouth of the Zambezi River, near Quelimane in present-day Mozambique.[37] Their demographic prominence in the city was matched by their critical role in labor regimes.

Even with the emancipation of enslaved Makoa (or Masombika, as highland officials referred to them) in 1877, Merina authorities continued to rely on forced labor regimes. By the late nineteenth century, an exhaustion of labor reserves, sweeping economic troubles, and persistent hostility from coastal regions caused the highland monarchy to falter. Mahajanga's economic future had already waned in the 1830s and '40s following the onerous imposition of taxes and a shift in trade routes to Zanzibar as the new hub of regional exchange.[38] Throughout much of the nineteenth century, French scientists, diplomats, and travelers eyed the prospective riches that could be extracted from Madagascar, such as cattle, honey, gum copal, and minerals. Building on their long-standing trading presence along the northwestern shores and growing aspirations for imperial conquest, the French military capitalized on the Merina kingdom's weakened state and undertook a series of attempted invasions during the 1880s. If Mahajanga served first for Sakalava rulers and then for Merina authorities as the gateway to Indian Ocean trade streams, for the French it provided a portal for colonial conquest. In 1895, French troops invaded the city, traversed overland to seize the highland capital of Antananarivo (Tananarive), and established Madagascar as their nucleus of colonial power in the Indian Ocean until 1960.

Building projects were foundational to French rule in Madagascar. The raising of buildings, monuments, and infrastructure served not only to justify France's *mission civilisatrice* on the island, but also to mediate colonial power through forced-labor regimes, demonstrations of technological prowess, and extraction of ecological plenty. Architectural absence was, for French colonizers, an impetus and justification to begin the material construction of colonization and to magnify their overall presence in the urban landscape, masking the paltry numbers of colonizers on the ground and expanding the dimensions of their control over local populations.[39] If colonial-era cities in Madagascar were "laboratories" for French planners experimenting with solutions to urban problems, as they were across the empire, they were also brought about through the pluralistic labor and knowledge regimes employed by colonial subjects.[40] Under French colonial rule, however, a conceptual category of buildings—en dur—that mirrored past privileging of durability under Sakalava dynastic and Merina rule was worked out through encounters between colonial subjects and officials. Initially, colonial officials prohibited *en dur* (durable, permanent) structures in an effort to ensure that the laboring population remained temporary. But certain groups, especially Comorians and their Malagasy-Comorian children, found ways to bypass those regulations and to construct mosques and homes in hardened forms that materialized their collective (even if fractured) hopes for the city in architectural forms.

Planners in Mahajanga redrafted the city's layout into a linear grid by dismissing long-standing Malagasy practices of cardinal spatial orientation and engagements with the spirit world, appropriating private properties (often owned by Indians), and forcibly displacing whole communities of Malagasy, Antalaotra, and Comorians. These measures cleared the way for transforming the city into what authorities hoped would be an engine of extraction, "the capital of the west and the future great port of the whole island."[41] Although officials saw economic potentiality in Mahajanga, their grandiose ambitions continually collided with ongoing labor shortages.[42] Turning to labor recruitment abroad, French rulers sought laborers from China, India, and Comoros, and streams of migration intensified from the Comorian archipelago in particular, bringing the Comorian population to some 50 percent of the city's residents by the 1950s.[43] By the mid-twentieth century, Mahajanga held the largest concentration of Comorians *worldwide*, including within Comoros.[44]

Comorians and their mixed Comorian-Malagasy families were particularly adept at integrating, partly through acknowledgment of the "customs of the land" (*fomban'tany*) associated with Sakalava ancestral presences that long inhabited the landscape. Featured as key protagonists in this material history, Comorians had for centuries traveled to and from Madagascar as traders, established Islamic communities, and exchanged linguistic practices with the Malagasy. With their long-standing ties to Madagascar and shared cultural lexicon, Comorian migrants ardently shaped the city's spatial and cultural terrain, marrying into existing Malagasy families, constructing mosques, and animating the street life. By pouring their vital energy and hard-earned capital into built forms, Comorian migrants positioned themselves as prime architects in the remaking of Mahajanga during the twentieth century. Contracted as wage laborers and joined by other migrant workers, they constructed roads, tin-roofed marketplaces, and a reinforced, cement wharf that, among other structures, ultimately overlaid the city's existing connective tissue. In bold, emotively infused ways, Comorians and their Comorian-Malagasy children leveraged these built forms to remake themselves into insiders of the city, weaving themselves into new lexicons of belonging that revolved around the concept of *zanatany* (children of the soil). Yet the durability of their emplacement was disputed by newer waves of migrants in a violent expulsion in the 1970s, exposing the ephemerality of their belonging.

Building Presences: Temporalities, Labor, and Indigeneity

In thinking about how and why urban buildings become political (and how urban politics are built), this book builds on a valuable inheritance of scholarship on urban pasts in Africa. This scholarship has traditionally been characterized by two overarching themes. On the one hand, scholars have shown how political institutions have instrumentalized built forms and urban designs to exert control and order society. Their work has explored how rulers—precolonial, colonial, or postcolonial—have drawn on urban space to perform their authority; set in motion economies of extraction; gather, separate, and discipline "unruly" subjects; harness heritage; and experiment with spatial solutions to urban problems on the continent and metropole.[45] In a second line of inquiry, urban studies scholars have explored the creative ways residents inhabited spaces of the city, carving out niches for sociality and self-determination, whether through leisure, conspicuous consumption, and expressive cultures; labor, religious, and nationalist movements; or associational ties and commercial endeavors. This work has revealed how city dwellers across the continent developed liberatory imaginaries and vibrant collectivities that animated everyday life and, at times, exceeded the scope of state governance.[46]

More recently, scholars have drawn together these two perspectives to grasp how urban spaces were transformed through the friction-filled encounters between inhabitants and political institutions and (especially when state presence faded into the background) among competing groups of inhabitants.[47] As historian David Morton notes in his important study of Maputo's built environment, urban space in much of colonial and contemporary Africa "constitutes a kind of multilateral politics that has not always announced itself as politics—or even in words."[48] This work has revealed that the dichotomized lens of "colonizer versus colonized" leaves in the shadows the ways subordinated groups have appropriated spaces and architectural forms to defiantly refuse dehumanizing conditions of racial capitalism through acts of construction, albeit with varying degrees of success. Large-scale urban planning projects were not technocratically driven, top-down processes, but rather were profoundly shaped by local officials, on-the-ground knowledge and praxis, and regional ecological conditions.[49] Scholars have shown how urban dwellers have constituted their claims to belonging and challenged colonial and contemporary regimes of power through the erection of domestic structures at times "illegally" and on the margins of the planned city.[50] More broadly, anthropologists have demonstrated how urban inhabitants construct buildings as an affectively saturated political act within creative repertoires of urban life.[51] Collectively taken, this body of work has shown how built forms are not only symbolic reflections of asymmetrical socioeconomic relationships, but also integral to the making of political lives and imaginaries.

Children of the Soil extends this burgeoning field of urban studies by offering a fresh approach to understanding urban becoming as a *material* process in which power, labor, and affective ties are woven and interwoven through built forms over time. Bringing together the world of materials and the world of symbols, this analysis attends to how people sought to build themselves into power, presence, and indigeneity through material forms, while buildings simultaneously shaped the conditions of urban possibility over time. If material forms are historical processes that have emerged from (and necessitated) particular conditions, then a fundamental task is untangling how the specificities of building materials and design have brought forth uneven sociopolitical relationships. Attention to materiality across several fields, including anthropology and archaeology, history, and science and technology studies, has shown how following objects across overlapping networks, geographical spaces, and timescales can help illuminate patterns of socioeconomic and political life in specific times and places.[52]

My approach draws inspiration from this scholarship by tracking the trajectories of particular materials—limestone, *satrana* palms, mangrove—over time as they were alchemically transformed from earthly matter into built forms, imbued with meanings that reflected emotive attachments, and gradually gained or lost import. For instance, limestone structures that enunciated authority under Merina rule in the late nineteenth century contrasted with earlier meanings of limestone as the realm of the dead, the material of ancestral tombs, and forbidden for the abodes of the living under precolonial Sakalava rule. The increasing use of limestone over the course of the nineteenth and twentieth centuries required specific technical know-how held only by some masons, shifted the temporality of maintenance, and reduced the frequency with which collectivities were brought together to restore structures and reenact their shared ties. Employing this approach to understand Mahajanga's history reveals how built forms and materials can become unhinged from their original associations, and then taken up and infused with novel meanings by historical actors in reconfigured constellations of agency. As material devices, buildings may be entangled in governance regimes rooted in particular logics—whether by Sakalava monarchs tethering veneration to ephemeral construction, or by French colonial authorities linking calculated standardization and notions of propriety with obdurate homes. Building materials were never exclusive instruments of *architectural governance*, however, and could just as easily be employed in acts of *architectural refusal*, such as when colonial subjects invoked their stubborn stone and rigid sheet metal houses to lay claims on French officials for compensation during the first half of the twentieth century. Even the most energetic efforts to radically transform urban spaces, whether from "above" or "below," were stymied by *architectural inertia*— the resolute resistance buildings impose through their material properties of malleability, porosity, or brittleness.

Centering the composition of buildings—whether ephemeral or lasting beyond generations—challenges conventional historical periodization and invites us to ponder multiple temporalities. The temporalities of matter— that is, the speed at which palm thatch decays, limestone crumbles, or corrugated tin roofs become brittle—stand incongruously with the finite lifespans of political dynasties, colonial rule, or successive postindependence republics, let alone the undisciplined temporality of ancestral spirits who intrude continuously on the living. As Anooradha Iyer Siddiqi recently noted, architecture is a "form of knowledge" with a distinctive "capacity to draw arrows to the past and, from there, the future."[53] Though building materials do not possess agency of their own accord, Tim Ingold has pointed out how they can "threaten the things they comprise with dissolution" through their comingling, decay, and intentional or unintentional destruction.[54] Once infused with vital substances (umbilical cords, animal fat, and bodily effluvia) and the vestiges of lives lived within their walls, moreover, building materials can carry residues that transcend generations and temporal passages. They can also serve as anticipatory devices through which different groups work to bring about their dreams—in the case of Mahajanga, for the revivified presences of past ancestors, the prosperity of their progeny, or the preservation of European dominance.

This book builds on the work of historians who have argued that objects are "vital sources of historical knowledge" that lodge the memories and experiences, emotions, ideologies, and intellectual aspirations of people "beyond" that which can be inscribed in textual or representational sources.[55] Although historians have considered material things as emotionally-laden "sources," I extend this to built forms, excavating how they can be ascribed overlapping, contradictory, and sometimes unspoken (though widely known) affective meanings through both everyday and ritualistic interactions of people and places.[56] This move coalesces with increasing attention among architectural historians to the nature of evidence and builds on earlier insights that buildings are revelatory of the moral valuations of those who produced them.[57] By privileging multiple, oft-marginalized voices—those of builders, caretakers, dwellers—I work to counter dominant narratives about the significance of spaces to show the pluralistic perspectives and knowledges at play. Like Mama Nasra described in the opening vignette, the labor of building construction and ongoing repair, which often stretched across family generations, enabled people to establish strong, emotive ties and enduring memories to the forms they inhabit.

What remains visible after the passage of time are the hardened forms—durable constructions of stone, brick, and concrete—that testify to compressions of aspiration, geological time, and particular assemblages of power. But if the city is an archival tableau, then, like the documentary archive, it holds not just political potentiality but also layered silences. Rather than latent, static things, the durable built forms that persist give credence to subsequent claims to authority and shape how historical facts are created, assembled, and narrated.[58] And like archival documents, these structures offer only partial insights into the past. How then does one apprehend the ephemeral, fleeting forms that have been effaced from urban horizons? This book offers one answer by attending continually to patent traces *and* willful erasures, and by charting *transgenerationality* and *ephemerality* as intertwined tactics through which builders, migrants, and governing authorities struggled to determine the built archive of the city. At times, the explicit choice to use ephemeral, vegetative building materials by Sakalava ritual practitioners afforded the fulfillment of unceasing, obligatory ties between the living and the dead, and assured the reconstitution of sociopolitical hierarchies through continual engagement in building maintenance.[59] At other times, architectural absence signaled the refusal of coerced laborers to build roads and civic buildings under conditions that stripped them of personhood during French colonial rule. As Saidiya Hartman has pointed out for archival silences in the Atlantic world, absences in the landscape sometimes signal violence that forever extinguished the hopes, thoughts, and dreams of those who once inhabited a particular place.[60] This study adopts a holistic approach that yokes together absences and presences, unbuilding and building, abandonment and transformation as relational practices that unfolded within the same spatial field of the city, but often to very different ends over time.

This attention to material statements and silences is particularly important in order to shed light on the agentic role of African builders and the valences they ascribed to materials. Cities are continual processes of dynamic struggle between competing groups, each of whom etch their presence on the archival tableaux of the built world through the (intellectual, political, ecological) means at hand. *Children of the Soil* takes successive waves of migrants—Sakalava ancestors and ritual experts, Islamic traders, Makoa captives, Merina soldiers, Comorian migrants and their Malagasy-Comorian families—to be the memorialists, each possessing varying degrees of latitude to construct epitaphs in the city's architectural history. The second half of the book, in particular, examines how acts of emplacement—whether through the building of a sturdy house, the burial of a newborn's placenta, or the suffusion of human excrement underground—involve not only reckoning with the accrued sediment of human, ancestral, and geological time, but also projecting into the past and the future claims to identity and belonging. Here, the book engages with and contributes to scholarly debates on ethnicity and citizenship by exploring how material designs and places have been tied to articulations of nativism and indigeneity—most often through the slippery concept of *zanatany*, which I examine in depth in chapter 5.

African societies have long been organized by paradigmatic principles of native and newcomer, even if ethno-racialist discourses have increasingly saturated debates over belonging in more recent times. Ethno-racial thought has been an important dimension to studies of the formation of indigeneity and to contemporary categories of ethno-territorial belonging in Africa. Recent studies have departed from the persistent but constraining questions of whether and to what extent ethnicity was "invented" and reified by colonial regimes; instead, they have investigated the ways local intellectuals have propagated and negotiated ethno-racial consciousness for the realization of exclusionary political projects.[61] While some scholars have tracked the convergence of violent new forms of exclusion and intensified discourses of indigeneity as relatively recent phenomena linked to African postcolonial political crises, neoliberal reforms, and globally circulating identity discourses, others have emphasized the layered, not-so-new histories of nativism.⁶² Work in both streams, however, has primarily privileged the world of symbols and discourses and has not adequately addressed the significance of materiality in processes of collective association. My approach builds on recent work that unsettles rigid binary frames of insider/outsider by signaling how people have performed affiliations with multiple communities of practice in material ways.⁶³ Architectural labor, that is, building, repair, and restoration—and at other times, architectural *refusal* to build in a certain place or to use certain materials—has constituted a central way Mahajanga inhabitants have expressed their moral standing as constituents of the Sakalava polity and established affective ties to the city.

Informed by the everyday theories and historical struggles of city dwellers, this book centers *zanatany* as an emic concept that contributes to scholarly understandings of indigeneity, the politics of urban space, and the significance of labor and affect by providing a fuller understanding of cities as ever-unfolding material and discursive historical processes. The multigenerational Comorian-Malagasy families who guided this research offered up the idiom of *zanatany* as a mode of life and historical category of belonging that is forged through struggles over placemaking in Mahajanga. Mahajanga inhabitants signaled *zanatany* as a category of urban citizenship, an intergenerational process of physically building one's presence into the city, and a critical mode of urbanism inflected by solidarity and conviviality. I ask: How has the concept of *zanatany* been redefined and constituted across shifting historical contexts? How have material designs and place—and their appropriation and reworking—been tied to articulations of *zanatany*-ness? What are the "techniques of the body," the bodily engagements with the material world of the city, by which *zanatany* has been rendered visible and made to appear natural?⁶⁴ These questions guide the latter chapters of the book, where I probe the historical construction of "names of belonging" in Mahajanga.⁶⁵

Like terms of belonging elsewhere, identifying as zanatany has historically been part of a forceful claim to insider status. Deriving from *zanaka* (offspring, but also plants, trees, or bushes that have been transplanted) and *tany* (earth, terrain, soil, land, country, kingdom), *zanatany* has an explicit autochthonous valence.⁶⁶ *Zanatany* is a slippery term full of contention about who can identify as an insider and which material indices authenticate zanatany claims. By tracing the genealogy of the idiom *zanatany*— which defies easy categorizations of autochthony, *créolité*, or cosmopolitanism—in Mahajanga, *Children of the Soil* reveals that nativist idioms can be much more capacious, encompassing far more than simply a reference to first-coming. *Zanatany* was not simply an autochthonous category; it was rather, as some residents suggested, a morally informed way of urban life replete with particular assumptions about consumption, habitus, and public decorum. As a category it implied a whole host of material, spatial, and bodily practices rather than just a claim to belonging by which some differentiated themselves from their neighbors.

The story of zanatany in Mahajanga offers a parable on the ethics of being a good settler. Interrogating the category of *zanatany* across time reveals a particular conception of belonging that is intrinsically anchored in spatial transformation and undertaken with reverence for earlier-dwelling (human and spirit) beings rather than in occupancy, property-holding, or nativist rhetoric alone. Self-identified zanatany inhabitants in Mahajanga emphasized repeatedly that the material realm and the symbolic, moral realm are mutually constitutive—one cannot be severed from the other. For many zanatany, being a settler came with a weighty moral responsibility to explicitly recognize the presence of those who already inhabited the land—the living and the dead—and to act responsibly toward the ritual prescriptions that governed those spaces, most of which were often associated with Sakalava political forebears and spirits. Unlike other documented cases of newcomers-turned-natives, zanatany claims to belonging were not constructed as negations of the presence of earlier groups, but rather were bound up with mutual recognition of ongoing reciprocity between living humans and already-there spirits in situ.

Methods and Sources

This book emerges out of the space between the animate presences in the city and the material vestiges of the past and the ways those architectural and archival remains are recapitulated, remembered, and effaced. In large part, the project was guided and shaped through my encounters with the living in Mahajanga, who then taught me how to attend more purposefully to the dead—to listen to their voices arising in the dusty archive, in *tromba* (spirit possession) gatherings, and in places inhabited by irksome spirits, throughout the city.

Children of the Soil draws on more than a decade of historical and ethnographic research, of which three years were spent in Madagascar, between 2011 and 2014. My family and I visited Mahajanga briefly in 2009 for preliminary research and then returned in December 2011 for twenty-nine months of intensive fieldwork. With our two young children in tow, we rented a home in the small fishing village of Amborovy-Petite Plage, just outside of Mahajanga, and we soon formed relationships with our neighbors and with families in town. Although I had studied Malagasy language for three years before arriving, I quickly encountered the politics of regional dialects and the shortcomings of using standard highland Malagasy in Mahajanga. Owing to ongoing tensions between coastal dwellers (*côtiers*) and highlanders and the historical dominance of highland polities across the island (discussed in chapter 2), standard Malagasy often carries negative connotations in the city. My search for a language instructor who could teach me the northwestern dialect spoken in the city led me to Ben Taoaby. Taoaby quickly became a dear friend and crucial intellectual collaborator. Born and raised in Mahajanga, Taoaby was from a mixed Comorian-Malagasy family that traced its roots across the region and to the Comorian archipelago. He was equipped with exceptional linguistic sensibilities and deftness for navigating social dynamics across ethnolinguistic lines. My first meeting with his parents, Mama and Papa Taoaby, revealed that our encounter was one knot in a broader tapestry of timescales and generations. Upon learning that I was an American researcher, Mama Taoaby fondly recalled her family's friendship with an American and her family who had lived for several years in Mama Taoaby's hometown, Analalava (some 430 kilometers [270 miles] away), in the 1970s. The realization that she was speaking of my mentor and dissertation advisor, Gillian Feeley-Harnik, brought us instant recognition and kinship; Mama Taoaby later insisted that our meeting was not happenstance but had been "destined" (*voa-soratra*; literally, "prewritten").

My collaborations with Ben Taoaby and his family shaped the course of this research in profound ways. During the early period of my research, Taoaby and I conducted many interviews together, and thereafter we spent countless afternoons with his parents on their veranda discussing the city's complicated social geography and layered histories. Mama and Papa Taoaby offered our family moral support, parenting advice, and stimulating intellectual provocations; our close partnership guided every step of my inquiry into how the past was remembered, invoked, and harnessed in contemporary Mahajanga. Their positioning as self-identified zanatany immersed me in the genealogical background and pressing concerns of this group of city inhabitants. A decisive shift came when Mama Taoaby facilitated my introduction to two *fikambanana*, which invited me to join them. She and the fikambanana members introduced me to other Comorian-Malagasy families who traced their ancestry to the unions between Malagasy women and migrant men from present-day Comoros. Comprising women from varying generations and class levels, the fikambanana was historically an important social institution through which large events were organized. Most but not all of the fikambanana members observed Sunni Islam to varying degrees, and a small but noteworthy group engaged in Sakalava spirit possession.

In addition to ethnographic encounters through the fikambanana, I sought out families of varied backgrounds, including newer migrants of different geographical, ethnic, and generational positions, to provide a wider purview of the contested ways people have negotiated the politics of space in the city. Our family's immediate neighbors and their daughter introduced us to many more recently arrived migrant families and invited us to consultations with ritual practitioners as well as to funerals, burials and exhumations (*famidihana*), marriages, and circumcision celebrations. Several times we travelled with other migrants to their ancestral lands (*tanindrazana*) and family tombs in the northwest region and as far as the highlands. These overlapping networks enabled multiple entry points through which I met and spoke with long-standing residents and newer migrants from wide-ranging backgrounds. Altogether, I conducted more than 120 semi-structured interviews with city inhabitants, urban planners, shopkeepers, ritual specialists, and religious leaders in Mahajanga. Within these personal accounts, I tracked how and when narratives congealed around key events, people, and concepts—and where they diverged.

Buildings and crucial sites—their design, material composition, residues, and destruction—are the book's primary portals into the past. Although oral accounts and ethnographic fieldwork shed light on contemporary concerns, remembered pasts, and the historical consciousness of those living in the city, extensive archival research formed the base for accessing the sedimented histories of built forms. The National Archives of Madagascar in Antananarivo hold incredibly rich correspondence between Merina government officials and provincial representatives detailing wide-ranging attempts to rule and manage the northwest region. Authored entirely by Malagasy administrators from the 1820s (when highland monarchs conquered the coastal city of Mahajanga) to the 1890s (when French colonial authorities were encroaching), these precious sources illuminate the micro-political struggles over urban sites and the ways city dwellers drew on built forms to negotiate colonial occupation by highlanders, long before French military troops arrived. To learn more about key terms and concepts that emerged, I juxtaposed these sources with historical dictionaries, historical linguistic studies, and collections of proverbs (*ohabolana*) and poetry. To render biographies of places and built forms during French colonial times, I collected documentary records, including city council records, regulatory acts, reports and correspondence, maps and blueprints, newspaper accounts, and photographs from the Centre des archives d'Outre-Mer in France and from multiple archives within Madagascar, as well as nineteenth-century missionary reports, shipping logs, and detailed diaries of two Europeans envoys collected at archives in North America and the United Kingdom. Personal family collections of photographs and land deeds, and discussions with families about the documents I gathered in the French colonial archives, generated collaborative, ongoing conversations that indelibly shaped this book.

My role as a researcher in this urban archive fluctuated, and the genres of this book reflect those changing roles. At some moments, I was a medium transmitting what people told me to write down—transferring relatively raw, firsthand oral narratives to curved letters on the page. At other times, I was an observant interpreter working with Malagasy collaborators to track how residents inhabited their houses, breathed life into them, and drew on them to craft subjectivities and navigate competing demands of nurturing life, hospitality, and protection. But built forms are not only singular, living places; they also have textual counterparts in government files and offices.[67] In that vein, I was also sometimes a sleuth, scouring through dusty municipal land deeds and records to pursue the documentary life of these selected buildings. Thus this book weaves together a variety of genres, including first-person narrative, textual sources, theoretical analysis, maps, and visual images, to tell a broader story of competing urbanisms, informed by affective ties, materials, and moral expectations.

This research was propelled by a desire to reckon with the material and ideological legacies of colonialism and racial capitalism, processes with which my personal family history is deeply entangled. The journey of writing this book was filled with profound uncertainty about how best to navigate the political weight of writing from my subject position—as a white Dutch-American woman, a descendant of colonial settlers, a privileged beneficiary of global systems of violent extraction—and from afar about people's lives and struggles in Madagascar. No words can resolve the material gap that enabled me to gather the recounted histories and far-flung documents of Mahajanga's past in ways wrongly denied to residents of the city. Encouraged by friends and collaborators in Mahajanga and emboldened by my vast ethical debts to them, I have chosen to write this book to chronicle overlapping histories of belonging, exclusion, and city-making that are still unfolding. It is my hope that this book calls into question how urban societies, replete with conviviality and coercion, are made over time, and aids reimagined possibilities for building a different, livable world.

My positioning as an outsider and as a secondary-language learner of Malagasy both constrained what I could know and understand and allowed me to move across different social, linguistic, and status groups in Mahajanga, opening conversational lines that were more difficult for city residents to initiate among themselves. Yet this was not without risks and challenges. As my relationships with families of different backgrounds deepened, I found myself pulled into a tension-filled field marked at times by jealousy and allusions to the ethical dubiousness of the other families. When friends questioned my whereabouts or why I was spending time with families of suspect character, I continually explained that my purpose was to understand how Mahajanga's history (*tantara*) was remembered by different groups in the city. My account reflects my attempts to navigate these different loyalties and ongoing debts of knowledge production.

Writing histories of Mahajanga is an especially fraught endeavor within the contemporary context, when many Comorian-Malagasy families find themselves on the margins of political power and, in the aftermath of an expulsion of Comorians in the late 1970s, vulnerably marked as a religious minority in a predominantly Christian national context. Memories of the expulsion of Comorian and zanatany residents in 1976–77, which I address in the epilogue, are sometimes said to have been expunged from popular historical consciousness, but I found them to be still palpable and raw among older inhabitants, many of whom expressed explicit desires for the recuperation of early Islamic, Sakalava, and Comorian contributions to the city's history. As a scholar interested in lived memories and historical ethnography, I found myself burdened to expose the political fault lines on which partial apprehensions of the past unfurled, while attending to what David William Cohen called the forces at "the edges of our stories and of the stories being told to us."[68] This book reflects my attempt at historical bricolage, at bringing together the multiple, sometimes incommensurate, fragments of the past, sifting through and amalgamating them into a textured reinterpretation of lives lived.

Throughout this project, I take the city as a site of archival struggle—an accumulation of sediment, ever morphing and shifting, in which some deposits adhere and solidify, while others erode with passages of time or active processes of neglect. There are very real geological processes of sedimentation of the city, but there are also human interventions in this sedimentation, where people layer their building materials, waste, memories, and personal belongings into a plastered palimpsest abounding with imprints of lives in transformation. If the city is a laminated archive, then its inhabitants are the archivists, curating—whether through preservation and repair, burial and destruction—their homes and mosques, streets and parks, as well as their personal photographs, documents, and possessions that bear witness to some pasts, while forgetfully effacing others. Interrogating this archive requires privileging Malagasy and Comorians as the primary knowledge-makers and brokers, the intentional curators of their architectural archive, and the anticipatory casters of their city.

In the end, it is just one story among the many that could be told.

PART I

Building Power

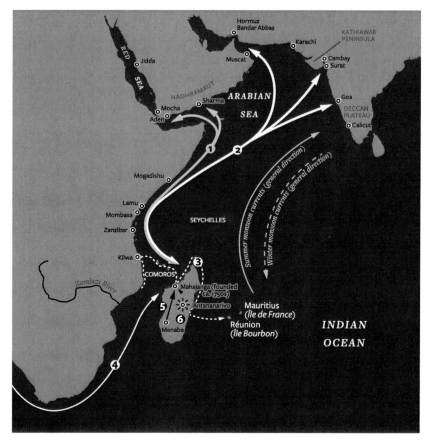

1 2 Migratory sailors, merchants, religious scholars, and captives circulating between trading settlements in

    1 Southern Arabian Peninsula (encompassing Hadhramaut region) from 1000s, with intensified traffic from 1700s

    2 South Asian region (encompassing Kathiawar Peninsula) from 1300s

3 East African captives (Makoa) traded in, across, and around Madagascar and beyond, accelerating in late 1700s (dashed lines)

4 European traders, beginning in 1400s

5 Andriamandisoarivo [posthumous name of Tsimenata] traveled from Menabe to found Boina kingdom, ca. late 1600s–early 1700s

6 Andrianampoinimerina consolidated Imerina kingdom, ca. late 1700s

MAP 1.1 Circulations, Madagascar in the Indian Ocean, fifteenth to eighteenth centuries. Map by Tim Stallmann.

1

Casting the Land

Architectural Tactics and the Politics of Durability

There are many genealogies by which to trace the forging of a city and many moments in which to locate the temporal edges of Mahajanga's history. One could begin with the tentative sixteenth- and seventeenth-century trading encounters that brought first Portuguese and Dutch, and then English and French, sea captains to Antalaotra traders and Sakalava monarchs in the region; the spectacular 1895 storming of French troops onto the city's shores in the dawn of colonial conquest; or the rise of Malagasy nationalism in the 1950s and '60s. But these approaches might obscure the immensity of deep time, the contingencies through which cavernous and shallow contexts have shaped each other, and the movements of those left out of textual, paper records. Instead, this chapter takes elemental forces—wind, water, sand—as the starting point for understanding Mahajanga's lineage, plumbing the earthly archive for the slow-moving geological and climatic processes that produced conditions hospitable to human thriving. As people arrived on the coast, they harnessed the things of the land—grass, thatch, mangrove trees, clay, and limestone—to creatively foster assemblages for human dwellings. Digging deep into this past requires rethinking inherited epistemological taxonomies, moving beyond documentary sources, and bringing in insights from archeological, genomic, biological, and paleontological research.[1]

Yet how to find one's way through this deep past? Toponyms are curious, instructive wayfinding guides through the morass of layered lives and events that comprise a place, and they cast light on the shifting perceptions of the city's past. Scholars have shown how naming is a profoundly political act. Systematically renaming places has been constitutive of settler-colonial violence, erasing traces of indigenous histories, expressing the ideological goals of colonizers, and reflecting entitled dominance. Within African historiography, scholars have complicated conceptions of naming as a top-down, ideological force rooted in colonial or postcolonial statecraft, showing instead that naming, in the words of Garth Myers, is one way competing groups "speak with space" to express intersecting, historical relations of power.[2] African cities are often home to multiple street-naming systems that expose conflicted memories of the past and, as anthropologist Stephanie Love notes, "mourning for the unrealized ideals of independence . . . and grievance toward the [postcolonial] state."[3] Yet, less critical attention has been devoted to the contested meanings embedded in precolonial place names in Africa and the ways they enfold ideas about rights, responsibilities, and possibilities of emergent landscapes for early migrants, long before the arrival of European colonizers.[4]

Building on this literature, this chapter opens by exploring Mahajanga's placename history to illuminate how the "world-making and world-destroying" capacities of toponyms stretch across time, accruing and building on each other.[5] It unpacks three competing narratives about the city's origins—each associated with a slightly varied toponym—to interrogate different conceptions of the city's past, but also to explore the moral and ethical dimensions of Mahajanga's toponym. As anthropologist Keith Basso signaled, place names not only reflect notable events specific to geographic site and social collective, but they can also serve as "a repository of distilled wisdom" through their ability to "condense into compact form their essential moral truths."[6] Each of the three origin stories discussed in this chapter reflect contrasting dimensions of the city's past and present—salient ideas about proper ethical norms, the imprints of consequential human and ecological events, and the significance of more-than-human forces in the making of a settlement. Notably, each also contains distinctive attributions of responsibility for the city's founding, and throughout my research long-time residents often recounted these narratives to implicitly make claims about *who* precisely were the original inhabitants of the town. Although these narratives have surely transformed across time, they appear to have stabilized and circulated contemporaneously since at least the mid-nineteenth century, during which time they were recorded by European travelers and missionaries.

In what follows, I bring together these competing parables about the city's toponym with the left-behind traces of the city's earliest dwellers (including geological sedimentary layers, seeds, bone fragments, and epigenetic maps) to shed light on how different groups sedimented their presence on the earth's archive through negotiations with the climatic, hydrological, and geological conditions at hand. From its very inception, and like other Indian Ocean towns of the period, the city was enacted by multiple groups: Muslim traders from Eastern Africa, Surat, Oman, and the Comorian archipelago; Sakalava royal leaders; spirit mediums; and commoners who brought their own overlapping, and sometimes competing, knowledge practices, strategies, and sensibilities. These intersecting groups braided together their social worlds—at times binding themselves in knots of marriage and alliance that frayed or snared. This chapter argues that through rituals and everyday practices, early coastal dwellers drew on affordances of the landscape—thatch, limestone, cloth, rice, rum, mud, and metal—to organize themselves, form affinal bonds, execute conflict, and create enduring architectural practices that persisted for decades and centuries (and with which city dwellers in later times were obliged to contend).

Though long marginalized from scholarly literature on Indian Ocean networks, which are oft-centered on the Swahili Coast, Mahajanga's history reveals the deep integration of this region into oceanic trade nexuses. In the earliest times of settlement, Muslim and Indian traders gave meaning to the land by founding villages and large towns, naming places, carving paths, planting trees and bushes, and constructing dwellings of thatch and stone. They did so by drawing on repertoires of knowledge and experience informed by long-standing ties across the Mozambique Channel and farther north to Comoros, East Africa, Arabia, and South Asia, and through productive, friction-filled encounters with aspiring Sakalava political rulers. Madagascar, like other islands of the southwestern Indian Ocean, is at once a "microcosm of larger continents" and an ecologically unique, highly endemic island, and its northwestern coast has witnessed the arrival of settlers from wide-ranging origins stretching to nearly all corners of the Indian Ocean (see map 1.1).[7]

Mahajanga's architectural history has much to tell us about the bundled knots of labor and expertise, moral registers, and political praxis of everyday life that defined the city's precolonial urban development. I contend that the city's urban spatial domain can be understood as a field of architectural tactics in which groups with competing aspirations sought to define new conditions of political possibility through building practices, while they continually negotiated the more-than-human world of geological, climatic, and spirit (ancestral) forces. Like other early African rulers, Sakalava monarchs assembled a broad range of experts and workers as well as ancestral spirits to legitimize their power. Long-standing monarchal prohibitions on hardened building materials served as vectors of architectural governance through which rulers codified political values and ensured their political import was undeniably visible across the city's material milieu. Yet, Muslim traders' influence and architectural defiance grew and, with the overturning of the royal prohibition on durable buildings in the 1770s, gave rise to newly constructed calcified homes that condensed merchants' moral orientations and served as leverage for claiming unfettered autonomy from the state. Throughout these fitful movements of the late eighteenth and early nineteenth centuries, competing groups were obliged to wrest stone, grass, and wood from the sedimented, undulating bounds of the earth's archive as they worked to transform the shoreline into new kinds of worlds.

Mahajanga: Braided Origins

Recollections of Mahajanga's founding are enmeshed in the braided threads of reposited memory and narrated oral accounts that often sit uneasily alongside documentary and archaeological traces. The first account is grounded in an arresting image: Andriamandisoarivo, the aspiring but unsuccessful claimant to the throne of the Menabe kingdom, is by the seaside, pondering the chances of future prosperity for his burgeoning Boeny kingdom in the aftermath of his conquest of the northwest. Knowing that the propitious future of his people is tied to the favor of the more-than-human world, he demurely appeals to the spirits (by some accounts the creator god Zanahary, and in other accounts ancestral spirits) to convey whether his kingdom and descendants shall flourish in Boeny. He determines to offer his dearest granddaughter—the firstborn daughter of his son, who is key to "preserving the purity of royal blood"—by setting her to sea.[8] If she survives, it means that the spirits accept his gesture and the future of his dynasty will be promising; if she perishes, it means the spirit world is angrily unsatisfied and the monarchy's future is doomed. Andriamandisoarivo constructs a small wooden box, layers it with grass, and climbs with his granddaughter aboard his tottering pirogue on the shores of Katsepy, a small peninsula town at the mouth of the Boeny (Bombetoka) Bay (map 1.2). Full of anticipation, he rows deep into the watery, liminal interstices in

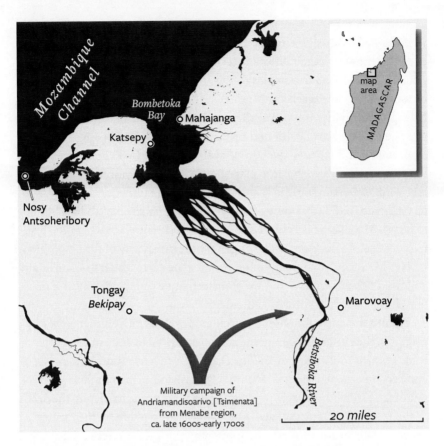

MAP 1.2 Key landmarks and towns referenced in chapter 1. Map by Tim Stallmann.

which his dynasty's fate will be determined, sets his encased granddaughter in the water, and returns to land. Gently stoked by the lapping waves, and "thanks to the protection of God and the ancestors," the living, entombed royal granddaughter is gradually pushed to the eastern riverbank, where the local fishermen seize her, raise her up, and sing praise songs, in jubilant celebration of their auspicious fortune. Upon learning of her fate, Andriamandisoarivo commands the construction of a city, which he names "Moudzangayeh" (chosen place), drawing on the power of naming and the spirit world's sanction to stake a political claim to territory in the emergent kingdom.[9]

A second account emphasizes the role of divination in political destiny and the relationship between divine, corporeal, and social wellbeing. In this account, we find Andriamandisoarivo in the northwest region (it is unclear whether he has already established the Boeny kingdom), ailing and weakened. Yearning for regained vitality, Andriamandisoarivo beseeches his appointed diviner (*moasy, ombiasy*), and together they embark on a journey by foot. When they reach a freshwater spring at the site of present-day Mahajanga, the diviner urges Andriamandisoarivo to drink, and soon thereafter he recovers his health and proclaims the site "Mahajanga" (derived from *maha*: to make; *janga*: cured, healed, restored). This conception of the city as a healthful, healing place persists in contemporary times, with many inhabitants reporting that the intense heat cultivates their strength. Crystallized in the city's motto, *Ho velona fa tsy ho levona* (To live, but not to bury), Mahajanga is conjured as a living, resilient place where the healing properties of land and water engender the prosperity of future progeny. These two accounts signal the importance for early leaders of spiritually endowed power (*hasina*) and the transformative capacities of water in establishing a viable territorial settlement.[10]

Finally, the most ubiquitously circulated oral narrative situates the city's origins in the cultural and migrancy amalgamations of ancient Islamic trade routes of the southwestern Indian Ocean. In this account, Muslim traders identified as "Antalaotra" founded the city following conflicts with the reigning Sakalava monarch, possibly Andriamandisoarivo. Upon the death of the monarch, the Antalaotra traders refused to abide by the custom of shaving their heads to mark the mourning period for deceased Sakalava royalty. They were ousted from a nearby town (likely Antsoheribory) by Sakalava royal followers and fled to the neighboring shores, where they founded Mahajanga. Drawing on their Swahili-inflected linguistic base, they called their newfound city "Mji-angaia" (*mji*: town; *angaia*: flowers) after the copious trees, vines, and especially luscious, fragrant flowering blooms visible from the bay. This telling exposes the tensions Antalaotra seafarers faced between their adherence to Islamic tenets and the requisite expressions of political loyalty to Sakalava monarchs that characterized their ambivalent position in the region.[11]

Collectively taken, these accounts portray the city's birth as intimately tied to the qualities of the land, the movements of people across the sea, and the weight of ancestral and divine power in crafting new political-economic assemblages. Yet each of these parables contains implicit moral lessons and claims about the original founders of the city. In the first two accounts, we witness Andriamandisoarivo reckoning with the more-than-human world of ancestral spirits as a critical step toward land occupation, following the long journey of conquest. The first telling affirms that appropriation of land was predicated on intersession with, and agreement of, ancestral spirits; without their accord the kingdom's "days were numbered."[12] Royal progeny, in this case the royal granddaughter, are the conduit through whom this engagement between the living and the spirit realm takes place, suggesting a tight connection between the corporeal body of royalty and the vitality of the political corpus. And the gender of the granddaughter is significant, perhaps added later, for women have held important roles as queens in Sakalava polities of northwest Madagascar from the eighteenth century onward. In the second account, the presence of the diviner (*moasy*) implicitly affirms the significance of ancestral concordance in claiming and naming the space of the city. Water is critical—in the first account it is a transitory substance and space that enables engagement between the living and the dead, and in the second account it is a healing substance that has an effect on Andriamandisoarivo. Both parables clearly anchor Mahajanga's founding in Sakalava political history and suggest that Sakalava political leaders were bound by an ethic in which the intertwined power over people and power over land was established on responsible relationships with the more-than-human domain.

Woven throughout these accounts are references to the marked ecological attributes of the region that enabled human settlement, which warrant brief attention. The Sakalava political rulers and Muslim traders who found their way to the shores of the Bombetoka Bay (known variously to European traders as Maringaan or Maningaar) in the seventeenth century were not the first to discover the island's northwest coast. Before them lay a riverine landscape already curated, already in motion. Long before the first humans arrived on the island's shores (at least some 2,000 years ago, and likely even earlier), profound geomorphological processes were underway that would shape the inhabitability of Madagascar's northwest region.[13] Andriamandisoarivo's act of layering the pirogue with "grasses" not only melded sea and land, but pulled on earlier geological histories of the northwest region. Contrary to colonial-era assumptions that the island was blanketed in dense tropical forests prior to human occupation, tenacious grasslands took root across Madagascar's ecosystems. In the northwest region, humble grasses anchored themselves in the alluvial soil and swathed the silty sandstone, giving way to patches of shrubland and dry, deciduous forest.[14] Early settlers who eventually established villages in the northwest were likely attracted by the rambling expanses of life-giving, verdant grasses that could preserve their grazing cattle herds and nurture their everyday socioeconomic lives. Proverbs offer a glimpse into time-travelled Malagasy conceptions of grasses as remarkably able to outlive harsh conditions and support animate life across entire lifespans.[15] We cannot know for sure, but these conceptions may very well have informed Andriamandisoari-vo's choice to include grass with the offering of his granddaughter to the ancestors.

The third telling of the city's toponym converges most explicitly with the archaeological accounts and writings of European traders and explorers in the nineteenth century that situate Mahajanga's founding as a kind of compromise, a site of uneasy alliances that afforded Islamic merchants latitude for conducting trade and establishing themselves, while allowing monarchal rulers to maintain a degree of control over trade and revenues. Drawn by the favorable tide and plentiful freshwater in the northern part of the island, maritime traders began to settle in northwest Madagascar between 900 and 1100 CE, building coastal communities that exhibited the varied cultural and linguistic admixture that characterizes Madagascar's exceptional cultural history. Unlike in East Africa, where many settlements emerged from encounters between mainlanders and oceangoers, early migrants came to Madagascar's northwestern coast exclusively from the sea—bringing along honed repertoires of culinary, subsistence, political, and economic practices with which they shaped a new coastal landscape.

Archaeological remains suggest that during the ninth and tenth centuries people resided in small villages along northwest Madagascar, but by the eleventh and twelfth centuries, Muslim traders (whose descendants would identify as the Antalaotra) built large-scale settlements, enriched by dense webs of connection and trade with Comoros.[16] Like Swahili coastal merchants, they utilized the rhythms of the monsoon winds to travel south toward Madagascar, where they resided and fostered enduring ties of affiliation with coastal dwellers through exchange, sharing Islamic practices, and casting architectural projects. The thalassic economy, which expanded to reach from East Africa and Madagascar to the Hadhramaut region in the Southern Arabian Peninsula and South Asia, revolved around the trade of ivory, skins, and tortoiseshell in exchange for pottery, glass vessels, and stone bowls. Recent archaeological research suggests that whereas early settlements in coastal northwest Madagascar were linked to Indian Ocean commercial flows, most of these ties were probably through Comorian (especially Nzwani) Muslim traders who would have served as important intermediaries with the early Islamic World.[17] These Indian Ocean traders came to northwest Madagascar for general provisions, but also in search of commodities deriving from the island's distinctive ecology, including carved chlorite schist and rock crystal vessels, rice, copal resin, soapstone, and mangrove stakes as well as, later, captives for enslavement.[18]

Ties with Comoros and the Indian Ocean trade networks were already underway in these early times, according to linguistic, genetic, and archaeo-botanical traces and evidence of shared rice-farming and cattle-tending techniques that stretched across the region.[19] Coastal dwellers in both Comoros and northwest Madagascar nurtured these regional trading re-lations, shared technical knowledge, and developed agricultural skills as they contemporaneously established early, large coastal towns in the ninth and tenth centuries. As settlements such as Mahilaka (north of present-day Mahajanga) grew from the tenth and eleventh centuries, early colo-nists contributed to discernable shifts in the biome conditions. Hauling not only boatloads of goods for trade, but also dormant and living species of all sorts, they altered the landscape in ways both intended and unintended. Early migrants brought technical knowledge in metallurgy, stonework, and ceramic production influenced by Southeast Asian practices; crafted iron tools that were eventually used in preparing the land for rice paddies; and formed stone and pottery vessels that facilitated food storage.[20] Early set-tlers possessed knowledge in riziculture and brought two distinct varieties of rice to Madagascar—*japonica* (originally from the Yangtze River basin and subsequently Southeast Asia) and *indica* (from northern India)—perhaps as early as the late ninth and early tenth centuries.[21] Establishing rice fields required a considerable investments in labor and time and thus was undertaken only in larger settlements, beginning in Comoros during the eighth century and in Madagascar as early as the tenth century, where inhabitants were able to dedicate effort to riziculture.

From Nosy Antsoheribory to Mahajanga

In the sixteenth century, Antalaotra traders settled in what was ultimately the city that preceded Mahajanga—Nosy Antsoheribory, in the Bay of Boeny (Boina, from Swahili, "the place of stones") (see map 1.2), which offered protection from invading Portuguese traders—as well as other sites across northwestern Madagascar, each under the tutelage of a distinct leader. Pottery sherds and archaeological artifacts, coupled with oral testimony, signal that these towns enjoyed vibrant trade relations with seafarers com-ing from the Indian Ocean world—both Islamic and European. English,

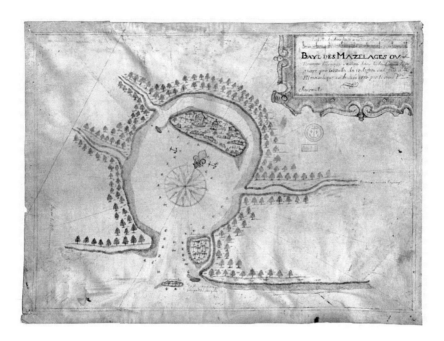

FIGURE 1.1 "Baye des Mazelages" (Antsoheribory), 1673, Map by Pere Louis Chervreuil. Note the extensive settlement and double-storied buildings on Nosy Antsoheribory. Courtesy of Bibliothèque nationale de France.

French, and then Dutch slavers also knew of Nosy Antsoheribory (which they called Massailly or Massalage) in the mid-1600s (see figure 1.1), and it later became regarded as Madagascar's leading slave-port. By 1676, however, Nosy Antsoheribory was destroyed by the Portuguese ship the *Nossa Senhora de Miragules*, devastating its inhabitants. Dutch skipper Aryaen van Asperen noted afterward that the tiny island had been governed by Sultan Hamet Boebachar, "a circumcised Arab aged 36" who was fairly proficient in Portuguese, and his people (numbering some 300 households) had taken refuge in a nearby village (see figure 1.2).[22] These coastal dwellers distinguished themselves as Muslim, in contrast to the hinterland communities. Traders and their families returned soon thereafter to Nosy Antsoheribory, only to face further confrontations with groups—later designated by the ethnonym "Sakalava"—moving northward from the Lahe Fouti (Sakalava Menabe) kingdom in the south, with whom they eventually intermingled and crafted new lifeworlds.[23]

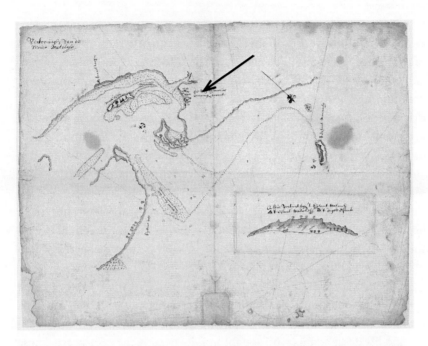

FIGURE 1.2 "Drawing of the River Matelesy," 1676. Map drawn from the Dutch slaving ship *Voorhout*. The arrow indicates the settlement where Boebachar and his people took refuge following attack by the Portuguese. Courtesy of Nationaal Archief, Nederlands.

These northerly moving factions were led by Andriamandisoarivo, the leading protagonist in the first two parable tales of the city's founding. A young twenty-something son of the Lahe Fouti king of the Menabe kingdom to the south, Andriamandisoarivo was keen to establish a new kingdom in the area around present-day Mahajanga.[24] Around 1684 he initiated an incursion by those from Menabe northward across the vast lands "where cattle are kept," toward Nosy Antsoheribory, drawing along the way on time-honored tactics for building political bases through military conquest and subsequent lamination of their political ideologies of sacred kingship onto newly conquered communities.[25] Royal dynastic groups in the western region had long transformed themselves into masters of the land (*tompontany*) by anchoring the geographically disparate body politic in the centripetal force of the monarch's corporeal body (and sacred royal compound), which derived its power from its intermediary role between the living and the invisible, ancestral forces (*hasina*). Through participation in key ceremonies of ancestral veneration, commoners and foreigners alike could demonstrate their political allegiance, claim the inclusion of their lineage, and, importantly, gain access to land.[26] Although political entities along the northwest coast were historically made up of semimobile communities, rather than clearly demarcated geographical territories, Andriamandisoarivo was able to cohere them into one of the most successful kingdoms in the island's history. Yet once they reached the trading port of Nosy Antsoheribory in the Bay of Boeny, Andriamandisoarivo's honed strategies of absorption of foreign populations through collective ritual observance failed to succeed. And violence ensued. Oral accounts recorded more than a century later suggest that Andriamandisoarivo's successors blisteringly battled the Islamic trading families in the region, possibly with the aid of European slavers, culminating in a devasting "massacre of Muslims" between the 1730s and 1760s.[27]

Although scholars are not completely certain that this conflict ensued in Nosy Antsoheribory, the island town's architectural splendor suggests it was a key site for encroaching, warring camps under Andriamandisoarivo and his descendants who sought to fully occupy the northwest. These conquerors allowed Muslim traders to remain there in the decade or so that followed, and evidence exists that the town's wealth grew at least partly through the intensifying slave trade in the late 1600s. Nosy Antsoheribory's archaeological remains testify to the island's economic flourishing and offer important insights into the architectural practices of Islamic trading communities in northwest Madagascar just before Mahajanga's founding. The island was home to some forty-five tombs, two stone houses, and a mosque containing some coral remnants at the qibla and openings for doors (see figure 1.3). Most houses were composed of thatch and vegetative matter, and stone structures—erected with masonry of "beachrock" and coral lime (mortar from burnt coral)—were largely reserved for the dead and for holy Islamic sites.[28] Travel accounts from the late seventeenth century affirm the importance of Muslim sacred structures in Antsoheribory, especially the presence of a stone mosque running north-south in which adherents prayed daily, as well as "superb tombs, cisterns and houses, all built of stones."[29] Some wealthier families may have built stone homes on the north-central side of the settlement, near the mosque. But within a century, merchants abandoned Antsoheribory and shifted their locus of trade to the newly established port town of Mahajanga.[30]

FIGURE 1.3 Archaeological remains of Nosy Antsoheribory. Courtesy of Martial Pauly, Société d'histoire et d'archéologie de Mayotte.

Anchoring Trade: Mahajanga as a "Sanctuary Allowed ... by the King"

Documentary traces affirm that Sakalava monarchs sought to conserve relationships with traders who could provide commercial expertise and connections to the monarchy, and these close affinities culminated in the merging of some lineages through marriage from the early 1700s. Throughout the seventeenth and eighteenth centuries, Muslim traders gained a monopoly over trade to the interior, to the exclusion of competing groups from the highlands.[31] Once established in the mid-1700s, Mahajanga was an important node of economic activity in the region, linking the sea to the hinterland, but it remained secondary to Tongay (Bekipay), the seat of divine power and core of ritual life. Sakalava political leaders understood their ritual power as bolstered by the strategic display and consumption of key commodities, but also by the auspicious spatial alignment of their royal compounds. Like other precolonial African monarchal structures, the spatial layouts of Tongay and other early Sakalava royal compounds were physical representations of the cosmologically informed networks of authority made incarnate through acts of construction, performance, and exchange.

One glimpse into this early architectural practice comes from the account of Hendrik Frappé, a Dutch merchant aboard the *Leijdsman*, who (like all incoming traders) was required to pass through the royal Sakalava upriver capital of Foelenak (possibly Marovoay) to conduct slave-trading negotiations with King "Tokaf" (Toakafo, the successor to Andriamandisoarivo) in 1715.[32] He described a square-shaped mountain-top royal compound aligned with the four cardinal directions and framed by wooden poles and gateways "in which 18 to 19 dwellings have been built."[33] Dwellings in the emergent Boina kingdom were generally made of heavy, hardwood beams with bamboo walls and thatched with "leaves of rushes."[34] The persistent natural and human-induced fires since the turn of the first millennia furnished builders with the ideal, abundant palm leaves for constructing thatched roofs in the area that surrounded the Bay.[35]

The large poles and beams described by Frappé would likely have been head- or shoulder-loaded by slaves or royal commoners from thickly forested areas in the hinterlands of Marovoay, where baobabs (*reniala* [Malagasy, mother of trees]; *Adansonia digitata*), rosewood (*Dalbergia*), and fast-growing deciduous (*Hildegardia)* species existed.[36] Builders utilized hardwood trunks to construct buildings of varying heights that correlated to social class; dwellings could reach 6 to 7.5 meters (20–25 feet) for nobles and royalty, and 3 to 4.5 meters (10–15 feet) or less for commoners.[37] This physical staggering of elevation reminded commoners daily of the constraints on their autonomy, while projecting the grandeur and omnipotence of royal ancestors and their living progeny who ruled the region. To be under another's roof (*tafo-trano*) signaled a power relationship characterized by deference, indebtedness, or even coercive control, as suggested in the nineteenth-century expression for an emancipated slave who was said to be "liberated from under the roof of nobility."[38] We cannot know for certain, but it is possible that the extensive ceiling height created a particular sonic environment in which voices were amplified, while eliciting a sense of physical diminution for passers-through in relation to the towering wooden pillars. Although Frappé did not specify, the royal compound was likely built along the directional axis that Malagasy have historically drawn from to express sociopolitical hierarchies of everyday life, in which the northeast is associated with elder, living men, patrilineality, and ancestors, whereas the southwest is associated with women, children, and the dead. These cardinal orientations have been carried through Malay-inflected linguistic genealogies of early settlers dating back to the seventh century and imprinted in the realm of the dead.[39] Sakalava tombs dating from the eighteenth century also demonstrate this cardinalized approach to sepulchral space in the consistent eastward positioning of deceased men, and westward positioning of women and children.[40]

Frappé did not mention stone, and this may have been because he glimpsed the structures of the living. Stone—enduring, resolute, obdurate— was generally reserved for the world of the dead, although some Sakalava parables suggest living royalty could dwell in "beautiful stone houses."[41] Archaeological remains at Bezavodoany (near Tongay) of the sacred shrine containing the royal relics reveal a stone interior and mortared stone wall enclosing the tombs, which were fashioned using techniques attributed to Antalaotra masons and built in a similar fashion to Islamic buildings in Antsoheribory and along the coast.[42] Elsewhere in Madagascar, Susan Kus and Victor Raharijaona have illuminated the relationship between stones and durable, sovereign power within the building projects undertaken by highland monarch Andrianampoinimerina in the late eighteenth century.[43] Even if often reserved for the ancestors, stones have had multivalence in Madagascar, as archaeologist Zoë Crossland has shown, serving as communicative mediums between the living and the ancestors, signifying legal arrangements from the eighteenth century, and symbolizing the fixed rigidness of the dead.[44] Though Frappé's account and archaeological records are sparse on the presence of stone, it is likely similar associations with stone were in circulation in northwest Madagascar.

In exchange for nine *reals*, the reigning monarch permitted Frappé and his crew to build small temporary structures along the seaside for conducting trade, including one building for storing merchandise, another for trading and imprisoning slaves, and a third for housing the crew. Most European captains hired local builders to construct and later dismantle these structures, while sailors often stayed in tents by the seaside (see figure 1.4). All these structures, however, were constructed of vegetative materials, and the Dutch crew deliberately burned them to the ground before their departure. It is not clear what the purpose of destroying the buildings was, whether to thwart competing traders from using the site or following a directive given by the Sakalava monarch. Burning the structures may have provided a way of controlling access to competing traders, but it equally could have constituted maintenance work to allow for fresh building of new structures on subsequent visits.[45]

Between 1710 and 1730, Sakalava political leaders shifted their capital from Tongay to Marovoay (some 60 kilometers [40 miles] upriver from Mahajanga), in the Bay of Bombetoka. Otto Luder Hemmy, a senior mer-

FIGURE 1.4 Bombetoka village, Dutch trading post on eastern edge of bay.
Source: "Quelques renseignements sur Madagascar, par Fr. Valentyn, en 1726," in
Grandidier et al., *Collection des ouvrages anciens*, 5:168.

chant aboard the Dutch East India Company's slaving ship *De Brack*, visited
in 1741 and described this settlement as much larger than what Frappé had
observed some decades earlier, containing thousands of houses and "a huge
crowd of inhabitants."[46] In keeping with the use of built borders to delineate
sacred and common spaces, a fence surrounded the town. Upon the invi-
tation of reigning monarch Andriamahatindriarivo, Hemmy and his crew
visited the impressive hilltop royal palace, which vividly communicated
the kingdom's worldly connections and trading prowess: "Larger than the
governor's residence at the Cape [of Good Hope]; it is surrounded by four
or five rows of concentric fences formed of large pointed stakes at the end,
inside of which stand five masts for the French, Dutch, British, Portuguese
and Danish ships, and several cases and cupboards packed full of all kind
of goods."[47] Inside the palace, Hemmy glimpsed many treasures: a porce-
lain vase from Japan filled with alcoholic spirits, more than one hundred
"beautiful and good quality muskets," a full chest of vases and objects of
silver, and a large lacquered and gilded throne—testimonies to the polity's
cosmopolitan trading and diplomatic connections.[48]

If the palace and its sumptuous array of exotic objects served as an expression of Andriamahatindriarivo's political potency, the palace's spatial
arrangement enacted a knowledge regime that constrained visitors' passage into the vital core of royal power. Hemmy noted that "the house of

the king and those of his wives are at the center, in the interior courtyard which is surrounded by a strong fence." The careful placement of the Andriamahatindriarivo and his wives served to symbolize their central positioning in the cosmic ordering of eighteenth-century Sakalava political life, which the monarch projected through carefully staged, incremental access of foreigners into the palace's private chambers over the span of several days. The progressive sequencing of fences, pens, and enclosures constituted and amplified royal power in the eyes of commoners and visitors through curated displays of concealment and visibility. Once Hemmy met the king, who was flanked by his wives on each side, they sat face-to-face on benches "covered with a scarlet cloth," the flaming color further projecting divine power through the association of red with ancestral forces.[49] While monarchs built themselves into power at the royal compound at Marovoay, however, the buzz of economic exchanges grew at the coast.

Sometime around 1750, the trading hub shifted to Mahajanga largely because of the growing presence and influence of Muslim traders, and perhaps also mandated by the king. By the 1760s, with the locus of exchange firmly situated in the city, the ruling monarch afforded traders more autonomy to conduct trade.[50] A 1764 account from the British slaving ship *The Fly* indicates that Mahajanga was by this point apparently "a large town chiefly built after the Indian fashion," but from these earliest days it was also ethno-linguistically diverse and inhabited by "native mores [moors, likely Antalaoatra and converted commoners of the Sakalava polity], and others from Surate, Johana, Mosembeck [Mozambique], and the Comoro Islands."[51] Although this account is tantalizingly bereft of details on the city's architecture, later European observers noted that the hinterlands were abundant in tamarind and palm trees, "called *sathan* [satrana palms] whose leaves are used to cover houses, and to fabricate sacks."[52] *Satrana* leaves could be artfully interwoven to create water- and heat-protective covertures for homes; they functioned as well to cool interiors, soften acoustics, and gave off earthy scents (especially following heavy rains), but they also accommodated unwanted rodents and insects.

Ready sources of fresh water replenished the growing population, and the soft, muddy seafloor made for facile docking for incoming boats.[53] As found in some West African trading centers, this separation of the trade activity in Mahajanga from the royal-ritual center in Marovoay can be understood as a spatial strategy in the service of an alliance between Muslim traders and Sakalava political leaders.[54] The traders, and likely others involved in trade, experienced Mahajanga as a "sanctuary allowed ... by the king of this country."[55] These traders enjoyed the liberty of movement along the coast and to the Comoro Islands, as well as easy anchorage at Mahajanga's deep port for their "large boats."[56] But the "King's purser" kept controls in place, operating under the king's authority.[57] The incorporation of Islamic constituents into the royal domain thus served as the most effective means for Sakalava royals to mitigate any threat and make use of commercial knowledge.[58]

Intensifying alliances between Sakalava monarchs, Muslim traders, and European seafarers accelerated the formation of the Sakalava (Zafivolamena) dynasty in Boina, alongside the augmentation of trade revolving around slaves and crucial food provisions, such as rice and cattle, beginning in the seventeenth century. As the demand for laborers on Portuguese, Dutch, British, and primarily French plantations in the Mascarene Islands intensified, Mahajanga became increasingly entrenched in competing global economies of chattel slavery, and Sakalava political leaders demanded even higher prices, often paid in silver coins and arms, for slaves. By the end of the eighteenth century, traders from northwest Madagascar began transporting captives, primarily east Africans, across cattle paths from west to east, where they were then sent on French vessels to the Mascarenes.[59] Yet the concentration of wealth in the space of the burgeoning city of Mahajanga raised new challenges, and architecture became a key forum in which town dwellers and rulers debated the contours and limitations of political authority.

Building Power

Mahajanga's leading traders and elites consolidated their position within the robust global and regional trading networks, and by the 1770s they increasingly articulated desires to transform their largess into architectonic symbols of longevity, trustworthiness, and prestige—especially whitewashed, storied houses and mosques. As traders moved within regional mercantile spheres throughout the eighteenth century, they witnessed the compelling rising of vibrant entrepôts across eastern African shores and the Comorian archipelago and sought to entrench Mahajanga in this littoral nexus. Such aspirations were among many that animated a strategic forcefield in which state rulers, traders, and inhabitants grappled with the bounds of political authority, economic autonomy, and the temporality of everyday life through the city's architectural fabric.

At the core of these debates was a long-standing prohibition on durable materials for building forms in the northwest region, enforced by Sakalava royal leaders throughout the seventeenth and eighteenth centuries.[60] Stone construction was strictly limited by Sakalava monarchs (as well as by their counterparts in the highlands) to tombs, as amply evidenced in archaeological traces along the northwest coast, the historical privileging of stone for tombs across Malagasy past and present, and anthropological accounts of Sakalava royal rituals.[61] Impermanent buildings in Mahajanga, as Labelle Prussin showed for communities on the African continent, enlivened everyday life and signaled "renewal, rejuvenation, and rebirth."[62] At the same time, the ephemerality of ritual structures allowed loyal adherents to measure and regulate the monarch's power (as well as that of the ancestors), reminding royal leaders and followers that their monarchal authority was bound up with the volition of the people.[63]

Critical to the maintenance of royal power across early Malagasy polities, as it was also for their counterparts in continental Africa, were cosmological conceptions of power as bestowed by ancestors and secured only through proper acts of reciprocity and devotion.[64] Architectural structures themselves signified and evinced royal power, and the spectacular ceremonies that took place in these built forms (re)enacted hierarchical political relationships. Moreover, through ritualized acts of building and construction with ephemeral materials, royal presence could be elicited, performed, and imbued into the material world. The sheer ephemerality of key architectural features in royal structures ensured repeated successions of building and rebuilding, which required specific labor regimes and enacted social hierarchies among royalty, commoners, and enslaved persons. For instance, in the *menaty* service, documented from the nineteenth century, royal followers methodically rebuilt the wooden fence encircling the royal tomb, thus affirming their attachment to ancestors and revitalizing ancestral presence.[65] Royal followers could "serve" (*manompo*) through the gift of building, signaling their allegiance to royal leaders and receiving ancestral blessings.

In an assertive tactic of architectural governance, early Sakalava monarchs in the Boina kingdom sought to retain these enduring, circular, relational exchanges, by which they garnered authority, through regulation of the textures, contours, and material forms of the city. Durable homes, mosques, and shops threatened royal authority because they constituted a transgenerational emplacement of outsiders that foreclosed the critical cycles and rhythmic temporality of production, decay, ruin, and reproduction that sustained Sakalava sociopolitical formations. As Guillain described, "In recalling the difficulty that Andriamandisoarivo encountered when he attempted—and finally succeeded—to seize the island of Boeny . . . [Sakalava rulers] had always forbidden the Antalaots [Antalaotra] to construct houses in stone (*pierre*), fearing that they would strengthen the city and evade [Sakalava royal] authority."[66] After a series of less remarkable Sakalava royal successions in the early to mid-1700s, a turning point came with the ascension of Queen Ravahiny (known during her lifetime as Andriamamelonarivo) to the throne around the early 1780s.[67] Her reign marked a profound movement away from male rulers and toward female leaders in the Sakalava polity, one that lasted into the twenty-first century. Critically, for our purposes, Ravahiny diverged from her lineage and authorized traders to erect hardened buildings—thus offering architectural collateral to increasingly powerful Muslim traders.

Queen Ravahiny, ascending at the height of the kingdom's power, seems to have been particularly attuned to the political possibilities and constraints of building materials. Although little trace remains about how and why Ravahiny radically departed from her predecessors, this shift came during a critical period of strengthening in kinship ties between Antalaotra leaders and the Sakalava royal family.[68] Guillain interpreted Ravahiny's change of course as evidence of the significant degree of influence that Muslim traders (whom he specified as "Antalaots") acquired under her reign. Indeed, by Ravahiny's time, monarchs had scaled back control over European traders, who apparently dealt directly with Muslim merchants without the presence of intermediaries.[69] Although we cannot be sure, it is possible that traders were already beginning to construct their homes using stone, and if so, these building acts would have constituted tactics of determination, of *architectural refusal*, which may have contributed to Ravahiny's growing sense that the maintenance of royal power depended more on control of commodity flows and ritualized performances of loyalty and reciprocity than on the material composition of everyday homes and buildings. In support of this latter point, at the turn of the century, Sakalava monarchs solidified their authority and enhanced revenues through the mounting overseas and domestic demand for cattle, especially cattle hides and tallow for American consumers.

In the last decades of the 1700s, the city of Mahajanga was transformed. The stretch of alliances that comprised the loose confederation under Sakalava leadership reached deep into the hinterlands and well across the seas. Owing in part to the accumulation of wealth generated through trade in provisions, slaves, and other commodities, Sakalava monarchal rulers and the city's Muslim merchant elites were well-heeled. Ravahiny's reign catalyzed the broadening of the architectural possibilities through which town dwellers could establish households, express aesthetic preferences, and accrue capital, both sociopolitical and economic. Although hints of encroachment from the competing highland monarchy emerged during this time, Mahajanga's material milieu was for the time composed by the presence of overlapping, allied spheres of authority.

Peopling the City

The late eighteenth century was the zenith of the town's prosperity, a halcyon moment before the rise of the Omani empire, the shift to Zanzibar as the locus of trade in the western Indian Ocean, and the increasing conflicts with—and later colonization by—Radama's highland monarchy. French trader Julien-Pierre Dumaine noted the mushrooming population of "more than 6,000 Arabes and Indiens," each of whom contributed distinct skills, labor, and technical acumen, as well as architectural influences, which collectively forged the topographical and aesthetic contours of the growing city.[70] Yet Dumaine's categorical ethnonyms masked the wide-ranging heterogeneity of these groups: "Arabes" included those from Surat, Comoros, Hadhramaut, and East Africa as well as those from Antalaotra families of mixed Comorian, Sakalava, and sometimes Hadhramaut descent. These families thrived through their generations-long involvement in regional and oceanic trade in rice, live cattle and bovine products, mangrove poles, and human captives. Antalaotra families, long aligned with reigning Sakalava political leaders, made their livelihoods by trafficking goods up and down the coastal waterways, and they dwelled in a large seaside settlement stretching east from Marofoto (near present-day Port aux Boutres) to the western quarter of Marolaka, the vibrant boat-building community. Conceptions of private property circulated in the town's earliest times, as evidenced in one European description of wealthy families' strong attachments "to the ownership of their land" as well as to their "most valuable possession"—cattle.[71]

The Antalaotra were not only leading traders but also builders who developed a vibrant boat-construction industry, memorialized in the seaside neighborhood's contemporary toponym Marolaka (*maro*: many, *laka/lakana*: boats; see map FM.3).[72] Shipbuilders constructed double-decked boats capable of carrying up to 150 barrels between Madagascar, Comoros, and East Africa, as well as dugout outrigger canoes for regional travel, which were artistically hand hewn of hardwood trees, such as takamaka (*Calophyllum inophyllum*).[73] Artisans' renowned techniques and selection of hardwood species reflected the circulation of expert knowledge that connected Mahajanga to the highly-frequented maritime trading routes across East Africa, Comoros, and northwest Madagascar.[74]

Small numbers of Gujarati Muslims (some of them Bohras) comprised the "Banian" or "Indian" community, who, together with Antalaotra traders, conducted an "astonishing" volume of trade with merchants from Surat (Gujarat region), trading wood, shells, wax, and enslaved persons for cloth, silks (*acoutis*), and merchandise from Arabia, East Africa, and the Comoros.[75] "Banian" (who quite possibly were Vāniyā merchants) were "established among Arabs" in the city, yet they were discernable to European observers by the volume and technologies of their trade.[76] Indian traders facilitated the "best commercial operations" with Europeans, employed Makoa and Swahili sailors who knew the coastal waters, and utilized double-masted *pala* boats to facilely navigate the difficult passages between the Comoro Islands and Madagascar.[77] Although travelers' accounts are frustratingly vague on precise locations, we know that Indian communities, as well as other Islamic sects (probably Sufis from Hadhramaut and Antalaotra families), constructed mosques and "houses of education" (likely *madrasa* schools) for their respective congregations in the late eighteenth century.[78]

The dead, like the living, were placed according to religious and kinship affiliations, creating a lasting, spatial archive of the sometimes-fleeting encounters between these diverse ethnolinguistic groups. Bohra congregants constructed their own cemetery in the late eighteenth or early nineteenth century, whereas Antalaotra and Hadhramaut migrants hailing from the Southern Arabian Peninsula were buried separately in stone tombs in Marofoto, due east of the Bohra cemetery. Archaeological traces signal an additional "great burial place" at which "Indians, Antalaotse and Arabs" were interred, apparently in a mixed fashion, but on which now stands the public high school, College Charles Renel.[79] In Mahajanga, as for Hadhramaut traders described by Enseng Ho, these tombstones were part of the agile repertoire used by Antalaotra as exemplary "local cosmopolitans" to continually express local affiliations and generate lively connections to diasporic communities through a material signifier of their interstitial insider-outsider status.[80]

The increasing demand for slaves in the eighteenth century, especially to work the French sugar plantations of the Mascarenes, accelerated the slave trade and transformed the city's demography (see map 1.2). Beginning in 1780s, forcibly captured East Africans described as *Makoa* (known in the highlands as *Masombika*) flooded into the city and pushed forward new forms of building erection. The vast majority were captured as prisoners of war or in slaving raids and categorized as enslaved persons (*andevo*), though some might have been absorbed as royal slaves (*sambarivo*) tasked with key service for Sakalava monarchs. Those Makoa who dwelled in town performed Islamic practices, were often active members of congregations, and likely contributed to the construction of mosques. Unlike the builders of "stone" construction along the Swahili Coast, who used coral rag, Antalaotra masons relied primarily on limestone, sand, and shell, and over time Makoa masons apparently acquired knowledge of these locally specific properties and techniques.[81] Makoa builders may have already been familiar with techniques for fabricating lime for building projects, but variances in the chemical and ecological attributes of the lime would have obliged them to adapt their techniques.

Those loyal to Sakalava political leaders were present in the town in the late eighteenth century, but Dumaine claimed that "not a single Sakalava cohabited with the Arabs." Rather they were transient, coming into town for the main purpose of purveying commodities from the hinterlands.[82] It is important to note that although European accounts gloss "Sakalava" as a discrete ethnic identifier, it was in large part a political affiliation during the nineteenth century. People in Madagascar have historically formed collective identifications through engagement with multiple communities of practice and have drawn flexibly on bilateral (from both parents) claims of descent.[83] Scholars have often emphasized the Islamic ambiance of the town, to the exclusion of a "Sakalava presence," as inscribed on the landscape in the many mosques and visible Islamic dress and religious practices."[84] But the diversity of Muslim communities, and the long-standing practices of intermarriage and affiliation between "Arabes" and "Sakalava," undermines simplistic characterizations. Regardless of the town's precise demographic composition, Mahajanga eventually became widely recognized as *tany Sakalava* (Sakalava land), governed by ancestrally proffered legal norms and regulations, and by capricious, more-than-human spirit forces capable of accommodating assimilation or unleashing consequences for willful ignorance.

Ravahiny's approach to governance seems to have taken into account the noisy communion and productive argument among the different ethnolinguistic communities, legal systems, religious orders, generations, and social hierarchies that constituted a kind of "middle ground," rather than being a top-down, brute exercise of power.[85] One chief and three overseers shared the management of interior affairs of the city and administered justice in nuanced processes tailored for "Indian," "Sakalava," and "Arab" communities. How this arrangement came about, whether it was spatially aligned, and whether respective figures secured their involvement in the process through contestation are impossible to say. But Ravahiny at least accommodated the involvement of the respective prosecutors ("Indian," "Sakalava," and "Arab") and sought to balance her sovereignty with diplomatic concessions intended to secure the fidelity of her ethnolinguistically diverse constituency.[86]

There was a darker underside to Ravahiny's practices of architectural governance, however—one bound up with violent pasts and present. "Arabs" resented her authority but found themselves obliged to her because of their existing "federative treaty," which granted them a "considerable cession of land where they initially settled, and from where they came to Mouzangaye [Mahajanga] following the hostilities."[87] The specter of these earlier violent conflicts reemerged in spectacular markers on the landscape, such as gruesome displays of cattle thieves' heads on wooden pickets on the outlaying pathways of Mahajanga. Although there is much of significance in Dumaine's account, what is notable is the selective emplacement of the severed heads *on the city's margins*, which may have served to lay monarchal claim to a liminal territory. Such staged performances of Ravahiny's power constituted a thin veneer over the seething contestations that pulsated across the body politic, and it temporarily masked the ongoing struggles and irksome refusals unfolding across the city's tableau.

How might we understand the complex nature of the political configuration writ large on the city's architectural tableau in late-eighteenth-century Mahajanga? Under Ravahiny, a nexus of multiple, distributed, and convergent spheres of influence emerged in which Antalaotra, Indians, and Sakalava groups held overlapping claims to different kinds of authority and carved out dynamic spaces for enduring networks of exchange, leisure, and religious practice. As traders, merchants, appointed district chiefs, and Sakalava royal figures moved through the multicentric landscape, they accessed varying degrees of authoritative license and latitude over political, economic, and customary matters, and employed reciprocity as a key tactic. In fact, ceremonial exchange and reciprocity were cornerstones of Ravahiny's strategy to maintain sovereignty, which she employed in royal rituals of rebuilding and in trading negotiations with European partners from the late seventeenth century, in ways similar to African leaders elsewhere on the African continent.[88]

The 1790s were a critical period in the southwestern Indian Ocean, during which regional trade was disrupted by conflicts in Comoros and by increasingly frequent raids on villages in Nzwani, Mayotte, and East Africa by ocean-going Malagasy raiders who seized captives for enslavement. By some accounts, subjects of Queen Ravahiny "took part" in the raids, though their participation was not sanctioned by royal leadership; in fact, Ravahiny apparently warned the Governor-General of Mozambique about preparations underway to raid the Kerimba Islands. Historian Jane Hooper suggests these raids can be understood as "aggressive manifestations of the increasing role of the Malagasy" in regional oceanic trading networks in which Mahajanga was a critical node.[89] British authorities glimpsed these raids and the ascension of Malagasy trade as a prime impetus for cultivating a stronger regional presence and tighter rapprochement with Malagasy authorities, and French traders simultaneously aspired to expand their footing in the region. It was precisely in the context of this shifting terrain that Ravahiny negotiated relations with foreigners while managing the allegiance of her polyglot political constituency and maintaining the legitimacy of her sacred power through architectural vectors.

Conclusion

Leading up to the eighteenth century, the Sakalava polity gradually established an orbit of influence in the northwest region through conquest and coercion, the cultivation of new affiliations, and the gathering of others into overlapping sets of economic and political-cosmological practices. The city's founding—like any city's birth—originated in the contingent convergences of the seventeenth- and eighteenth-century expansion and consolidation of the Sakalava Zafivolamena dynasty founded in the Boina kingdom, reaching a pinnacle under Ravahiny's reign: the violent conflicts, displacement, and subsequent reconvening of Islamic trading communities in the face of mounting Sakalava rule; newly developed boatbuilding and navigation technologies that made possible longer sea journeys; and the unfolding, historical ecology of the northwest coast, born of centuries of compression, climatic forces, and human-induced terraforming that created conditions favorable for planting a city, sustaining a growing population, and cultivating regional and oceanic trade relations.

With the growing enmeshment in western Indian Ocean trading constellations, goods, ideas, and people flowed increasingly into Mahajanga through the oceanic trade channels, the pathways winding inland and into the hinterlands, and the finger-like, grooved waterways of the Betsiboka river basin. Yet there were also limits to the integration of Mahajanga in the global Indian Ocean nexus. Madagascar's relative geographical remoteness to the heavily trafficked ports of Surat, Mocha, Aden, Kilwa, and Cape Town during the eighteenth century gave rise to distinctive Malagasy language and cultural practices, the former of which later became a lingua franca for diverse enslaved and free communities across the western Indian Ocean.[90] Perhaps more importantly, the city's proximate positioning hastened the early flourishing of abiding exchanges between northwestern Madagascar and its nearest archipelagic neighbor—Comoros—of goods, technical knowledge, and religious affiliation that would profoundly shape the city over the centuries to come.

Mahajanga's material transformation can be likened to a process of gathering, of accretion, through which the earthly, material traces of the city gradually accumulated and compiled into a calcified, even "reluctant," landscape.[91] Migrants bringing varying linguistic, genealogical, and commercial sensibilities sedimented the landscape; they gleaned from the sea, reaped from the soil, and collectively conjured new worlds within the urban topographies. They drew on the spatial offerings and affordances of the ecological landscape to assemble communities, curate the contours of everyday life, and negotiate new vistas with which they could reimagine their futures. Like the historically emergent narrative of Shaka Zulu described by Carolyn Hamilton, the built environment of Mahajanga was incrementally established through processes that "set limits on the extent and form of its manipulation in the service of politics."[92] As multiple waves of migrants drafted the variform textures and invoked the more-than-human world, they brought about an enduring urban terrain animated by the dead, the living, and indeterminacy that would shape new possibilities for political action and the (re)constitution of communal ties in the century to come.

Collectively, early settlers inscribed artisanal, economic, and political endeavors on the landscape, forging associations between places, people, and earthly things that have endured into the present. Marofoto, the seaside port neighborhood for the town's traders, crystallized as the town's gathering point, the beating heart of economic exchange and Islamic religious encounter. Even if the original mosque structures were torn down and rebuilt, several of the Muslim congregations, including the South Asian Bohra (and the later-arriving Kodja) communities, have continued to convene in the quarter's narrow, sandy passages. Marolaka persists as the seaside ship-repair and shipbuilding yard, and the ancient Antalaotra and Indian cemeteries and tombstones still lay scattered throughout town—occasionally intruding on the aspirations of contemporary dwellers and planners.[93] In these early decades, city dwellers, Muslim traders, and Sakalava rulers honed architectural tactics—of refusal, governance, and the assemblage of expertise—and strove to craft spaces for autonomy and political agency in the built landscape, though they did not do so equally. Some of these groups prevailed over others, and some practices carried forth, like durable building as a defiant signifier of self-determination; but they would also take new forms in the nineteenth century. Successive generations in the nineteenth century would seize the foundational physical and metaphorical scaffolding of the city to generate, experiment with, and contest practices of belonging in a more-than-human landscape.

2

Vibrant Matters

The Rova *and More-Than-Human Forces*

"Look here. You see this? This was the gate to the old rova, and just over there," he said pointing westward, just a little afield, "that was Sakalava *doany*."[1] It was March 2012, and we stood at the hilltop of Mahajanga in the blinding morning sun, with the bustling seaside town at our feet. Bachir had brought me here. I had met Hadj Soudjay Bachir Adehame, a tall, dignified, retired schoolteacher and politician, through a mutual friend. Learning of my interest in the city's past, he set about to instruct me on Mahajanga's early history from our first meeting. Over the course of several months, we met weekly in the airy stone home he shared with his hospitable, elegant wife in La Corniche, an expansive elevated quartier historically inhabited by elite Malagasy and Europeans. During these sessions, we drank fragrant black tea and ate crumbly vanilla biscuits while Bachir, ever the commanding intellectual, narrated the city's emergence from ancient Indian Ocean trade routes, to the early inhabitance by Antalaotra traders, and finally to the contemporary social geography of the town. He drew on a remarkable range of sources—historical linguistics, maps, archaeological sites, and published scholarly sources—to compose compelling narratives in the fashion of a veritable "homespun" historian.[2]

Our visits culminated on this day. I had proposed a drive through the city for the last of our scheduled meetings, hoping that a journey through the city's spaces might elicit more personal memories from Bachir— recollections of his younger years growing up and living in the town, memories largely absent from his scholarly renditions. Bachir showed his characteristic enthusiasm, and he had clearly taken deliberate care to craft our route. The only moment that came close to personal reflection occurred when Bachir pointed out his boyhood home. Still, I could scarcely be disappointed, as he took me to an array of landmarks reflecting the diverse historical actors animating the town's past: Sakalava sacred spaces, shophouses owned by South Asian families, French colonial-era civic buildings and houses, many now in ruins, the city's industrial past and rich maritime history.

At last we climbed the town's steep, prominent hill, now crowned with a sprawling public hospital and a gated military encampment but also with the material traces of a key historical nexus. It was on this hilltop, Bachir explained, that Sakalava monarchal leaders first established their *doany*, or royal compound, in the city's earliest days in the seventeenth century. Together we stood at the foot of a towering fig tree, swathed in brilliant, scarlet-red cloth to honor royal ancestral connections.[3] Across Madagascar, trees have historically been important gathering points, sites of reckoning, "calling places"—in sum, "geopolitical centers of communities"—that express the linkage between petrified ancestries and time-stretching claims to land.[4] Mahajanga's gigantically thick-trunked baobab tree, which sits not far from the hilltop, for instance, was one among the many reportedly planted by Islamic traders some 700 years ago and now serves as an arboreal metaphor for their enduring ties to the northwest coast and the city's best-known landmark (see figure 2.1, and map FM.4).[5] This particular tree on the hilltop was a fig tree, known to be related to sacred fig species (*Ficus lutea*) planted by highland royal leaders as acts of territorialization at their ancestral tombs and in newly conquered lands throughout the eighteenth and nineteenth centuries.[6] Although the exact origins of this tree remain shrouded in mystery, its adornment with the distinctively vibrant red swaths associated with Sakalava royalty manifested an expression of resolute ancestral presence on this site. Beyond the wrapped tree, no physical trace of a dwelling or structure remained. Standing just a few hundred feet away, however, was a massive stone gate that marked the entrance to the nineteenth-century fort erected by Radama I's soldiers (see figure 2.2). If Bachir's account was true, it was no accident that Radama's highland-based forces, upon invading the city in 1824, selected this hilltop on which to construct their fort. By appropriating this paramount place, Radama I's soldiers invoked the politics of altitude to spatially assert their dominance over the city's inhabitants and the reigning Sakalava royalty.

I was intrigued that Bachir found it important to show me this place. Friends and acquaintances had implicitly warned me that Bachir might

FIGURE 2.1 Baobab tree, Mahajanga, ca. 1900. Courtesy of Foiben-Taosarintanin'I Madagasikara.

deliberately lead me astray by indoctrinating me into a historical narrative skewed toward outsiders, especially Antalaotra and Islamic traders. One high-ranking administrator at the Université de Mahajanga impressed upon me the importance of finding "other" learned people (*mahay*) who could educate me in "the Sakalava"—and thus "true"—history of the city.[7] At times, Bachir's narrations *did* seem to overemphasize the role of Antalaotra traders—his own ancestors—in the city's formation. But our arrival at this hilltop site affirmed Bachir's heartfelt investment in the city's myriad histories and exposed the futilities of such neatly cast historical narratives. Although I'd read about the location of Radama's fort and knew that the current military compound was located there, I knew nothing of the old tree associated with the doany or the struggle that had ensued there. But the story of this hill and the competing constructions of built structures turned out to be emblematic of a deep-rooted history of conflictive and mutually constitutive place-making in Mahajanga. This hill was a kind of metaphorical knot on the undulating landscape, revealing the entanglements of multiple historical protagonists—Sakalava monarchal leaders and ritual specialists, Islamic traders, enslaved Makoa, Radama's mili-

FIGURE 2.2
Entrance Gate
to the rova,
Mahajanga, ca.
1886. Courtesy
of Archives
du Ministère
de l'Europe et
des Affaires
étrangères—
La Courneuve,
Serie P-Afrique,
A009325.
Photographer:
Albert Pinard.

tary forces, migrants from across the island, and European explorers and travelers.

This chapter chronicles how the more-than-human world was a crucial force in shaping the architectural possibilities for aspiring rulers and everyday city dwellers as they sought to build themselves into the city's landscape during the politically and economically tumultuous nineteenth century. Anchored at one of the city's key sites, the Saribengo hilltop, I offer a biographical excavation that sifts out the ways competing groups harnessed their uneven access to ecological affordances and refashioned labor and knowledge regimes to advance their morally infused visions for the future in the landscape. To understand the significance of this hilltop is to reckon with the successive struggles over architectural governance to which it bore witness. Throughout the first quarter of the nineteenth century, the hill was scarcely settled, a residential afterthought to the whirling node of economic trade at the seaside quarter of Marofoto. After the conquest of 1824–25, newly arrived Merina colonizers seized Saribengo to establish their rova (governor's palace and fort), cognizant as they were of the hill's natural attributes and the symbolic power of verticality. To construct the rova, and to compensate for the scarcity and refusal of local laborers, Merina rulers instituted forced-labor regimes and obligatory tributes from town residents. As powerful as they were, the Merina rulers depended not only on the expertise of Antalaotra masons and the ready availability of limestone, mangrove timber, and *satrana* palms, but also on the ancestral realm to legitimatize their authority. Once construction was underway, Merina soldiers confiscated the royal relics of the Sakalava ancestral monarchs—the material sources of political power—from Marovoay, planning to bring them to the hilltop rova, where they would construct a shrine to which they could regulate Sakalava access. Along the way, however, their aspirational plans were disturbed and manipulated in unexpected, irrepressible ways by the crisscrossing interventions of unruly ancestral spirits, purposeful Sakalava ritual experts, and creative town dwellers. Perhaps more than anywhere else in the city, the hilltop and its built forms gathered the past into the present and enfolded the living and the dead, the animate and inanimate, into the unceasing pleats of time.

In recent years, historians and archaeologists have developed new analytical apparatuses for understanding the ways that precolonial political elites produced power and cultivated authority, especially through built forms, in early African societies. Early engagements foregrounded how power was diffusely disseminated across collectivities, converged in alliances, and embodied in cosmological, ritual devices, rather than emanating from centralized political institutions exercising primarily coercive means.[8] Architecture was understood as a vital expressive and symbolic form through which elites demonstrated and asserted sociopolitical hierarchies. More recent scholarship, moreover, has offered heuristic approaches that emphasize how built forms were enmeshed in the gatherings, ritual performances, and economic exchanges through which hierarchical relationships were forged.[9] This perspective has been critical for grasping how authority in early African polities was continually negotiated through spatial-material *and* discursive domains, but the role of the more-than-human world in architectural assemblages has remained underexplored.[10] We know of the long-standing, tightly knit relationship between the spirit realm and creative power (that is, the kind of power that generates new meanings, compels people to believe, and is elicited through ritual) in Madagascar and across the African continent.[11] But how can we understand the significance of other-than-humans in conditioning the contours of possibility for architectural inscription and governance, for building a concrete presence in the world?

In this chapter, I argue that we need to see built environments not simply as collective material, political, and economic processes but as emerging from entanglements with ancestral spirits, otherworldly forces, trees and stones, and vibrant substances as well as from specific regimes of labor and expertise that are embedded in political economies. By juxtaposing a rich trove of official nineteenth-century correspondence (between Merina rulers in Mahajanga and Antananarivo, the highland capital) with past and contemporary ethnographic accounts, I explore how spiritual entities were understood as active presences in the unfolding biographies of built forms on the Saribengo hilltop. At times these intractable forces constrained the tempo of construction, or they gathered ritual specialists and royal followers together. At still other times, they prompted new moral vocabularies with which city folk could contest authoritarian Merina rule. In scanning the archival city and the documentary trail that remains, the hilltop protrudes as a particularly crucial site of negotiation with the spirit realm. Though certainly not the only such place in the city, the hilltop's trajectory reveals how architectural bundling, shrouding, and encasement necessitated specific forms of ecological and ritual know-how as well as arduous, varied labors. By building Saribengo hill, city dwellers inscribed their aspirations in the earthly tableaux, laminating over the traces of those and that which had preceded them, and—much like their Swahili counterparts at the time—curated spaces from which to negotiate the economic and political fluctuations of the nineteenth century.[12]

Seizing the Saribengo Hilltop

In the early 1800s, at the pinnacle of its trading activity, Mahajanga underwent seismic political upheavals, key among them the invasion by military forces of highland monarch Radama I (1810–28) in 1824–25. Nestled in a constellation of southern Indian Ocean entrepots, Mahajanga was at the time of the Merina invasion a thriving port with a lively exchange of goods and an astonishing ethnolinguistic diversity of inhabitants. Jutting into the sea, the peninsular city boasted easy dockage and convenient proximity to the Betsiboka River, where dhows and smaller ships traded with villages upstream.[13]

Estimates of the town's population in the 1820s suggest modest demographic growth since the late 1700s, to around 8,000–12,000 Antalaotra, Sakalava, Makoa, Hadhrami Arabs, South Asian Hindus and Muslims, Comorians, and Malagasy.[14] As in the eighteenth century, the diverse city was governed by a representative tripartite council consisting of a "Malegash" leader, a "chief of the Arabs," and a third responsible authority for the protection of "strangers," who apparently shared power in a relatively heterarchical fashion.[15] British navy officer Thomas Boteler, who passed through the town in 1824, noted that these leaders "consulted together for the benefit of the place" and sought consensus in legal cases brought before them.[16] Although Sakalava monarchal figures and the royal Sakalava do-any were rooted in Marovoay until the 1820s, trading activity was clustered in Mahajanga with commercial tentacles stretching deep inland and out to sea.

Political leaders in Imerina, based in the highland region, glimpsed Mahajanga's economic richesse and sought to expand the kingdom's territorial reach to the city (among other coastal regions) in order to capture raw materials and trade imports, expand access to labor, and eliminate competing rivals through military expeditions in the early 1800s. At the same time, Radama I strategically cultivated a relationship with British officials as a means of gaining leverage to extend his rule domestically. For their part, British authorities hoped to gain a foothold in the region to counter the expansive French and Omani influence in the Indian Ocean. By 1820, the British offered their support to Radama to submit the entire island to his control and recognized him as "king of Madagascar" in exchange for Radama's agreement to abolish the slave trade.[17]

In 1824, buttressed by British support, Radama boldly initiated military expeditions to the northwest coast, which had hitherto remained beyond his control. Two years earlier, expeditions to the southerly Menabe region were carried out with a sizeable standing army (by some accounts 100,000 strong), yet troops were ill-prepared and poorly supported, and upward of half were lost through death and desertion.[18] Nonetheless, in a strategic mission to overtake Mahajanga and the Boina region, Radama forcibly conscripted more troops, employed British agent James Hastie as a diplomatic envoy, and set off on foot for the expedition. Once in the vicinity of Mahajanga, Hastie attempted to secure the city through diplomatic and economic negotiations, during which time he learned that Andriantsoly (known as Andriamanavakarivo while living), the reigning Sakalava monarch, had absconded from the royal capital Marovoay to Mahajanga, and "many of the traders and residents" had scrambled out of Mahajanga with their belongings.[19] Radama's troops forged ahead, killing Hussein ben Abdallah, the Antalaotra leader of Mahajanga, and marching into the city, where they hoisted the Imerina flag on the highest hilltop. After briefly halting trade, the newly arrived administrators resumed economic activity and increased taxes on ships anchoring at the port.[20]

At the heart of Radama's military conquest of Mahajanga were articulations of property and property norms, hinging on performances of violence and dispossession. Against the advice of Hastie, Radama offered a reward for the capture of Andriantsoly and declared that "all the property" of Andriantsoly and Hussein, which included enslaved persons, cattle, and their homes, now belonged to the royal treasury.[21] At the same time, Radama instructed his soldiers that private property belonging to commoners "should be respected" and assured residents that soldiers who pilfered or pillaged would be strictly punished—a promise he kept when the ringleader of a small group of soldiers subsequently accused of theft was swiftly "taken to the beach and shot."[22] If Radama hoped to intimidate both highland soldiers and local inhabitants through the public execution, he was partially successful. Antalaotra leaders privately expressed their shock to Hastie at the harsh punitive measures for a "trifling" crime.[23] Other measures to consolidate power were more obviously corrupt. Radama requested that town elites "send him an estimated value of [their] property" to enable him to choose a governor from among them.[24] Though it's unclear how many property owners actually sent the information, Radama apparently drew on these declarations to implement a five percent property tax on property owners across the city, and then installed his cousin Ramanetaka to serve as provincial governor for the Boina region.[25] He did show some mercy on the then-deposed Andriantsoly, however, allowing him to remain in the vicinity of Mahajanga in an area on the outskirts of town known as Anfiaounah, where Radama funded the construction of an exile home for the monarch and provided him a living allowance.[26]

Within the city, Radama's troops immediately set to work building themselves into power. Drawing on long-held cosmological practices of architecture on the island, they quickly identified the Saribengo hilltop just near the port as the ideal setting for the rova to house some 1,100 troops.[27] The summit was the highest point in the city, some 160 feet (50 meters) above the seaside, and military troops cleared a large road leading there. Radama's approach to managing space resonated with those of his predecessors in Imerina and of many African political leaders in early modern times. It was one of altitudinal power, in which elevation and ample breeze was tied to political authority.[28] Seizing the hilltop was a way of monopolizing verticality with all its strategic, aesthetic, and symbolic advantages. The peak served multiple functions: a strategic look-out for visitors, traders, and potential invaders; a visual proclamation of the dominance of the new Merina imperial rulers; and a performative space requiring visitors and commoners to physically ascend to the enclosed seat of power.

Much like the royal capital of Antananarivo at the time, the Mahajanga fort was circumscribed by a ditch.[29] Highland soldiers removed red earthen soil around the half-mile circumference of the rova, demarcating it as an exceptional, protected site, apart from the everyday spaces of trade and sociality at the seaside village.[30] Later observers noted a few years after construction that some sixty cannons, "all dismounted," lined the perimeter of the rova, carefully arranged in a display of military prowess.[31] Imported from Britain, the cannons also testified to the monarch's access to far-reaching trading networks and his ability to harness military equipment. Over time, a bamboo enclosure was added with two openings: one facing north into the countryside, and another south toward the seaside village.[32] The latter was equipped with three large-caliber guns (likely muskets), revealing the new regime's awareness of potential conflict with town inhabitants.

Sure enough, six months after the establishment of the Merina fort on the summit, the rova became a key site of contestation between Sakalava and Antalaotra, on one side, and Ramanetaka's men, on the other. Guillain recorded his account of the events some twenty years later; he wrote that the conflict was precipitated by a slave revolt organized by the enslaved laborers confiscated from Andriantsoly and given to Ramanetaka. We know little about these individuals' age, gender, or status, but they evidently wielded power through their voices and mobility. After complaining bitterly of the treatment they endured under Ramanetaka, thirty of them revolted, escaped, and established themselves with Andriantsoly in his residence at Anfiaounah. This led to a fierce dispute between Andriant-soly and Ramanetaka over the ownership of enslaved dependents and the purported customary laws dictating the norms for inheriting the enslaved people as property. Eventually, Ramanetaka took Andriantsoly's enslaved dependents by force, prompting Andriantsoly to organize a retaliatory at-tack on the rova with his men.[33]

After Andriantsoly mobilized the Sakalava who had dispersed across the region, his armed Sakalava and Antalaotra faction grew (some say to 2,000) and finally arrived in Mahajanga after about one week. As the armed conflict erupted, some trading families and inhabitants of the city managed to flee with their belongings to other nearby ports. Suddenly, however, Ra-manetaka set the city alight to repel his attackers. As fire engulfed the town, most of the town residents abandoned their thatch properties and traveled on "fifty-three boats and sixteen Arab dhows, as well as many boats and canoes" to the town of Katsepy, across the bay.[34] Andriantsoly, his closest aides, and the majority of Antalaotra traders fled and eventually settled on the island of Mahore (Mayotte) in the Comoros Islands. Others with lim-ited ties to Mahajanga opted to return to their homelands of Mozambique, Zanzibar, or the Comoros Islands (see map 2.1).[35]

Ultimately, the tumult destroyed the once vibrant seaside town, turn-ing it into "a mass of cinders, roofless huts, and walls blackened by fire; the herbage was parched, the gardens destroyed."[36] Ramanetaka honored some of the small number of inhabitants who remained in the smoky embers of the city by granting them chiefdoms for their "loyalty" to him and by des-ignating two Antalaotra as leaders of their constituency.[37] In addition to the few Antalaotra traders and Sakalava who stayed behind, a number of resident American traders remained, apparently unaffected by the fire.[38] Al-though the town's population was thought to be between 8,000 and 12,000 before the 1824 invasion, it dwindled to near desertion after the conflict and remained that way for several decades.[39] By the 1840s, according to tax collections, the town had only some 950 Antalaotra traders and enslaved dependents, 113 Sakalava inhabitants, and 30 Indians and their families, in addition to Merina soldiers and officials—reflecting the enduring demo-graphic impact of the violent conflict of 1824.[40] Ramanetaka had fallen out of favor with Radama's successor and reigning monarch (Ranavalona I), and he too fled to Comoros, where he was crowned sultan of Moheli. New gov-ernors succeeded him, but Mahajanga remained plagued by the ghosts of the past.

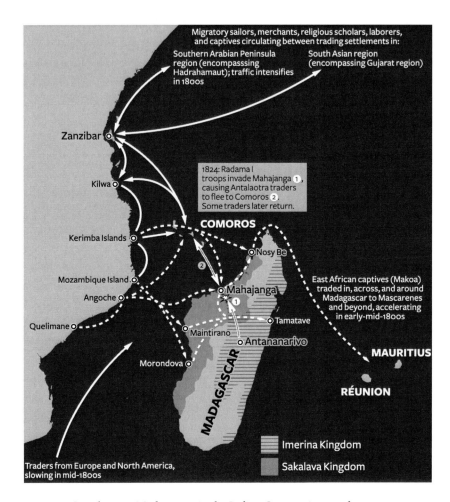

Migratory sailors, merchants, religious scholars, laborers, and captives circulating between trading settlements in:

Southern Arabian Peninsula region (encompasssing Hadrahamaut); traffic intensifies in 1800s

South Asian region (encompassing Gujarat region)

Zanzibar

1824: Radama I troops invade Mahajanga ①, causing Antalaotra traders to flee to Comoros ②. Some traders later return.

Kilwa

COMOROS

Kerimba Islands

Nosy Be

②

Mozambique Island

East African captives (Makoa) traded in, across, and around Madagascar to Mascarenes and beyond, accelerating in early-mid-1800s

Angoche

Mahajanga ①

Quelimane

Tamatave

Maintirano

Antananarivo

MAURITIUS

Morondova

RÉUNION

MADAGASCAR

Imerina Kingdom

Sakalava Kingdom

Traders from Europe and North America, slowing in mid-1800s

MAP 2.1 Circulations, Madagascar in the Indian Ocean, nineteenth century. Map by Tim Stallmann.

Ancestral Power

In the midst of the conflict, Radama's troops seized the sacred Sakalava relics (*dady*; literally, "grandparents") from the royal capital of Marovoay. Although accounts are patchy, we know that the relics were transferred to the hilltop rova at Mahajanga and stored "inside the Governor's stockade," which was guarded by soldiers bearing firearms.[41] The appropriation and possession of Sakalava relics—whether by an imperial highland monarchy or later French forces—were means of enunciating dominance and keeping

Sakalava inhabitants subordinate.[42] As the very substance of royal power, which endowed the possessor with legitimate "strength to rule," these relics were subsequently contested among competing Sakalava monarchs in the western region.[43] The dady were the source, substance, and center of ancestral power, enacted through rituals of spirit possession. Spirit mediums and the dady were the critical conduits through which ancestors could be placated, beseeched, and engaged. Linking past to present, the relics were (and are) the material accumulation of sedimented pasts and thus the "most vital resource" of Sakalava political authority.[44] Possessing the relics was tantamount to laying claim to the land, peoples, and things of the northwest. If, as archaeologist Zoë Crossland rightly points out, "to seize a territory was to capture its ancestral past" in nineteenth century Madagascar, then the inverse was also true in this case: to seize the ancestral past (embodied in the royal relics) was also to seize a territory.[45]

The ancestral spirits associated with the relics, however, exerted their own irksome force on highland administrators by stalling and foiling their aspirations for dominance. Soon after seizing the relics from Marovoay, builders (unidentified in the archival record) constructed a small square shrine (zomba) intended to house the relics—the teeth, nails, and hair of past Sakalava monarchs, including Andriantsoly's grandfather. According to the young British agent John Studdy Leigh, the shrine was designed in a square configuration with four corners aligned to the cardinal points, in keeping with historical norms of sacred architecture in Madagascar.[46] By constructing the shrine using satrana palm and wooden poles adorned with "many pairs" of oxen horns, the shrine builders created a composite of animate and inanimate traces, in which earthly things enclosed the living artifacts of royal power.[47]

Yet when the time came to transport the relics, the ancestors hindered the process by apparently invoking a politics of refusal. The soldier entrusted with physically transporting the reliquary from Marovoay to the zomba at Mahajanga became ill en route. His body became stiff, and for almost one week he was completely unable to move. The association of bodily rigidity and death was not lost on highland administrators, who likely interpreted this fearsome event as evidence of the perilous strength of Sakalava ancestors. It was only after a week's delay that "the relics consented to proceed," possibly after ritual experts interceded, though Leigh's account does not say.[48] The disruption caused by the ancestors' refusal impressed on ruling highlanders not only the potency of Sakalava relics, but also the urgency of placating ancestors through proper ritual intercession.

Radama's appointed governor Raen'zaro (successor to Ramanetaka) and his men immediately regarded the relics as "objects of veneration" and found themselves beholden to the obligations and vulnerabilities associated with the royal objects.[49] The new authorities went to great lengths to venerate the dady in elaborate, public ceremonies, even while expressing their dominance by enclosing the shrine within the rova. Among the key ritual events observed at the rova was the performative fanompoa, or "care of royal ancestors" and their property, which included their relics, tombs, and artifacts.[50] Leigh witnessed this "remembrance of departed kings of Malagasy," as he called it, after ascending the hilltop fort with American trader Vincent Marks in 1836.[51] Leigh and Marks were led into the zomba, where they found many young women seated on the ground, as well as several male relatives of the highland royal family. In the corner (probably the northeast, following with cosmological norms governing space) sat the arc containing the black box of "mysteries." After the first layer of drapery covering the relics was pulled away, the women began a "melancholy chant," intermixing whispered prayers and mournful incantation. Leigh noted that the relics were nestled into boxes, set atop "ebony sticks and hung with black drapery." As an aesthetic strategy of hiddenness, the layers of cloth and wood encasing the relics obfuscated the visual field. Concealing the relics signified both the precious, powerfully generative nature of ancestors and the elusive (and thus even more valuable) ancestral knowledge.[52]

Performances of piety and deference to powerful Sakalava ancestors, to which Merina authorities were subject, persisted over time. In 1839, Leigh witnessed a similar ceremony in which a group of twenty women gathered before the relics, with the governor and a half dozen male highland administrators standing at attention.[53] With hands covering their faces, the women knelt before the relics, praying in lowered voices; in adherence to proper bodily comportment, they pointed their feet away from the shrine.[54] Leigh did not mention how the men positioned themselves, but he noted that one male relative of the highland Queen Ranavalona I finally "addressed a long prayer to the objects." As the festivities intensified, the women began to dance; a few became possessed by ancestral spirits and were obliged to "practice various rites to please" the spirits.[55] When Guillain arrived in the 1840s, he observed similar, sustained formal veneration of the relics by the then-governor Raen'zaro throughout the year, culminating in the annual washing of the relics (*fanompoa be*): "Raen'zaro maintains piety [toward the relics] by, at various times in the year, taking them to be ceremoniously washed in the sea, with much pomp and gunshots."[56]

On these yearly occasions, the governor cleaved open the gate enclosing the rova and enjoined free and unfree inhabitants to grand feasts, during which the ordinarily hierarchical, routinized space gave way to the abandon of spontaneous, charismatic play and staged performances of patronage relations.[57] Raen'zaro likely hosted these feasts in the hope that the possession of the relics would attract Sakalava inhabitants to remain in the area rather than disperse.[58] Keeping the relics perhaps offered a degree of protection to highland administrators, who perceived that Sakalava adversaries would be reluctant to strike the rova and risk destruction of the relics. Imerina and Sakalava monarchies shared linguistic and cultural registers that framed ancestral relics as sources of power. This shared schema, in turn, allowed for a degree of mutual legibility between the two monarchies regarding the norms governing proper treatment, emplacement, and honoring of ancestral remains.

These accounts shed light on the relationships among material objects and built forms, the spiritual realm, and political practices in the early to mid-nineteenth century. The sensory dimensions of the shrine's material composition lent itself to the enunciation of particular collective rituals, which congealed over time into durable communities of practice. Constructed of wood, the shrine protecting the relics allowed the chants and prayers within to echo outward, thus constituting an aural ritual community and announcing the collective, energetic power within to those outside. The presence of oxen horns—sedimented expressions of generations of Sakalava royal strength, durability, and wealth—indexed the historical importance of cattle as a source of wealth and animate power for Sakalava royalty. How these ritual encounters shifted the subjectivity of Merina officials is hard to say, but their efforts to honor Sakalava ancestral relics at the zomba persisted for decades. Not only did they continue to participate in the fanompoa be, but eventually many Merina soldiers and officials also used Sakalava *sampy* (amulets or charms) to activate the protective powers associated with the Sakalava spirit world—much to the dismay of Merina administrators and British missionaries who arrived in the latter half of the century.[59] If seizing the relics was, at first, a strategy for subjugating the Sakalava territory, the ancestors' encroachment into the present ultimately stymied Radama's plan.

Beyond the zomba and the ancestral realm, the rova was a locus for negotiating the earthly relations between ruling elites, free and unfree inhabitants, and strangers. The rova stood at the end of a broad avenue that was shaded with abundant orange, mango, and cocoa trees (figure 2.3). It was

FIGURE 2.3
Avenue to the
rova, Mahajanga,
ca. 1886–89.
Courtesy of
Archives du
Ministère de
l'Europe et
des Affaires
étrangères—La
Courneuve,
Série P-Afrique,
A009327.
Photographer:
Albert Pinard.

surrounded by a wall that marked the space node of power and was expressive of the unrivaled superiority of highland authorities. Several armed
soldiers guarded the walled enclosure itself, and admittance was strictly limited to approved visitors and Merina officials. European passersby, driven
by curiosity and sometimes charged with imperial scouting, often sought
unsuccessfully to penetrate the fort.[60] Popular festivities such as weddings
and Eid (the end of Ramadan), by contrast, unfolded in the streets, where
subalterns could more freely claim spaces for political inversion and constitute their social collectivities. For the most part, the rova remained an
exclusionary space in which Merina rulers privileged highlanders, traders,
and select Sakalava ritual experts, while marginalizing everyday inhabitants. Like any architectural enclosure, the rova's wall and forbidding gate
(figure 2.2) simultaneously constrained and generated social formations
and political negotiations.[61]

FIGURE 2.4 Houses to the north of the rova, Mahajanga, ca. 1886–89.
Courtesy of Archives du Ministère de l'Europe et des Affaires étrangères—
La Courneuve, Série P-Afrique, A009323. Photographer: Albert Pinard.

The rova contained houses intended for military troops, a small church, and the governor's home, each differentiated by strategically selected materials that reflected the internal hierarchies of the elites and military troops charged with surveilling the city.[62] Shortly after establishing the rova, soldiers hauled heavy timbers from the wooded hinterlands and mangrove stalks from the swampy coast, with which they framed the houses designated for elite military troops and their families, as well as the houses in the surrounding "village" occupied mostly by highlanders (see figure 2.4).[63] The roofs of these commoner homes were constructed from *satrana* palms, widely abundant in the vicinity.[64] Woven palm walls—permeable and airy—enabled sound to travel and thus allowed for a degree of surveillance over troops, "all of whom were under the orders of the Governor."[65] Radama's approach to maintaining power hinged on strict discipline within the military, enforced with speedy and capital punishment, which extended into requiring fastidious interior conditions in soldiers' homes. An Austrian traveler in the 1870s described the "extraordinary elegance and cleanliness" of the soldiers' peak-roofed, wooden houses and the elaborately, tightly woven patterns of satrana palm–paneled walls.[66] Inside, most homes contained a *kitanda* (bed) with wooden frames and raffia-twine netting, as well as several low chairs; those of greater means and importance might also have had "European furniture."[67] Such distinctions in domestic interiors reflected the many gradations of status within Radama's rigidly hierarchical military bureaucracy. Soldiers derived their income by serving as the state's tax collectors, a practice that generated differential incomes among soldiers and surely fueled town dwellers' animosity toward the military presence.

The governor's home, by contrast, was built of limestone. The home's exterior was said to have been guarded by a door with "two crossed spears" opening onto a foreyard.[68] Beyond the yard stood a second guarded gate, and beyond that a "capacious yard"; this sequence served to orchestrate visitors' incremental access to the political sanctum and to visually remind visiting officials of the differential field of power.[69] Only after passing these thresholds were visitors received in a room of 14 × 16 feet, supported with pillars and with a "black wood" (likely ebony) floor; the room was filled with a large table and chairs.[70] The thick stone walls created a cool, buffered environment contrast to the sweltering heat of the city, enabling Merina officials and their guests to craft an alternative space in which they could temper rhythms and negotiate exchanges.

In this innermost chamber, the Merina governor ceremoniously received European traders, ship captains, and emissaries and lavished them with gin, champagne, and vermouth; extravagant feasts; leisurely conversation; and choreographed festivities. Leigh remarked, for instance, that the Merina governor initially welcomed them into a meeting room, served them wine, and conversed through his interpreter, General Raiengo.[71] Over the course of Leigh's multiple stays, they shared meals with increasingly copious amounts of beef, sherry, and port wine.[72] Visitors in later decades described elaborate banquets replete with "bottles of Médoc, soup in a willow-pattern tureen . . . rice, curried fowls, chicken kabobs, roast beef; geese, beef olives, dry, sweet sausage, and wild ducks in great abundance."[73] These demonstrations of hospitality served as vivid spectacles in which Merina authorities' access to global trading connections was on full display and European traders were positioned as pliable consumers. As scholars of Africa have shown elsewhere, these feasts were not only moments that rendered conspicuous the political and economic power of the ruling elites, but also dynamic "arenas within which power and authority became possible."[74] The ambiance of these ritual events was engendered by the architectural contours at hand, and ruling administrators expended considerable efforts to construct the governor's house as a suitable site for leveraging negotiations. The rova's architectural forms summoned the dense entanglements of political power—expressed through the gathering of material ancestral relics and living humans, thatch, stone, wood, and cloth, agricultural bounty and slaughtered animals—and stood as a material performance of otherwise invisible potency.

Transforming People, Place, and Nature

Merina performances of trading finesse, their access to wide-reaching regional and global networks, and the manifestation of their power into built forms were predicated on their violent disruption of long-standing systems of exchange and labor norms. After the 1824 invasion of Mahajanga, Merina officials wrested control over trade in the city. Endowed with bountiful pasture, Sakalava pastoralists in the northwest kept large herds of distinctive humped cattle (*Bos taurus indicus*), which were not only the economic foundation on which Sakalava dynasties grew to acclaim, but also the source of strategic alliances with Antalaotra traders throughout the eighteenth and early nineteenth centuries. Antalaotra and Gujarati traders were the key intermediaries in regional networks and long-distance trade, channeling through Mahajanga and other northwest ports key commodities from the interior such as bananas, sago, salt, rice, copal, beeswax, sandalwood, and tortoiseshell.[75] Consumers in Mahajanga demanded a wide range of imports, including silver coins, furniture, cloth, beads, muskets, alcohol, glassware, and even "musical boxes."[76] Merchants in Mahajanga drew global repute for their voluminous, high-quality cattle products—tallow (rendered fat), prepared hides, and dry jerky—which New England traders and consumers increasingly demanded in the early nineteenth century.[77]

The photograph in figure 2.5, captured by French photographer Alfred Pinard, offers a striking glimpse into this cattle-driven world, albeit at a later moment in the 1880s. Piles of parched hides, from zebu presumably brought in from the hinterlands and slaughtered at the nearby slaughterhouse, are strewn about the open-air square. Laborers are absorbed in the feverishly paced, intensive work of stripping and processing the hides, under the watchful gaze of white-robed Indian merchants seated in the distance. The varying building facades in the background—some whitewashed with lime plaster, others of barren stone, and still others of thatch—suggest

FIGURE 2.5 Disembarkation of beef hides, Mahajanga, ca. 1886–89. Courtesy of Archives du Ministère de l'Europe et des Affaires étrangères—La Courneuve, Série P-Afrique, A009278. Photographer: Albert Pinard.

differences in the economic means among merchants and perhaps also the duration of their establishment in the city. Once Merina troops occupied Mahajanga, however, they shifted the cattle trade away from Sakalava rulers and gradually marginalized Antalaotra traders beginning in the late 1820s.[78] Over the course of the nineteenth century, highland administrators seized land and cattle from Sakalava by increasingly violent means. Wealthy Sakalava were gradually purged after being falsely accused of various crimes and put to death. Ruling officials then confiscated their property and eliminated them as political opponents, a practice found in the highlands as well.[79] The larger network of highlander-dominated trade relied on Indian and some Antalaotra traders as key intermediaries, but the vast revenues from cattle, taxes on commodity trading, and property taxes in the city were largely funneled into the coffers of the ruling Merina elites.[80]

Construction projects doubly served as critical sites for constituting labor regimes that enacted new sociopolitical hierarchies throughout the city. Merina monarchs had long relied on *fanompoana*, a system of forced labor of free men over thirteen years of age, to carry out farming and infrastructure projects in the highlands. Under Radama I (1810–28), the scope of fanompoana widened to intensify recruitment for the army, while en-slaved persons increasingly undertook agricultural work. In Mahajanga, the situation was slightly different. Early on, Sakalava were apparently obliged to supply wood and service boats for royal projects, but once Merina elites recognized their fragile hold on power, they grew reticent to impose forced labor on hostile Sakalava inhabitants for royal projects.[81] Rather than risk a massive uprising, the Merina officials in Mahajanga adopted what histo-rian Micheline Rasoamiaramanana called a "policy of conciliation" marked by negotiations involving concessions to subjects to maintain their tenu-ous grip on the region.[82] As part of these concessions, free town inhabi-tants might avoid forced labor themselves by offering either their enslaved workers to labor on their behalf or other resources.

Leigh's accounts of the forced-labor schemes rarely mention Sakalava. Instead, Karana, Antalaotra, and their dependents, as well as Merina sol-diers and reinforcements, appear to have been the target populations for fanompoana. In November 1839, for instance, when the Merina governor mandated that all town residents haul sand up to the rova, some hundreds of Antalaotra men and women complied, but Karana "sent their slaves," most of whom were women, to labor on their behalf.[83] A few weeks later, the governor signed an order calling all Karana and Antalaotra, or their dependents, to build the cattle enclosure at the rova. This time "very few went," and consequently many faced fines.[84] Fanompoana invoked coercive regimes that moved across scale from kingdom, to region, to household and individual bodies. The practice was not only about insisting on the Merina monarch's dominion over a region and its subjects; it also entailed free persons' assertions of dominance over the enslaved persons in their households. Within households, calls to pay tribute to the queen reinforced social hierarchies through the reallocation of labor and the designation of differential roles in the service of the state. Conversely, these calls could also be met with free and unfree inhabitants' collective refusal, for which the governing regime had little recourse apart from fines.

By and large, the burden of labor for royal building projects fell on the enslaved population, largely made up of East Africans collectively, though not unproblematically, and referred to as Makoa in written sources.[85] De-spite Radama's official pledge to end the exportation of enslaved captives in 1820, the forcible movement of captives from coastal East Africa to Co-moros and Madagascar, as well as within the island, persisted well into the 1880s.[86] Like other Indian Ocean entrepôts at the time, Madagascar was both an importer and exporter of enslaved persons.[87] Many slaves landed on the shores of Mahajanga and remained there with Karana, Antalaotra, highland, and sometimes Sakalava families, whereas others were taken on foot to the highlands or to the east coast ports for further sale. Their position as property went unquestioned until the 1870s, and—unlike land and livestock—they were considered inviolable property of their owners by the Imerina state.[88]

Within the everyday life of the town, Makoa markedly shaped the cultural tableaux of the city. Many observed the Islamic practices of their slavers' families and were key figures in Eid festivities. Leigh described how "slaves of Mozambique extraction," for instance, traversed the streets, singing and dancing and dressed "in their best," during the Eid celebration in December 1839.[89] Rival groups (whom Leigh called "Marduco" and "Marfuto") competed against one another in musical and dance competitions that sometimes ended in physical fights.[90] Makoa apparently seized the streets as capacious spaces of potentiality and unabashed visibility, where they conjured spirited diversion, temporarily upended the strictures of social hierarchy, and claimed the city as their own.

Enslaved Makoa, however, were much more than drivers of street festivities. As the city's main laboring population, they emerged as experts in construction techniques and technologies. Like their counterparts in Mauritius, Mahajanga's enslaved population gradually accumulated an intimate and critical knowledge of how to transform the hardened matter of the earth—shells and stone—into durable built forms.[91] Makoa were charged with the fabrication of lime, a central component of "stone" architecture used for the governor's house. Like cities along the Swahili coast, Mahajanga had an earlier history of construction from lime tied to transoceanic trading commerce.[92] Wealthy merchants in Mahajanga commissioned the construction of "stone" houses out of lime, coral, limestone, and "argamass" (a mortar of lime, vegetation, sand, or clay; from Portuguese *argamáça*), which stood as physical manifestations of their economic status, trustworthiness as traders, and connections to global networks of exchange (see figures 2.5 and 2.6).[93]

The archival record of techniques and knowledge transmission among masons is patchy, beyond the mention that "Malagasy" masons constructed stone homes that belonged primarily to "Hindo and Arabs."[94] Traders with the wealth to do so commissioned laborers—possibly Antalaotra or Makoa—to collect rocks from the quarries of "neighboring mountains" for construction of their homes in Old Majunga, the neighborhood just near the port.[95] Images from later in the century suggest that builders recuper-

FIGURE 2.6 Porters from the highlands, Mahajanga, ca. 1886–89. Note whitewashed lime cement construction on right; wood, argamass, and coral stone construction in middle and far structures. Courtesy of Archives du Ministère de l'Europe et des Affaires étrangères—La Courneuve, Série P-Afrique, A009269. Photographer: Albert Pinard.

ated coral rock from the sea, which they used to fortify walls (see figures 2.6 and 2.7). These two-story homes stood in sharp contrast to the many single-story dwellings occupied by Antalaotra, Comorian, Sakalava, and Makoa families. Such homes were constructed of mangrove wood frames and satrana palm panels, with slanted, thatch roofs composed of interwoven palm and cocoa leaves (figure 2.8). They also differed from homes built by Merina migrants, which were supported by mangrove poles and padded with yellow mud and raffia fibers.[96]

By the 1830s, according to Leigh's journal, "Masombika" (Makoa) were charged with the production of the lime that was so critical to the construction of durable forms in the city. Lime production involved traversing multiple geographies and geological timescales. Laboring groups, composed of both men and women, traveled considerable distances by foot, up to 40 or 50 kilometers (25 or 30 miles), to collect limestone from Mahajanga's hinterlands.[97] There, limestone beds held the hardened rock, solidified from sedimented layers of marine organisms over sixty million years old.[98]

FIGURE 2.7 Unloading rocks (likely coral), Mahajanga, ca. 1886–89. Courtesy of Archives du Ministère de l'Europe et des Affaires étrangères—La Courneuve, Série P-Afrique, A009290. Photographer: Albert Pinard.

Workers then hauled the stone back to the seaside, where they collected cockle shells that they transformed with the limestone in a multistep incineration process. In a square, mud-brick oven filled with red-hot charcoal (processed from hardwood trees in the region), they placed the cockle shells, which they then covered with more charcoal. Using indigenous bellows, which Leigh described as "peculiar to this part of the world," they supplied a steady stream of air to the fire until the shells became "well-calcined."[99] The shells were then dropped into water-filled coconut shells to cool. Ultimately, Leigh noted, this process produced "excellent lime."[100] This lime was an ideal mortar, which could either bind together the mined limestone rock or be fabricated on its own into hardened bricks used for construction. Workers then hauled the "lime" in these forms from the seaside to the governor's hilltop home, where it was used to build walls that would last.

The many steps of the process drew on reservoirs of geographical, chemical, and technical knowledge accrued through diverse exchanges and refined over time. Fabricating lime hinged on knowing where to locate limestone

FIGURE 2.8 Three Makoa women, Mahajanga, ca. 1886–89. Note the woven thatch and wood construction of the home. Courtesy of Archives du Ministère de l'Europe et des Affaires étrangères—La Courneuve, Série P-Afrique, A009186. Photographer: Albert Pinard.

deposits and the footpaths that led to them; which chunks of limestone and cockle shells would yield the highest quality, hardest lime; and how much combustion and heat were needed, as well as burning and cooling times. All these layers of enskillment required proximate, tacit knowledge of the offerings of the natural environment and the ways skillful intervention might bring about chemical reactions and material transformation. Anta-laotra, who were entrusted with the construction of the governor's house and would have had more specific knowledge of the properties of limestone and shell in the Mahajanga region, joined the Makoa.[101] Just how the two groups exchanged knowledge and the differential roles they assumed in the construction process (whether laborer and overseer, or a more egalitarian arrangement) remain unclear. By the 1860s, royal orders for fanompoana continued to enroll a portion of the town's population but gradually shifted to rely more on Merina soldiers and reinforcements sent from the high-lands.[102] Collectively, these masons drew on techniques long known in the region and exerted arduous effort to transform ossified, buried sediments of the earth's past into future vestiges of the living.[103]

Crumbling Ruins, Splintering Rule, and Architectural Aspirations

Over the years, the cumulative forces of scorching sun, pounding rains, and saturating humidity metamorphized the once-proud masonry of the rova into crumbling decay. By the latter half of the nineteenth century, weather exposed the lifespan of lime, revealing its brittle nature and the ever-growing need for labor to resurrect it. The Imerina monarchy, too, was splintering. Ranavalona I (1828–61) had fashioned an autarkic regime marked by cessation of diplomatic and trading ties with Europeans, strict controls on commerce, and intensification of tributes and ritual practices (such as the *fandroana*) to sustain royal power.[104] Weakened by devastating military losses and increasing cattle raids by warring groups in the western regions, the labor base in the highlands was detrimentally depopulated. As enslaved people and other forms of wealth were increasingly concentrated in the hands of highland military and royal officials, the free population carried a greater burden of the dreaded forced labor service for the queen, prompting many to migrate away from the center of power.[105] Demand for enslaved laborers intensified in the highlands during the mid-century, and infrastructural and agricultural projects slowed. In Mahajanga, too, the monarchy administrators drained the population first through the expulsion of wealthy and influential Sakalava and then through the onerous conscription in forced-labor schemes. Royal subjects in Mahajanga, like other provinces on the island, were required to pay heavy financial tributes to the highland monarch to support ritual events and building projects in Antananarivo.[106] At least every four months, royal officials in Mahajanga sent caravans to Antananarivo with cattle, enslaved dependents, and "the king's belongings" as an additional tribute beyond the routine taxes.[107]

These heavy tributary systems led the Imerina monarchal regime down a self-devouring path, which gradually brought about popular dissent, sweeping economic crises, and vulnerability to European imperial predations. In the 1850s, an emergent cadre of reformists within the court, some educated in mission schools, pushed for opening the circumscribed relations with Europeans. These efforts gained momentum with the ascension of Radama II (Ranavalona I's son) to the throne in 1861. With the backing of progressive-minded counselors, Radama II lifted the prohibition on Christianity, invited British missionaries to resume their educational programs, reestablished diplomatic ties with Europe, and sought to entice European concessionaires to the island.[108] Port cities like Mahajanga were set to gain importance in this era with the re-expansion of Madagascar's activity in global trading networks.

At just this moment of intensified optimism for the empire's (re)ascension in the global market, ruling Merina leaders renewed their concern with the *materiality* of architecture. Radama II, anticipating a glorified epoch on the horizon, ordered his men in Mahajanga to prioritize the rebuilding of the collapsing rova in 1863. Drawing on centuries-long aesthetic practices among Merina monarchs who dedicated extraordinary resources to stone construction in the highlands, Radama II emphasized that the rova in Mahajanga ought to be *durable*. He instructed the governor at the time, Rainivoanjo, to enlist town inhabitants to restore the rova's enclosure back to its impressive state, one befitting the kingdom's image. Radama II worried that the deteriorating structures would "bring shame" (*mahamenatra*) on the monarchy, especially in the eyes of visitors arriving on the shores.[109]

Faithful servant that he was, Rainivoanjo conscripted town laborers to repair the rova, but several weeks later the king was assassinated. Radama's abrupt and zealous methods of reform, undertaken in the span of a single year, fomented opposition and unrest; in the end, he was strangled during a palace coup orchestrated by his key advisors and was succeeded by his wife, Rasoherina.[110] But Rainivoanjo reassured the widow-now-queen that the restoration of the rova had been fruitfully seen to completion. "The rova was built," he wrote in a letter in 1863. "It was beautifully finished." He was sure to emphasize that it was "hard" (*mafy*). What was more, according to Rainivoanjo, the whole town population, including the "officers, soldiers, Silamo and Sakalava," had contributed labor to the rebuilding effort.[111] He hoped the rebuilding of the rova would signal the imminent reconstitution of the now-waning kingdom's body politic.

But in the early 1870s, a series of fires devastated the rova, damaging the military housing, destroying half of the governor's house, and partially incinerating the Sakalava zomba.[112] After one of the fires, highland administrators reported to the monarchy that Sakalava royal servants collected "precious woods" from nearby forests and constructed a "flat-roofed structure" to house the relics, which had apparently remained unscathed.[113] Eventually, the doany (including the shrine) was rebuilt in the renowned seaside boatbuilding quarter Marolaka, the first of several moves until settling at its current site in Tsararano. This shift may have come about because the Merina monarchy had officially turned toward Christianity (initiated by the crown conversion in 1869) and sought to disassociate the shrine from the government seat, or because Sakalava ritual experts seized the opportunity to uproot the relics from the rova, the Merina nerve center in Mahajanga, or both.

At any rate, British missionaries began to infiltrate the northwest region, and churches rose up in Mahajanga's sacred landscape long dominated by mosques and the doany. Like the removal of relics to Mahajanga decades earlier, church-building did not go without contestation among the living or dead. In the 1880s, British missionary W. Clayton Pickersgill reported that converts arranged for men to collect wood from nearby forests and that the walls were quite costly, composed of "rubble and lime firmly put together" by "Arab workmen."[114] Determined to infuse the acoustic realm of the city with ecclesiastic sounds, converts sought to emplace the church "in a central location" near the hilltop and collectively raised funds to purchase a bell.[115] But after particularly heavy rains, the church structure was reduced to a pitiful heap of rubble. Sakalava royal followers "and their companions in faith among the Imerina-born" understood this destruction as an expression of ancestral anger about the proximate (and thus offensive) placement of the Christian edifice near the shrine.[116] Once again, ancestors had disrupted the well-laid plans of the living to build themselves into the landscape.

Even more than the difficulty in constructing a church, the adherence among highlanders to Sakalava ritual practices alarmed British missionaries. Not only were Sakalava dwellers reluctant to send their children to the newly founded mission school, Pickersgill complained, but highland soldiers strengthened the importance of Sakalava ancestral practices.[117] Merina residents in the city, whom Pickersgill had hoped would be paragons of Christian piety, instead regularly petitioned and assuaged ancestral spirits through sampy (or what Pickersgill called "fetishes").[118] Increasing Merina observance of Boeny Sakalava rituals during this time resonates with scholarly observations that Merina leaders over time reinterpreted Sakalava royal ancestors as the forebears of their Merina royalty; at times this materialized with marriages between Sakalava and Merina monarchies.[119] Yet, this appropriation had a cost. Merina administrators and their allies wrote back to the queen that obeisance to the fetishes among highlanders was coupled with a concerning decline in Sakalava attendees at ritual practices at the shrine. Sahid Aly, a Silamo leader appointed *andrianambaventy* (deputy judge) in Mahajanga, noted in 1881 that "very few" Sakalava, namely those living nearby, carried out the weekly service (fanompoa).[120] This decline of Sakalava ancestral customs (*fomba*), he worried, threatened the very "security of the kingdom."[121]

Diminishing degrees of observance of Sakalava ancestral customs suggested that Merina control over the northwest territory—via the relics—

was weakening. Though Aly did not indicate why Sakalava followers were more disinclined to carry out regular service for the ancestors, significant migration of Sakalava into the hinterlands to escape onerous Merina authoritarian rule is one possible explanation. The emancipation of Makoa by the Imerina crown in 1877, after mounting pressure from European countries, further reduced the number of attendees at the Sakalava shrine. Many Makoa who had once joined in Sakalava ritual practices migrated to the highlands, where the monarchy granted them land, or embraced Christianity, which provided them with new possibilities for social mobility.[122] These demographic shifts, coupled with an economic turn toward wage labor and European-controlled capitalist trading systems, helped pull human energies and resources away from the royal service of building.

In the decades that followed, the royal relics traveled in unexpected trajectories. Some archival accounts suggest that at the time of the French invasion of the city in 1885, discussed in the next chapter, Merina authorities seized the relics and took them to Antananarivo; eventually the French returned them to Mahajanga and used them to "control the population."[123] Contemporary oral accounts from Bemihisatra and Bemazava followers, however, suggest that the relics were taken to Antananarivo at an earlier time by Ndramfefiarivo, a descendant of Ravahiny, who married King Radama I to protect the Bemihisatra.[124] At any rate, the relics appear to have been relocated to Mahajanga around 1897, and a new shrine was constructed in the Mahabibo-Marolaka neighborhood. The new shrine was marked by an altered design that centered the reliquary rather than the monarch's house.[125] Over the years that followed, the shrine was moved several times, owing to the challenges of enforcing norms in the increasingly congested and ethnolinguistically diverse city and fractures within Sakalava royal lineages.[126] The latter resulted in ongoing contestations between two adversarial factions—the Bemazava and Behimisatra—beginning in the 1960s, and the construction of a secondary shrine, though the relics are currently kept by the Bemihisatra at Doany Ndramisara (Miarinarivo) in Tsararano-Ambony.[127]

Conclusion

The fortunes of the rova reveal how the Saribengo hilltop served as, at once, a fallible architectural instrument of top-down empire-making, a contested site of mediation, and a vibrant cluster of different knowledge regimes. Building the rova was key to conceptions of Merina imperial rule that pivoted on extracting labor power—from the conscripted laborers who toiled to hew limestone rocks and cleave mangrove timber, to the designers and planners who crafted their visions into architectural form, to the ritual experts and royal followers who animated the rova through performative, purposeful inhabitance. Collectively, these countless inhabitants enacted different modes of knowledge and, in so doing, brought the hilltop into being as a meaningful physical and symbolic presence.

Laboring—whether traversing into the satrana-filled savannah to winnow palm leaves; appraising and mining the optimal limestone deposits in nearby hills; or alchemically transforming earthly things into building materials through proven and nascent masonry techniques—comprised ways of knowing. Expertise in matters of the supernatural realm—specifically, knowing by what means, by whom, and when unyielding Sakalava ancestors could be engaged at the newly constructed hilltop shrine—were critical forms of ritual knowledge on which nascent Merina rule depended. Moments when these experts put their knowledges to subversive ends, though not as readily apparent in archival traces, were also key. Yet the periods during which rulers and their built empires existed were fleeting. Sakalava fled and then returned. Karana and Antalaotra opted to send their enslaved dependents as forced workers or paid fines. Freed Makoa eventually left behind the rova and the city. Although built durably, the rova failed to endure as a revered site in the city. Inhabitants and visitors today seem to hardly notice the remains of the lofty, crackled stone gate (figure 2.2). Instead, the royal compound that holds the relics (now in Tsararano-Ambony) has long been back in Sakalava hands, and, although relations with Merina participants are equivocal, it endures as an abiding site of ritual congregation in the city. For its part, the Saribengo hilltop bore witness to multiple afterlives: it was seized by French colonizers and transformed into military encampment; then during the 1920s a large public hospital was built adjacent to the military camp, which today bears the name of Hôpital Androva.

Most of what my friend Bachir told me was right, but he was wrong about one thing. The Merina soldiers had not appropriated an already-existing Sakalava shrine on the hilltop, but instead opportunistically claimed the unoccupied land for their fort and brought the relics later. Highland officials took considerable efforts to *uproot and implant* the Sakalava relics, melding together ancestral Sakalava power and Merina military authority into a hybridized, materialized political center in the city. Merina administrators understood the specific geographies of ancestral spirits, that the

FIGURE 2.9 Sakalava procession ascending to the rova during the "festival of the relics" (fanompoa be), Mahajanga, ca. 1886–89. Courtesy of Archives du Ministère de l'Europe et des Affaires étrangères—La Courneuve, Série P-Afrique, A009320. Photographer: Albert Pinard.

place was tethered to ancestors and that it was *Sakalava*—not Merina— ancestors who governed the land and demanded concessions in Mahajanga. Archival stories of possession, "fetishes," and attacks by unruly beyond-human forces, as Florence Bernault has argued, illuminate people's "engagement with theories and technologies of power."[128] In Mahajanga, even fragmented accounts of intractable spirits and the labors of appeasement demonstrate not only the impactful presence of ancestors in shaping Mahajanga's urban space and the demands they placed on rulers and commoners alike, but also the conceptions of distributed power that came to life in architectural processes.

Much as Merina rulers sought to codify, surveil, and manage the cityscape, the ecological, human, and spirit topographies constrained the composition, tempos, and conditions of possibility for architectural spaces. This chapter has argued that more-than-human forces are worthy of attention, together with humans' aspirations to build their worlds anew in narratives of power, space, and urban becoming. Attending to labor and otherworldly forces in this spatial history allows us to see how spirits were not solely an instrumental resource for indigenous political entrepreneurs claiming authority; they were active elements in a complex topography in which humans were one set of participants. Reckoning with ancestors and other-than-human forces, as we will see in the following chapters, was critical not only for terraforming the landscape but also for projecting affective ties of belonging and attachment to the city.

For their part, Sakalava ancestors have continued to impress themselves on town dwellers long after the Merina hold on Mahajanga dissipated in the 1880s, and they unfailingly exhort royal followers to return to the doany year after year.[129] Those of Sakalava descent did (and still do) return for the annual bathing of the relics (fanompoa be), despite the shadow of Merina and then French rule (figure 2.9). Each year, the living and the dead come together, enlivening gatherings that serve as vibrant forums of interpreting the past, heterochronic nexuses that collapse linear notions of time, and indeterminate reckonings with the possibilities of futures.[130] In so doing, Mahajanga is reconstituted as a sacred Sakalava center, filled with raucous singing, drinking, and ritual performances, animated by the specter of ancestors—and rooted by the relics in the shelter of the zomba.[131]

PART II

Anticipatory Landscapes

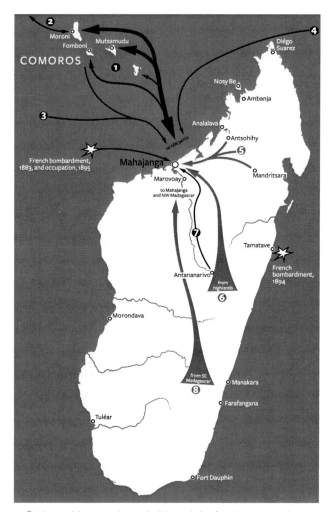

1. Migratory laborers, traders, and religious scholars from Comoros, accelerating early 1900s

2. 3. Continued movements of migratory sailors, merchants, religious scholars, and laborers circulating, by way of East Africa and Comoros, from trading settlements in

2. Southern Arabian Peninsula (encompassing Hadhramaut region)
3. South Asia (encompassing Gujarat region). Among this group were around 200 indentured laborers from Porbandar to Mahajanga, 1901–5 (chap. 3)

4. Recruited laborers from China to Mahajanga, 1901–5

5. Migrant laborers, from ca. 1920s

6. Migrant laborers, from ca. mid to late 1800s

7. European Christian missionaries based in Antananarivo, from ca. 1880s–90s

8. Migrant laborers to northwest region from ca. 1900s, and increasingly to Mahajanga from ca. 1920s

MAP 3.1
Circulations, Madagascar in the Indian Ocean, late nineteenth to mid-twentieth century. Map by Tim Stallmann.

Storied Refusals

Labor and Laden Absences

In 1900, a thirteen-year-old boy named Nanji Kalidas Mehta and his cousin
left their home village of Gorana (Gujarat) to board a dhow in Bombay
bound for Mahajanga. Born to a family of grocers with modest means,
Mehta had long been drawn to the siren "call of the sea" and the imagined
adventures that awaited him. When his older brother established a shop
in Mahajanga and summoned him to join as a domestic worker and shop
assistant, Mehta seized the opportunity. After an arduous five-month-long
journey resulting in a near shipwreck and an unplanned detour to Comoros,
Mehta's boat finally reached Mahajanga. Weary, but still full of enthusiasm,
Mehta encountered a "neat, trim and elegant" city propelled by its sociable
ambiance and thriving mercantile activity (for a view similar to that which
Mehta encountered, see figure 3.1). For more than a year, he devoted himself to building his brother's flourishing business, mastered trading tactics, and joined spirited Indian festivities. Then in 1902, the town suddenly
was gripped by bubonic plague. Mehta later recalled that the French "secretly accused Indians" of causing the plague. Colonial eradication efforts,
he recounted, targeted newer migrants from South Asia who dwelled in
wooden and corrugated sheet-metal houses and were said to have "unhy-
gienic way[s] of living and unsanitary habits." Indian families (including
Mehta and his brother) were moved to a temporary camp some 3.2 kilometers (two miles) away from the city, and their homes were destroyed.
Mehta calmly weathered the changes until he hastily departed the city in a

FIGURE 3.1 Entrance to the port, Mahajanga, ca. 1886–89. Courtesy of Archives du Ministère de l'Europe et des Affaires étrangères—La Courneuve, Série P-Afrique, A009249. Photographer: Albert Pinard.

mass exodus of Indian families, burdened with a "half-expressed and half-suppressed" dream of his unrealized pursuits.[1]

Mehta's peripatetic route to Mahajanga was at once an inheritance of the many thousands of journeys undertaken by Indian migrants across the Indian Ocean basin and a personal foray into an "era of colonially inscribed mercantile expansion."[2] For centuries, old diasporic trade routes brought Indian artisans and traders to Madagascar and East Africa, where they infused cities and towns with wide-spanning connections to new crafting techniques, desirable commodities, and invigorating ideas (see map 3.1). Within African historiography, Indians have been portrayed as marginal actors, legible primarily through their economic roles in colonial and postcolonial societies. Yet, as Sana Aiyar has recently argued in the case of Kenya, the "paradoxical invisibility of ever-present Indians ... can be located in contestations over a shared political space" that began long before colonial times.[3] As diverse Indian migrant groups made their way to African ports, they negotiated local and global attachments and engaged in strategic alliances with their old and new homelands by drawing on the affordances of their historical conditions. Despite their diverse religious and regional origins, erased in European colonists' racial categorizations, Indian communities found themselves relatively more privileged than Africans were, with access to land, credit, and citizenship. But they were still subject to colonial regulations over their everyday, ritual, and political lives. The resonances of racial hierarchies persisted well into postcolonial times, as Indian families navigated the tensions over inclusion in African nationalist movements and the uncertainties of postindependence African nationhood.[4]

Even as they maneuvered the perils and possibilities of belonging, Indian families were key builders, designers, and memorialists of the places they inhabited. In cities and towns across East Africa and the Mascarenes, Indians transformed the topography through building projects, collective ritual practices, and performed urbanism. They helped build road and rail infrastructures, extracted harvests from plantations, and portered goods across vast distances. They raised shophouses, animating them with everyday bartering and trade. They constructed places of worship and erected community centers, language and religious schools, and libraries that gave rise to new knowledges and social networks. They built and maintained cinemas, where wide-ranging city dwellers gathered in darkness to marvel. Those with ample means sponsored public-works projects and sometimes served as officially enlisted architects and planners. Indian communities across Africa were characterized by immense disparities of wealth, prestige, and social status. While some Indians emerged as benefactors, the majority infused their adopted cities with vitality through everyday place-making practices, labor, and aesthetic styles. Still, all Indian families were subject to colonial urban-planning efforts, and some endured violent displacements in the service of spatial segregation that were justified as public health measures.[5]

Scholars have demonstrated how colonial authorities sought to control the messiness of African cities, exacerbated by unemployment and increased mobility, through what Frederick Cooper called the "mask of city planning and urban architecture."[6] Colonial efforts to create visible, grid-like spaces conducive to pacifying and exploiting local populations manifested in urban segregationist schemes designed to create separate residential spaces for colonizer and colonized. Planning initiatives were designed to constrain the creative energy of urban migrancy points and to curtail the ideologies, including anticolonial resistance and nationalist political mobilization, that were produced in dense gatherings. Political configurations and modernist aesthetic theories gave rise to new conceptions of architecture as an experimental device for domination or, alternately, for cultivating sympathies among colonial subjects through heritage preservation, even if efforts were stymied in bureaucratic fractures.[7] At times, as Anthony King and Garth Myers have shown, cocreative endeavors between colonizer and colonized gave rise to architecturally syncretic forms of housing that interwove vernacular and colonial aesthetics.[8] We know less, however, about the architectural forms that were destroyed or *never built*—ephemeral constructions that left little trace in the archival and archaeological records—in sum, *absences* in the city's archive.

This chapter opens the nested stories embedded in Mehta's nostalgic account of Mahajanga to attend to both durable built structures *and* ephemeral or never-built forms in the early colonial moment. Between 1895 and 1920, the precise possibilities and contours of the colonial project were being worked out on the ground, and French officials were obliged to contend in very material ways with the preexisting built environment and competing forms of urbanism. Among the durable outcomes French officials imagined were large-scale technological projects—roads and railways, canals and ports, telegraph lines and irrigation systems, and civic and military buildings—intended to facilitate economic extraction, perform imperial domination, and emit colonial sublimity. Owing to a scarcity of willing local workers, French officials were reliant on labor recruitment abroad, for which Indian traders were instrumental conduits. Yet these established Indian families and the calcified structures they built over time hindered French technological dreams to inscribe their own visions of the future on the city's architectural tableaux.[9]

Just as materialized buildings have stories to tell, so too do *unbuilt* forms. Alongside the visible "biographies" of Mahajanga's durable built structures, including Indian double-storied limestone homes, streets, and French colonial civic buildings (some of which were subsequently destroyed and some of which still stand today), are the "shadow histories" of ephemeral forms, such as temporary housing for migrant workers, half-finished roads, and an unrealized railway.[10] Scholars have shown how failed building projects expose the limits of colonial rule in Africa, namely, the bureaucratic inefficiencies, insufficient state-financing, and labor scarcity that characterized urban-planning interventions. We know that many large-scale colonial infrastructural projects went awry when subaltern groups opposed them through rich practices of everyday resistance, such as flight, foot-dragging, sabotage, and negligence.[11]

Recently, anthropologists Audra Simpson, Carole McGranahan, and others have enriched our conceptual vocabulary for understanding subversion by introducing forms of *refusal*, distinct from resistance, that open up generative possibilities for social solidarities and new political spaces.[12] Unlike *resistance*, which foregrounds reactive opposition to dominant power structures, *refusal* exposes the creative ways people challenge political constraints by reimagining their futures, reinventing categories of classification, and prioritizing the "vitality of one's immediate social relations."[13] As Tina Campt puts it, the "practice of refusal is a striving to create possibility in the face of negation . . . and terms of diminished subjecthood with which one is presented."[14] Resistance and refusal can be taken as interrelated tactics in a wider repertoire of subversion that people have historically employed, with the former characterized by opposition and the latter by rejection and reimagination.[15] To this, I would add that refusal and resistance have been material, spatial stances, as much as imaginary, intellectual tactics, through which people have to varying degrees powerfully shaped their architectural, ecological, and political conditions. Exploring moments of unbuilding can reveal not only mishaps and colonial visions of urban planning informed by persistent ideologies of modernism, but also the "half-expressed dreams" and desires for futures sought in moments of what we might call *architectural refusal*.

With a focus on practices of refusal, this chapter interrogates lasting, fleeting, and never-built forms to gain insights into the agentive tactics and utopian imaginaries of hidden historical actors who shaped their architectural world amid and in tandem with beyond-human, material forces of the ecological world. It provides the historical context of key events in the progression of French colonial presence in Mahajanga's landscape. Following two successive attempts at conquest, French military troops appropriated major sites in the city, including the rova (governors' palace and fort), and aspired to transform the streets and buildings in the center for overland conquest. French colonial dreams of constructing new civic buildings and infrastructure, however, were hindered by the fundamental lack and refusal of laborers, the unyielding terrain, and the entrenched stone structures built by South Asian families, who wielded the architectural inertia of their hardened homes against colonial-run efforts to displace them. By attending to the city's built presences and absences, this chapter argues that structures both realized and only imagined constituted a site of encounter through which competing groups—Indian inhabitants; Islamic traders;

Sakalava royal leaders and followers; laborers from China, India, and Comoros; migrants from across Madagascar; and French officials—negotiated colonial transformations with the architectural, ecological, and political-economic affordances at hand.

Militarizing the City (1880s–1890s)

Throughout the convulsions of colonial encroachment and the rise of modern global capitalism, the Merina monarchy retained its hold on Mahajanga, maintained a remarkable degree of autonomy, and garnered long-standing international recognition as a sovereign state, partly through its proficient negotiation in consular matters of significance to France and Britain. French traders and diplomats inserted themselves along the east and northwest coasts throughout the nineteenth century, where they made loose alliances with local Sakalava royal leaders in opposition to the rival highland monarchy.[16] Enticed by trade opportunities and abundant raw materials, and aspiring to secure a political foothold in the southwestern Indian Ocean, French agents mounted a steady campaign toward colonization.

Eventually, elaborate legalistic arrangements between the Kingdom of Madagascar and France gave rise to disputes. These disputes, coupled with popular resistance to obligatory labor and the refusal of northwest groups to acquiesce to highland royal authority, led to the demise of the Merina dynastic power. In 1883, following a treaty dispute over French rights to land, French troops prepared to bombard the west coast and carry out an overland conquest. Perceiving Mahajanga as a critical portal in this early military campaign, Admiral Pierre and his officers set the city as their primary west coast target. On May 16, following the unwillingness of the city's highland administrator to surrender, French troops bombarded the city for more than six hours. So critical was this attempted conquest in the late-nineteenth-century French public imaginary, that the battle scene was prominently featured on a chocolate wrapper, effaced of any hint of the battle's violence and ultimate outcome: temporary occupation, but an initially failed colonization (see figure 3.2). After taking possession of the city, the French troops seized the customhouse (figure 3.3), a key building for the Merina authorities that had been constructed and repaired over decades with the support of an important Indian benefactor.

French military officials immediately began refashioning Mahajanga's landscape through the appropriation of existing knowledge and labor re-

FIGURE 3.2 "Seizure of Mahajanga (Majunga) Fort," ca. 1895–1900. Chromolithograph print. Chocolaterie d'Aiguebelle, Drôme, France.

FIGURE 3.3 "Customs house" (left), Mahajanga, ca. 1886–89. Courtesy of Archives du Ministère de l'Europe et des Affaires étrangères—La Courneuve, Série P-Afrique, A009309. Photographer: Albert Pinard.

FIGURE 3.4 View from the height of the rova, with the French diplomatic residence in the distance, Mahajanga, ca. 1886–89. Courtesy of Archives du Ministère de l'Europe et des Affaires étrangères—La Courneuve, Série P-Afrique, A009237. Photographer: Albert Pinard.

gimes and the occupation of symbolically important nodes throughout the city. Beginning with the rova, the contested seat of political entanglements, French officers transformed material design to inscribe their ambitions on the landscape. Drawing on the knowledge and labor of Makoa builders, the French reinforced the hilltop rova with fortified stone walls and planted wooden stakes and thorny bushes to hinder retaliating highland troops. Lush mango trees were cut down to ensure clear lines of sight for sentries (see figure 3.4). French troops invaded a sacred Karana cemetery near the north side of town and transformed it into a defensive bulwark by constructing a chest-high fortification. They employed Makoa (and perhaps other) inhabitants to construct three encampments along the shoreline—sleeping shelters, a washhouse, and a dining structure—using the plentiful satrana thatch found throughout the region. But progress on building construction was lethargic, and these projects were short-lived. Troops spent most of their time procuring basic provisions and fresh drinking water. Frequent drunkenness among soldiers consuming locally brewed "arrack" further enervated work efforts. Troops reportedly lost their minds, owing to heat and exhaustion. Moreover,

FIGURE 3.5 "European cemetery," Mahajanga, 1888. Courtesy of Archives du Ministère de l'Europe et des Affaires étrangères—La Courneuve, Série P-Afrique, A009239. Photographer: Alfred Pinard.

high mortality rates among French troops led to many burials, thus transforming the city into a foreboding necropolis (figure 3.5).[17]

The outright refusal of town inhabitants to aid the imperial conquest, as well as the lack of troops and military equipment, dashed French aspirations for an immediate colonial invasion into the highlands. Highland monarchs temporarily regained control of Mahajanga in the 1885 treaty ending the first Franco-Malagasy War. Rather than thoroughly rebuild the rova and fort, highland military officers based themselves in the hinterlands. During this time, Sakalava villages flourished along the coastal hinterland, allowing easy access to Muslim, "especially Comorian," traders, "who long held a monopoly on commerce" in the region.[18] Inhabitants throughout the northwest demanded high wages, which foiled ongoing attempts by French would-be concessionaires to develop plantations in Mahajanga's hinterlands. Although France laid claim to the island, its imperial declaration remained symbolic until 1894, when the French Assembly voted in favor of funding the Corps expéditionnaire, the military cadre tasked with conquest of the entire island.[19]

In 1895, French military administrators launched the Corps expédi-tionnaire from Mahajanga. They perceived Mahajanga as the ideal por-tal for overland passage to the highland capital city of Antananarivo due to the former's "healthier climate" and "less bellicose" local population.[20] Officers and troops would depart from Mahajanga's port, traveling either by land or boat up the Betsiboka River; they would then follow Malagasy footpaths some 250 kilometers (150 miles) to the capital. Officers took eight months to prepare for the invasion, and pulled together a corps of 14,773 men, composed of some 11,000 European soldiers and nearly 3,800 "in-digene" soldiers, as well as 6,000 to 8,000 Malagasy porters to serve the corps. Among the "indigene" soldiers were a sizeable group of West African "Hausas, Dahomean tiralleurs," who arrived with their wives and children. French soldiers pushed highland military leader Ramasombazaha and his troops out of the city and bombarded Tamatave.[21]

French soldiers quickly militarized the city's landscape, overhauling the city to create an instrumental nerve center for the Corps expéditionnaire. Streets overflowed with officers, troops, oxen, and donkey carts. Hous-ing was crowded, and military officers and soldiers alike camped in tents. Troops seized open land to construct large wooden buildings for storing supplies and food provisions. At nightfall, gas lamps illuminated the streets, dissipating the nocturnal darkness once familiar to town inhabitants. Once again, French troops occupied Mahajanga's hilltop rova, laminating their claim to authority over the city and affirming the rova as a key symbolic site of power. Although the French colonial army would soon take thou-sands of lives in the overland campaign, Mahajanga was buffered from violent attacks and instead was engaged as the primary seat of military operations.[22]

From the moment of conquest, French military officers were beset by labor shortages. Male domestic workers were frustratingly "fickle," com-ing and going at their leisure. The French preferred hiring "Arabs," whose dhows were able to traverse the shallow waters (unlike the larger French ships) for transporting cargo.[23] "Arab" operators, however, "found little advantage" in the work and soon abandoned the French.[24] More pressing was the dire need for porters and dockers to unload massive cargo arrivals from France. Where the French saw lack and hindrance to their campaign, traders, artisans, and town dwellers understood the economic opportu-nities inherent in the fragility of French conquest, manifest in their need for goods, supplies, and labor. One French observer wryly noted that local inhabitants hiked prices on everyday commodities, sought new business

FIGURE 3.6 "Disembarkation of troops," Mahajanga (Majunga), ca. 1900. Chromolithograph print, Chocolat Poulain.

ventures, and insisted on "dearly paid work."[25] Local builders demanded "incredible prices" to construct an officers' meeting center and cable office.[26]

These accounts suggest not so much a resistance to French military conquest as a dogged refusal among some city dwellers to accept the terms presented by French agents and a quiet resolve to leverage capital, form alliances, and assert alternative norms around the value of manual labor. But political and economic stratification in the city created differential possibilities among town dwellers to shape their encounters with French military officials. In the absence of willing local laborers and a viable wharf, Somali and Comorian "coolies indigène" were hired to undertake the grueling work of unloading supplies across the muddy sea flats (see figure 3.6).[27]

Even the sea refused to cooperate with French plans. For thousands of years, the Betsiboka River had carried enormous amounts of sediments from upstream and deposited them at the edges of the city. Over time, the river flows and intense seasonal rainfall shifted the clay and sand into ancient channels throughout the estuary, and generated sediment-rich slurries in Mahajanga's port. Local seafarers learned how to navigate across the thick layers of silt-clay mud to reach the seaside by appraising tide rhythms and developing wooden dhow boats well suited for shallow waters (see figure 3.7). Sakalava ritual specialists understood that the mud in the estuary con-

FIGURE 3.7 Boats at the port, Mahajanga, ca. 1886–89. Courtesy of Archives du Ministère de l'Europe et des Affaires étrangères—La Courneuve, Série P-Afrique, A009284. Photographer: Albert Pinard.

tained life-giving mineral deposits of white kaolinite, a clay-like substance known as *tanimalandy* that materialized ancestral sacred power (*hasina*) and constituted a critical substance for healing, spirit possession, and ritual blessings. Mud could be a multivalent material force—a presence with which to reckon, or a medium enabling the straddling of the living and ancestral domains.[28]

For newly arrived French military officers, however, the muddy terrain of the city obstructed logistical operations that relied on local navigation expertise and the bodily labor of porters. Once cargo ships arrived from abroad, smaller boats brought goods to the sandy peninsula, where dockers "carried [goods] out . . . more or less easily, depending on the state of the sea, which rises up to 4.5 meters, and the nature of the load. At low tide, there is little water and the boats are stranded; but even at high seas, the coolies are forced to work in the water."[29] Reliance on local laborers not only presented risks to supply chains integral to violent conquest, it also highlighted the need for capital investments—most immediately a wharf—that would allow larger ships convenient dockage and enable large-scale, economi-

FIGURE 3.8 The wharf, Mahajanga, 1898. Courtesy of FR ANOM 44PA/123/55.

cally viable trade. Preliminary studies by military engineers determined that underlying this boggy mire lay a hard rock bottom that would prevent speedy construction of a wharf. Building the wharf required manipulating an uncooperative seabed and constituted an "immense labor," which persisted for years beyond the immediate events of the conquest (figure 3.8).[30]

Above all, the French military invasion was slowed by the island's unforgiving land, which voraciously consumed the lives of troops. Beginning in May 1895, thousands of troops from France and across the empire arrived on Mahajanga's shores. After nearly two months of preparations, the Corps expéditionnaire began its overland journey (see figure 3.9). The 15,000-man legion first traversed vast stretches of swampland in the Betsiboka River valley that were saturated with malaria, and soon encountered an austere landscape devoid of vegetation, where soldiers were overcome with dysentery, typhoid, and malaria. The seemingly malicious Malagasy land "devour[ed] the soldiers," and military convoys left behind a "streak of cadavers."[31] French observer Nathaniel Aubanel described the island's red, laterite soil as a hostile terrain of "lost lands with the bloody hues of clay, deep and dark sites like tombs inhabited by reptiles, beasts and human monsters."[32] French observers made explicit links between the island's

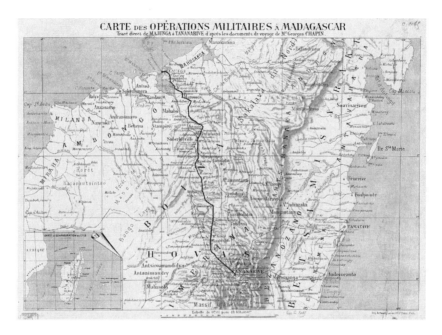

FIGURE 3.9 "Military operations in Madagascar direct route from Majunga [Mahajanga] to Tananarive [Antananarivo] from Georges Chapin's travel records." Courtesy of Bibliothéque nationale de France, département Cartes et plans.

environment and the bloodshed of violent conquest, but as Gillian Feeley-Harnik argues, far from being daunted by the landscape, the French drew on ecological images to justify colonial occupation of the island. The spilling of French blood would "fertilize the plain and mountains" and leave an "ineffaceable red print of their [the Malagasy] defeat."[33] According to this logic, French blood served as a sacrificial substance that not only marked French presence on the geological and political tableaux, but also constituted the basis of colonial claims to their newfound territory. If the island was not initially a kindred landscape, French officials saw the mixing of blood and soil as the grounds for transformation.

The French succeeded in capturing Antananarivo, but at an enormous human cost. Contrary to sunny predictions about the healthfulness of the northwest region and the perceived ease of the overland passage to Antananarivo, the operation resulted in the deaths of 4,500 European and West and North African troops and 3,000 Malagasy porters. In French popular and military memory, Mahajanga became synonymous with the death and devastation of the conquest. Journalist Étienne Grosclaude noted that the town emitted a kind of melancholy, dotted with ruins that spoke to the more prosperous and populated period of the early 1800s. The seaside was "saddened by the perpetual twirling of an infinity of these birds" [vultures] that swooped over the beach, which was littered with old scrap metal, leather bits, Lefebvre wagon parts, and other detritus from the invasion.[34] Mahajanga's sprawling cemetery was symbolic of the "providentially completed but infernal expedition" of French colonial conquest. Mahajanga had become a "city of the dead."[35]

Planning for the City to Come

Despite French lamentations about the faltering start of the imperial project, commentators optimistically proposed that the infusion of roads, railways, water systems, and buildings would resuscitate the cadaverous town. Given the city's prime location for trade, agriculture, and industry, officials prioritized Mahajanga as a key site in island-wide infrastructural plans. Streets were to be lit and stone-paved. The construction of a telegraphic line between Mahajanga and Antananarivo, along with an elongated jetty that would allow cargo ships to dock and a fluvial transport system linking Mahajanga to the nearby town of Maevatanana, promised to knit together the island colony. Rails were purchased in anticipation of a railway to Tananarive (Antananarivo). As historian Rudolf Mrázek points out, infrastructure was alluring as a conceptual foil to the sluggishness officials perceived in colonized spaces and bodies. Roads, railways, and water systems were pathways to modernity and technological panaceas for materializing futuristic colonial visions of prosperity.[36] A majestic residence for the provincial governor would serve as a symbolic testimony to colonial prowess and help attract needed administrators from the metropole to this distant frontier town.

Before embarking on large-scale infrastructure and building projects, authorities inventoried the existing built forms and the communities that inhabited them. Using ranked architectural categorizations of hard and soft, durable and ephemeral, impervious and porous, surveyors noted that the western bank of the rova, which was "half in ruins," extended the neighborhood of Marofotona, in which Sakalava, Makoa, and Comorians inhabited wooden, stone, and daub homes.[37] Wall and roof panels were artfully woven from fan palms, some with corrugated metal roofs (tôle), which would have been imported (see figure 3.10). In the far east of town, flanking the shoreline,

FIGURE 3.10 Mahajanga (Majunga), likely Marofotona, 1895.
Courtesy of FR ANOM 8FI435.

was the neighborhood of Marofototra ("place of many roots"), inhabited by
Antalaotra, Makoa, highlander, and Sakalava families. Farther east was Ma-
rodoka ("many shops"), where Sakalava and Comorian fishermen dwelled
and docked their vessels. Just inland, Antalaotra, Sakalava, Makoa, Comorian, highlander, and Betsimisaraka (from eastern Madagascar) families were
clustered in the Village des Mangues ("Village of Mangos," locally known as
Bostany) and the Village de Mahabibo ("Village of the Cashews") (see right
side of figure 3.11). European observers classified earth, sand, and straw as
"rudimentary" materials comprising "unfinished" structures, rather than as
value-laden substances nested in a moral economy and building techniques
honed over time through intergenerational knowledge-transmission.[38] In
keeping with colonial narratives of technological lack, the colonizers saw
the vegetative architectural composition of these communities as a marker
of racial inferiority and as a justification for colonial occupation.

French plans were predicated as much on imagining future histories
as on willful erasure of past ones. Yet, as Michel-Rolph Trouillot reminds
us, silencing was always strategic, power-laden, and partial.[39] Take, for instance, the maps drawn by Henri Fillot, a colonial official, in 1895. The first

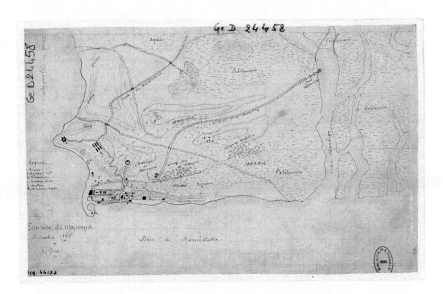

FIGURE 3.11 Mahajanga (Majunga) and surrounds, 1895. Map by Henri Fillot. Courtesy of Bibliothéque nationale de France, département des Cartes et plans.

(figure 3.11) portrays the town before French building projects, sketched lightly with a hesitant hand. The second (figure 3.12) confidently shows anticipated colonial construction plans, boldly delineated in sharp lines and heavy print. In an explicit lamination over preceding political regimes, Fillot effaced any trace of the rova in the second map, overlaying it with the town hall and the path to the French military camp ("chaussée militaire") on the same hilltop. Village des Mangues and Village de Mahabibo also are eerily purged from the second map. We can imagine the everyday rhythm of life in these quarters, where residents enjoyed the abundant shade of the mango trees, the proximity to marshland where rice was grown, and the muddy mangrove swamps rich with crabs and small fish. We can imagine neighbors meandering along winding paths dotted with wood and thatch homes, greeting one another and chatting on their way to and from the market. In an act of cartographic violence, the second map uproots these layered relationships and silences the murmured voices of these communities. Some streets are named for early French imperialists. The abattoir, customs house, ancestral tombs, and Indian and "Comorian" mosques, however, were to be left untouched, perhaps to avoid inciting rebellion.[40]

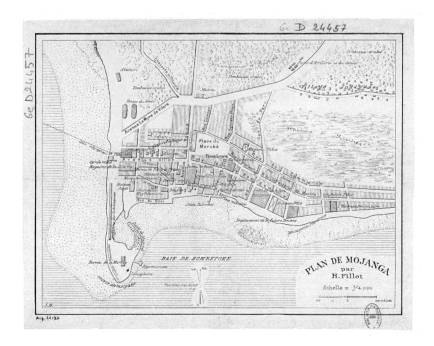

FIGURE 3.12 Mahajanga (Majunga), 1895. Map by Henri Fillot and J. Hansen.
Courtesy of Bibliothèque nationale de France, département des Cartes et plans.

As elsewhere in Africa, categorization and containment were key to colonial rule. Early colonial rulers in Madagascar sought not only to divide
Europeans and Malagasy, but also to distinguish between eighteen perceived
ethno-political groups (termed the "eighteen tribes"). Mahajanga's intermingled communities of Sakalava, Merina, Makoa, Indian, Zanzibari, and Ye-
meni descent, who altogether spoke five to six languages, confounded easy
disaggregation and undermined this logic. Comorians, moreover, comprised
a "quite significant colony" and contributed to the Islamic ambiance of the
town.[41] Authorities enacted a spatial strategy of governance, fabricating a
"colonial world divided into compartments," as Fanon shrewdly signaled,
"inhabited by . . . different species."[42] In Mahajanga, demarcation took the
form of a European neighborhood on the breezy hillside overlooking the
bay, and commercial facilities, with their effluvia, clustered some distance
away on the riverbank. French authorities forcibly removed the vegetatively
constructed homes in the Village of Mangos, which was located on "the
most beautiful" and pleasant site in the city, shunting its residents a kilome-

ter (half a mile) away, near the Village de Mahabibo. Soon thereafter, they designated a city dump on the edges of Mahabibo, rendering material the French conceptual relationship between excess people and refuse.[43] When officials shifted their gaze to Majunga Ancien, however, strategies of containment, effacement, and architectural governance collided with the entrenched, resolute structures that Indian families had built over generations.

Indians in Mahajanga: Salient Inscriptions and Resolute Architecture

By 1902, South Asian traders made up about 12 percent (around 600) of the city's overall population of 4,703.[44] Although their ancestors had crossed the Indian Ocean for centuries, the vast majority arrived in the nineteenth century. Though generalized by colonial officials as "Hindoos," "Banians," Karany, or Karana, they observed different religious practices (some Muslim and others Hindu) and came from diverse regions of Gujarat, including the Kathiawar peninsula, Surat, and Kutch.[45] With the rising demand for cloth in East Africa and northwest Madagascar, Gujarati merchants expanded their trading networks and leveraged their goods in overlapping circuits of ivory and slave trading. Khoja and Bohra Shi'a Muslim traders, however, comprised the majority of Indians in northwest Madagascar. They enjoyed alliances with Merina rulers in the city and, along with the Antalaotra, dominated the region's trade in the early to mid-1800s, and rising to prominence as key financiers of credit and commerce by mid-century. Together with Antalaotra traders, they established their households and based their commercial operations at the foot of the Saribengo hilltop where the customhouse was situated (figure 3.13), in what the French called Majunga Ancien (Old Majunga, known today as Majunga Be, see map FM.3).[46]

As historians of the Indian Ocean have shown, such trading networks thrived on a mixture of mobility and rootedness. Mobility allowed traders, freed slaves, and rulers to "buy time" for more optimal exchanges, establish new alliances, secure protection, and delay or evade debt-repayment; emplacement enabled the construction of homes and buildings, the accumulation of wealth, and the gathering of kin.[47] Capital was rerouted through built forms, and claims to legitimate belonging could be hedged through a community's visible, vertical markers of rootedness—houses, mosques, trading houses. If wooden boats (figure 3.14) were porous, buoyant vessels that enabled the flow of capital, houses were sedimented containers where

FIGURE 3.13 "Customs Road; trading galleries," Majunga (Madagascar), ca. 1886–89. The building on the right is likely the "Indian Mosque." Courtesy of Archives du Ministère de l'Europe et des Affaires étrangères—La Courneuve, Série P-Afrique, A009248. Photographer: Albert Pinard.

capital could accrue and solidify over time. In Mahajanga, as elsewhere in East Africa, trading transactions (re)produced social and economic differentiation, and capital congealed in the hands of traders and other elites. Yet, Indian communities in Mahajanga were pluralistic and characterized by caste, ethnic, and linguistic differences that defied easy categorization. Class distinctions also abounded, especially within Indian communities, and were often visible in the textures, durability, and location of homes—whether gleaming two-storied limestone shophouses or those "provisionally made of wood or corrugated sheet," as described in Mehta's account at this chapter's opening.[48] If stone houses enabled Indian owners to imagine the prosperity of their progeny and their enduring ties to the island, wooden and sheet-metal homes expressed either the hope for affluence to come or inhabitants' tentative optimism about their long-term prospects.[49]

During Imerina imperial rule (1824–96), some Karana families assumed important roles as benefactors of building projects throughout the city. In 1871, Governor Ramasy reported to reigning monarch Ranavalona II that

FIGURE 3.14 "Indian Boat," Mahajanga, 1899. Courtesy of FR ANOM 8F1562/38.

"Daosa," a Karana, funded the construction of the stone customs building (see figure 3.3).[50] While Daosa paid the labor costs and supplied most of the materials, the governor provided the lime that was extracted from nearby hills and processed on the shores, likely by enslaved Makoa. Earlier, Daosa had committed to funding the anticipated repairs to the customs building. Although Karana may not have regularly funded civic structures, they supported a number of other public health and charitable projects, including the provision of rice during food shortages and medicines in times of illness. Above all, Karana families poured considerable resources into erecting mosques, cemeteries, and double-story stone, mud, and lime homes from which they conducted trade in Old Majunga.

Tombs and mosques were particularly salient inscriptions made by Indian communities in early colonial times; indeed, some continue to stand today among the oldest stone structures in town. Oral accounts indicate that a large influx of Sunni Muslims from South Asia in the 1880s and 1890s assumed control one of the oldest mosques, constructed "by the Arabs [likely Antalaotra] in 1870" ("Mosquée Arabe" on figure 3.12).[51] Migrants constructed the Bohra mosque ("Mosquée Indienne" on figure 3.12) of

stone, and Khodja *ithna ashery* congregants pooled their funds and secured financial support from coreligionists across East Africa to construct
their stone mosque around 1897.[52] Khodja Ismailis established their first
cemetery in a garden owned by Amode Khodja, an important merchant
who directed the local branch office of Taria Topane, a Zanzibar-based fi-
nancier. As Nile Green shows for elsewhere in the Indian Ocean, mosques,
tombs, and madrasa construction projects were as much expressions of a
"religious economy" as they were animated by the influence wielded by Islamic firms in local networks.[53]

When French city planners delineated the borders of the town in 1898,
however, they left the tombs intact and accommodated the resolute presence of the dead entombed in the Khodja cemetery. Officials ceded new
terrain for the Khodja mosque and a new cemetery, and, with funds from
Aga Khan in Bombay, residents erected their mosque in 1912 on private
property belonging to "Bandjee Sandjee."[54] French authorities opted not to
enforce the permit requirements for the Indian mosques, in sharp contrast
to those required of Comorian mosques (see chapter 4), because adherents
were "Indian subjects" of the British state who did not "proselytize," whereas
Comorian adherents were not.[55] Indian traders drew on the hard, enduring
stone composition of their mosques and on French fears about the looming possibility of conflicts with British diplomats to deter anxious French
administrators from appropriating or destroying these precious communal
structures. In refusing the displacement of their dead and their religious
collectivities, Indian inhabitants asserted their intergenerational claims to
the land and affirmed an urban ethic rooted in ritual practice.

If mosques and tombs served as epigraphs to congregational pasts, Indians' limestone homes expressed generational histories, desires to "claim
belonging to a range of elsewheres," and—importantly for this story—
access to labor networks.[56] In the 1870s, some forty of these "high castellated"
homes existed, and more were built in the last decades of the century (visible
in figures 3.1 and 3.3).[57] Masonry techniques employed in the construction
of homes, which combined residences and storehouses, were said to be distinctively built on an "Indian pattern," with the ground floor raised above
the threshold from the front door (figure 3.15) and narrow passages leading to an inner courtyard.[58] As in other East African towns, many of these
homes were adorned with elaborately carved wooden doors inscribed with
prayers for fertility or prosperity. Though it is unclear whether they were
made locally or imported, such doors signaled ties to transoceanic Muslim
trading networks, where such patterns originated. Windows were tall and

FIGURE 3.15
Postcard, "Old
Quarter, Indian
House," Majunga
(Mahajanga), ca.
1900s. Author's
collection.

narrow, and wealthier families sometimes adorned them with shutters to block the intense sunlight. Thick walls, fortified with cement, using lime "dug from the hill," and coated with a white limewash, provided protection from the sweltering heat.[59] Crisscrossing mangrove planks, extricated from plentiful mangrove forests surrounding the shoreline and plastered with mud mortar, served as a supported ceiling. Many homes had a second floor, with a metal or wooden veranda that offered a view from above. Some exteriors were constructed with settees of stone, which created an atmosphere of relaxed sociality (see figures 3.13 and 3.15). Although little remains in the archival record about the construction process, British missionary Joseph Mullens noted that "Malagasy workmen" were the builders; these were likely Makoa and perhaps Antalaotra masons who would have exchanged ideas on aesthetics and technique with the Indian financiers.[60] The inclusion of such wide-ranging materials—mud from the bay, limestone from surrounding mountains, and lime from incinerated shells—was costly and labor-intensive; it served as a physical manifestation of the economic and social capital many Karana families garnered in the nineteenth century.[61]

Limestone cement construction enabled architectural verticality, and with such stone houses merchants could demonstrate their affluence and worldliness. Few written accounts exist describing the domestic interiors of these homes in Mahajanga, but the British naval captain P. H. Colomb, who visited the port in 1869, described the interior aesthetics of one Indian trader's home. After the governor-appointed interpreter led Colomb to a large stone house, he ascended to the top floor by climbing a ladder. He found himself in a large, impressively arranged room: "The floor was covered with pieces of matting; and the tables, of which there several, groaned beneath loads of glass and crockery . . . the whitewashed walls decorated with small looking-glasses disposed in contrast to varieties of saucers and plates."[62] In the confines of single-room living, beds were draped with curtains to allow for privacy. From one of these beds emerged an English-speaking woman, "swathed, Indian fashion in voluminous folds of pink muslin." She was adorned, with a pierced nose, "earrings of stupendous proportions in her ears, necklaces and bangles on her neck and wrists."[63] She was originally from the Cape Colony, but had lived for many years in the city with her husband, a "native of Kutch," a British subject, and a trader between Madagascar and the Comoros Islands. The interior aesthetic of homes like this, as Prita Meier described for the Swahili coast, foregrounded "the ability to displace objects and values across great distances."[64] Though rare, such accounts suggest that these homes were sites of mediation, in which owners and visitors calibrated their expectations of one another through the material objects displayed, which testified to Indians' wide-reaching oceanic connections.

In these built forms, French officials encountered an unyielding landscape inhabited by houses and families that refused to comply with colonial visions of urban space. Following the approval of a large-scale urban plan in 1898, officials attempted, with some degree of success, to purchase Indian-owned as well as the few European-owned properties in Majunga Ancien for public domain.[65] Falling short of gaining ownership, however, they rented Indian homes for public offices such as the Bureau of Domaines until permanent structures could be built. The entrenchment of Indian families and their intense trading activity in Majunga Ancien stymied not only colonial officials but also aspiring European merchants. Adding to colonial frustrations were the determined ways that Indian inhabitants shaped the sensorial rhythms of urban life. Jewelers in Majunga Ancien working into the late-night hours vexed city officials, who years later passed a prohibition against the use of jewelry hammers after nine in the evening.[66] Despite mounting efforts by French colonizers to impose a disciplinary order—one informed by early twentieth-century French norms concerning racial hierarchies and urban respectability—these traces suggest that the ambient built environment was a site of refusal through which Indian families in Majunga Ancien insisted on temporal autonomy and shared space. At the same time, when faced with labor shortages in the region, French officials found themselves reliant on these Karana inhabitants for labor recruitment.

Climate, Coercion, and the Politics of Refusal

Labor lay at the heart of French anxieties about the incipient colony. The unavailability of labor, considered the most troublesome of "the three elements needed to develop the colonies" (the other two being land and capital), was a source of concern across all French possessions, but some remarked that Madagascar's population presented *particular* difficulties for exploiting resources.[67] Consensus emerged early on that Europeans ought to avoid work "with [their] own hands."[68] Such taxing physical labor, one legal scholar asserted, must be left to the "local population" or "other people capable of withstanding climatic conditions."[69] Implicit in statements like these were racialized assumptions about the nature of different bodies—what they could sustain and what they could transform. Establishing distance between different populations enabled colonizers to maintain racial hierarchies and assert the prestige of French officials and settlers.

Colonial claims that constructed "the tropics" as unhealthy sites were constitutive of racial conceptions in the nineteenth century.[70] These racial categories were profoundly intertwined with labor recruitment, as authorities noted how "Hova," "Tanosy," and "Sakalava" (and later "Chinese," "Indian," and "Comorien") workers performed in different environments and climates. Like divide-and-rule approaches taken across colonial Africa, racialized categories were at the heart of Gouverneur Gallieni's *politique des races*, which designated leaders on whom officials relied for taxation and, by the 1930s, obligatory, unremitted work for the state (*prestations*). Imposed racial hierarchies and categories buttressed French efforts to extract labor by pressuring leaders to produce laborers from their constituencies— although communities often refused to recognize the authority of these French (and French-appointed) officials, and rural dwellers often resisted coercive labor by fleeing their jurisdictions.[71] Archival records contain traces of workers' narratives, filtered through French eyes, that explain why they refused to work.

Colonial authorities in Mahajanga agonized over the dearth of voluntary laborers. Between 1896 and 1905, inhabitants in the northwest region of Madagascar, largely comprising Sakalava, Makoa, Antalaotra, and Karana, were insufficient in numbers and demanded high wages for tasks. Of followers of the Sakalava polity living in the area, many "completely refused" to work on infrastructural projects, likening wage labor for the French to servitude and enslavement.[72] Thus, the prisons were among the most important sources for laborers in the young colony and in fact supplied the majority of the urban labor force in early twentieth-century Mahajanga. Administrators relied periodically on forced laborers (*prestataires* or *corvée*), later instituted under the Service de la main d'oeuvre des travaux d'interet général (SMOTIG), and the forced workers were supplemented with small numbers of wage laborers.[73]

Prison laborers and workers recruited from the highlands both enabled and constrained construction of several early colonial building projects. In April 1898, prison laborers cleared the site for the governor's residence (figures 3.16 and 3.17), a symbolic and administrative node adjacent to Majunga Ancien and overlooking the seaside. Administrators' desire to signal their enduring presence by constructing in stone necessitated adept masons, "several" of whom they recruited from Nosy Be and Diego Suarez in the north, and from Tananarive in the highlands. The highlanders failed to "produce good results" despite their apparent "eager willingness" to work, and five workers perished. Only three of the highland stonecutters survived, but these had united with family members in the area and managed to "acclimatize."[74]

French overseers noted that the highlanders were all ill and weak (*eprouvés*) from the excessively hot and humid climate, and suffering from intense homesickness and "nostalgia" (*nostalgie*) for loved ones left behind.[75] It is not clear whether the highlanders understood their illnesses to be linked to "nostalgia" or framed their explanation in terms they knew would be legible and persuasive to French officials with medical and geographical understandings of health. But one way to understand highlanders' refusal to

FIGURE 3.16 Residence for French colonial provincial governor, Mahajanga, 1903.
Courtesy of FR ANOM 44PA134/3.

work is as an agential creation of an opening, a space of longing, "an insistence on the possible over the probable."[76] Their distinctive role as masons,
critical to the materialization of the residence project, gave them leverage in
shaping the progress and pace of construction. The earthly conditions (in
this case, the hot, swampy coast), moreover, were a mediating force through
which the highland masons contested their condition—whether through
slow work as stubborn pushback or through vehement enunciation of attachment to home. Although the remaining masons and prison workers
eventually erected the residence, the highland masons slowed the pace of
construction through their explicit refusal and bodily limitations, exposing
the hairline fractures in coercive colonial building regimes and leaving French
officials scrambling to find solutions to the perpetual scarcity of labor.

As in other French colonies, roadbuilding in Madagascar was central
to refashioning cities and linking them to others, especially the capital in
newly renamed Tananarive (Antananarivo).[77] Unlike masonry work, which
required specialized knowledge, the backbreaking labor of roadbuilding,
which primarily entailed digging trenches and laying of stones, could be
done by anyone with strength and endurance. Frustrated with the shoddy

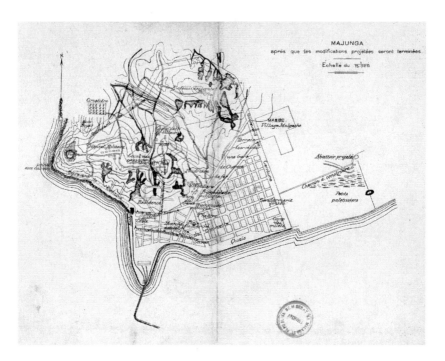

FIGURE 3.17 Mahajanga (Majunga), "after projected changes are completed," 1901. Courtesy of National Archives of the République Démocratique de Madagascar.

work of prison laborers and the "complete refusal" of local wage laborers, colonial officials sought to fill the ranks with laborers from China, India, and the Comorian archipelago for roadbuilding.[78] This was not the first time European imperial powers sought to secure indentured workers from China, which became an increasingly pervasive practice among European colonizers beginning in the 1850s.[79] Likely working through a French trader residing in China, French authorities secured approval from the Qing Dynasty to bring 764 Chinese indentured laborers to Madagascar in 1901.[80] As in the French Congo, Europeans in Madagascar assumed that Chinese laborers were "inherently docile," but were able to complete work only when subject to "very energetic discipline."[81] Under this harsh treatment, some fifty Chinese migrant workers and twenty-five prison laborers completed a large road and gutter project linking Mahabibo to Majunga Ancien. Soon thereafter, many of the Chinese laborers fell ill, and others were struck by skin infestations of "chiques" (likely sand fleas) serious enough to warrant their admission to the hospital.[82] With scarce numbers of Chinese recruits remaining, colonial roadbuilding projects stalled across the city, and French authorities soon abandoned Chinese recruitment efforts, turning to India and Comoros instead.[83]

Pests, Plague, and the Perils of Labor

In the early 1900s, French officials found a short-term solution to perpetual labor scarcity in Indian workers. Original efforts to recruit workers from sister French colony Pondicherry for infrastructure projects elsewhere in Madagascar proved disappointing owing to the significant number of evaders (*evades*) on site.[84] Cognizant of the "ancient relations between Madagascar and Porbandar" sustained through Indian merchants, officials shifted tack to work through Gujarati elites in Mahajanga for labor recruitment abroad.[85] Local Karana interlocutors possessed intimate knowledge of Mahajanga, including its climatic and dockage conditions, and some had already established agencies in the city to welcome and assist new migrants. Among the notables were two men, Ahmed Codja and Nathoo Premjee, both of "good standing in the community," with long-standing ties to Porbandar, who in 1900 brokered contracts for 200 workers from the Gujarat region.[86] According to the indentured workers' booklets (*livrets d'engagés Indiens*), laborers were obliged to work in public works projects for ten hours each day, with a monthly salary of twenty-five francs per month, for a duration of three years.[87]

That same year, some 214 men arrived in Mahajanga.[88] Newspaper accounts conjectured that new arrivals were all too happy to leave "Punjab where they're subjected to the plague and famine"; in actuality, recruits departed from several ports in Gujarat, including Jamnagar and Porbandar.[89] Made up of diverse religious affiliations (Hindu and Muslim), caste, and cultural practices, these laborers brought wide-ranging expert knowledge, as reflected in their declared professions: thirteen masons, eight cooks, five potters, five leatherworkers, three barbers, and two ironworkers; the remainder identified themselves as farmers and "workers."[90] New recruits were immediately put to work constructing the port, roads, and major civil buildings, and they reportedly "produced good results if trained and surveilled well."[91] Some toiled as stonecutters, carving out hefty blocks of limestone used to construct double-story homes and buildings (figures 3.18 and 3.19).[92]

Despite their utility, the migrants presented new problems. They placed material demands on the colonial regime for such things as housing and

FIGURE 3.18 "Stone cutters," Mahajanga, 1903. Courtesy of FR ANOM 44PA134/15.

FIGURE 3.19 "House in construction," of Mahajanga, 1903.
Courtesy of FR ANOM 44PA134/14.

sanitation facilities. Codja and Premjee obliged French authorities to institute an elaborate set of housing and meal arrangements to "avoid mixing" between the divergent groups possessing different prohibitions and religious practices, governed by a hierarchal regime of surveillance, as described by Moriceau:

> They have been split into 8 groups, each having a corporal and a cook, and live in 4 large, wood houses [each housing about 55 men] . . . which are easily surveilled. For some of them, meat is prohibited and others do not eat fish; it was thus impossible to make one common cook and kitchen. Each house has its kitchen which is equipped with 4 cast-iron marmites, 6 buckets and 1 knife for cutting the wood. Even if the rice [for both] is purchased at the market, it must be cooked separately.[93]

At the same time, the intensification of connections to a global industrial-capitalist trade network and the relative ease of dockage with the completion of the wharf brought new boats and diseases to the town. The late nineteenth century brought a surge in plague epidemics, in which nodes along heavily trafficked international routes were more vulnerable in the 1890s than they had been when the plague initially spread out of Asia. The first cases of bubonic plague in Mahajanga drew the attention of French doctors in February 1902. The doctors who observed that the victims were recent migrant workers immediately blamed them for bringing the plague from south India, where plague was rampant. The outbreak ostensibly originated in a group of homes inhabited by Indians in Majunga Ancien. Within the span of two weeks, eight Indians died. Several homes were incinerated, and families, including Mehta and his brother, were displaced to temporary encampments (figure 3.20).[94]

French officials quickly harnessed the plague outbreaks to materialize long-envisioned plans to spatially (re)engineer the city. They focused on Majunga Ancien, where the obstinate stone homes of Indian shopkeepers had long obstructed French attempts to radically rework the landscape. Since the approval of the aforementioned 1898 urban plan, officials hoped to expropriate three-quarters of the neighborhood. Although the city plan forbade residents from expanding or restoring their homes should they fall into disrepair, officials lacked sufficient funds to compensate landowners and actualize the plan.[95] As a result, the homes remained untouched until the plague outbreak in 1902 provided a new opportunity. Targeting the sedimented homes of Karana families, health commission officers conducted house-to-house visits and designated those that were dilapidated (and thus

FIGURE 3.20 Postcard, "During the Plague—Encampment of Banians," Mahajanga, ca. 1900s. Author's collection.

FIGURE 3.21 Postcard, "During the Plague—Infected house in the course of demolition," Mahajanga, ca.1900s. Strikingly, the handwritten note blithely sends "best caresses" but makes no mention of the plague, even while the postcard itself depicts the dispossession of residents of "infected homes." Author's collection.

supposedly vulnerable to infection) or "infected" for immediate incineration (figure 3.21).[96] The Municipal Commission reported that the epidemic had demonstrated that the "repugnant cohabitation of Indians" was a public health danger and recommended that they be moved to a newly designated three-hectare area where they were to construct "clean, more spaced apart, larger and better aerated" homes that would ensure the city's restored health.[97]

But Karana, and even some European residents who lived in the area, refused the derisive terms in which they and their homes were framed. Employing the durability of their homes as an architectural tactic, they countered French efforts to appropriate them. They petitioned Gouverneur Général Gallieni, arguing that the 1898 urban plan forbade improvements on their dwellings and that the city's restrictions on home improvement were responsible for the rampant plague. They also invoked the stone construction of their homes as grounds for the preservation of their homes:

> These buildings are still in very good condition . . . and could become very good habitations with some modifications to windows and doors to allow light and air to penetrate . . . they are always better than those in wood and sheet metal. For the moment, housing is lacking in Majunga and for this reason, Governor General, we ask you not to condemn to demolition of our Indian neighborhood, the only neighborhood in Majunga constructed entirely in stone.[98]

In so doing, residents harnessed the political power of their "obdurate" homes to obstruct French redesigns of the city's future through their material rigidity and the deep-seated relations around them.[99] Their efforts were successful. Officials ultimately permitted proprietors to make some hygienic improvements to the homes, including enlarging the doors and windows and whitewashing the walls. But, in a chilling afternote to the Gouverneur Général, head colonial administrator René Jules Édouard Moriceau glossed over the distinctive Indian and Antalaotra presence and their contributions to Majunga Ancien, and urged the authorities to "execute a plan of which the achievement is indispensable for effectuating the disappearance of the Arab character of our city."[100]

It's unsurprising that the eradication of an Indian presence in the Majunga Ancien was veiled under the guise of public health measures; such techniques of spatial engineering have been documented across the French and British empires. What is intriguing is the way in which building materials were considered constitutive of ethnic differences, and how—in a new twist—these differences were linked by authorities to the presence of rats.

Having been expelled from their burrows by the intensive construction of the city's infrastructure, rats took refuge in homes in Majunga Ancien that abutted the wharf in the years following the 1902 outbreak. After another epidemic in 1907, health officials discovered some 150 rat cadavers under the wooden floor of an Indian-owned house.[101] Authorities blamed the particular material construction of Karana-owned homes, noting that rats "dug their burrows in every way" in the composite of amalgamated stone, earthen mortar, sand, and wood, and found comfortable dens in the thick walls.[102] City officials drew on the materiality of Karana homes—the mud walls and wood rafters—to discursively equate their ostensibly unsanitary conditions with rats, essentially "making colonized people into pests."[103]

The plague outbreak of 1907, and the resultant destruction of large swaths of homes, signaled a metamorphosis in the spatial layout and aesthetic of the city. Home demolitions not only effaced the layered family histories of migration and emplacement but also opened spaces in which French officials overwrote past histories with new visions of futurity and engagements with the global, capitalist economy. Newspaper accounts described how demolitions had the "advantage of contributing to the beauty of the city which found itself cleared of hideous hovels."[104] Paradoxically, this supposed beautification campaign was born from death and destruction. The eradication of subalterns' homes and lives gave rise to a new imaginary of a colonial city in which colonized bodies were hidden. At the same time, labor scarcity compelled colonial officials to scale back their sweeping aspirations of transforming the city. Plans for a railway and train station in town were scrapped, and officials lamented the plodding pace of road, sewer, and building construction. The absence of realized projects exposed the incoherencies of the colonial bureaucracy and futilities of the colonial project, but they also revealed moments of workers' refusal, of their insistence on privileging the life-giving labor that came from sustaining kin relations and the anticipatory nurturance of dreams of alternative futures.

Conclusion

Mahajanga's cityscape—its presences and absences—was a tactile gauge of shifting relations, a communicative medium that expressed contradictory dimensions of colonialism, and a living epitaph that memorialized contested pasts. Riddled with material remains that testify to the pluralistic knowledges that comprised the city's archive over time, the city was, in Doreen Massey's words, the "multiplicity of histories all in the process of being made."[105] It was also a landscape profoundly shaped by human and nonhuman refusals. The situation of Mahajanga in the late 1800s and early 1900s reveals *refusal* in its myriad forms: the thick-clay seabed and malaria-ridden mire that impeded plans for a gallant military conquest; the nostalgic murmurings among homesick workers that affirmed attachments to kin and ancestral land; and the resolute conviction of Karana families, who asserted the value of the dynamic forms of urban life they had forged across generations. Tracking these forms of refusal helps us see how human agency unfolded in an ecological, more-than-human world that exerted its own forms of hindrance to projected plans.

The terrain of the city was (and continues to be) as much a struggle over who could harness resources to inscribe their presence into the architectural archive as it was a site for debating the contours of coercive colonial rule. If French colonial officials in Mahajanga initially envisioned the colonial project as the joining of "native work and European capital" in the service of producing "something fertile and durable," they soon saw their aspirations foiled by their inability to enforce coercive colonial labor laws.[106] But migrants from Madagascar, China, and India ultimately faced increasingly precarious conditions of dispossession in the face of shifting labor markets. By the early 1900s, French officials sought workers in nearby Comoros. In 1902, France attached the Comorian archipelago to Madagascar, further accelerating the movements of people across the silty channels.[107] The entrenchment of racial, global capitalism and the expansion of French colonial rule in the nineteenth century ensured the changing identity of workers who actualized colonial infrastructure projects.

Within the Karana community, some families were able to leverage the architectural inertia of their homes, their grasp on oceanic commodities trade, and their access to overseas labor markets not only to place demands on state officials, but also to shape the negotiating terms for colonial praxis on the ground. The unfolding encounters between Indian inhabitants and French authorities expose the limits of architectural governance, as well as the spaces cleaved open for imaginative refusals. French city planners who once imagined the cityscape as a malleable terrain that they could bring under colonial domain through property regulation were instead confronted with their dependence on Indians for labor and the immovability of the already-built landscape. Karana traders came to dominate the economic life of the city, especially when Europeans fled during the economic downturn of the 1930s. They expanded their export-import businesses and founded numerous large enterprises manufacturing oil, soap, and natural fibers. By the 1950s Karana families were said to have owned 80 percent of the city's real estate.[108] Although the home of Nanji Kalidas Mehta has long since disappeared, many gleaming white shophouses still tower in Majunga Ancien (now known as Majunga Be) as manifestations of the determined entrenchment of Indian families, past and present.

4

Sedimentary Bonds

Treasured Mosques and Everyday Expertise

September 23, 1912, began like any other day, but it ended in catastrophe. What likely started as a small cooking fire in a courtyard of a home quickly expanded into a mass conflagration. Sweeping northwestern winds carried the flames across the expansive village of Mahabibo, the crowded neighborhood that housed the diverse groups of Malagasy and Comorians who toiled in Mahajanga. In the end, the fire voraciously consumed some 580 homes, transforming a patchwork of tightly nestled thatch, wood, cement, and sheet-metal into heaps of ashes and angst. Beyond exposing the flammability of vegetatively constructed housing and the limitations of colonial policies, the fire raised new quandaries for city officials who had tried to keep the labor population temporary by limiting building materials. Echoing Sakalava monarchs from centuries earlier, French colonial municipal acts mandated in the early 1900s that inhabitants of Mahabibo construct homes from ephemeral materials (e.g., thatch, wood, and mud) to discourage migrants from long-term residence in the city. With the fire in 1912, colonial administrators were obliged to face the fragility of the temporary material landscape that they had so deliberately legislated.[1]

Casting themselves as benevolent protectors of the town dwellers, city administrators responded to the fire by appointing a French contractor to work with Malagasy and Comorian families, conflated under the single term *indigenes*, to construct in an "orderly" fashion homes made of hardened materials more resistant to the rapacious properties of fire. Officials seized the firestorm's aftermath to redesign the city's layout and expand the state's role in regulating property by identifying a terrain adjacent to Mahabibo to which some 2,000 victims without shelter would be forcibly relocated to build new homes.[2] Unlike the earlier settlement of Mahabibo, however, this space would be delineated into ethnic enclaves, so that "Comorians" lived with "Comorians," "Antaimoro" with "Antaimoro," and so on. Mahajanga Mayor Carron, who served from 1911 to 1913, proposed the construction of 1,000 new homes in brick or cement, with limestone whitewash and tin roofs, that would be offered in a rent-to-own scheme. This intervention, the mayor argued, would encourage home ownership among colonial subjects, promote colonial hygienic norms through "solid housing," and (in an about-face from earlier policies) foster a "sedentary Majungais population which is precious to the development of commerce and industry."[3]

Certain residents were made irate by this proposal. Among them was a group of seven "Anjouanais" migrants (from Ndzwani in the Comoros) who pooled their monies, hired a scribe, and crafted a petition to Gouverneur Général Albert Picquié in French, demanding that the state honor their property rights over their current land parcels. Significantly, the petitioners hinged their opposition to the forcible displacement not on the ghettoization of the proposed plan, but on the material composition of their dwellings. They made a distinct point of emphasizing the durable construction of their homes—and the economizing practices that had enabled them to build lasting structures that withstood the fire—on land parcels granted by authorities.

DEAR MONSIEUR GOUVERNEUR GÉNÉRAL,

We have the honor to kindly submit to you the following. We have resided in the city of Majunga [Mahajanga] since 1895, where we were given parcels on which we settled. Since then, we've constructed our homes there, some in cement, some in wood. These constructions are the fruit of our modest savings that we have been able to accumulate during this time in Majunga by doing some work. Today . . . a great part of the village has been burnt. The administration has decided that residents can no longer make any reparations to their homes and cannot remain on their parcels, even if their homes were not touched by the fire. We appeal to you to keep us in our current locations, since our homes are made of durable [*en dur*] materials, without a single change. Our sheet metal, wood and all our building materials will not be of a single value if we are displaced.

SIGNED,

Moucheda Ousseny, Youngca, Sidy Omady, Bakary Naouda, Abodou Boina, Salimon, Sidi Hamadi, Charifou Abdallah, and Boudoury, Anjounais Living in the Mahabibo Village (habitant tous au village de Mahabibo (Majunga)[4]

The Anjouanais petitioners slip out of the archival record after this letter, and we know frustratingly little about their livelihoods, families, or personal itineraries.

We do know they were among a broader wave of migrants from the Comorian archipelago during the late nineteenth and early twentieth centuries who, more than any other group at the time, were critical to the spatial thickening—the increasing density of building projects and expansion of vital practices of inhabitance in streets, alleys, and common spaces—of Mahajanga. Antaloaotra (of mixed Comorian, Sakalava, and sometimes Hadhramaut descent) long traversed the city, but French census records suggest "Comorians" were few in number early 1900s, although they grew to comprise around half of the city's population by the 1950s.[5] Building on generations of mobility, Comorians found grounds for experimenting with labor migration as a strategy for garnering wages, achieving adult status, and managing the temporality of their life cycle in the changing conditions of the late nineteenth and early twentieth centuries. Once in Mahajanga, they were particularly agile in securing land, integrating with local families (as we will see in chapter 5), and clamorously engaging with colonial officials around access to property. By the early twentieth century, with the encroachment of French colonial rule and the growing population of the city, built forms became critical sites in which Comorian migrants worked out politically and ethically charged ideas of urbanism.

Colonial urban rule was predicated on the assumption that urban planners possessed an expansive capacity to reconfigure cities. The policing of epistemic boundaries around expert knowledge of urban planning and architecture meant that Africans who designed, built, and engineered monumental and mundane forms were rarely recognized in the historical record as urban designers, architects, and engineers. Yet, time and again, colonized subjects—in this case migrants from the Comoros—did just those things and exposed the fractures in colonial rule by building the city anew, within the constraints at hand. Comorian and Malagasy designers and builders were recognized locally as experts, knowledgeable people (*olo mahay*) who built and repaired things (*mpanoamboatra*) and possessed the knowledge necessary to plan and construct buildings (*olo mahay rafitra, mpandrafitra*). This chapter offers a corrective to the epistemic erasures that were initiated by colonial officials and perpetuated by scholars. I contend that these everyday experts—designers, planners, and engineers—wielded legitimate power to reframe the conditions of possibility of colonial urban life. I argue that shifting who counts as a designer in urban histories allows for greater understanding of non-elites in architectural becoming and foregrounds pluralistic knowledge forms that have been sidelined in historical records.[6]

In early twentieth-century Mahajanga, mosque-building was the most conspicuous practice through which everyday experts showcased their technical acumen. Even before they constructed homes, newly arrived Comorians constructed mosques as collective abodes for Islamic practice and as living epitaphs of communal memories and shared hopes. For their part, French officials increasingly sectioned, surveilled, and regulated urban spaces in an effort to craft a distinctly French colonial city that would be not only invulnerable to disruption from colonized subjects but also economically viable based on extractive, dispensable migrant labor.[7] At first glance, mosque-building and the proliferation of colonial regulations appear to be opposing projects, in which Comorian communities and French authorities sought to render durable their competing visions for the city in the early twentieth century. But such binary framing of colonizer/colonized risks eliding the pluralistic constituencies (class, ethnolinguistic, sectarian, and gender) and ambivalent interrelations subsumed in categorial identifiers like "Comorians," let alone the "cacophonous . . . moments" that Chickasaw theorist Jodi Byrd flags, "where the representational logics of colonial discourses break down."[8] In other words, the complex, heterogeneous communities of people in Mahajanga that mosques brought together in epistemic and affective encounters were sites where the incoherencies of colonial rationales could be exposed.

Instead, this chapter takes mosques as relational nodes through which diverse Comorian congregants subverted colonial logics around property value and asserted alternative, anticipatory visions for the city grounded in religious conviction, fraternal sociality, and enduring ties of reciprocity. Over time, mosques became key mediums through which migrants from the Comorian archipelago developed discourses of *zanatany*, cohering in a concept of urban belonging steeped in solidarity even while saturated with intergenerational tensions. By following flashpoints when Comorian migrants acquired land, pooled their resources, and collectively summoned mosques, I investigate early-twentieth-century mosque-building projects as both *epistemic* and *affective* processes. Municipal records, property and regulatory acts, correspondence, and images shed some light here, but the architectural forms themselves—their stylistic forms, material composition, and textures—evidence pathways of circulating technical and architectural knowledge across the western Indian Ocean. Comorian migrants brought diverse knowledges of masonry techniques, economizing practices, and long-term project management to bear on the collective construction of mosques. Mosque-building enabled congregants to develop contingent technical and aesthetic capacities, to discern their positioning in the city's social geography, and to probe the fissures of colonial authority.[9]

Brought into being through the centripetal movement of builders, designers, ritual experts, tools, and buildings materials—limestone, sand, wood—and sustained by the everyday passages of faithful congregants, mosques were (and continue to be) weighty emotive repositories. Comorian and Comorian-Malagasy families (who were in many cases the descendants of mosque builders) described to me the affinal connections and emotional experiences of love (*fitiavana*) and desire (*faniriana*) forged through communal construction events. Mosques offered Comorian migrants possibilities for remaking their lifeworlds. Yet, much as mosque-building communicated condensed relations and abiding attachments, the construction of a mosque could equally signal the centrifugal forces that drove people apart, the bitter fractures and noisy dissensions among Sufi congregants resulting in yet another newly founded congregation.

Mosques were places that emotionally *moved* people. Drawing on documentary records in French colonial archives, postcard images, ethnographic research—including interviews with descendants of the historical mosque builders—and recent scholarship on affect and built forms, this chapter contributes to scholarly understandings of the powerful role of emotion in historical transformations of material, architectural, and ecological landscapes in African contexts. Historians have productively probed the past for shared norms and experiences of emotions, yet scholars of Africa have been less inclined to excavate regimes of affect, especially love.[10] The act of apprehending the vivid emotions of subalterns embedded in colonially authored archival fragments is replete with methodological challenges, but I also piece together oral accounts and chart linguistic valences to help bridge evidentiary gaps. Here, Sara Ahmed's capacious conception of "emotion" as directional movement that might repel or attract, "hold us in place, or give us a dwelling place," is generative for grasping the propelling forces of city-making and tracking affective expressions across time and place.[11]

In what follows, I first chronicle the historical conditions in the Co-moros that led young men to migrate to Mahajanga, attending to how the expansion of racial global capitalism, the rise of French imperialism, and ecological changes in the archipelago created the conditions of possibility that accelerated Comorian migration beginning in the first decade of the 1900s.[12] Migration for wage labor intersected with expanding Sufi networks throughout the southwestern Indian Ocean as part of broader, contemporaneous Islamic reformist movements. Once settled, Comorian migrants found work and established Sufi communities (which coexisted alongside the already-established Shi'ite Indian communities discussed in chapter 3), transforming Mahajanga into what one descendant of mosque-builders called the "cradle of Islam" in Madagascar.[13] The latter section of the chapter meditates on the role of everyday experts and emotive forces in the forging of mosques as archival epigraphs and living testimonies to anticipated futures.

New Iterations of Comorian Mobility
under French Rule (1900–1920s)

Comorians crossed the choppy, churning waters of the Mozambique Channel in wind-powered boats, full of anticipation about the lives they might pursue in Mahajanga. Emerging from nearly a century (from the 1840s to the 1920s) of political turmoil, ecological disaster, and French encroachment on agriculturally productive land in the Comoro Islands, migrants fled the strictures of their homelands. But they also built on long-standing migratory ties, seasonal trade patterns, and cultural exchange between northwest Madagascar and the Comoros, evident in linguistic imprints in both Malagasy (an Austronesian language) and Shikomoro (closely related to Swahili and with strong Arabic influences).[14] Many migrants were drawn to northwest Madagascar by the possibility of wealth accumulation, which would enable them to support their kinship networks and strengthen their relative social standing in their Comorian home villages.[15] The historical flow of the Comoros to Madagascar, however, reveals the problematic nature of inherited analytical concepts of "voluntary" or "forced" labor and the ideological distinction between them, which, Frederick Cooper reminds us, is inherent in the making of global capitalist economies.[16] In the twentieth century, a Comorian migrant to Mahajanga could conceivably move across a range of labor modes over his lifetime—from a position of servitude and subordination to senior men, French officials, and employers, to relative economic authority and seniority in the household. Yet Comorians' "choice" to migrate for work emerged from the ecological, economic, and political upheavals that shook much of the Comorian archipelago in the nineteenth century.

Several critical shifts in the archipelago and the Indian Ocean basin radically disrupted existing livelihood practices and led some men to migrate abroad. Prosperity in the archipelago waned, especially over the course of the nineteenth century, when European trade routes shifted away from the Comoros as a key provisioning site and internal conflicts erupted between and within elite lineages in Ndzwani and Ngazidja. Weakened by infighting, local leaders sought support from the French. French horticulturalists and entrepreneurs seized the opportunity to negotiate commercial treaties with local leaders; establish cash-crop plantations of ylang-ylang, cloves, and sugar in Ngazidja and Ndzwani; and implement French protection of the islands in 1887. By the early twentieth century, the globalized capitalist system and French imperial expansion in the Indian Ocean basin had destroyed existing modes of land use and disrupted economies of social production rooted in kinship relations. Former slaves and commoners bore the burden of agricultural work on French-owned plantations, while young men who could not find wage labor on these plantations, or who refused submission to European employers, sought contractual work in northwest Madagascar. As the ruling classes in the Comoros lost their power to French-backed sultans and foreign plantation owners, families scrambled to find new avenues for retaining influence and prosperity. Although sources are patchy, it seems most probable that elite men comprised a large number, if not the majority, of immigrants to Mahajanga (figure 4.1), in a manner similar to Soninke migrants in French West Africa.[17] The decline of sugar plantations in northern Ndzwani in 1905, due to the global drop in sugar prices, further precipitated an exodus of young men from the archipelago.[18]

Migratory streams were hardly uniform throughout the archipelago, with most migrants hailing from Ndzwani and Ngazidja. Early official attempts to recruit workers to Mahajanga from Moheli, for instance, yielded negligible results, because adult male laborers were scarce and officials in the Comoros worried about weakening the "already diminished" population.[19] Young men in Ndzwani, by contrast, were numerous and eager to pursue work in Madagascar. The streets of Moutsamoudou, Ndzwani's capital, were filled with young men from rural land-owning families, "dressed elegantly in white robes, adorned with necklaces of perfumed flowers."[20] When

French medical geographer M. Lafont asked these young men—appearing rich—why they would want to work abroad, they described how class norms paradoxically hindered their possibilities for income generation. "It is dishonorable for us," they explained, "to work in our countryside, in front of our former slaves."[21] Lured by the possibility of superior salaries, Ndzwani men came to Mahajanga in droves, and by 1901 there was an "important Anjouanais village," although few traces remain of its whereabouts.[22] Young male migrants recognized the shifting affordances of historical sea change—namely, the rise of plantations in Comoros at the expense of agricultural production and the expansion of French domination at the turn of the nineteenth century, which transformed patterns of migration and residency—and their journeys to and from Mahajanga constituted anticipatory responses to the uncertainties at hand.

To sustain incoming streams of migrants, colonial authorities in Madagascar replicated a tactic they had employed with Indian intermediaries at the turn of the century: aligning with prominent figures to facilitate labor recruitment. French officials hoped that by appealing to Comorian intermediaries to find workers, they would not only entice men reticent to work for French enterprises but also forge tighter alliances with key Sufi leaders who could allay possible anticolonial sentiment among Muslim communities. One such mediator was Prince Saidina, captain of the boat *Étoile d'Anjouan*, who was so successful in sending laborers to Madagascar that French administrators granted him a governorship in the province of Mahavavy, near present-day Ambilobe.[23] The name of Saidina's boat suggests that he recruited laborers from Ndzwani, from where he likely hailed.

But Saidina may have been a more complicated figure. Historians have elsewhere documented that a noble named "Saidina," appointed as a local governor, was also a key figure in the propagation of *tarīqa Shadhiliyya*, an important Sufi order that spread rapidly across Indian Ocean networks in the late nineteenth and early twentieth centuries.[24] In these accounts, Saidina apparently began his missionary efforts to establish Shadhiliyya in the northern region of Madagascar among Ankaranana. He was considered by at least one French military officer to be the ideal candidate to temper the influence of Muslims (who by French estimations threatened to "dominate Sakalava") in northwest Madagascar, owing to his "devotion to the French cause" and the "high estimation of his co-religionists."[25] Whether the captain of the *Étoile* and the Islamic missionary were the same man is unclear. But these distinct accounts of elite Comorian men nevertheless reveal the overlapping projects of labor recruitment and Islamic missionizing in which they were involved.

French colonial encroachment in Madagascar and across Africa converged with, and in some ways spurred, sweeping reformist movements across Islamic communities worldwide. To understand how Comorian migrants peregrinated trajectories of commercial exchange, wage labor migration, and religious networks, some background on Sufism and how it spread to the southwestern Indian Ocean is relevant. Beginning in the latter half of the nineteenth century, Sufi reformists energetically propagated *tarīqa* (often translated as "way" or "path"), organized groups founded in early modern times that cohered around distinctive teachings, ritual practices, and spiritual leaders. As historian Nile Green has described, the late nineteenth century was characterized by a "massive increase in Muslim religious production," where new ideas and affiliations circulated widely, enabled by new communication and transportation technologies.[26] Starting from Hadramawt, Sufi missionaries circuited the Indian Ocean, moving along the East African coast, into northern Mozambique, and through the Comoros and northern Madagascar. Among the Sufi orders, Shadhiliyya gained strength in the Comoros in the mid- to late eighteenth century, and, through continued ties to northwest Madagascar, became the most important *tarīqa* in Mahajanga among Comorian settlers in the early twentieth century.[27]

Over time, migration from Ndzwani, Ngazidja, and the other Comorian islands to Madagascar intensified. It is difficult to determine the exact number of immigrants from the Comoros to northwest Madagascar, partly because colonial surveillance of human traffic was minimal and because many men avoided official scrutiny. Yet city census records attest that although "Comorians" comprised just 11 percent of the population in 1902, that number had grown to 20 percent by 1913; by the 1950s they reached around 50 percent of the city's overall population.[28] Ever elusive are the exact, disaggregated breakdowns of where migrants came from *within* the Comoros. French administrators were either unable or unwilling to distinguish the fine-grained detail in migration patterns, let alone the social networks and relations that specific migration dynamics indicated. French colonial ambitions to consolidate regional imperial holdings were realized in 1908, when the Comorian archipelago was linked by legislative annexation to the by-then-colonized Madagascar, captured in a vividly illustrated chocolate wrapper that circulated among French publics in the 1910s (figure 4.2). This legislative binding of the Big Island and the archipelago was partly a superficial grafting of colonial regulation onto centuries-long migratory movements between the two. But it also facilitated, channeled, and intensified the movement of (predominantly) male migrants and missionaries from Ndzwani and Ngazidja to Mahajanga during the period from the 1910s to the 1930s.[29]

Labor Niches, Sufi Networks, and the Making of a Comorian Community

Migrants from the Comoros worked a wide variety of jobs. In oral interviews, migrants and descendants of migrants described how many worked, at least for a time, on construction projects around the city.[30] Some labored as dockers, domestic workers, cooks, messengers, drivers, guards, and night

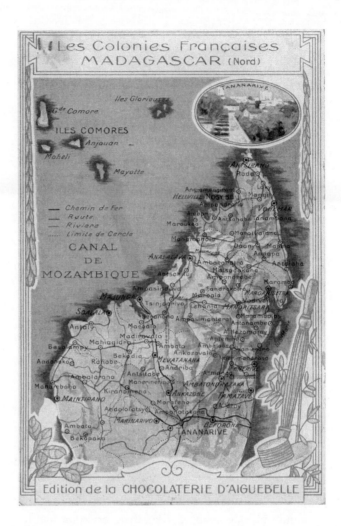

FIGURE 4.2
"French colonies
of Madagascar"
(North), ca. 1910.
Chromolitho-
graphic print.
Chocolaterie
d'Aiguebelle,
Drôme, France.

watchmen for Europeans (*mpiasa an'vazaha*), or as city workers charged
with street sweeping (*mpamafa lalana*).[31] Others worked as petty traders and
taxi drivers. Some took up the work of their itinerant ancestors, working as
sailors or traders, trafficking such commodities as coconuts and cowhides
between the Comoros and Madagascar (figure 4.3). Still others kept vege-
table gardens, farmed corn, and raised goats to supplement their income.[32]

Over time, they took other jobs tightly aligned with the French colonial
administration, such as municipal workers, court translators, and couri-
ers.[33] Some mixed Comorian-Malagasy children recollected that their fathers and grandfathers had worked as police officers for the French, who
favored them for their loyalty and reliability. Mama Beatrice, an iconic

FIGURE 4.3
"Comorian
sailors,"
Mahajanga,
ca. 1886–89.
Courtesy of
Archives du
Ministère de
l'Europe et
des Affaires
étrangères—
La Courneuve,
Série P-Afrique,
A009210.
Photographer:
Albert Pinard.

figure among mixed Malagasy-Comorian families and an important spirit medium in Mahabibo, recalled that her father had migrated from Ngazidja in the 1920s or '30s. He worked initially as a fisherman, until he secured coveted work as a police officer with the city. Mama Beatrice laughed as she recounted that the French hired him because they liked his uncompromising manner, even though he was not formally schooled (beyond Qur'anic school) and didn't really know how to read and write. "He was very strict (*masiaka*)," she said. "He would stand at the crossroads of Mahibo [Mahabibo] and pull people over. . . . They were scared (*mavozo*) of him!" Over time, characterizations of Comorian police as complicit in maintaining French colonial rule would abound and persist in Madagascar through the twentieth century.[34] The shift of Comorians securing jobs in colonial administration appears to have begun with police work; French officials increasingly approached Comorians who, perhaps by virtue of their relative "foreignness," were perceived by the French as trustworthy agents in the face of Malagasy resistance.[35]

But other Comorian civil workers worked quietly to subvert coercive colonial power, especially the surveillance and regulation over residents' mobility. Hasandrama, a revered healer and *fondi* (Islamic teacher) in his nineties at the time of our interaction, recalled one Comorian inspector charged with inspecting town inhabitants for identification cards and imposing fines on those lacking identification: "When he approached a household, he secretly motioned to those whom he knew didn't possess the card. . . . He looked as though he was calling them, but really he was telling them to flee and hide." Hasandrama nostalgically remarked that city dwellers interpreted the inspector's protective gesture as one born of affection and solidarity in the face of French colonial rule. "In earlier times, people loved each other" (*taloha, mifankatia olo*). He elaborated that these values of affinity, social camaraderie, and amiability were key attributes of a distinctive urbanism emergent in dense Comorian and Malagasy interactions, stressing that "this was the *zanatany* way of life" (*ny fomba zanatany izany*).[36] Undermining French power, thus, was at once a refusal of colonial logics and a generative building of solidarity.

If labor is anchored in space, then it is also an object of time. Men were motivated to migrate to Mahajanga by the possibility of wage labor, a sense of adventure, religious pursuits, or the promise of a fresh start in a new place. This final point was especially important for men coming from Ngazidja and, to a lesser degree, Ndzwani, where customary practices obliged junior men to parlay their savings into the lavish, opulent marriage celebrations (*āda* in Ngazidja; or *harusi* in Ndzwani) that marked adult masculinity and strengthened community ties in reciprocal "cycle(s) of indebtedness impossible to close."[37] In addition to their own marriages, brothers, uncles, and fathers were also expected to contribute to the marriages of their sisters, daughters, and nieces. Migration to northwest Madagascar offered young Comorian men the promise to gather wages with which they could return home and gain the status of elder, garner fame, and bolster their reputation in the Comoros.[38] In other words, time and money afforded "symbolic capital" that young men from the Comoros could use to propel themselves across life stages—accelerating their passage into adulthood through their newfound earnings.[39] Conversely, displacement to Madagascar also offered the possibility of circumventing onerous kin obligations and, instead, building a life in the newfound land. In so doing, junior men could secure some autonomy apart from senior men in the Comoros and defer (indefinitely) the morally weighted duties binding them to their communities of origin. No matter their choices, Comorian men negotiated competing temporal registers, ranging from the seasonal demands of trade or farming activity to the temporal order that French officials, driven by the frenetic demands of an insecure colonial state anxious to build itself into being, imposed on men's lives.

Not all Comorians migrated in search of wage labor. Some came primarily to spread their Islamic faith traditions, tapping into and augmenting the vibrant Sufi networks unfolding across the southwestern Indian Ocean. Mama Jaki, a woman whose family history is representative of broader migratory trends, described to me how her grandmother married a *fondi* (learned Islamic teacher) from Ndzwani who traveled in the northwestern region of Madagascar and was enmeshed in a broad network of Comorian religious leaders.[40] He was part of a small, flourishing congregation of the Shadhiliyya brotherhood that spread rapidly throughout Lamu, Zanzibar, northern Mozambique, South Africa, and the Comoros in the 1890s, building on existing commercial and personal relationships, and "transforming local conceptions and practices of Islam."[41] Indeed, as historian Anne Bang points out, the intertwined networks spanning the Comoros and Madagascar in the late nineteenth century can best be understood as "a southern extension of an established trade- and religious-pattern" anchored in the Comoros and stretching to East Africa and Hadramawt.[42]

Like other classical Sufi orders, Shadhiliyya emphasized practices rooted in chanting and meditation, fidelity to the group's *fondi*, and sentimental, fraternal bonds grounded in a shared path of piety. Collectively performed rhythmic songs and dances, known as *daira* (literally, "circle"), strengthened these affective ties (figure 4.4). The Rifa'i (Rifā'īyah) order, founded in ancient Iraq, also formed an important early Muslim community in Mahajanga. Early communities established new Sufi orders, often with founding members originating from the same home villages in Ndzwani or Ngazidja that helped sustain connections to the Comoros. Still other communities were founded by migrants yoked through collective study with prominent *fondi* known for their specialized Qur'anic knowledge and skills. As they did elsewhere in the Indian Ocean basin, Sufi orders gained traction in Mahajanga during the early twentieth century because they offered pathways to urban inclusion while connecting adherents to the Swahili and broader Islamic world. Through their ubiquity and sacrosanct fraternal ties, Sufi orders served as critical means for structuring social relationships and subverting French colonial rule.[43]

FIGURE 4.4 Postcard, "Comorian dance," Mahajanga, ca. 1920s.
Author's collection.

In our conversations, mixed Malagasy-Comorian Muslims emphasized that Mahajanga was historically the birthplace of Islam in Madagascar, nurtured by the streams of Comorians who brought Islam to the city.
One respected Muslim leader of mixed Comorian-Malagasy descent in the
Shadhiliyya community explained it this way: "Comorian workers came to
all parts of Madagascar, all the way down to Tulear in the south and Diego [Suarez] in the north...they were considered the nineteenth tribe of
Madagascar by Tsiranana [the first president after independence] and they
were really populous here, like today in Marseille. Mahajanga, though, was
the cradle (*berceau*) of Islam here in Madagascar."[44] In another discussion,
a retired electrician in his late 60s of mixed Comorian-Malagasy descent
emphasized the longevity of Comorians in the city by referencing the arrival of his father from Comoros to Mahajanga in 1907, and then noting they
[Comorians] really "carried" (*mitondra*) Islam here: "Just look at the city's
name 'Moudzangaie'... it's an Arabic word!"[45] Devout Comorian migrants
demonstrated their piety through public gatherings for Islamic festivities,
Islamic instruction for their children, and cultivation of fraternal networks.
They infused the Malagasy language with a religious lexicon influenced by
Comorian and Swahili dialects, such as *motromy* (prophet; from Como-
rian *mtrume*; Swahili, *mtume*); *mikosoaly* (to pray; from Comorian *huswali*;
Swahili *kusali*); and *mikofotoro* (to break the fast; from Comorian *hufuturu*;

Swahili *kufuturu, fungua*). Most importantly, however, they built mosques (Malagasy, *maskiriny*, from Comorian *msihiri*; Swahili *msikiti*).[46] Over and again in their oral accounts, long-term residents described the primacy of mosque construction for early Comorian communities—prioritized even before the building of homes. The burgeoning Sufi orders' extraordinary collective projects to construct mosques testified to the significance of Islam in the city, but also to the Comorian migrants' intentions for emplacement and community-building. It was precisely these robust place-making endeavors that overwhelmed French administrators and evinced their incapacity to curtail the forceful migratory streams they had once encouraged.

Building the "Cradle of Islam" in Madagascar

Mosques were enduring landmarks on Mahajanga's horizon for more than a century before newer Comorian migrants arrived in the early twentieth century and were observed by European travelers passing through the town as early as 1792. Many of these original mosques resolutely continue to mark the city's landscape today (see map 4.1), as both artifacts of historical migration and vibrant social nodes. Maskiriny Zanatany (also known locally as Maskiriny of Makoas), founded in the Al-Shafi'I tradition in 1897, stands in its original site in Ambovoalanana.[47] Indian communities built several mosques in Majunga Be, as discussed in chapter 3, including the gleaming, cream-colored Khoja Shia Ithna Asheri Mosque, founded in 1897; the Saoudi Bohra Mosque, built in 1897; and a smaller Sunni mosque.[48] But unlike Indian Muslim mosques, which largely predated French colonial rule, most of the mosques constructed by Comorian migrants were built in negotiation with French colonial policies. Indian and Comorian congregations remained segregated, and congregants rarely if ever visited one another's mosques. Thus while Karana mosques were important in Majunga Be (Old Majunga), Comorian communities in Mahabibo were at the forefront of twentieth-century Islamic place-making.[49]

Like their coreligionists in town and across the Muslim diaspora, Comorian congregants referred to the Prophet's foundational act of mosque-building as the political and religious bedrock of building vibrant communities. Throughout a period of intensive mosque construction along the Swahili Coast in the late nineteenth and early twentieth centuries, congregants were driven to build mosques as an expression of piety amounting to "one of the greatest acts of Islamic charity and civility."[50] From Lamu to Zanzibar,

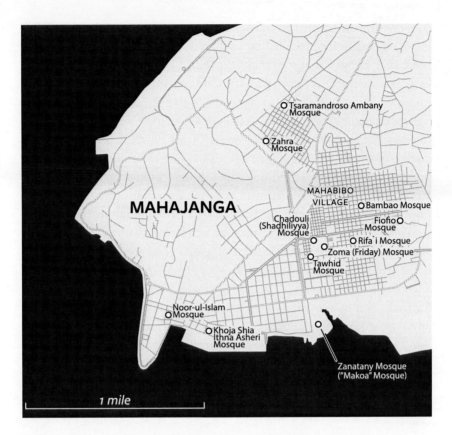

MAP 4.1 Mosques of Mahajanga. Map by Tim Stallmann.

Durban to Mahajanga, building a mosque helped newcomers adapt to their new surroundings, form relationships with coreligionists, and attest to the "permanent, rather than transitory, nature of Muslim settlement."[51] More than mere sites of prayer, mosques were centers of gravity for educational, cultural, and religious life that nourished burgeoning communities across the Islamic world. Likewise mosque builders in contemporaneous Mahajanga affirmed their enduring ties to Comorian Muslims and the broader Swahili world.[52]

Little remains known about the informal conduits that early Muslim Comorian immigrants navigated in Mahajanga to acquire the land on which they built their substantial network of mosques. Oral accounts suggest that the practice of *mamaky tany* (literally, "to go over," "divide," or "break" the land, implying the allocation of land on various grounds) was critical to early land acquisition. *Mamaky tany* is a customary practice of usufruct (use-based) land tenure throughout Madagascar in which unoccupied, fallow land can be appropriated by any family and reworked in productive ways, such as by farming or building an edifice. Comorian migrants in the early twentieth century would have found resonance between *mamaky tany* and long-standing historical practices of usufruct land use in the Comoros, guided by matrilineal practices that kept most property in women's lineages and from which men enjoyed usufruct rights. In Mahajanga, precisely *who* owned the land on which various Sufi congregations ultimately built mosques was obscured not only through colonial appropriations of land that dispossessed earlier owners, but also through oral narratives that posited congregants' rights to claim fallow land for pious purposes.[53]

Through *mamaky tany*, but also through formal petitions to the French state for land concessions, Sufi congregants of various brotherhoods— namely Shadhiliyya, Qaddiraya, and Rifā'īyah—established themselves and cultivated a following. The earliest congregants erected the Maskiriny Zanatany, which was led by Mohamadi Cadi, a former police agent, and attracted at least one hundred followers in 1912, according to French surveys.[54] Migrants from Ndzwani founded the Maskiriny Shadhiliyya, known previously as the "Anjouanais Mosque" (figure 4.5). The most imposing mosque of all was Maskiriny Zoma (previously known as "Mosque of Comorians"), which served as the religious home for migrants from Ngazidja (figure 4.6). Altogether, Comorian congregations successfully pressured city officials to grant land concessions and authorize building permits that enabled eight mosques to be erected by 1912—in contrast to two Christian churches and one Hindu temple.[55]

As the Islamic presence in Mahajanga grew, French administrators became increasingly bewildered by "Comorians' great success" in propagating Islam among the Malagasy.[56] Officials remarked that Comorian men often married Sakalava women who came from local trading families, further expanding their Islamic presence through their Muslim progeny. The legislative annexation of the Comorian archipelago to Madagascar as a single colonial territory in 1908 smoothed migratory pathways and dispossessed local colonial officials of the means to curb Comorian migrants' penetration into the city. "It is regrettable that not a single regulation permits us to prohibit their entrance to the colony," the mayor commented in 1912, lamenting that though migrants claimed to be seeking work, they actually drew "most of their resources by exploiting the local population." Comorians exerted a "real influence" over Sakalava converts, he exasperatedly reported, noting that "Sakalava . . . want to imitate them and follow their

FIGURE 4.5 Maskiriny Shadhiliyya, Mahajanga, 2014. Photo by David Epstein.

FIGURE 4.6 Maskiriny Zoma, Mahajanga, 2014. Photo by David Epstein.

advice." Elided in the mayor's account were the exploitative colonial undertakings that hastened mass migration to the island, as well as the complexities of kinship relations in the Islamic communities of Mahajanga.[57] Even more, such characterizations failed to account for the long histories of intermarriage between ethnolinguistic groups, and the complex ways people invoked multiple identities and strategically interwove Islamic and Sakalava ritual practices.

Property regulation appeared as one means of architectural governance for colonial authorities who sought to manage Comorian migration. By the mid-1910s, French administrators conjectured that they could stem the tide of Comorian migrants by restricting the allocation of permits for new mosque construction and tightening ordinances that allowed the expansion of existing mosques. Mosques were not the only religious edifices that French officials sought to control through property regulation; churches were also required to secure permits for land tenancy and building construction. But in the case of mosques, colonial authorities made explicit linkages between stricter controls on mosque construction and their objective of suppressing undesirable Comorian migration. In contrast to Muslim Indians who, according to French authorities, posed little threat because they ostensibly did not "proselytize," Muslim Comorians were particularly worrisome because of their inclusive practices, which many Malagasy converts found attractive, and their frequent intermarriage with Malagasy women (as we will see in chapter 5).[58]

Authorities used the power of paper (permits) to counter the power of limestone (mosques) as a convenient means of maintaining the appearance of *laïcité*, the French republican value of secularism. Because urban terrain came under the jurisdiction of the city administration, land use and building construction were legitimate arenas for state intervention. But even Mayor Carron admitted that such regulatory undertakings could be stymied and that existing mosques could not be appropriated. These Muslim communities had "already existed for a long time" in the city without any state regulation, he confessed in a 1912 report, which would render any new regulatory initiative very difficult to implement.[59] Carron was right. Efforts to shape demographic composition betrayed the limited reach of colonial rule. Migration from the Comorian archipelago to Mahajanga had much deeper roots, and it gained momentum through ongoing demands for laborers caused by French capitalist ambitions. Mosque construction continued to serve as a critical strategy through which migrants obstinately emplaced themselves and forged ties of sociality and solidarity in the city and beyond.

By the 1920s, Mahabibo was home to many Comorian-Malagasy families and mosques (see maps 3.5 and 4.1). It had more than tripled in size since 1900 and was so crowded that "every last parcel was occupied."[60] Immigrants sought new areas surrounding the city to settle, and city administrators scrambled to find secondary sites for another "native reserve." The vision of a planned city, in which French authorities could graft tidy gridlines on vacant spaces and deliberately channel the local population, was fading away. Instead, city officials raced to keep apace of the expanding city, teeming with newcomers and families who sometimes compelled administrators to recognize their established settlements.[61]

Perhaps recognizing the futilities of bureaucratic management of exuberant mosque construction, or perhaps realizing the importance of freedom of religion to their hold on power, the colonial city council loosened its policies on building permits and land grants to Muslim congregations. In 1920 the Maskiriny Shadhiliyya (also known as the Anjouanais Mosque) was reconstructed on a centrally located plot of land near the present-day town hall. In the mid-1920s an observer noted the presence of at least two more mosques, one for "Sunni Zanzibaris and Comoro natives" and another for "Shi'ite Indians."[62] And in 1936 a group of Muslims from the "Refaky" congregations (the Rifā'īyah brotherhood deriving from Syria) congregations successfully won the concession to a parcel of land in the center of town on which they could construct their mosque, known as Maskiriny Rifa'i. In 1944, the existing community of an unnamed "Comorian" mosque (likely Maskiriny Zoma) was authorized by the city to take possession of 144 square meters (172 square yards) of adjacent land to enlarge the structure.[63] Though there must have been unsuccessful attempts that escaped the archival record, these cases indicate how congregants drew on the compelling presence of their already-built mosques to animate (ultimately successful) claims on the state for official recognition of their communities.

The proliferation of mosques—many of them in limestone—between 1897 and 1912 indicated the remarkable growth of Comorian migrant communities and showcased their robust place-making initiatives. But their multiplication also signaled the increasing factions and divisions within the "Comorian population" so homogenously represented in official documentation. Migrants held different economic means and ambitions, ethno-linguistic and religious practices, statuses, and places of origin; and competing understandings of norms around leadership and unified Islamic practices. Migrants from Mayotte and Moheli comprised a tiny minority of the population. They purportedly remained in Madagascar for a few months, just long enough to garner funds to celebrate the extravagant "grand-marriage" (*āda*) in Comoros. Those from Ngazidja likely comprised the majority of Comorian migrants. They had less access to arable land at home and therefore settled on Madagascar for longer terms.[64]

Yet even when congregants shared many attributes, tensions grew, at times erupting into confrontations that divided the fraternal bonds tying adherents together. One particularly instructive example, recounted by the *fondi* son of locally famous mystic Tsepy (figure 4.7), unfolded in the Rifa'i congregation, where contestations over succession tested the bounds of fictive kinship. During the 1920s and 1930s, the Maskiriny Rifa'i in Abattoir was led by two sons of a well-respected *fondi* in Mutsamudu, Ndzwani, who grew the congregation through well-honed strategies of absorbing newcomer migrants from Ndzwani. Among the new arrivals was Tsepy, a trenchant, committed Qu'ranic student from an impoverished background who had been encouraged by the *fondi* in Mutsamudu to join his sons and bolster the community at Maskiriny Rifa'i. Shortly thereafter, Tsepy ran into conflicts with the two sons that some attributed to jealousies: Tsepy was apparently a charismatic and dynamic teacher who forged strong sentimental ties to his students and quickly became beloved among young congregants, much to the chagrin of the two sons. Others suggested racial hierarchies were at play: Tsepy was *mainty be* (very black), whereas the sons were from an elite, lighter-skinned family. When tensions escalated, the *fondi* told him, "You're not my blood-child, but my child of shared ancestry (*tsy zanaka'lio, fa zanaka'foko anao*). . . . You should leave and join the Shadhiliyya community instead."[65]

Seeking to avoid conflict (*tsy mila miady amin'olo izy*), but emboldened to make his own path, Tsepy broke off from Maskiriny Rifa'i and opened his own madrasa for the study of the Qur'an sometime in the late 1930s. Tsepy found unoccupied land (*malalaka*, suggesting it was spacious and ample) for purchase in the nearby quarter of Ambalavola, where he built a madrasa that he gradually transformed from a wood structure to sheet metal (*trano toly*), and then to brick (*trano biricky*). Gaining the favor of not only parents but also local French officials, who rightly perceived him as an instrumental and persuasive leader, Tsepy and his coreligionists sought to establish a new Shadhiliyya mosque in Fiofio. With the subsidies of supportive parents and beneficiaries, fellow congregants (*mpivavaka*) undertook the manual labor of building the mosque, hauling cinder blocks (*parpaing*) one by one from Tsepy's house and eventually elevating the mosque that stands today. The disputes between Tsepy and his teacher's sons reflect how

FIGURE 4.7 Tsepy, seated in the middle, ca. 1940s. Courtesy of the family of Ali Mohammed.

the social hierarchies that historically had shaped religious congregations in the Comoros—organized around age sets and status—were contested among emergent migrant communities in Mahajanga. Although the founding of Maskiriny Fiofio may have signified a triumphant disruption of long-standing inequalities, we can imagine the many ways in which social hierarchies continued to persist within congregational communities.

At other times, congregational fractures ensued into conflicts that spilled into the archival record, especially if they involved anticolonial activities. One such incident described in colonial records as the "Abdulatif Affair" involved the ousting of the imam of the Anjouanais Mosque in 1934 by his congregants for his strong separatist, "anti-French" discourses that often "deviated from religion."[66] He was subsequently welcomed into the Maskiriny Zoma (made up largely of migrants from Ngazidja) and was accused of seeking revenge on his adversaries at the Anjouanais Mosque by instigating dissent. Tensions between the two communities, referred to in colonial reports as "Grande-Comorians" and "Anjouanais," erupted in a hostile confrontation that required police intervention. Several years later, in 1941, a series of conflicts came to the attention of officials at the "Mosque Anjouanais" following a large, communal meal between "Said Allaoui" and "Rako-toharitsifa."[67] Although less is known about Rakotoharitsifa, Said Allaoui was known as a former student of the prestigious École le Myre de Villiers in Tananarive, and he had risen to Chef de Canton in the nearby town of Boanamary. Along the way, however, he espoused strong anticolonial sentiments and became a "hot partisan to the Ralaimongo movement," referencing the famed anticolonial leader Jean Ralaimongo.[68] Rakotoharitsifa apparently reported Allaoui to French authorities for these treasonous remarks, and they immediately undertook an intensive investigation into the matter. Although the investigation took another direction and yielded revelations into other issues (as I will discuss later), the swift official response exposes how mosque-builders and congregants posed serious threats to colonial powers. Through the enclosure of sacred space, Comorians and visitors who might bring anticolonial ideas situated themselves in a safe refuge beyond the reach of colonial authority structures.[69] As along the Swahili coast and parts of West Africa, mosques in Mahajanga were "intensely politicized places for resisting" the compression of colonial power.[70] In short, colonial authorities found that the task of surveilling anticolonial activities and whisperings uttered within thick, limestone walls was frustratingly elusive, and they were obliged to rely on key interlocutors for information.

Over time generational differences also emerged and intersected with political divergences, namely between Shikomoro-speaking early migrants (known locally as "Old Comorians") and the mixed Comorian-Malagasy Muslims who spoke Malagasy and would eventually self-identify as zana-tany.[71] Following the incident involving Allaoui, a heated feud emerged between two factions at the Anjouanais Mosque at a pivotal moment of a looming, contested succession for the next community leader.[72] At the heart of the conflict, according to colonial reports, was a long-standing tension between two key groups of constituents in the congregation. On one side were "pure Anjouanais," made up of those born in Anjouan, who claimed to follow "religious orthodoxy" and who largely harbored anticolonial sentiments. On the other side, were "métis" who positioned themselves (to French authorities) as victims of exclusion by the Anjouanais, who reproached the "métis" for their lack of Qu'ranic knowledge and their lack of support for Ralaimongo's anti-French movement. Despite these apparent divisions along generational, ethnolinguistic, ideological, and religious lines, these boundaries were porous, because there were "métis" found among "pure Anjouanais" and vice versa.[73] When both sides failed to reach an accord, the "métis" appealed to French officials to intervene and resolve the pressing issue of representation in the leadership and to ensure their continued authority over religious matters.

Although the final outcome appears to be that the community resolved to stay together, it reveals the overlapping interests and competing agendas that shaped the diversification of Muslim Comorian communities during the critical juncture of late colonial rule. Disputes and fractures among mosque congregations in Mahajanga were akin to those found in diasporic communities across the southwestern Indian Ocean. The splintering of communities and construction of new mosques can be understood, as anthropologist Sophie Blanchy pointed out for early twentieth-century Comoros, as "a language in which to express political rivalries or divisions," where enterprising religious leaders might expect to unsettle rigid status hierarchies and claim previously unattainable leadership roles.[74] Yet such conflicts also demonstrated diverging ideas about what constituted Sufist corporeal practices, ideal leadership, pedagogical approaches, and broader relationships to the French colonial state at a pivotal juncture in global, Islamic reformist change. As shown elsewhere in the Islamic world, rifts among congregations and leaders during this time were weighty intellectual debates in which scholars grappled with predicaments of modernity and developed new forms of religiosity and social organization.[75]

Affective Architecture and Everyday Experts

Long-term residents with whom I spoke glossed over the factions and fraught discord that undermined Islamic solidarity in Madagascar, and instead narrated mosque-building projects with affection. They emphasized the distinctive Shadhiliyya spirit of continual gratitude (*shukr*), fraternal solidarity, cooperative economizing practices (*shikoa*), and building expertise that made mosques possible. On a breezy July afternoon in 2013, Maître Youssef, a retired mathematics teacher in his seventies, described how Comorian efforts to build enduring structures in the mid-twentieth century were tied to their diligent work ethic (*mazoto miasa izy ireo*) and industrious opportunism. He and others explained that at the heart of Comorian migrants' building enterprises, whether mosques or homes, were cooperative economic practices that enabled household accumulation of means while ensuring equitable distribution of wealth among members. Comorian migrants brought with them habituated sensibilities of economization, manifest in a cooperative sharing arrangement called *shikoa*, similar to rotating savings and credit associations described elsewhere on the continent and beyond.[76] Historically, in rural Comoros shikoa served as a ceremonial exchange system in which groups—either age-sets (cohorts of people from roughly the same generation, known as *shikao*) or entire villages—reciprocated gifts of food, livestock, and money in predesignated amounts.[77]

Comorian migrants formed collective mosque-building projects by expanding shikoa to include congregants from across generational and gender lines and from different villages in order to generate funds, material, and labor. Shikoa relied on a shared moral lexicon in which asceticism, frugality, and collectivism were emphasized. Adherents constructed ideas about their distinctive virtue as Muslim Comorians and mixed Malagasy-Comorian progeny, building on Sufi conceptions of ascetism and moral propriety, in contrast to the perceived corrupt social mores of the "Malagasy." Whereas "the Malagasy" wasted their wages on "alcohol, food, pleasure and women," migrants from the Comoros knew how to "work hard, save money," and abstain from bodily pleasures to pursue material improvement and moral virtue. "They didn't always have to eat abundantly, or well," one man explained about Comorians. "They could go hungry and work and work."[78] Built on mutual trust, familiarity, and affinity, these saving circles proved remarkably effective, enabling the raising of durable mosques across the city, even if there were also fractures and misunderstandings. For self-identified Comorians and their Malagasy-Comorian progeny, such invocations served not only to attest to the attachments forged within, but also to constitute difference between themselves and "Malagasy" and to tentatively claim urban belonging in a dynamic city marked by an ever-mounting stream of migrants. Shikoa was nestled within a broader repertoire of reciprocal practices that enabled dynamic relationality.[79]

Mosques were rendered affective structures through the centripetal movement of people and things toward construction of sacred architecture. Like elsewhere on the African continent, mosques encoded the long-standing presence of Islamic communities through the development of building (and rebuilding) projects that assembled congregants in collective forms.[80] Take Maskiriny Shadhiliyya, for example. The congregation was initially founded by men from the region around Mutsamudu, Ndzwani, in about 1897, and congregants collectively generated labor and materials through shikoa to construct their mosque over several decades. By 1920, construction began. Maître Youssef emphasized that congregants gathered funds from their work as cooks, gardeners, and guardians for Europeans, driven by pious yearning: "They didn't have much means, but they longed for this mosque . . . so they worked hard!"[81] The effort to construct Maskiriny Shadhiliyya was so energetic that it attracted fellow migrants from Mutsamudu and as far as Marovoay (90 kilometers [60 miles] from Mahajanga) to join the collective building. Daughters, sisters, and wives provided key labor—hauling rocks, providing sustenance, and cooking collectively in large cauldrons. Building was not simply a logistical or physical process to fabricate a mosque, but an emotive experience in which mosque builders experienced themselves as bound through shared affective ties, modes of emotional expression, and values, amounting to what historian Barbara Rosenwein termed "emotional communities."[82]

Building gatherings were emotive encounters because they were moments of material commingling. Youssef described how mosque builders brought cement, hoisting overstretched sacks onto their backs and "sweating, working so hard, because they so *desired* this mosque."[83] Hauling limestone (*tsoka, chaux*) likely mined from nearby quarries, teams of men mixed it with sand and water to adhere the chalky, crumbly stone. Walls were built thick, up to 50 centimeters (20 inches), to withstand the intense heat and powerful tropical rains. Animating their energetic building efforts, their descendants emphasized, was desire and shared love (*fitiavana*) for the divine, for one's Sufi order, and for their adopted city.[84] On September 4, 1921, Maskiriny Shadhiliyya opened. By melding their lifeforce with limestone, the builders undertook a powerful alchemy of urban transformation, materialized in an architectural bestowal for living congregants and their anticipated progeny. Through construction, congregants and their descendants were bound to one another, to faraway Sufi communities, and to the city— bonds realized in the stickiness of sweat, mortar, and limestone. If, as Sara Ahmed reminds us, emotions entail "what sticks . . . what sustains and preserves the connection between ideas, values and objects," then congregants' emotional ties were imbued into the very walls and minarets they molded.[85]

Critical here was the role of everyday experts—the "simple people" (*olo tsotra*)—who poured their labor and energy into designing and constructing the mosque. Expertise was described as akin to habit, emergent from repetition and practice, which enabled the expert to gain a familiarity (*mahazatra*) with how to make or do, rather than something passively received through instruction. To be an expert was to possess profound tacit knowledge— that is, knowledge gained by doing, rather than through written or verbal explication. "You know," Maître Youssef emphasized, "those that founded and constructed the [Shadhiliyya] mosque, these were everyday people, not learned people or elites. These were people accustomed (*zatra*) to building things!" Similarly El Had, son of the renowned mystic imam Tsepy, described how his father mobilized the support of the congregants (*mpivavaka*) and "not a private company" (*tsisy enterprise*) to build the Fiofio mosque. Again and again, people narrated the absence of outside experts, companies, or state officials, instead emphasizing how ordinary congregants were the primary builders and designers of mosques.[86]

Comorian architects, designers, and builders brought technical know-how honed over generations, but they were also informed by historical aesthetic practices found in the constellation of exemplary mosques across the Comoros and East Africa. The ability to replicate sacred mosque features found elsewhere signified a triumph of expertise, and designers and builders proudly borrowed from the construction techniques used in beloved mosque architectures in the archipelago and beyond. As in the Comoros, hardened materials—stone, coral rag, and corrugated metal—were preferred as construction materials by builders, even for simpler, smaller mosques (figure 4.8). For centuries, Comorians in Ndzwani and Ngazidja rebuilt wooden mosques into enduring "stone" structures using timber, basalt cobbles, reef coral, and lime plaster. As found across the Islamic world, clay was historically a default building material—an expressive extension of the "Qu'ranic emphasis on the clayness of Adam" and the transformation of the creation of humans to humans' creation of buildings.[87] Like their counterparts throughout the Swahili world, Comorians designed mosques with rectangular prayer halls (rather than the courtyard styles found in North Africa and the Middle East) and oriented mosques and burial sites toward Mecca in accordance with Islamic norms of directionality.[88]

As renowned architectural historian Nasser Rabbat points out, mosque builders across the Islamic world historically relied on "no single model . . . as sole inspiration," but instead selectively borrowed architectural attributes from existing precedents and refashioned them according to their spiritual, political, and ecological exigencies.[89] For Comorian migrants in Mahajanga, nostalgic recollections of mosques in the Comoros, as vital central pillars sustaining communities, informed their building aspirations. "No matter where they migrate," one prominent Shadhiliyya leader, "Khalil," asserted one afternoon, "Comorians don't forget their religious roots."[90] This dutiful sense of remembrance, or coercive force to not forget, was built into the very architectural forms and norms of the mosques themselves, constructed through layers of hardened cement and limestone that would resist the pull of wind and whim as the city unfurled over time.

FIGURE 4.8 Mosque, Ngazidja (Comoros), 1890–96.
Courtesy of FR ANOM 8FI15/46.

Maskiriny Rifa'i, for instance, is nestled on a small hill in Abattoir, a neighborhood long dominated by Comorian and mixed Comorian-Malagasy families. Its striking green-and-white minaret towers rise above the corrugated steel–roofed homes of the city (see figure 4.9). In 1936, a group of Comorian migrants hailing from Ndzwani (also from Mutsamudu, but from the "Refaky"—Rifa'i brotherhood) appealed to the city for the parcel of land on which this mosque is now located. They won. In designing their mosque, congregants took inspiration from their home mosque in Mutsamudu, which was built of "white coral rock"; indeed the end product is nearly identical (see figure 4.10).[91] More remarkable than the white façade, however, is the rounded style of the single minaret, known as a pillar minaret. Circular, single minarets are distinctive across East Africa, whereas double, often square, minarets are typically found in West African mosque structures.[92] But tapered, conical pillar minarets like that found on Maskiriny Rifa'i are distinctive features of select Swahili coastal mosques, famously found at the Mnara and Mandhry mosques in Mombasa, at the Lamu Shela mosque, and at the Zanzibar Malindi mosque. Pillar minarets' form and meaning, as art historian Prita Meier points out, have been contested over time on the Swahili coast, yet their presence in the Comoros

FIGURE 4.9
Maskiriny Rifaʻi,
Mahajanga,
2014. Photo by
David Epstein.

and Mahajanga demonstrates the capaciousness of Sufi ties between diasporic Muslims in the Swahili world.[93]

Similarly, Maskiriny Zoma was fashioned in the style of the fifteenth-
century Ancienne Mosquée de Vendredi, found in Moroni, Ngazidja, which
had long been "the heart of the city."[94] The resemblance between the prototype in Moroni and the architectural descendant found in Mahajanga is
striking, replete with the same white, limestone façade, embellished edg-
ing, and squarish, triple-storied minaret with rows of two openings (figures 4.11 and 4.12). Originally constructed of wood and corrugated steel in
1897, Maskiriny Zoma was rebuilt over time using limestone cement, like
its counterpart in Moroni. According to French reports, Maskiriny Zoma
was sustained by the largest congregation in the city, regularly frequented
by some 400 congregants in the 1910s.[95] Today, Maskiriny Zoma is a notable landmark in Mahajanga, towering above shops and homes, and serving as a central gathering point where people sit on the *baraza*, a typical

FIGURE 4.10 Friday Mosque, Mutsamudu, Nzwani (Comoros), 1955.
Courtesy of FR ANOM/30Fi97/35.

Swahili-style, built-in bench at the front of the mosque (or home). Though few records exist on the mosque's architectural borrowings, the clock on the minaret is notable and may have been inspired by church aesthetics, as was likely the case among West African mosque designers in the nineteenth century.[96] By incorporating the clock into Mahajanga's Maskiriny Zoma, mosque designers drew selective inspiration from their beloved homeland mosques, but also took creative latitude to refashion the prototype according to their aesthetic preferences.

By reenacting architectural features from Comorian mosques in the mosques of Mahajanga, congregants were able to (re)create fraternal ties

among themselves and to affirm solidarity with the Comoros. Such acts of architectural borrowing resonate with what Liisa Malkki describes as people evoking "homes and homelands in the absence of territorial, national bases—not in situ, but through memories of, and claims on, places that they can or will no longer corporeally inhabit."[97] Comorians conjured religious and social homes in the material, architectural forms of mosques, and imagined themselves connected not only to their land of birth, but also to broader transnational, transoceanic Sufi communities. Yet in their oral accounts, descendants of mosque builders were careful to point out that similarities in mosque architecture were separate from nationalistic identification. One man insisted, "For Comorians, there was never really a spirit of nationalism, of Comorian nationalism, but rather the spirit of religious fraternity which has always revolved around [a shared] Muslim faith."[98] If anything, their fraternal ties superseded nationalistic identifications and suggested a kind of "national indifference."[99]

FIGURE 4.12 Moroni, Ngazidja (Comoros), 1948 (Friday Mosque at center).
Courtesy of FR ANOM 30Fi97/32.

Comorian mosques in Mahajanga were materialized sites of exchange
in which congregants shifted between the past and present, memorializing
moments of earlier Sufi history and infusing borrowed architectural features
with fresh aspirations for the future. Islamic architectural historian Kishwar
Rizvi describes mosques' dialectical nature as resulting from their being
built with "several temporalities in mind . . . looking backward and forward
simultaneously."[100] As everyday experts crafted their visions for mosques
in the city, they conserved fragments of Sufi legacies and captured fleeting
moments of epistemological transmission and material intermingling in
the walls and minarets they molded. The project of remembering sacred
pasts through architecture can be situated within a broader Islamic historical sensibility in which the "sanction of past authority was of overwhelming
importance."[101] Yet what from the past is valorized, memorialized, and invoked shifts and changes over time, and likewise mosques could be flexibly
rebuilt, deconstructed, and restored depending on communities' needs and
interests. Resonant designs across mosques in the Indian Ocean allowed
congregants to reference—and, at times, contest—Sufi traditions of trusted
knowledge, but also to feel "at home in the world" through collective solidarity with communities across the Mozambique Channel and beyond.[102]

Conclusion

By the 1910s, French officials expressed increasing anxieties about their simultaneous reliance on Comorian migrants and the mounting threat migrants posed by virtue of their religious and political influence in the region. Administrators noted that, with few exceptions, Comorians were the mainstay providers of manual labor for industries and for commercial shipping and trading companies in Mahajanga. They drove the petty commerce, fishing economy, and dockwork in the city. And they routinely paid taxes. As a diverse collectivity, Comorians had quickly become indispensable to the economic vibrancy of the city. Yet officials fretted about the far-reaching sway Comorians enjoyed through their intensifying relationships with multiple groups in the city, including formerly enslaved Makoa families and those of Sakalava descent. Especially concerning was frequent intermarriage among Comorian men and Sakalava women—particularly into royal Sakalava families. As key interlocuters in these influential families, Comorians threatened to destabilize the tenuous authority French held in the northwest region during the early years of colonial rule.[103]

The upsurge in mosques throughout the city in the early twentieth century was a continual reminder to colonial officials of the enduring Islamic presence of Comorian communities and the inadequacies of colonial bureaucracy. While property regulations initially appeared to be an ideal instrument through which officials could constrain mosque construction—and, consequently, the city's burgeoning Comorian migrant population—officials were soon frustrated with the limitations of such regulation. Continual efforts to rebuild more durable structures—moving from wood to limestone—expressed migrants' intentions to steadfastly settle in Mahajanga, as well as their aspirations for an urban life animated by Islamic practice and communality. Mosques are brought to life through the multiple temporalities at play: congregants amalgamated remnants of their pasts, invoking architectural traditions running through their Comorian homelands; performed morally informed visions for the city steeped in affective, reciprocal relations; and enunciated their anticipatory longing for the longevity of their kin and Sufi networks.

City dwellers' retrospective accounts of mosque-building suggest that emotions—love, desire, attachment—spilled beyond discourse and embodied bounds, infusing the material, sacred spaces of the city in ways that continued to exert affective charges on religious progeny. With a shared conviction that love (*fitiavana*) for the divine and for one's Sufi order was best expressed through the shrewd, sweat-filled labor of mosque construction, builders sedimented their affinal bonds in the thick, compacted walls. Critical in this history was Comorians' choice of building material: limestone. Abundant in coastal regions of northwest Madagascar, limestone gains its hardened, sedimentary texture through the compression of shell and bone fragments over the course of millennia. Though durable, limestone is also highly porous and vulnerable to decay, serving as a reminder that even the most obdurate communities can erode and fracture over time.

Mosque construction in twentieth-century Mahajanga, I suggest, was an inherently ardent, and even excessive, phenomenon that eclipsed the bounds of the state and subverted colonial logics. While capitalist, colonial paradigms framed property as an economic device and a vessel for investment, such instrumentalist approaches to regulating religious edifices (and later homes) were confounded by the generative nature of communal construction projects. In contrast to the economizing logics of colonial regime, Comorian congregations were informed by particular ethical positions—ones inspired by Sufi norms concerning the value of labor, the importance of reciprocity, and the virtue of disciplining the body. Through the living structures of mosques, migrants anchored their conceptions of collective property in affective ties to fellow congregants, both living and dead, nearby and beyond the sea.

PART III

Residual Lives and Afterlives

Garnered Presences

Constructing Belonging in the Zanatany *City*

In August 1913, the head colonial administrator in Analalava, some 430 kilometers (125 miles) north of Mahajanga, wrung his hands in distress about the abiding influence of "Silamos," whom he characterized as "one of the worst elements of our coastal population." Among them, Comorians most arrogantly "treat the northwest coast as their conquered country," arriving on the coast, "which they never leave for the interior."[1] Established and newly arrived migrants from the Comorian archipelago congregated in Mahajanga, especially in the city's Mahabibo quarter, he noted, where they disdained wage work and seemed to live "parasitically" with local families. Unlike the ostensibly autochthonous Sakalava pastoralists who practiced "vagabondage" attributed to cattle-raising, officials were particularly worried about the "special kind of vagabondage" of Comorians who spent their hours roaming the city, loitering in streets, and socializing in groups.[2] It was this form of "vagabondage"—marked by unfettered mobility, inclusive kin-making, and spontaneous sociality—that French administrators found most threatening to their paper-thin hold on power.

Frequent French references to Comorians as "parasites" and "vagabonds" in contrast to the other migrant groups exposed the logics of profit undergirding the colonial, racial capitalist state in the first half of the twentieth century. "Vagabondage" can be understood as a historically constructed category, a conceptual slot necessary for framing the desired colonial worker, and a racialized marker defining who could circulate freely in the city and who posed threats to European presence and to capitalist

FIGURE 5.1 Postcard, "Mahabibo Village, Game of Cards," ca. 1930s. Note men in distinctive Comorian garb. Author's collection.

efficiency. Inverting the colonially constructed category of "vagabond-age" exposes key relational strategies that Comorian migrants prioritized over wage labor, including political bantering (*mikalezy*), visiting kin and friends (*mamangy trengo*), performing Islamic rituals, and studying texts. Comorians often conspicuously appropriated urban spaces on the edges of mosques (*barazas*), street-facing steps, and parks in Mahabibo, where these performances of masculinity, status, and piety could be fully displayed (see figure 5.1). One official wryly remarked, "It is never surprising to see them always well dressed, passing their days playing cards or 'katra' and their evenings dancing or reciting the coran."[3]

Though French colonial officials saw such practices as disruptions of the spatialized order and as frivolous distractions from capitalist endeav-ors, Comorians' sociality can be understood as a critical form of work, akin to what anthropologist Julia Elyachar calls "phatic labor," to refer to those "future-oriented activities that foster channels for circulating resources which ensure social reproduction."[4] Sociality was a strategic resource by which enterprising Comorian migrants survived and thrived as settlers in Mahajanga, enabling them to forge connections with more established Comorian and Malagasy families in the city. To the extent that their inter-

actions combined ongoing, circular exchanges of money and goods, pragmatic know-how, and emotive experiences, they brought into being a set
of overlapping "affective circuits" through fleeting, repetitive encounters
between settlers new and old.[5] Comorians produced these emotionally
laden networks between northwest Madagascar and Comorian hometowns
by continuously sending and receiving ideas, monetary support, and kin,
while they concurrently charted new pathways to social-kin relations and
wealth acquisition in the city through marriage with Malagasy women.

Marriage to Malagasy women from local families, often followers of the
Sakalava polity, enabled Comorian settlers to integrate into existing kin networks, accrue capital, and establish households—thus transforming themselves and their progeny from strangers to kin, from visitors (vahiny) to
children of the soil (zanatany). For many Malagasy families, the marriage
of their daughters to Comorian men offered possibilities for expanding kinship constellations and augmenting household support through labor and
income. While inheritance norms prevented most Comorian husbands from
acquiring land, marrying into a wealthy or well-connected Malagasy family could ensure conditional access to land and credit, secure social capital,
and provide some authority in the household. Following marriage, a mixed
Comorian-Malagasy couple could conceivably acquire land and construct a
home, a critical material device for rooting themselves in the city. Situated
within lively circuits marked by continual exchanges of things, ideas, and
emotions, Comorian-Malagasy houses became pivotal sites where these
material and affective flows snagged, settled, accrued, and were reworked
over time. Houses were integral means through which Comorian-Malagasy
families anticipated their futures, weathered moments of economic austerity and political uncertainty, and expanded their kin networks spanning the
Mozambique Channel in the nineteenth and twentieth centuries.

If a house is a "topography of our intimate being," as Gaston Bachelard
noted, what kinds of ideas, imaginaries, and political significances did
city dwellers in Mahajanga build into their homes?[6] How did Comorian-
Malagasy build their presence into the city, and what kinds of presence did
they infuse into the intimate spaces they inhabited? Building on chapter 4,
this chapter charts how Comorian-Malagasy families drew on home (re)
construction in the mid-twentieth century to materially manifest specific
theories of how social collectivities flourish. Like migrants in many other
African cities, Comorian-Malagasy families developed creative, improvisational practices to sculpt the city as their own, reworking the meanings
of building materials over time to render tangible their conceptions of

kinship, inheritance, and proper urban norms.[7] Home construction was a profoundly anticipatory undertaking, an act of hope in which families enfolded their visions for an urban life grounded in ethical sensibilities, transgenerational investment, and ardent conviviality.

Yet houses were also a medium through which Comorian-Malagasy families sought to differentiate themselves from other groups in the city and claim autochthony through laminated, accruing building practices. In oral accounts and ethnographic exchanges, Comorian settlers and their mixed Comorian-Malagasy families emphasized that domestic homes were the material and metaphorical expression of being *zanatany*, an idiom intimating indigeneity, connection to earth, and cognizance of those human and other-than-human beings that dwell in place. They described how transgenerational investments of labor (*asa*) and "stone" (*vato*)—brought from Mahajanga's hinterlands—and incremental transformation of their ancestors' thatch homes (into wood, metal, and then cement structures) brought about their collective transformation into zanatany and legitimated their rightful place in the city over time.

The story of *zanatany* reframes scholarly understandings of belonging as both a set of ongoing intellectual debates *and* a spatial-material-affective process, lived through embodied modes of place-making and informed by contested moral norms. Historians of Africa have documented the ways categories of difference are produced in discursive, ideological debates informed by multiple, overlapping genealogies over time.[8] Material worlds offer rich, relatively unexplored terrain for tracking how people infuse and transform distinctions into material forms, giving them substance or, conversely, neglecting and destroying their physical vestiges and ideological import over time. By taking seriously house-building as a material, transgenerational undertaking, and by tracking the historically contingent emergence of the concept of *zanatany* in the archival record and popular memory, I show the intricacies of the social-historical process through which claims of belonging and nativism were made (and disputed) and how they manifest in physical presences. Attending to the materiality of home construction—the ways people infused and mixed labor, vital bodily fluids, ecological materials—provides an empirical path out of binary categories of inclusion/exclusion and insider/outsider by showing how people cleave to shifting collective identities while also differentiating themselves within and beyond those collectivities. In so doing, I push for broadening the aperture beyond human actors in producing differential categories, by emphasizing the earthly materials and bodily substances people enlist, and the labors those matters entail, in collective efforts to articulate, bundle, and render cogent distinctions and new histories of belonging.[9]

The forging of belonging could be understood as one of *deposition* (to borrow a geological term) in which people gradually transform their ephemeral earnings, energies, and even effluences into the lasting, material form of the house. Over generations, migrants in the city labored, layering accretions of wood, stone, and tin, and slowly sedimented their homes as a material embodiment of their ties to Mahajanga.[10] Yet these senses of belonging accrued with an awareness among Comorian settlers and their Comorian-Malagasy progeny that the city's terrain was Sakalava land, beholden to the ancestral norms, ritual practices, and ancestral presences associated with Sakalava polities. As zanatany homes took durable forms, they shaped the everyday lives of their inhabitants, serving as repositories of past memories and containers of hopeful anticipations of the future. But like all processes of sedimentation, homes-as-belonging could also be ruptured—as the 1976–77 expulsion known as the *rotaka* tragically exposed.

Roots of the "Comorian City": Migration, Marriage, and Inheritance

Between 1920 and 1950, the Comorian population swelled across the island. Mahajanga, more than any other city, quickly became the epicenter of Comorian life within Madagascar. In 1900, French censuses tracked some 1,000 "Comorians" in all of Madagascar.[11] By 1912, Mahajanga was home to 2,030 "Comorians," "Zanzibaristes," "Somalis," and "Makoas"; by 1936 French census records disaggregated these groups and counted 9,220 "Comorians." In the late 1950s, around 34,000 Comorians lived in the city (about 50 percent of the city's overall population).[12] Contemporary residents in town described how during this time Mahajanga became a "Comorian city" distinguished by its many mosques, strong Islamic presence, and the boisterous comportment of young Comorian men in the streets. Indeed, Mahabibo—the historical labor reservoir—contained the largest concentration of Comorians anywhere, including cities in the Comorian archipelago, transforming Mahajanga into the "first Comorian city in the world" (see map FM.4 and figure FM.2).[13]

Who exactly were these Comorian migrants? Notwithstanding some discrepancies between oral recollections and colonial-era population statistics, the total sum of evidence suggests most migrants were men.[14] French census records for Mahajanga suggest slightly more women than men within the "Comorian" population, but this figure likely reflects descent-based forms of colonial recognition in the early- to mid-twentieth century in which racial identity and nationality generally followed from descent-based paternal lines, based on *jus sanguinis*.[15] Children born of "Comorian" and "Anjouan" fathers, regardless of their mothers' categorization, would have probably been classified by French census takers as Comorian, following their fathers' line.[16] Even if French census records failed to capture the male-dominant migratory stream from Comoros, by the 1950s and '60s, official statistics concurred with popular perception; Comorian men were definitively immigrating to Madagascar far in excess of Comorian women.[17]

By the 1920s, Comorian settlers inhabited an urban and regional landscape that was rapidly becoming populated with newly arrived migrants from across Madagascar (see map 3.1). Diverse streams of migrants from southeast Madagascar, often grouped together under the umbrella ethnonym "Betsirebaka," came between 1900 and approximately 1940 to work on French-owned agricultural plantations and industrial enterprises throughout the northwest region.[18] Amounting to some 10,000 in total, most of these migrants were young men seeking to earn money and then return home. Some sought to purchase cattle for bridewealth, others simply to raise their prestige in their home communities, and still others to contribute to elaborate funerary events for their elders.[19] During the 1930s, famine in the deep south prompted migration of men from the Antandroy areas to the city, where they kept dairy cows on the outskirts of town, selling milk each day in town to accumulate funds for bridewealth.[20] Joining longer-standing settler groups of Merina, Betsileo, and Tsimihety descent, these new arrivals filled important labor voids in road-building and public works projects. In some cases they worked side by side with Comorians, whereas others took jobs that Comorians had left to pursue more lucrative opportunities.[21]

Having come at an earlier time of labor scarcity and established their expertise, Comorians enjoyed relatively high earnings compared to other migrants. They continued to be disproportionately represented in the city's police force, to the point that city council members decided that vacancies left by Comorians should be filled with "natives of other races" to correct the ethno-racial imbalance.[22] Migrants from elsewhere in Madagascar appear to have been more vulnerable to exploitative labor schemes, and this exploitation would sow the seeds for long-standing resentment toward Comorians.[23] Whereas new migrants from within Madagascar were forcibly conscripted into the *corvée* labor scheme to build public works projects and roads, during the 1920s and '30s, "Comorians and Silamo," as well as "Europeans" and "Indians," were exempt.[24] Comorians thus occupied a favored, middle position relative to migrants from Madagascar in the broader colonial racial hierarchy.[25]

Comorian men's relative privilege and access to wages positioned them as attractive marriage partners for Malagasy women in town. Descendants of mixed Comorian-Malagasy families explained that Comorian men understood and respected Malagasy norms of inheritance practices, generational relations, and complex, transregional family histories. Malagasy families appreciated the addition of an enterprising junior man to the family network and valued the disciplined and communally minded approach to work espoused by Comorian men, which many felt had been key to their families' prosperity. When I asked children of Comorian-Malagasy unions about the interests of Comorian men in seeking Malagasy brides, many mentioned the women's superior aesthetic beauty, "strong character" (*toetra*), calm demeanor, or even cleanliness in comparison to Comorian women.[26] One zanatany woman in her fifties said that Comorian women failed to tidy up (*mampierna*), and that their kitchens were always messy.[27] Still others reasoned that marrying a Malagasy women was less expensive (*mora*) than marriage to a Comorian woman; in Ngazidja, marriage was indeed often costly for men.[28] Some Comorian men said that courtship conventions in Comoros were onerous, and romantic relationships with Malagasy women were simply more accessible and easier.[29] More than their historical accuracy, these explanations reveal the range of considerations for prospective partners and how descendants recalled these unions.

Even more, mixed descendants commonly emphasized that Comorian men specifically pursued marriages with Malagasy women whom they thought had a "Comorian sensibility" (*manana Comorian sens*).[30] These "moral sensibilities" were performed in embodied practices such as collective celebrations, pragmatic economizing, and vibrant solidarity inflected by an Islamic ethos of reciprocity.[31] Comorian-Malagasy families cultivated this shared moral sensibility through negotiated and improvised embodied and material practices rooted in the everyday, even as they built on deeper histories of cultural and linguistic exchange between northwest Madagascar and Comoros. Women from Sakalava and Antalaotra families were those deemed most compatible with Comorian social norms, yet Comorian men recalled difficulty securing brides from these families.[32] One man recalled, "Even if you had money, or worked for Europeans (*vazaha*), and you asked for the hand of marriage of a Sakalava woman, they often wouldn't agree.

[Sakalava women] were snobby (*miavona*)." Nonetheless, the commonality of Islamic practices eased the way, in many cases.[33]

Many families of Sakalava descent shared Sufi practices with Comorian settlers, and families emphasized the import of shared customs (*fomba*), such as prohibitions (fady) on pork and eel.[34] In other cases, because wives and children were expected to follow the religion of husbands and fathers, marrying non-Muslims (or those who were minimally observant) was a way for Comorian settlers to expand Islamic ties. Indeed, one Christian missionary remarked in 1914 that in the northwest coast "most of those who turn to Islam are women."[35] At the same time, for many Malagasy, conversion to Islam *expanded* the field of, rather than replaced, collective ritual practices. Given the propensity of Malagasy to engage in pluralistic practices, colonizers in the late nineteenth and early twentieth centuries questioned the veracity and depth of Islamic piety among Malagasy converts; French ethnologist Gabriel Ferrand noted in 1891, for instance, "Malagasy converts . . . still keep their old beliefs and continue to worship national [royal] gods."[36] But such accounts elided the nuanced, fluid ways in which people negotiated their relationships to multiple communities of practice—Islamic, kin-based, residential, and royal-ancestral-political—to navigate everyday life through political and economic changes. This agility has persisted in contemporary Mahajanga, where inhabitants continue to selectively draw from repertoires of coexisting communitarian practices.[37]

Openness and polyphonic observance of multiple traditions, however, was not without tensions. Many descendants of mixed Comorian-Malagasy families remarked that wives' and mothers' adherence to Sakalava royal ancestral practices and spirit possession ran counter to Islamic tenets and practices, which at times gave rise to conflicts within families.[38] Although not mentioned specifically by descendants, such disputes would have intensified in the late nineteenth and early twentieth centuries as Islamic reformists spread universalist and legalistic approaches and attempted to stamp out what they perceived as local heterodoxies across the Indian Ocean.[39] Some converts negotiated the conflicting rights and obligations arising from pluralistic practices by ascribing them varying degrees of importance at different life stages. Several grown children of Malagasy-Comorian parents described their mother's Muslim piety during her lifetime but noted her strict instructions to bury her on ancestral land (*tanindrazana*) following the funerary customs associated with her *kind* of people (*karazan'olo*). Even if such designations were intended to be "acts of completion" to resolve the ambiguities of myriad loyalties and competing obligations in one's lifetime, death rites were frequent sites of familial discord over which norms should be observed.[40]

For many Comorian migrants, marriage into Malagasy families (literally, *mangala olo*, or the "taking of people") was made possible primarily because of their shared Islamic connections.[41] Although some Comorian men quickly located already established family members, most drew extensively on their neighborhood and religious connections to identify respectable marriage partners.[42] These relations were initiated and sustained through the spontaneous, lively sociality of street life—playing games, discussing and debating (*mikalizy*), and festive celebrations—precisely the activities that French colonizers dismissed as "vagabondage." Many older Comorian-Malagasy couples noted the significance of serendipity or "destiny" (*voa soratra*; literally, "already written") in bringing couples together. Some noted that after a man glimpsed a beautiful woman in the street, he would approach a learned Islamic leader (*zanatany foundi*) or a long-time resident and "ask about her respectability."[43] Young Comorian men depended on older men who were familiar with a prospective bride to approach the family.

Parallel practices between those of Comorian and Sakalava descent regarding inheritance encouraged the establishment of mixed households and lasting lineages. Unlike most Muslim societies in history, Comorians have observed matrilineal descent and privileged bequeathal of wealth to *daughters* over sons.[44] Communities throughout the Comorian archipelago have historically observed matriliny and matrilocality, in which the matrilineal house is "composed of several generations of siblings and headed by the elder married women and their brothers."[45] Even amid Islamic reforms and the rapid spread of Shadhiliyya and other Sufi orders in the early twentieth century, leaders and missionaries inhabiting the shores of northwest Madagascar continued to observe these practices, as did their counterparts in Mozambique.[46] For Sakalava, who had bilateral conceptions of kinship, either daughters or sons could inherit, but bequeathing to daughters only was not unusual and was seen as a means to avoid generational competition between fathers and sons.[47] As a Sakalava spirit medium in his seventies explained, "For Sakalava, the inheritance should go to the daughter (*zanakavavy*), just like the Comorian, because . . . if the parents pass on the house to their son, then the son will always be chasing after the father's wealth, he'll never seek his own fortune (*mitady vola, mitady harena*)."[48] A bias toward female inheritance set the Sakalava apart not only from most Muslims worldwide, but also from other groups in Madagascar, in which only sons inherited or the inheritance was evenly divided among all children.[49] In theory, this commonality has helped prevent family disputes.

Even if both families shared inheritance customs and practices, these marriages could be messy. Comorian-Malagasy children often debated with one another in interviews, and gave conflicting, wide-ranging accounts of the customs and technical rules governing legitimate marriages. Marrying within the extended family (*havana*) could ensure retention of wealth.[50] Likewise most families asserted that casual sex or promiscuity (*frandata, manao si-pasipa*) between extended kin was absolutely forbidden. Zanatany families, however, debated under what circumstances first cousins could marry. Some maintained that for Comorians—unlike for Malagasy—first cousins could marry so long as their sibling parents were different genders (cross-cousin marriage).[51] Others argued that children of sisters could marry, but not children of brothers, because of the disproportionate strength (*matanjaka, mahery*) of the father's side that would be "too much" for resulting children.[52]

Some descendants recalled that Comorian fathers and grandfathers had strategically sought wealthy Malagasy women to marry in order to enhance their access to resources and prestige.[53] Mama Taoaby, a retired schoolteacher in her early sixties, drew on the example of her own family history to illustrate this. Her father, originally from Ngazidja, arrived in the Analalava region around the 1920s.[54] There, he sought out her mother for marriage. Her mother came from a wealthy family, and many prospective suitors had been declined. At the time, husbands were expected to contribute the customary bridewealth of *vodi-ondry* (literally, "the sheep's rump"). "[The sheep's rump] wasn't very expensive," she explained, and wealthy families could be choosy about their daughters' husbands. But many families were "willing to give their daughter in marriage to Comorian men, even if they lacked funds, because they were hardworking (*mazoto*)." The family accepted the appeal of her father, not because he was wealthy, but because he was educated, gainfully employed as a nurse in the state hospital, and had a promising path to prestige and stability.

In sum, marriage was foundational for Comorian-Malagasy families seeking to build their presence in the city. Not only could Comorian husbands gain conditional access to land and other forms of support, they could leverage such support to establish their own households. Mama Taoaby patiently explained that Comorian migrants were content to not inherit land from the families they married into, that "they just wanted to lower their expenses." By living with their wives' families, they could save money on "housing and possibly food," which left more funds to invest in business, save to buy land, or remit to Comoros. When I naively asked whether Comorian men found living as the junior man with their fathers-in-law discomfiting, she said, "No, this was the custom for Comorian men. When men marry, they join their wife's family, even though their religion and other customs (*fomba*) follow (*manaraka*) from their father's side. Moving in with Malagasy families presented no major challenge to the Comorian men's custom or ego. But, Mama Taoaby added, there were times that the Malagasy family might think the Comorian man was a gigolo (*jaoloko*), because some Malagasy have the custom for daughters to move out and stay with their husband's family."[55] Although some children of Comorian-Malagasy marriages disputed the notion that Comorian men sought Malagasy women from wealthy families, they agreed that Comorian men pursued women from "respectable" or "noble" families.[56] Comorian-Malagasy inhabitants emphasized that Comorian migrants were self-made men. Dadilahy Kassim, a well-regarded son of a Comorian father and zanatany mother, claimed that "often Comorians married modestly and grew their lifestyle through hard work. Their prestige only came *after* their hard work."[57] Marriage was one of a multitude of tactics to get ahead.

Genealogies of Zanatany

Comorian-Malagasy families distinguished themselves by funneling most of their earnings into the construction of domestic homes, which were then incrementally rebuilt by future generations in increasingly obdurate forms. Built forms were not only material expressions of urban inclusion and economic mechanisms for accumulating capital; they were also the *anticipatory* means through which Comorians and their progeny transformed themselves from outsiders (vahiny) to insiders (zanatany). The concept of *zanatany* reveals critical perspectives on the bundled material and imaginative practices through which Comorian-Malagasy constituted urban belonging through affective and labor relations that nourished relations between the living, the dead, and urban places. Comorian-Malagasy invocations of *zanatany*, however, sit within a deeper historical field of grammars, to which I will now turn to explore how ideas of indigeneity emerged, circulated, and took hold in homes in Mahajanga during the twentieth century.

 Zanatany is used in contemporary contexts to mean autochthones, natives, or those born in the land in which they live—and it explicitly links blood and soil; it literally means "children of the soil." It is a derivative of *zanaka* (offspring, plants, trees, or bushes that have been transplanted; figuratively, an object that is smaller than another) and *tany* (earth, terrain, soil, land, country, kingdom).[58] First noted in the 1830s, *zanatany* seems to have been a relative lexical latecomer in a linguistic field inhabited by several other key terms of indigeneity.[59] According to nineteenth-century dictionaries and European travelers' accounts, Malagasy speakers had long used *tompontany* (*tompo-* "master"; *-tany* "land") to denote "a native, a citizen," "masters of the land," or "first occupants" across different parts of the island.[60] Anthropologists have signaled that tompontany were ostensibly the descendants of the first ones to "break open the land (*mamaky tany*) for planting," set in contrast to vahiny—visitors, newcomers, strangers, or guests.[61] Throughout much of northwest Madagascar, the Sakalava polity has been historically regarded as the tompontany whose descendants buried their dead in the land and who thus enjoyed the privilege of dialogue with the ancestors who were at the origin of the land they occupied.[62] *Tompontany* continues to be widely used in all parts of the island to refer to those who not only hold land (for simply possessing land does not confer tompontany status), but who also "act responsibly on the land," which is often closely tied to royal authority.[63] In some parts of the northwest, people use *teratany* (*tera-* is likely from *teraka*, or offspring, so "offspring/children of the soil") to similarly indicate land occupancy.[64]

By the 1880s, and likely reflecting longer-standing oral practice, *zanatany* appeared with increasing frequency, as noted in dictionaries, where it was defined as "native" or "native to the country/land" (*indigène, natif du pays*). By the close of the century, zanatany became hitched to modern nationhood and denoted "citizen" (*citoyen*), "native" (*indigène*), and "national" (*nationaux*).[65] Under colonial rule (1896–1960), French authorities appropriated the term zanatany to describe Malagasy as the children of the French motherland, infantilizing Malagasy as the children of the metropole. As early as 1896 colonial authorities proclaimed that Madagascar had become "Zanatany Frantsay" (children of French soil), thus equivocating the past and still-to-come brutality of colonial appropriation and violence.[66] Colonial administrators sought to bring the island under the metropole's domain in an imagined, affinal network that sutured together colonized and colonizer; the declaration of Malagasy as the French zanatany was a thinly veiled attempt to foster paternalistic loyalty among colonial subjects while maintaining the hierarchical distinction between colonized and colonizer. Conversely, French nationals who remained in the country after independence described themselves as zanatany or *vazaha zanatany*, in a claim of belonging to the Malagasy soil.[67]

In Mahajanga, and in northwest Madagascar more broadly, *zanatany* increasingly referred to those born locally but of mixed parentage (of a stranger and a native, vahiny and tompontany).[68] By the 1940s and '50s colonial authorities invoked *zanatany* in official reports to refer to the first-generation offspring of Comorian migrants (usually men) and their Malagasy partners (often women of Sakalava descent).[69] In 1957, a small group of self-identified zanatany petitioned and were granted authorization to organize the Association des Zanatany Majungais (AZAM), a mutual-aid group dedicated to zanatany, whom they defined as "Comorian natives to Mahajanga."[70] The founders of AZAM occupied a relatively comfortable economic position as traders, salaried teachers, and office clerks, and they advocated for the fee-based membership association as a means to garner funds for social and religious-civic needs.[71] Although the paper trail on AZAM is thin, evidence suggests that the group grew rapidly to nearly 200 members over two years, held regular evening meetings in Mahabibo, and was devoted to fundraising for mosque construction, organizing parties at venues, including the well-known Ritz Cinema, and hosting homecoming celebrations for returnees from pilgrimage to Mecca.[72]

Within the broader social geography of the town, AZAM was one among several other mutual aid societies organized for the benefit of Comorian migrants hailing from specific towns of origin in the archipelago—Iconi, Bambao, and Fomboni—as well as societies dedicated to migrant groups from across Madagascar. The composite of these mutual aid groups provides a glimpse into the categories of difference circulating in 1950s and early 1960s, the importance of maintaining ties to one's place of birth, and the access to and accrual of capital (however modest) and state recognition through collectivities defined by origins. The presence of AZAM in the late 1950s, alongside groups tied to villages in Comoros, however, suggests the growing importance and self-conscious positioning of this emergent generation of children of Comorian descent. This generation of mixed progeny increasingly referred to themselves as zanatany to starkly distinguish themselves from their Comorian fathers (*vieux Comoriens*) and to draw on the connections with their matrilineal ancestry to make claims to the spaces, jobs, and opportunities of the city.[73]

While *zanatany* gained traction in overlapping linguistic fields—as evidenced in government reports, clubs, and popular memory—it is critical to note its genealogical roots in an earlier ethnonym: Antalaotra. As discussed in chapters 1 and 2, the ethnonym *Antalaotra* circulated in the eighteenth and nineteenth century to denote Muslim seafarers and their families of diverse Comorian, Malagasy (usually Sakalava), and perhaps Hadhramaut origins. Although relatively few inhabitants in Mahajanga identify themselves and their ancestors as Antalaotra today, and although census figures no longer track ethnolinguistic categories of this kind, documentary traces and my ethnographic research in the 2010s suggested that *Antalaotra* waned as a salient identifier, just as *zanatany* gained traction in the early to mid-twentieth century. Though more linguistic and historical research is needed to clarify the precise relationship between these categories, both terms signal a collective consciousness of belonging to a community of shared descent—one with the deeply rooted migratory and marriage practices linking Comorian and Malagasy families. Attending to this "precolonial intellectual inheritance" goes some distance, as Jonathon Glassman importantly argues more broadly, to foregrounding the role of Comorian-Malagasy intellectuals—rather than, say, the colonial state—in creatively fostering lexicons of difference and collective consciousness over time in Mahajanga.[74]

Despite this deep history of long-standing ties between Comoros and Northwest Madagascar, many residents in the town insisted on *zanatany* as a novel generational identity definer. Natasha, a woman in her late forties (not of Comorian descent) who was born and raised in Mahajanga, explained, "Zanatany are really the product of Comorian-Gasy mixing (*mifangaro*), they were the next generation born here."[75] Some cast *zanatany* not only as a generational category, but as one saturated with ethnic identification. Pastor Toky, also in his late forties, recalled, "Comorians came and mixed with Gasy. This gave rise to a new ethnic group (*foko-vaovao*), a new way of life, new customs (*fomba vaovao*), and this is zanatany."[76] During my research in Mahajanga in 2011–2014, newer Malagasy migrant groups and youth sometimes self-identified as zanatany in bold declarations of their urban citizenship that were often questioned by older generations of mixed Comorian-Malagasy inhabitants.[77]

But identities in northwest Madagascar have never been singular, unilateral, or mutually exclusive, and thus people have invoked *zanatany* alongside other identity affiliations. While *Antalaotra* and then *zanatany* circulated as a differentiating concepts in earlier times, under French colonial rule the latter term crystallized as an identity category in the convergence of French bureaucratic practices tied to racial hierarchies. At the same time, Comorians and their mixed Malagasy-Comorian progeny actively harnessed the term and tethered it to their transformation of the city through building, as a form of distinction from newer waves of migrants. Within the rich lexicon of Malagasy words signifying various forms of inclusion, Comorian-Malagasy uses of *zanatany* in Mahajanga during the twentieth century are particularly distinctive because they hinged on what stands on the soil and the transmutation of soil into material form, rather than on occupancy or mere possession.

Building a Zanatany Presence

Striking in the seeming shift from Antalaotra ("people of the sea") to zana-tany ("children of the soil") is the spatially specific change in geographical point of origin—from sea to soil. This linguistic shift perhaps reflects the particularly grounded emplacement practices—houses set in soil, made of stone—of Comorian-Malagasy families that took new shape in the mid to late twentieth century. House-building, namely in the Mahabibo area, including Abattoir, Manga, Morafeno, Ambalavola, and Ambovoalanana, figured centrally in narratives about the emergence of zanatany (see map FM.3).[78] "Comorians, they built so many houses in town," one man remarked. "Many Malagasy thought Comorians were boastful because they built big houses, they were carpenters and knew how to build."[79] Comorian-Malagasy families framed their narratives about the establishment of their homes—as zanatany households—in moral registers about the value of work and frugality, contrasting the foundational ethical norms of their kin with those of other migrant groups in the city. Older self-identifying zanatany recalled that their Comorian forebears distinguished themselves from their Malagasy neighbors by upholding idealized notions of fastidious bodily cleanliness, asceticism, and scrupulous economizing practices.[80] In these narratives, Comorians and their progeny became zanatany through the acquisition of property enabled by their energetic toil, faithful perse-verance, clever economization, and savings (*manao economie, miafy*).[81] As with mosques, home construction relied on accumulating wealth—and strengthening of social solidarity—through the Comorian social institution of *shikoa* (savings groups), which required members to pay an allocated sum each month and then rotated the recipient monthly.[82] Anchored in a logic of reciprocity and indebtedness, shikoa brought together Comorians and Malagasy in disciplined, short-term austerity for long-term material gain.

Mama Mariam, a widowed owner of a *hotely* (snack bar) in her sixties, offered an emblematic account of the sedimentary process through which her parents successively hardened their home and established themselves as zanatany insiders. Mama Mariam's mother, born to a Sakalava mother and Comorian father, was considered zanatany, whereas her father was a Comorian migrant from Nzwani (Anjouan). Mama Mariam's mother inherited her land from her parents, following the customary inheritance practices to daughters that Comorian-Malagasy families observed, much as Mama Mariam then inherited the house in turn. When Mama Mariam was a child, her father held a well-paying civil service job, and her mother cooked and sold her prepared foods outside the home. Although Mama Mariam emphasized her mother's role in successively rebuilding and then hardening their family home (in line with her family's matrilineal practice), she clarified that her parents together accrued capital, consolidated their earnings, and collapsed their assets into the lasting, material form of the house: "My mother, she built this house because she was economical. She did shikoa . . . that's how she finished the house. She built the house from sheet metal (*toly*), before I was even born. By the time I was a young woman (*efa misy jery*; literally, "already with mind/sight/consciousness"), we'd already rebuilt the home in concrete (*vato*; literally, "stone," but in this sense, "cement"). And then she built three other houses in the city [in Manga and Ambalavola]. It's also how she bought all her furniture (*fanaka*). She was very clever (*fetsy*) [clicking her tongue]."[83] In Mama Mariam's retelling of her house's history, changes in the house's composition from *toly* to *vato* were temporal markers through which families narrated the lifespan of the home. There was an unabashed teleologism threaded through these accounts, wherein cement was the peak in the house's trajectory, although it must be rebuilt anew after years, because even cement crumbles in the stifling heat and unrelenting rains. Mama Mariam's dwelling can be understood at once as a repository of memories and a kind of living presence, with a biography that has extended beyond the lifespans of its inhabitants.[84]

Comorian-Malagasy families understood their ancestors as particularly inclined toward private property ownership and durable home construction as anticipatory acts designed to ensure intergenerational prosperity amid inevitable vicissitudes of fortune. Descendants' morally saturated histories of house-building and the rise of zanatany ways of urban relationality can be understood as what John Lonsdale terms "moral ethnicity," driven by "internal discourses of social responsibility."[85] Equally, these implicit norms—described as a zanatany sensibility—of industriousness and wealth accumulation in hardened homes were frequently contrasted with those of other migrants.[86] Some characterized the corrupt social mores of "Malagasy," who ostensibly wasted their wages on "alcohol, food, pleasure and women," in contrast to Comorians, who knew how to abstain from bodily pleasures to pursue aspirations for material improvement.[87] When I pushed back on these generalizations, most Comorian-Malagasy acknowledged that architectural differences—whether a house was built of mud or stone—were tied to economic means; they also signaled that different conceptions of forms of wealth were at play. As Mama Amelie explained, "For Tandroy migrants [from the island's deep south], a mud house (*trano motramotrakwa*) is acceptable. If there aren't cattle, then you're considered poor (*raha tsy misy omby, dia mahantra*). So they take their money and place it there. Also, the tomb (*fasana*) is very important for them, they need a nice tomb. And those from the highlands, if you don't have a rice field (*tanimbary*), then you're poor."[88] Mama Amelie's description reflected ideas that anthropologists working across the island have long documented about the diversity of wealth production and accrual practices. But in reality, many migrants struggled to accumulate enough earnings to send back home. Dadilahy Saondra, who migrated from Vangaindrano (in the south) to the east and then west coasts in the late 1950s, described how fleeting wages were: "Back then, you got your salary, filled your belly, sent a little to your children, and it was—gone!"[89]

Yet it would be a mistake to suggest that *all* Comorians yearned to acquire land and build homes, and indeed those of Comorian descent internally differentiated themselves through the vector of house-building. According to oral accounts, many Adzudzu (those from Ngazidja) pursued temporary labor migration and retained ties to Comoros, with an eye to returning home to Ngazidja.[90] Residents ruefully recalled the propensity of Adzudzu men to abandon their Malagasy wives and children, captured in the saying, "the value of a *gasy* child is less than a gunnysack of rice"[91] Papa Taoaby, a retired civil servant in his early seventies, had been treated this way by his Comorian father, and he acknowledged a long-held resentment and desire for revenge (*kankay*) that he left aside when he had his own children. But many from Ngazidja *did* establish households and build homes, even as some preserved ties to kin in Comores.

Those from Nzwani (Anjouan), by contrast, were regarded as zealously ambitious in land acquisition, home construction, and permanent settlement in Mahajanga (figure 5.2). Take Papa Raissa's family. His father migrated from Nzwani to Madagascar as a soldier in the French army in the 1940s; he then met Papa Raissa's mother, a Sakalava woman originally from the nearby town of Boanamary.[92] They purchased a parcel of land in

FIGURE 5.2 "Anjouanais" migrants in Mahajanga, 1904. Courtesy of FR ANOM 4PA 135/83.

Manga from a South Asian (Karana) family and lived in the existing sheet metal home (*trano tôly*) while Papa Raissa's father gathered funds by buying and selling wood, and participating in shikoa. His father purchased a second land parcel in Mahabibokely that he kept as a rental property. Many residents commented on Anjouans' abilities to build up a "kind of enterprise" of rental properties, yet they had nothing like a monopoly on rental housing and hardly constituted a "rentier" class in the sense scholars have described for Indians in East African cities.[93] More often, Comorian migrants concurrently pursued wage labor and small-scale trade via their ties to the archipelago, alongside home construction, as a set of nested, anticipatory strategies for building their presence in the city.

Calcifying the City

Long-time residents of varied backgrounds narrated the city's unfolding as a process of increasing hardening in the city's material topography, which was closely linked to the growing presence of Comorian-Malagasy families in the early to mid-1900s. Historically, followers of the Sakalava polity across northwest Madagascar fabricated their single-story homes with widely abundant palm leaves (*satrana*) and rafia branches, supported by wooden poles and covered with interwoven palm fronds.[94] As discussed in earlier chapters, inhabitants deliberately constructed these dwellings of vegetative materials to distinguish them from enduring royal Sakalava dwellings and tombs.[95] Although migrants to the city from elsewhere in Madagascar brought extensive knowledge of adobe mud brick home construction (*trano fotaka*), many followers of the Sakalava royal family generally eschewed these structures, associating them with mud and filth.[96] Over time, families with the means to do so increasingly employed techniques of fabricating limestone from mixing coral and stone, which was overlaid on wooden frames, as was commonly found in Zanzibar and Mauritius.[97] Regardless of the construction materials, most islanders shared a cosmological sensibility rooted in spatial orientation along the four cardinal directions, in which north and northeast were reserved for elites, sacred figures, ancestors, and men, whereas southern and western parts were designated for women and children.[98] As one proverb exhorted listeners, "Aza mijery tany avo avaratra!"—literally, "Don't look to the land in the north," meaning "Don't envy the powerful."[99]

As in the case of Indian-owned homes in Majunga Be, French colonial rulers sought to rework intimate dwellings and spatially engineer the neighborhoods of Mahabibo to conform to French moral norms of propriety. Like colonizers elsewhere, French officials seemed to assume that markers of domesticity were "straightforward reflection(s) of the inner state of the individual's soul and the family's moral state."[100] Officials carried out their housing policy ("la politique de l'habitat") by instilling new regimes of proximity. At times this meant distinguishing separate spaces for cooking and waste disposal, whereas at other times it meant propagating windows, doors, and commercial hinges to create impervious enclosures.[101] At still other times, it meant controlling the very materials from which homes could be constructed—policies that affected long-standing mortuary practices that had sustained communities in the city.

The ephemerality and flammability of thatch housing construction was key to maintaining distinctions between the living and the dead—and between purity and filth—and to ensuring flourishing in ancestrally centered cosmologies among followers of the Sakalava polity.[102] In 1911, Dandouau described how Sakalava families in the northwest anticipated the death of a sick relative by first attempting to move the person to a temporary shelter, or *trano ratsy* (literally, "bad" or "poor quality" house).[103] Following the relative's death, the *trano ratsy* was torched, and those who had prepared the dead bathed in the river to purify themselves afterward.[104] Homes were burned if people died in them, and no further edifice could be erected until diviners (*moasy*) deemed the site free from troubled spirits, in order to safeguard the living from ancestral wrath and the spiritual pollution associated with death. Elders with whom I spoke vividly recalled these practices and the frantic efforts of families to gauge the timing for transporting sick relatives to the *trano ratsy* to ensure they were moved *before* their death.[105]

Guiding conceptions of purification and protection persisted with the forging of hardened homes among mixed Sakalava-Comorian families and increasing pressure by the French on residents to build in hard, durable materials (*en dur*); but practitioners adapted rituals to the changing materials of construction. Dandouau noted that if the original home of the deceased was of great economic value or if the family was reluctant to incinerate it, a diviner would ritually purify the site using *tany malandy* (white earth) to absolve the living of any wrongdoings against ancestors.[106] Elder residents confirmed this and noted that Sakalava ritual specialists resolved to shift away from house burning and toward ritual cleansing, some time before the 1950s.[107] Perhaps pressured by French colonial restrictions and the urban nature of tightly nestled homes, families in Mahajanga heeded the counsel of ritual experts and turned increasingly to these ritual blessings rather than to incineration in the aftermath of death.

Comorian-Malagasy families establishing new households and building homes in the early decades of the 1900s negotiated these evolving colonial urban planning initiatives by melding together cultural norms, technical knowledges, and cosmological conceptions actively practiced in Mahajanga with those brought from Comoros. Migrants from the archipelago brought to their new families in Mahajanga specific carpentry skills, drawn from generations of constructing homes in wood, with supporting posts of coconut trunks, walls of raffia panels, and thatched, gable roofs of coconut leaves or vetiver (a woody, aromatic long-sheathed grass).[108] Elite families, from whom many migrants hailed, constructed hardened, limestone cement homes, described by one traveler to Ngazidja in 1864, as gleaming "mansions built from volcanic rock and decorated with luminous lime."[109] These dwellings were composed of lava stones carved to reach four feet high, on which supporting poles rested (see figure 5.3). "All the houses have on the front a veranda," reported one visitor to the archipelago in 1870, "and on the back a courtyard planted with coconut and sugar apple (*Annona squa-*

2. GRANDE COMORE. — Une rue de Moroni.

FIGURE 5.3
Postcard, Street
in Moroni,
Ngazidja
(Comoros),
ca. 1930s.
Author's
collection.

mosa) trees, surrounded by a high fence of tightly braided coconut leaves
to stop the prying eyes of passers-by."[110]

Residents recalled that their Comorian ancestors initially built their transgenerational homes of satrana thatch and wood (*trano ketikety*), which they
lived in until such time as they amassed funds to purchase cement and corrugated tin.[111] As processes of historical becoming, homes could be found
in various stages of bricolage—creatively patched and pieced together with
a medley of corrugated tin, thatch panels, mangrove reeds (*ketikety*), and
mud slip. Throughout the northwest region, Comorians constructed their
homes with a stone threshold, built walls of wattle and daub, and covered
their roofs with *ravinala* (traveler's palm) leaves.[112] Gabriel Ferrand visited

Mahajanga in the 1890s and described homes occupied by Comorians as "quite different." He noted that "the exterior is almost elegant, the leaves of the *rafia* . . . intermingle symmetrically and form a design quite graceful to the eye." Yet, he continued, unlike many other houses in the city, "the door is always hermetically closed like that of any Moslem house; but through the reeds or the leaves which are used as fence, the *vazaha* [European] who passes can glimpse, as behind the moucharabiés of Cairo, the eyes of the inhabitants . . . who follow him so much that he seems not to suspect the curiosity of which he is the object."[113] These enclosures—doors, fences, inner courtyards—were increasingly important architectural features, informed by Islamic architectural styles from Comoros and beyond, that distinguished Comorian-Malagasy homes in the early to mid-twentieth century.[114] Houses configured in this way contained nested layers of visibility, protecting inhabitants from the peering eyes of curious or even malicious passersby, including, as Ferrand observed, intrusive French authorities.[115]

Within the rectangular parcels designated by colonial urban plans, Comorian-Malagasy families designed their homes by drawing on Islamic-informed aesthetic traditions that stretched to Comoros and the Swahili coast. Descendants of Comorian-Malagasy families described the adoption of the double-roomed configuration so distinctive to Comorian homes. One room often opened onto the street and served as a reception area and a sleeping area for men, replete with chairs and mats. Behind a connective partition lay a second room, reserved for women as a sleeping space, filled with beds, mats, shelves, and a mirror, that led to the inner, enclosed courtyard, in which cooking and washing took place.[116] Yet the materiality of room partitions enabled a shared sensorium that stretched across the household compound. French observers in the nineteenth century noted that the partitions separating the rooms were often made of raffia reeds, and in contemporary Mahajanga many families hang semisheer, embroidered cloth known as *ridao* (modified from French *rideau*) in connecting doorways.[117] These porous partitions afforded aural and olfactory communality, a "flow of sociality," and a shared sensorial index that encompassed all inhabitants of the home.[118] Conversations could be overheard, fragrant cooking scents could be smelled, and a broader awareness of other individuals' presence on the home could be sensed. Like Swahili homes, these so-called zanatany homes were designed in incrementally tightening circles of intimacy—moving from the street to the innermost sanctum of abode—even as they were connected to broader geographies of economic, religious, and cultural life.[119]

Although friction-filled negotiations over different domestic inhabitance practices, including gendered norms and cosmological orientation, must have taken place in Comorian-Malagasy households, they have largely slipped into the historical abyss; few contemporary residents intimated these conflicts in our conversations, and that which remains are the material forms to which they gave rise. Instead, most enduring in popular historical consciousness were the memories of how Comorian-Malagasy families hardened the city over time, efforts that coincided with increasing pressure by French colonial authorities toward durable home construction for smoother governability and fire prevention.

Long-time residents credited Comorians with the widespread proliferation of corrugated tin (*tôly*) as a staple, solid building material, which indelibly changed the city's landscape. The genealogy of corrugated tin, and how it arrived on the shores of Mahajanga, suggests that it was not only critical to the transformation of the city—it was fundamentally constitutive of the colonial project. Corrugated tin spread across the world in the late nineteenth century, owing to its lightweight and portable form.[120] It emerged within the twin axes of colonial expansion and industrialization as a key material for prefabricated structures that were modular and thus highly mobile.[121] Portable corrugated tin was a material manifestation of colonial aspirations to implant European presence abroad, and the material propensities of corrugated tin allowed authorities to establish their presence with speed. Much like the "hard and clean" roads described by Rudolf Mrázek in colonial Indonesia, gleaming sheets of corrugated tin promised to bring modernity to the dusty, humid roads of Madagascar in reassuringly standardized forms.[122] Corrugated tin was nothing short of essential to the making of empire.

In places like Madagascar, where labor was scarce, corrugated tin was a particularly critical component of colonial construction, because it could be assembled easily, requiring few workers.[123] Sheets fitted together to make rooftops, groove into groove. More than that, the sweeping circulation of corrugated tin encompassed a premise that corrugated tin could physically carry and instantiate the accompanying ideals of the civilizing mission. But if mass-produced corrugated tin seemed to officials a gratifying marker of the replicability of colonial imperatives (or even of European places themselves), these fantasies were shaken by the specific conditions on the ground. Ecological factors—heavy rains, unrelenting sun, pervasive humidity—flattened out the promise of prefabricated tin as an enduring marker of shiny cleanliness, dissolving lustrous metallic surfaces into rough, ruddy

Photo G. Charifou

MAJUNGA. — Une Rue du Village indigène.

FIGURE 5.4 Postcard, "Street view of Mahabibo," ca. 1910s. Note the extensive use of corrugated panels (*tôly*) in home construction, and tôly combined with wood (*ketikety*), front left. Author's collection.

rust. Climatic forces revealed to colonized subjects the indeterminacy of French colonial rule as much as the ephemerality of technological imports.

Even more than the climatic forces, it was the aspirations of Comorian-Malagasy builders that challenged the colonial meanings of corrugated tin on the ground. In their able hands, tôly became a cosmopolitan technology of self-determination and an architectural statement of inclusion to the city.[124] Tôly arrived in Mahajanga sometime between the late 1890s and early 1900s, when colonial administrators used it to erect temporary housing for labor migrants.[125] But tôly quickly went from the province of the colonial state to a commodity through which colonized subjects could reshape their everyday lives and urban environments (see figure 5.4). To be sure, tôly was costly for most city inhabitants and, unlike thatch or wood, required a sizeable up-front investment. From at least 1912, Comorians were among the first to use their relative economic capacity to prioritize the purchase of tôly, which they mixed with thatch and wood.[126] The transduction of economic capital into obdurate, transgenerational home construction became synonymous with the transformation of Comorian-Malagasy families into zanatany in the mid-twentieth century.

Beyond construction styles and design, Comorian-Malagasy families brought distinctive conceptions of the value of land and homes informed by established practices in Comoros. One self-identified zanatany, a retired electrician in his seventies, attributed Comorians' propensity toward land acquisition in the mid-twentieth century to "the strong Arabic influence" and to the high population density coupled with the "smallness" of Comoros, which led to "everyone wanting their own place."[127] Kassim commented that for Comorians, "unlike the Malagasy . . . the house of the living is precious . . . no one can come and insult you in your home."[128] A house contains and reflects "value" (*trano am'valeur*)—not just monetary investment, but enhancement of one's personhood. This was particularly salient in the city. Whereas in the countryside, cattle was the marker of wealth ("Amin'ny brousse omby tresor" [In the countryside, cattle is wealth]), in the city people said, "The house is the cattle" (*Trano ao omby*). Without a house, there is no value, no treasure.[129] As Mama Amelie described, "In Comoros, if you don't have a house, it's a big problem (*problem be*) and you're a disgrace (*tena manompa anao*)."[130]

Conceptions of value extended beyond landed property, however, to the very material substance of the home. When I asked older friends about the attraction to tôly, given Mahajanga's scorching hot climate, they cited both its nonflammability and its "value" (*valeur*) as a marker of status. One woman explained that people shifted away from building with wood and thatch because tôly was a "prestige symbol," deemed more "respectable" than wood (*ket-ket*).[131] Investing in a *trano tôly* or *trano vato* (figure 5.5) that would endure over generations offered financial security and longevity for the family. One man explained, "a house won't get ruined [like other investments]. For instance, if there's a car, then one day you're in an accident—everything is lost, ruined . . . The first thing to do, should be to build a strong house . . . in a home, there's value, and you can bequeath it."[132]

A hardened house signaled not only accumulated economic wealth, but also anticipated wealth-in-kin, including future progeny. Given the norms of matrilineal inheritance and matrilocality, providing for daughters was a critical imperative for zanatany families, further motivating Comorian fathers and their families to build a house (if not more than one) for their descendants. Comorian fathers were obliged to construct a home for their adult daughters or risk shame and the possibility that no suitors could be secured for marriage (*tsisy olo manambady*).[133] Building a home was, in

FIGURE 5.5 Postcard, "Majunga—Indigeous village of Mahabibo," ca. 1940s, with predominantly "stone" houses (*trano vato*). Author's collection.

other words, not only the fulfillment of a father's ethical responsibility to care for his girl children but also foundational to social reproduction and continuation of the family line. In turn, those children would be similarly obliged to perform their ethical duties of caring for elders. Durable houses were and are an anticipatory expression of affective attachments between parents and beloved children, a material rendering of intense devotions that go beyond words and travel across time.[134]

There was also a moral connotation to owning a home for many self-identified zanatany, as expressed in the proverb "Jaolahy [or jaolboto] manana trano, sarotra lazaina olona ratsy" (If a thief has a house, it's difficult to say he's a bad person). Homeowning zanatany often described that owning one's home was linked to a "good character, a clean character" (*toetra tsara, toetra madio*). Mama and Papa Taoaby and their eldest son, Taoaby, explained this to me one sunny afternoon. Mama Taoaby remarked,

If you have money, the first thing you should do is to build a house! This is not the same for people from the highlands (*afovoantany*); for them the house *and* the tomb are both very important. And for Tandroy, the tomb (*fasana*) is the most important, and the house matters little. But for people from the coast, the house is of utmost importance. . . . If you rent a house, even a big, luxurious house, you're still insignificant (*tsy considere*), you're unimportant (*tsy masinteny*; literally, "don't have the right to speak"). You should rather take that money and build yourself a house. If you rent a house, it shows that you're a newcomer (vahiny). But if you own a house and you go afar, say to Diego or Ambanja [both cities in the north] and introduce yourself to people, they may very well recognize you, place you as, "Oh, you're the owner of that double-story house in Abattoir. . . ." Having a house is what gives you prestige and value in society. [135]

As the conversation continued, however, it was clear that homeownership offered not only social prestige, but also protection against those who might wish to do harm to you. Mama Taoaby explained:

All of your secrets, they are inside this house. The house is a kind of protection, if someone wants to do something bad (*manao zavatra ratsy*), they will hesitate to enter the courtyard. But if you rent, then you're more vulnerable because there are probably other renters there, more traffic in and out. You may also have the landlord coming and entering your home, trying to get the rent that you're late in paying. This is also why it's important to stay in one house . . . if you move a lot, then it's like you leave a bad reputation in those places where you stayed, like you left a trace of yourself, then everyone knows your business.

When Mama Taoaby mentioned that people leave "traces" of themselves in homes, she signaled the intimate ways in which inhabitants impress themselves on their domestic spaces, blurring the boundaries of containment between persons and places.[136] Mama Taoaby did not mean that people leave traces only figuratively, but also quite literally. The home was not only the keeper of secrets, but also the container for bodily fluids and matters connected to critical moments in the lifecycle. For example, families described the importance of the father or grandfather burying the infant's placenta (*tavony*) and umbilical cord (*foitra*) in the courtyard of the family's home, where it would remain protected. Burying an infant's placenta in the family courtyard rooted the child to the household, literally emplacing them in the soil.[137] Failure to do so could leave a child's heart in an unstable, easily startled (*titra*) state.

The home played an important role in death, as well. The relatives of deceased Comorian-Malagasy followed prescribed Muslim norms of washing and purifying the body, and these rituals generally took place in the privacy and protection of the home. Those knowledgeable about mortuary rituals explained that at the time of death (literally, when the "lifeforce leaves the body"), family members warmed the water for the bath (*rehefa lasa ny fofokaina, dia mamana ny rano*). Junior family members were sent to retrieve a special rope cot from the mosque, which would allow the drainage of fluids from the body. Same-gender family members (*havana*) performed the ritual cleansing. Ideally, postmortem fluids were then deposited in the home. As one woman described, the fluids from the dead should be poured into a dugout hole in the center of the home, "because those fluids . . . they're sacred, and if they're seen or taken outside the house, then people can begin to talk about the dead disrespectfully, remarking on how much filth left the body."[138] A ritual cleaning of the home, which some zanatany described as Sakalava or "Malagasy" in origin, would follow.

Protecting the dead (and their family) from social harm at this most critical juncture was contingent on invisibility and interment, afforded by the barriers—fences, walls, and protected courtyards—of the home. When I asked other self-identifying zanatany families about the use of the dugout hole, they confirmed that it had a long history. Some maintained the custom and even built their homes with this in mind, leaving an unfinished dirt opening in the concrete slab of the floor for this purpose, but most no longer observed the custom, although many families still carried out ritual washing of the home itself following death. Older residents lamented the loss, noting that in-home burial of these fluids was better.[139] What these discussions and practices suggest are the multiple ways through which zanatany homes were made and remade. Perhaps more than any other dimension, the entombment of precious bodily fluids and substances into the home signified the sedimented, processual way in which Comorian-Malagasy families built their presence into the soil of the city.

Zanatany houses were brought into being through acts of burial, the interring of precious bodily liquids, and the melding together of the living and the dead with the physical structure of the home. In these acts, inhabitants infused the fleshy and fluid substances of the living and the dead into the fixity of the (tin and concrete) home, transforming it into a secret, sacred vessel; layering it with histories of lives lived and lost. These practices of emplacement and home-making enabled Comorian-Malagasy to understand themselves as transformed from migrants into *children of the soil*, but these practices are not unique to Mahajanga. An abundant anthropological literature documents the processual nature of houses, how the "material world" of the home is constructed over time through the cumulative interventions of social actors.[140] And, to be clear, Comorian-Malagasy families did not cite these practices as necessarily the definitive markers of their autochthonous position or "zanatany-ness." Rather, it was the combination of these ritual practices, their family genealogies, and the commanding presence of their homes (replete with histories of their own) that created their legitimate status as those who belonged to the soil of the city.

Customs Sit in Places ('Mipetraka An'toerana ny Fomba)

When Comorian-Malagasy recalled how their ancestors came to occupy land, they almost always referenced *mamaky tany*, which means "dividing up" or "breaking" the land—the same term used for acquiring and preparing land acquisition and mosque construction.[141] *Mamaky* is multivalent, also meaning "to read," and indeed some town dwellers described the need to *read* the land, to converse with ancestral spirits before and during the early stages of house-building and before taking occupancy. The practice of consulting a diviner to discern the optimal orientation and day for constructing a home is well-documented throughout Madagascar.[142] But for most Comorian-Malagasy, *mamaky tany* denoted their ancestors' useful occupation and cultivation of otherwise fallow land. Many described that when Comorians arrived the land "wasn't titled" (*tsy borné*), and so they staked it out using stones or by building a palm leaf fence (*manao valavala satrana*).[143] Others described how their parents and grandparents cleared the forests of mango and palm trees to claim land.

Comorian-Malagasy families described the land as vacant prior to the arrival of their ancestral Comorian settlers. At first glance, these references to vacant land resonate with discursive practices of belonging and nativism found elsewhere. Scholars working across African contexts have noted how claims to belonging, whether to a geographical or political space, have been increasingly framed around "first-coming" (autochthony) and have intensively animated public debates about claims to citizenship in the nation-state across Africa (and beyond).[144] Now and in the past, friction-filled claims to being first-comers often entailed reworking a group's origin stories and, at times, effacing their earlier histories of mobility and migration.[145] Nativist narratives performed by settlers consistently emphasized the emptiness, and thus ostensibly available nature, of the lands first occupied.[146] But self-identified zanatany often described first-comers as followers of the Sakalava polity, and they almost always referenced the journeys undertaken by their parents and grandparents from Comoros, Nosy Be, or Analalava to Mahajanga. Recognizing these histories of movement did not seem to challenge their legitimate claims to nativism. Autochthony here was not the "mystification of ancestry," but rather the revelation of ancestry—specifically the ways in which ancestors' marriage and labor practices produced a veritable claim to belonging to the city.[147] Zanatany cited the value their ancestors added and the labor they invested as what secured their "rightful place in the city."[148] These transformative efforts to add a material, built presence to the land, rather than first-coming status, were pivotal to the staking of autochthonous claims by zanatany.[149]

Indeed, zanatany understood the region as belonging to Sakalava royal followers through the presence of Sakalava royal ancestral spirits. Quite a few inhabitants, both of and not of Sakalava descent, adamantly asserted that the "true masters of this land" (*tena tompony/tompontany eto*) were Sakalava and (for some) Makoa, *not* Comorians.[150] Self-identified zanatany and other contemporary residents of the city frequently pointed out that although Sakalava followers were the "masters of the land," they had gradually exited the city to escape exploitation from the French or to avoid conflicts with incoming groups of migrants.[151]

There is much dispute and dissonance between colonial reports and census records, as well as within contemporary accounts concerning the constitution of the ethno-category "Sakalava" and the extent to which the purported population emigrated from the city over the twentieth century. For our purposes, what's important are the ways zanatany narrated a nuanced conception of their belonging to a place that itself retained distinctive Sakalava character. A prominent theme in these narratives centers on prohibitions and norms around land use. Residents argued that customs ought to remain tethered to the land—regardless of the preferences and habits of the current occupants. As a former state worker and local dignitary in his early seventies named Said Hassan explained, "Customs are tied to the place (*fomba mipetraka*; literally, customs "live" or "sit" in place). Mahajanga has long been a Muslim town, and people coming here [meaning migrants and visitors] should respect norms like not consuming pork, especially in certain parts of town."[152]

Others explicitly indicated the rootedness of fady (taboos) in place through specific Sakalava histories and the presence of royal ancestral spirits. Ancestral (and thus historical) associations with land imbued it with certain Sakalava properties, taboos, and expectations that migrants

FIGURE 5.6 Sakalava *doany* (royal compound), Mahajanga, 2014.
Photo by David Epstein.

and later-comers have an obligation to respect. And the active presence
of royal ancestral spirits (and their mediums) helped maintain the sense
of Mahajanga as "Sakalava land," in ways similar to cases described elsewhere in Africa.[153] This was especially the case in parts of town where
observance of prohibitions and norms were critical—even necessary for
one's survival. These areas included the *doany* (sacred Sakalava compound;
figure 5.6), but also the seaside in the areas of Village Touristique (Atsa-
habingo) and Petite Plage, where the consumption of pork was absolutely
forbidden.[154] During vacation months, the seaside attracted large crowds
of vacationing highlanders and outsiders who often violated this taboo.
Long-standing residents remarked on vacationers' carelessness toward the
fadys, which angered Sakalava royal ancestors and resulted in the deaths
of several people each year—by drowning or by the *lolondrano* (ghost/
spirit of the sea). Dadi'Elio, a Tsimihety woman in her late seventies, explained, "The lolondrano has long been in the sea, but before it didn't take
people (*maka olo*). Ndriamisara (an important royal Sakalava ancestor)
became angry because of the *bourzany* (perjorative term for highlanders) coming to the sea and eating pork. Then, things spun into chaos (*lasa
mikorontana*)."[155]

These accounts illustrate that key sites in Mahajanga, and sometimes the city as a whole, are what Mikhail Bakhtin termed *chronotopes*—places in which time and space intersect, "time thickens, takes on flesh, and becomes visible; likewise space becomes charged and response to the movements of time."[156] They reflect deeper, overlapping histories through which zanatany calibrate their own positionality and deliberate social norms. In this conception, the land of the city has never been a static substratum, but rather is ever-animated by the permeation of more-than-human presences and historically constructed practices.[157] And as Keith Basso beautifully demonstrated for Apache in North America, places are sites in which wisdom is embedded and which thus offer ethical instructions from tales of the past: "Knowledge of places is therefore closely linked to knowledge of the self, to grasping one's position in the larger scheme of things, including one's own community."[158]

Many of Sakalava descent contrasted newcomer migrants' brazen disregard for the city's prohibitions with the practices of Comorian migrants and Comorian-Malagasy residents, who were seen as cognizant of their position in a city populated and governed by ancestral forces. In this frame, Comorian-Malagasy inhabitants understood themselves as beholden to ancestral spirits and already-there presences across the landscape whom they were obliged to recognize; this understanding made them distinctively able to gain acceptance among longer-dwelling families in the city. Herman, a self-identified Sakalava musician in his late fifties, framed it this way: "It's absolutely necessary (*tsy maintsy*) for outsiders (vahiny) to adapt to Sakalava customs (*adapte fomba Sakalava*), for example, by avoiding pork, which is prohibited here. Comorians knew this. They adapted, they knew the customs. But other groups haven't adapted like this, but rather expect to carry on with their customs here. This is where we have problems."[159] By abiding by the standards distinctive to Mahajanga as "Sakalava land" and thereby establishing harmonious social coexistence, Comorians and their mixed progeny were able to not only gain legitimacy among many as zanatany, but also to bolster their claims to urban citizenship. Self-identified zanatany expressed coexisting—if competitive, at times—articulations of Comorian and Sakalava history.[160] Remembering early histories of Comorian migration and settling did not preclude the recollection of Sakalava ancestors and histories, nor did it necessarily invalidate zanatany claims to belonging. In fact, recognition of these existing presences bolstered their claim to autochthonous zanatany status, because it indicated an intimate knowledge of place and an awareness of the obligations to royal authority.[161] Thinking about historical narratives around autochthony this way may also move us away from thinking of nativism as a sum-zero field in which winners are natives and losers are strangers.[162]

In the mid-twentieth century, *zanatany* came to denote an identity category distinctive to Mahajanga. Inflected with nativism, to be zanatany was to have long-standing roots in the city, to have made the city one's own, and to have been made *by* the city. To be zanatany was also a categorical refusal of affiliation with a Christianized, highland conception of Malagasy-ness and a spirited assertion of an Islamicized coastal urban political subjecthood. This was not a refusal in opposition to superior, colonial institutions (and therefore not "resistance"), but rather at times levelled against fellow "Malagasy" city dwellers. These articulations of refusal, and the insistence on moral economies made visible in houses and building projects, animated zanatany collectivities. It was through the cumulative processes of fabricating homes that Comorian-Malagasy families established themselves as zanatany and claimed their ties both to the land and to broader networks of sociality and reciprocity. It's critical that *zanatany* was not simply a genealogical identification, but also a signifier of spatial transformation rooted in material and moral practices. *Zanatany* was inherently about emplacement, about "the soil" and rooting oneself in situ through the transformation of that site, rather than the sheer possession of land.

By assembling stories of house-building, zanatany children made connections across genealogical expanses. Houses have served as memory devices, as evidence of the moral righteousness of their inhabitants, and as testimonies to the strenuous labor, collective solidarity, and fierce determination of zanatany ancestors. Within zanatany families, durable houses were expressions of hopeful anticipation of the progeny yet to come, and critical vessels through which kin continuity stretched across generational and temporal bounds. Generations of children and grandchildren regenerated these houses materially, infusing and interning them with the bodily substances of the dead, the young, and the just-born. Layering and laminating new deposits was not only a way to link generations, but also a form of affirming the moral norms by which zanatany distinguished themselves and their ancestors from their neighbors and adversaries. In building homes, Comorian-Malagasy families sought to laminate over the past, enunciate their visions for an anticipated future, and proclaim themselves as zana-tany in recognition of the more-than-human world. Yet, in the decades to come, these transformative acts would incite contestation and disputes among newer waves of migrants about their legitimacy—revealing that even hardened claims can crumble.

Violent Remnants

Infrastructures of Possibility and Peril

On an oppressively humid afternoon in October 2013, Alain opened a figurative door and guided me through the stakes of living with colonial-era infrastructural remnants. A resident of Mahajanga in his early fifties and married with three children, Alain spoke with me many times before and after that day. He was short, agile, and quick with a smile. A skilled electrician, he had helped our family with some irksome electrical wiring problems in our home over the span of several months. I wanted to learn more about his migration journey from Mandritsara and his experiences of daily life in the city since he had settled in Mahajanga in the early 1980s. He agreed, and that afternoon, on our verandah, he recounted how he had been born in Mandritsara, north of Mahajanga, into a comfortable family, well-supported by his father's position as a schoolteacher and his mother's access to land. Our conversation moved fluidly as he recalled how he migrated to Mahajanga in his early twenties and quickly secured work at SOTEMA (Société Textile de Majunga), the massive cloth manufacturer, after easily passing a test as a mechanic. He worked there until 1998, when the factory closed. In the years that followed, he'd worked intermittently at the French School, as a guard for a *vazaha* woman, and as an electrician and handyman.[1]

But when I asked him more generally about the historical linkages between kinds of work and kinds of people (*karazañolo*) in the city, his tone shifted entirely. He told me that in the past Tandroy and Betsirebaka worked as *pousse-pousse* (rickshaw) drivers. "It was Comorians who did the work of cleaning the city," he said slowly. "Comorians did most of the filthy work (*asa maloto*) of emptying the latrines (*visy*)."[2] They usually worked at night, he explained, because "perhaps they were ashamed (*mety menatra*)." "Who does this work now?" I asked gently.

Suddenly, Alain grew silent. After some moments, he began sobbing. He confessed that in recent years he had been obliged to clean his family's latrine; there was no other choice because of the family's poverty, and this brought him deep shame (*menatra, fahamenarana*). The profundity of Alain's expression of sorrow hung in the hot, thick air, seemingly beyond words. I sat helplessly with him, filled with regret for ignorantly probing into such a sensitive spot. At the same time, I was grateful that Alain had revealed to me the fraught relationship between personhood, waste matter, and infrastructure. He exposed the far-reaching affective experiences of sanitation work in the city. The labor of emptying the sewage pit was loaded and layered, and it frayed Alain's fundamental sense of what it meant to be a proud, dignified human.

If Alain's maintenance of his family's latrine was a "material vital doing" for his family, and a distasteful, though ethically laden, obligation, then it was also tightly tied to experiences of harm and susceptibility.[3] Informed by historical, hierarchical ideas of the kinds of people and kinds of work in the northwest region, Alain had not thought of himself as someone who would clean the pit of overflowing waste, and doing so challenged his underlying sense of himself as a person of respectable standing. Alain's infrastructural labor exposed him to affective experiences of shame and constrained his anticipations of prosperity in the immediate present, but it was entwined in a thorny history of colonial infrastructure that repeatedly instantiated violence and dispossession, laying burdens of infrastructural labor on some but not others. Alain's story emerges from a deeper history of colonial space and infrastructural design, and it complicates assumptions about urban technological systems in the African past and present.

This chapter attends to the material configuration of waste and water systems to parse out the multiple logics, constraints, and affordances that generated these systems over the city's longue durée. Here, I track the *peopling of infrastructure*—the process by which human beings became entangled with infrastructural forms in Mahajanga's past. I diverge from urban studies and infrastructures scholarship focused on citizenship and "rights to the city," differential access to services and goods, and the symbolic and imaginary dimensions of infrastructure.[4] An ever growing body of work emphasizes the *immaterial*, creative interventions of urban dwellers who improvise in the absence or perpetual breakdown of infrastructure—crystalized in the concept of "people as infrastructure."[5] This literature has helped challenge developmentalist assumptions, but it has not yet addressed the material implications of built forms and infrastructures in specific historical contexts.[6] Building on a growing body of vibrant work that documents the politics of urban infrastructural labor, waste systems, and urban belonging, I head in a different direction—focusing the aperture on *who* exactly "becomes infrastructure" and who does not.[7] If we understand people's relationships with infrastructure to be imbricated in uneven sociopolitical landscapes, when and under what conditions do people become more or less infrastructurally engaged? For those like Alain, what are the consequences of these infrastructural engagements—whether through labor, use, adaptation, or destruction?

As elsewhere in Africa, colonial engineers in Mahajanga inscribed normative assumptions about labor—availability of workers, forms of acceptable work, and appropriate human–technology interactions—into the physical makeup and morphological layout of the city's waste and water systems.[8] Within the constraints of colonial rule, many city residents refused sanitation work as degrading to bodily, communal, and cosmological integrity. But others were obliged to take part. Human workers, however, were not the only vexatious agents enrolled in water and waste systems. There was also bodily waste, animal discharge, rainwater, soil, and debris—in short, the mundane substances so central to the rationale for these systems. Water and waste systems registered colonial assumptions about earthly compliance— about the ostensibly predictable behavior of the matter that they were to contain and move along. French colonial engineers tried in vain to construct two discrete systems, one for water provision and the other for waste deposition. Yet the physical dynamics of the matters integral to these systems (urine, excrement, sandy soil, rainwater) stymied their efforts to construct and regulate the boundaries between water and waste. Earthly and corporeal substances coagulated, stagnated, and accumulated in household stone-lined pit latrines. In the wet season, waste mixed with rainfall and drained into groundwater. When pits could not contain the oozing urine and excrement, the waste leached into the sandy soils, overflowed onto streets and paths during the rainy seasons, and contaminated the aquifer in unanticipated ways.

This chapter takes a diachronic approach to water and waste systems in Mahajanga, from the earliest times to present day, and focuses on one of these systems—waste removal—through photographs, archival records, ethnographic observation, and oral recollections to understand the peopling of the city's material infrastructure and the ways this infrastructure was articulated through bodies and earth. I contend that French colonial sanitation infrastructural design enacted enduring forms of violence and exploitation, in large part through requisite labor regimes. Once emplaced, colonial technologies—including water pumps, communal standpipes, and bucket and cesspool latrines—exerted their own force on the social and physical landscape through their durability and layout, leaving little room for radical modification in the decades to come. Sanitation workers have, over the past century, been entangled in worrisome ways with these colonial-era technological materials. Infrastructural repair at times expressed affective ties to kin and even afforded some expanded possibilities for acquiring political and economic capital; at other times, it eroded senses of personhood. Over time, sewage laborers have employed a range of techniques—ancestral rituals, ablutions, silence, and distancing—to mediate harm. They have strategized to avoid becoming marked as wasted, shameful people (*olo ratsy*) and to manage their embeddedness in uneven, ongoing structural violence. But critical here is the materiality of human waste. Workers negotiated harm and their sense of their own humanness, partly because of the excrement's viscosity, stickiness, and residuality—it clings metaphorically (and literally) to human bodies and invites forms of governance and sociality that "treat people as residual."[9]

Human wastes—like other kinds of residues—are "transgressive."[10] In a landscape of cesspools, pit latrines, and sandy soil, they permeate and spill across boundaries, going places they don't belong and re-entering human and animal bodies and aquifers with disastrous consequences.[11] Colonial sanitation technologies were designed to manage human waste as a singular substance, but once released, excrement and urine interacted with soil and water—and collectively triggered indeterminate processes that unfolded slowly over time.[12] Throughout the twentieth and twenty-first centuries, Mahajanga bore witness to outbreaks of cholera and dysentery, contaminated freshwater sources, and polluted oceanic waterways. Bodily and earthly vessels, channels, and cleavages were critical sites for the displacement and accrual of water and waste. The unruliness of human waste matter as it travels along inserted technologies and mixes with earth, water, and living beings demands that we attend to forms of technopolitical violence that unfold through long-term earthly, bodily, and material interactions. Bodily and earthly matters complicated colonial aspirations for architectural governance and continue to present unforeseen challenges to postindependence city administrators and urban inhabitants alike.

Preserving Life in Early Mahajanga

Bits and fragments of evidence tell us little about how early inhabitants of the city secured freshwater and managed human waste. Muslim settlers likely selected Mahajanga not only for its favorable natural port, but also for its proximity to freshwater. Early written accounts from British slaving ships mention the availability of freshwater but do not indicate the locations of sources.[13] References to human waste removal are even more scarce. One European visitor in the nineteenth century described the town as "unwholesomely dirty," owing to the pervasive stench of rotting offal from the city's thriving cattle trade.[14] Others, by contrast, described the city's thoroughfares as "sandy and generally clean."[15] No descriptions or archaeological traces relating to human waste have been found to date. It may be that city dwellers in early Mahajanga had relatively sound practices for disposing of waste out of sight. The town's 2 kilometer (1 mile-long) stretch along the seaside, coupled with its population of five thousand to six thousand at the turn of the twentieth century, afforded a separation between domestic dwellings and human waste.[16] Overgrown areas in the nearby hills and mangrove forests would have provided ideal sites to deposit human excrement, where it would decompose relatively quickly or be consumed by scavenging animals.

Nevertheless, sometime in the late eighteenth or early nineteenth century, city inhabitants harnessed the flow of a natural spring by building a fountain. In the early 1840s, the French commercial agent Charles Guillain noted that the natural spring was located some "200 steps" from the edge of the hilltop fort (rova), on the northwestern side of town.[17] The built fountain was an engineering feat in which designers sculpted the topographical contours to construct a water collection and channeling system, adorned by the flora offerings of the landscape. It revealed designers' understandings of hydrological flow, of the behavior and temperament of the spring, and of the capacity of constructed materials to alter the water's directionality. Amalgamating limestone, wood, and palm fronds, early designers and builders of the reservoir and fountain turned nature into infrastructure.[18]

Channeling the earth's fresh waters enabled the provision of nourishment and thus the social reproduction of early town dwellers, for whom the fountain served as a site for water collection, bathing, and ritual washing. People of "different sexes, ages, and clothing" frequented the fountain, coming from a variety of ethnolinguistic and economic levels, to engage in conversation, gossip, and suggestive intimations.[19] Given the city's Islamic presence, the fountain was also an enduring purification site where, Guillain observed, "the believers [Muslims] came to cleanse themselves."[20] By the time of Guillain's visit from August 1842 to January 1843, the water source apparently replenished both the highland soldiers housed at the garrison and the inhabitants of peripheral villages. It served as the primary source of water, as the city did not yet have wells, and there was only one cistern for storing water located at the military fort.[21] Water was at times scarce—or at least arduous to obtain—for ships seeking refreshment. European seafarers had long remarked that although the hinterlands were abundant in springs and streams, the "principal defect" of this "magnificent harbor" was the lack of potable water.[22] Arriving vessels would drop anchor to the southwest of the city, where they would find "excellent drinking water," in contrast to the brackish water at the seaside urban settlement.[23]

Beyond survival, water was incorporated into Islamic-inflected practices of daily ablutions and bathing, and it served as a critical purifying substance in rituals central to social reproduction for Malagasy of various backgrounds. Throughout Madagascar, elders have performed *tsodrano* (blowing of water)—taking a small amount of water in the mouth and blowing it on or toward a person to reconstitute kinship ties and as a benediction at lifecycle events, such as circumcisions and weddings.[24] Ritual bathing of ancestral relics in northwest Madagascar have historically featured cleansing with water and honey-filled jugs (*sajoa*), and sacred Sakalava funerary sculptures (*aloalo*) depicted women head-loading sajoa in evocations of ancestral blessings for prosperity.[25] Not all water, however, was the same. Certain bodies of water, such as select rivers and lakes throughout the northwest region, held sacred properties anchored in the presence of water-deities known as *vazimba*, who demanded adherence to ancestrally prescribed prohibitions.[26] Near the Ankarafantsika forest and the Tsiribihina River basin, for instance, Sakalava royalty derived their authority through their connection to vazimba spirits, facilitated through entombment in the river. These acts of burial for the dead of royal Sakalava descent, who were set afloat in dug-out canoes, served to reconstitute them as *tompon-drano* (masters of water).[27] Throughout the northwest region, Sakalava political followers historically disposed of the liquids deriving from bodily decomposition of the royal dead into sacred lakes or the sea (*rano masina*).[28] Water in these contexts was understood to have an agentive property—to transform the mundane into exceptional and the dead into vibrant ancestors who reified the authority of living Sakalava monarchs.

Mahajanga's emergent water system was organized around nested containers, which enabled the movement of water from the fountain to the

FIGURE 6.1 "Mabibo [Mahabibo] Manufacturers of Pottery," ca. 1900.
Courtesy of Archives départementales de la Réunion.

seaside.[29] Late nineteenth-century accounts noted the thriving artisanal industry of pottery production by both Malagasy and Indian migrants (for the latter, see figure 6.1). Indian migrants brought new techniques of pottery construction and were key producers of the clay jugs and containers that town inhabitants used for daily water transportation and storage. Yet these jugs were only the primary containers in a broader system. Although jugs allowed families to construct households far from the freshwater spring, in-home standing barrels enabled households to store water over longer periods of time and manage the temporality of household labor. By the late 1880s, wells were added to this system and became increasingly omnipresent (see figure 6.2).[30] "There are more than a hundred in the city or in its immediate vicinity," one military officer observed in 1895. "Every Indian or Arab house has one. There are others dug in the middle of the streets."[31] Sources do not reveal the norms that governed use of the wells, or how the presence of "household wells" intersected with competing conceptions of property that circulated at the turn of the century. But it is evident that containers allowed people to maneuver the inconstancy

FIGURE 6.2 "At the well, an Antalaotra and two small Makoises," Mahajanga, ca. 1886–89. Courtesy of Archives du Ministère de l'Europe et des Affaires étrangères—La Courneuve, Série P-Afrique, A009190. Photographer: Albert Pinard.

of freshwater flow, terraform the city's emergent spaces, and move across geographical scales in the town's earliest days.

Water carriers were at the heart of this water system. Because the work was so fundamental to household activities, a wide range of people would have assisted with water provisioning. Some accounts from the mid-nineteenth century suggest that children, especially young girls, and women hauled or head-loaded sajoa filled with water from streams to homes in Mahajanga and the hinterlands (see figures 6.2, 6.3, and 6.4).[32] This was certainly the case elsewhere in Madagascar. In southern Madagascar, girls undertook the majority of water-carrying work, at times refashioning toil into diversion, infusing it with playfulness—"singing and splashing in the stream."[33] Yet, by the late nineteenth century, Makoa women and eventually men were gradually enrolled, first as unfree and then as emancipated laborers, into hierarchies of care-labor that provided water to households. Makoa women were said to take up the work of "drawing water," among other odd jobs (including making mats, carrying stones, and serving as nurses and cooks), through which they could provide for their families.[34]

FIGURE 6.3
Women
returning from
the "tap with
freshwater in
their sajoas,"
Mahajanga,
ca. 1886–89.
Courtesy of
Archives du
Ministère de
l'Europe et
des Affaires
étrangères—
La Courneuve,
Série P-Afrique,
A009244.
Photographer:
Albert Pinard.

By the late nineteenth century, water hauling and waste labor shifted to young boys and adult men in Mahajanga. Some late nineteenth-century observers described "small Sakalava boys at the service of [French] officers" who would have been responsible for drawing water for military officials among their other domestic duties.[35] Makoa men were also observed drawing water from wells in town (figure 6.5).[36] By the turn of the century, the *paid* work of water hauling was reshaped into a masculine enterprise, and over time the gradual transformation of water carrying into masculine, wage-earning work was marked by the Malagasy word *rano-dahy* (water man).[37] Unpaid work of hauling water for households in Mahajanga was not necessarily gendered, but was rather organized generationally, in which junior household members had primary responsibility.[38] Overall, the historical role of Makoa in these assemblages of toiling care-work to collect and haul

FIGURE 6.4
"Woman from
Comores,
Madagascar,"
1908. Courtesy
of Société de
Géographie, SG
WE-289.

water—thus nurturing everyday life in the city—reveals how water provision was deeply inscribed by histories of collective violence and displacement associated with the slave trade from the city's early times.

Waterscapes: Crocodiles, Wells, and Subterranean Veins of Life

Water—its appraisal, consumption, and storage—were at the heart of France's conquest of Madagascar, akin to "hydroimperialism" elsewhere on the continent.[39] With the exception of one freshwater source in the southwest

FIGURE 6.5
"Makois
[Makoa]
water carrier,"
Mahajanga,
ca. 1886–89.
Courtesy of
Archives du
Ministère de
l'Europe et
des Affaires
étrangères—
La Courneuve,
Série P-Afrique,
A009191.
Photographer:
Albert Pinard.

part of town, and despite the town's location at the mouth of the Betsiboka River, French soldiers complained about the quality of water for consumption.[40] Despite the city's matrixed water provision system—visible in the containers and laborers that maintained it—French colonial administrators unsurprisingly did not classify it as a viable, veritable system. They noted the presence of human water carriers and wells, but, if anything, these impressions informed broader mythologizing about African technological lack; in the estimation of the French, a water system was defined by the presence of pipes and canals, spigots and pumps, in other words by *thing-conduits* (not people or nonhuman animals) that moved water. European colonizers arrogantly invoked "industrial inferiority" as a central tenet for affixing new technological things that collectively exploited the very labor regimes they critiqued.[41] Colonial administrators' failure to grasp Mahajanga's water system as a *system* was also rooted in a particular "regime of perceptibility" informed not only by engineers' available grammars and conceptual understandings of networked conduits for water provision, but also by racialized tropes of African technological incapacitation.[42]

Appraisals of Mahajanga's hydrological terrain in the 1890s were shaped as much by the violent establishment of rule as by French imaginaries of subterranean worlds. As part of broader efforts to apprehend the island as a singular territory under Gouverneur Général Gallieni's pacification campaign, colonial hydrographers surveyed the rivers and tributaries of the northwest coast between 1885 and 1895. Drawing on local knowledge of water sources—which were later effaced in colonial reports—hydrologists sketched the boundaries of the watersheds of the main rivers and the paths of watercourses.[43] These regional and island-wide geographical reports, however, were less helpful to the on-the-ground military technocrats charged with appraising the freshwater sources to supply a growing settler population and laboring pool. French city planners relied on the work of explorers who had, in years preceding the 1896 military conquest, charted some significant contours of Mahajanga's subterranean water field. Military planners working in the early 1900s drew from limited topographical studies that the Navy's hydrographic service carried out in 1892, and from Malagasy knowledge about where the freshwater sources appeared in the town and surrounds.[44] Mahajanga's position at the mouth of the Betsiboka River estuary meant that the underground hydrological network was extensive; yet although those who already lived there could likely locate and access precise nodes of freshwater supply, military officials struggled to do so.

Within a few years of the 1896 military invasion, officials charted the aquifer system, understood it as an arterial nexus, and identified one promising freshwater source at Ambobokekely and another at Ambobokabe, both some 5 kilometers (3 miles) from the town.[45] Hydrogeologists were astounded, moreover, to discover that the various freshwater sources in the city "seemed to be in solidarity" and drew from a "single water table."[46] The realization of the aquifer's profound connectivity, manifest in the knitted tangles of the fluvial furrows underfoot, did not appear to radically shape officials' plans for the city's water infrastructure. The public works records lack any mention of the ubiquitous household wells or individual well-digging entrepreneurs, nor of how their efforts to draw water could affect the supply of water through the city's well. Administrators seemed hardly concerned that the growth and demand of Mahabibo residents might eventually constrain flow in the European-dominated quarter of Old Majunga. Once tapped, the fluvial vein seemed to flow endlessly.

Appraising an ideal water source was entangled with colonial visions of the urban body politic—and contingent upon concurrent acts of calculation by racist metrics. Using measurements of water volume and flow, hydrogeologists calculated the hydrological needs of the small communities of "French," "other Europeans," "Creoles and Mauritians," and "Asians."[47] With this population hovering around 1,777, and an additional 1,000 or so troops and hospital employees, they surmised that the source of Ambobokabe would amply support the city's population with a yield of 13 liters (3 gallons) per second, or 100 liters (26 gallons) per day/person, for a population of 10,000.[48] As an afterthought, city administrators mentioned that there was also the "indigene" population of some 2,181 in Mahabibo (the city's native reserve), as well as at least 4,500 families in the villages in the city's hinterlands—but neither of these groups was imagined as fully deserving consumers of the envisioned water system. In French and British colonial cities, water infrastructure was, from its earliest design and implementation, unevenly and disproportionately allocated to key sites and neighborhoods largely inhabited by Europeans, assimilées, and South Asian families.[49] Mahajanga was no exception. Many homes in Old Majunga and other European-dominated neighborhoods were equipped with water taps and household latrines. Also prioritized for the installation of a pump and fountain was the city's abattoir, which was supplied by an "abundant well" and from which the wastewater washed into the swampy area near the indigenous neighborhoods in and around Mahabibo.[50] In other Malagasy cities, the arrival of the plague precipitated the installation of water piping and the expansion of access, but this was not the case in Mahajanga.[51] Despite the devastating plague outbreak in 1902 (discussed in chapter 3), city administrators instead prioritized the construction of paved roads, gutters and drain ditches, a large dike, and a fortified port.[52] Owing to these "improvements," officials in the region gloated that Mahajanga would soon "hold the record of rapid sanitation" among the urban centers of the colony.[53]

Following the devastating fire that decimated most of the homes in Mahabibo in 1912, the city's Commission of Hygiene began to prioritize water access in Mahabibo. Although residents had kept containers of water in their household compounds, these reserves were hardly sufficient to quench the flames that consumed the quarter. Certain that there would be more fires in the future—owing to the dry and windy conditions; flammable, thatch homes; and courtyard cooking fires—administrators turned to water pumps as a solution, allotting 10,000 francs for the project. Rather than installing household spigots, though, water distribution in Mahabibo was organized around a limited number of shared water pumps (*bornes fontaines*), on which hundreds of families relied.[54] With Mahabibo's population estimated at 5,700 in 1912 and continuing to grow, this system, organized around a few centers of distribution, was far less extensive than the individual household taps found in Old Majunga.[55] Such a configuration necessarily meant that, in the absence of pipes and household taps, French officials would require water porters to transport water to individual households, ensuring the stability not only of everyday life but also of colonial rule.

Enclaves and Enclosures: The Racial Politics of Water

In the decades to come, racist metrics undergirded colonial plans for allocating water across the city as well as designs for leisure facilities. One afternoon in January 1939, a group of city administrators gathered in the town hall in Mahajanga and deliberated the future of the city. They fretted over the many unfinished projects ahead: the digging of gutters, land reclamation of the swampy outlying areas, new construction of a municipal stadium, and improvement of the city's pool. The city's economic position was increasingly austere. The city council owed some three million francs to the colony's central administration, the Chef de la Colonie, for public works projects completed or underway, and the upcoming projects would cost "several millions" more.[56] The council could not imagine asking for the needed amount, and instead determined to ask for a small advance of 500,000 francs for a prioritized project or two. Councilman Orsini suggested that the gutter construction and land reclamation ought to take precedence, in light of their ability to improve "the hygiene of the city." But his fellow council members disagreed. In the end, they voted to fund the reconstruction of the pool and stadium—two key leisure sites emplaced in the predominantly European sections of town.[57]

The city council's dedication of municipal funds to the rebuilding of the swimming pool was informed by circulating ideas about "modernizing" colonial cities for the exclusive pleasure of European settlers. Contemporary swimming pools, along with other leisure facilities, were critical interventions through which city planners in colonial African cities could transform colonial towns into modern cityscapes and cultivate new spaces of affluence, while further enforcing racial hierarchies.[58] In the early 1930s, Europeans in Mahajanga had advocated for council members to implement much-needed "modern improvements" (*aménagement moderne*), including

FIGURE 6.6 Postcard, "Public Water Pump," ca. 1940s. Author's collection.

expanded water and electricity services, updated buildings and roads, and the planting of trees and gardens.[59] A swimming pool was seen as integral to this modernization program; proponents proclaimed it would stand as city's "most beautiful ornament" and assure Mahajanga's prosperity as a European tourist destination.[60] When the pool was finally constructed in La Corniche in 1932, an upscale seaside neighborhood, European town residents were delighted with it.[61]

Set in juxtaposition to one another, two anonymously authored postcard images reveal some insights about the valuations of space and bodies in the hydroscapes of the colonial-era city. Even if postcard images were (and still are) "capitalist commodities" steeped in violent relationships of power and appropriation, they offer hints about the imaginaries around colonial infrastructures.[62] In the first image (figure 6.6), from around the 1940s, young Malagasy men with pressed tin buckets gather around the water pump, seemingly at ease. Some are leaving, and one man toils on the side. The cement base for the standpipe appears rough, corroded by sunshine, wear, and dripping water. This image foregrounds the work dimension of the water system. Water is clearly a commodity, and it cannot be disseminated across the city without those who work to fill buckets and haul water to homes beyond the image's frame. The standpipe is erect, stationary, and reliant on people to extract water from its internal channels. This was

FIGURE 6.7 Postcard, "La Piscine," Mahajanga, ca. early 1950s. Author's collection.

conceivably a site of vibrant sociality, a place for exchanges of gossip and news, and later for fomenting anticolonial sentiments and actions.

In images of La Piscine (like figure 6.7), from the early 1950s, people are diminutive in relation to the gigantic pool. Some images show women perched on the pool deck, while small children splash in the cordoned, shallow section. All figures appear to be white Europeans. Dozens of changing rooms and toilets line the upper level. Constructed of cement at the sea's edge, the pool appears astoundingly enormous in depth and breadth—even by present-day standards.[63] Perhaps an early experiment in brutalist architectural style, the pool's impervious walls suggest a tidy, certain barrier from the irritations and disparities of everyday colonial life. The patchy archival record gives little information about the nuanced, social world of the pool as a site of bodily performance, intimacy, and regulation. But the thick, cool walls of the pool surely served to demarcate an exclusionary site of European life and to produce racial and social difference in the midst of the "indigene" society.

The sheer mass of water accumulated at La Piscine was not only a testament to the promise of architectural engineering in this colonial "backwater," but also a reflection of hydrological disparities writ large. At the time that civic administrators were channeling water into the behemoth pool for European pleasure, Malagasy and Comorian inhabitants around the city were contesting the scarcity of access to freshwater.[64] By 1941, city officials clamped down on nighttime "illicit acquisition" by removing existing standpipes and monitoring public usage.[65] This triggered an uproar from a city populace disgruntled with the constraints of water provision and increasingly determined to demand recognition from the colonial state. In Abattoir, one of the most densely populated quarters, families were particularly vociferous about the elimination of three of the four existing water pumps. They framed their dispute in terms of survival and calculation, pointing out that they were forced to choose between cooking water and personal cleanliness on a daily basis.[66] Colonial officials were eventually pressured into reinstating communal water taps throughout the Malagasy neighborhoods. But this logic of organizing public works systems around central nodes persisted, and communal, (now) commodified standpipes remain today the most prevalent form of water provision in the city. Yet the fundamental conception of a bounded water system, contained in pipes and pumps, remained ever elusive—entangled as it was in a porous and populated landscape.

Wastescapes: Pits, Buckets, and "Infectious Odors"

Colonial officials sought to ensure the health and contentment of the small, growing colonial settler population by refashioning the landscape into a more healthful place, a project predicated on an "imagined hygienic modernity" defined by a germ-free landscape of linear structures and impermeable surfaces such as paved roads, cement latrines, and metal waterpipes.[67] Colonial officials initiated a broad sanitation intervention over several years, encompassing the construction of canals, water standpipes, wells, public hospitals, and latrines. Organizing infrastructure around concentrated centers was the fundamental logic undergirding French colonial interventions into sanitation. Bringing their own conceptions of waste and their criteria for appropriate technologies, colonial authorities employed reasoning that diverged dramatically from local perceptions around managing filth. Town dwellers, especially those of Sakalava descent who influenced the everyday norms in the city, historically observed strict prohibitions against contact with and proximity to human waste.[68] These practices reflected a long-standing awareness of the potentially harmful effects of contact with human waste. And in the dispersed early landscape of Mahajanga, inhabitants could easily deposit human waste far from the city center without encountering problems.[69] But French colonial officials strove to bring excremental (and hydrological) matters under the domain of governmental purview, drawing defecation from "the open air" (*à l'air libre*) into confined, contained sites: latrines.

Unlike the French architects and urban designers who regarded the colony as a "terrain for working out solutions" to sociopolitical and aesthetic problems in the metropole, urban planners in Mahajanga were strikingly conventional—even unimaginative—in their approach to sanitation.[70] In surveying appropriate forms of sanitation infrastructure for the city, colonial officials applied contemporaneous norms of equipment in France. Following conventional practice in early-twentieth-century France, authorities in Mahajanga configured sanitation as a decentralized system based on individual, disconnected latrines constructed in two variations. Some latrines were conjointly built with a cesspool, essentially a dugout hole in the earth lined with rocks. Others were constructed with a moveable bucket system (*tinettes mobiles*), which consisted of a steel bucket placed atop or inside a concrete or wood platform. Both systems had drawbacks. In the former system, excrement could overflow into the topsoil or surface during heavy rains. But the latter system was labor intensive, requiring laborers to empty heaping buckets.

It should come as no surprise that French military and colonial authorities did not initially consider the construction of a city-wide, centralized sewage system in Mahajanga, consisting of underground sewers, pipes, and linkages. Human waste collection in European and American cities predominantly used the privy vault–cesspool system until almost the turn of the century.[71] In 1894, on the cusp of France's invasion into Madagascar, the French parliament approved the Paris city council's plan for an all-inclusive sewer (*tout-à-l'égout*), which would drain rainwater, street debris, and human waste.[72] Although some limited sewage piping was constructed in the capital city of Antananarivo, most fecal matter was deposited in cesspools.[73] But across the island, moveable bucket latrines were generally prescribed for colonial subjects and French authorities alike.[74] In this way, Mahajanga's sanitation configuration was similar to that of other provincial cities in France, as well as to those in other colonial cities in Madagascar in the early 1900s.

This network of latrines, rooted in a logic of containment and concentration of filth, ran counter to existing Malagasy practices of waste management. Quite soon after the construction of latrines in Mahajanga, French colonizers encountered unanticipated public responses. The movable buckets posed problems. People dumped the foul contents of heaping receptacles in undesignated places, despite surveillance. Although some officials reported the public latrines "are cleaned every morning and function well," others asserted the latrines were perpetually left in a "generally filthy state" despite multiple cleanings each day.[75] More troublesome was ruination, which officials perceived as vandalism, of the pit toilets. French authorities were dismayed to find that locals threw stones into the pit, which clogged the dugout cavity and risked waste overflowing onto the street.[76] The system's design, furthermore, lent itself to spillage and infiltration into the soil and eventually the aquifer.[77] The leaky design of the city's waste removal system troubled colonial efforts to create an encapsulated system for water provision, one that would be impervious to contaminants of human waste. And the viscosity, fluidity, and porousness of bodily and earthly matters undermined the very concept of waste removal and water networks as two *separate* systems that could be independently regulated, monitored, and controlled.

Early efforts to legally mandate households to construct in-home latrines hardly ameliorated colonial concerns about seeping flows of excrement. Municipal acts passed in 1913 and 1926 pertained only to the European-dominated sections of town, and officials relied on existing public latrines in Mahabibo, by then a fast-growing neighborhood of Malagasy, Comorians, and East Africans.[78] Public latrines were problematic, however, for many town dwellers for whom defecation "in place" translated to attacks on individual and collective well-being.[79] The need to manually discard the waste in the buckets denigrated long-held ideas about proper relationships between people and waste matter, the living and the ancestors. Objections to situating a polluting latrine near places of rest, cooking, and leisure stymied administrative efforts in the 1930s to enforce household latrine construction in Mahabibo. As one elderly city resident described in recollecting perceptions of earlier generations, most town residents initially perceived household latrines as a *vazaha* practice.[80] Building a small solid structure dedicated to toileting was considered bizarre (*hafahafa*) because durable (*mafy*) materials were historically reserved for tombs and ancestral shrines throughout Madagascar.[81] At play were conflicting spatial approaches to sanitation. Whereas the French colonial latrine system relied on concentration of filth near one's most intimate domestic dwelling, Malagasy practices hinged on dispersal (and avoidance) of excrement in surrounding uninhabited areas—far from sacred, lived spaces.

Despite past practice, however, more and more households in Mahabibo built latrines in the 1910s and 1920s. Archival sources are not explicit about how or why some groups incorporated latrines while others did not. But it is evident that by the late 1930s so many households in Mahabibo had constructed cesspools that officials attributed blame to these "poorly constructed" vessels for the spread of malaria in 1937.[82] They also blamed the insufficient amount of stormwater drains and the administration's still-unrealized project of paving over marshlands for the massive water pooling that attracted mosquito larvae. Finally, they concluded that the passageway recently constructed across the marshy southern area of town, named Digue Metzinger for a French general who led the conquest of Madagascar, prevented stormwater from draining from higher gradations. As with other cities worldwide, it is likely that the introduction of piped water, without a concurrent system to dispose of water refuse, played a major role in the pooling and flooding that plagued the city's low-lying areas in the mid-twentieth century.[83] Knowing little of the behavior of water and soil in Mahajanga's landscape—the temporal metrics of drainage, flows, and rainfall—colonial authorities built forms that failed to keep pace with patterns of inundation and drought. Unfamiliar with local climatic conditions and topographical variations, and subject to increasingly constrained budgets, French planners struggled, and largely failed, to engineer the city into an ecological homeostasis.

Labor Regimes and Infrastructural Engagement

By the mid-twentieth century, Mahajanga's sewage system—which persists into contemporary times—could best be characterized as an *anti-infrastructure*, or an infrastructure that does not afford the *movement* of human waste. Unlike sewage systems elsewhere, there were—and in fact still today are—no pipes, taps, or plants linking toilets or households to one another.[84] In a system like the one in Mahajanga, human sludge doesn't flow, but rather accumulates and creates other problems. Excrement stays put in the ground, mostly contained in underground holes and vats, but leaching slowly into the soil over time. Blockage and stasis have historically been the perpetual state of affairs. Mahajanga's sanitation system diverges from the now-classical definition of infrastructure as that which "enables the movement of other matter."[85]

If Mahajanga's sewage system challenges conceptions of infrastructure hinging on transmission, it also suggests a host of questions about the kinds of relationships such a material configuration affords. Mahajanga's sewage infrastructure, once idealized by colonial authorities as a harbinger of modernity, soon became a site of unfolding cycles of decrepitude, conservation, reconstruction, and upkeep. It has continually broken down, owing to the competing temporalities of its material composition. In the city today, sewage pits constructed of concrete, stone, and mud erode with time, accrue waste, and flood in the rainy seasons. The lifespans of these materials (and thus the system) took on new meaning with the human acts of restoration and reworking. And attuning to these moments of repair can offer us a deeper understanding of the creative, resourceful ways "stability is maintained . . . rich and robust lives sustained against the weight of centrifugal odds."[86] This brings our story to those historical agents who kept things going in the mid- to late twentieth century: prison laborers, wage-earning sanitation laborers, and ordinary inhabitants.

The sanitation and water provision systems French urban planners introduced to Madagascar were predicated on assumptions about the availability of laborers (to build infrastructural forms and keep things functioning), the value of wage labor, and the capacity of human bodies to endure certain forms of work. As with other building and infrastructure projects (described in chapter 3), a perpetual dearth of voluntary laborers obstructed these plans. Those who followed the Sakalava polity saw wage labor as akin to enslavement and were loath to undertake waged work for French infrastructural projects.[87] Indian traders generated income through commercial businesses and thus had little need to do manual labor for the French. Few archival traces remain about who constructed the public latrines, but at the time French colonial authorities were highly dependent on prison laborers, while also recruiting migrant laborers from Comoros, China, and the Kutch and Punjabi regions of India.[88] The first constructed latrines—utilizing the moveable bucket system—were built in Mahajanga in the 1910s, near public spaces such as the main marketplace and the slaughterhouse.[89]

After the initial construction of latrines, French authorities found few manual laborers willing to empty, transport, and dispose of steel vats of human waste from the congested areas of the city. Prisoners fulfilled the demand for workers prior to the 1950s.[90] As households constructed their own latrines, often by digging a catchment hole into which they inserted a steel drum (*bidon*), prison laborers were also called upon to empty those. A married couple in their sixties, long-time residents, recalled that "prisoners (*gadra*) would come at night because they were ashamed, and they carried the barrels of feces suspended between long poles of wood. If you dared to tease them, they would dump the waste on your doorstep!"[91] While the rebellious throwing of feces may have been a subaltern tactic in the face of deeply humiliating labor, others described the strategies prisoners employed to rid themselves of the stigmatized shame of their labor. Because handling excrement violated ancestral norms (*folaka razana*), some prisoners were obliged to purify themselves in the sea upon release from prison and before rejoining their families.[92] Those families with the means to slaughter a cow did so in order to appease ancestors angry about the exposure to filth and to ensure a more prosperous future.

Over the course of the first half of the twentieth century, however, French authorities sought alternative laborers to maintain the city's sanitation system. They found a solution in the growing migrant community from Comoros, especially in a small group of migrants from the archipelago—said to be those from the island of Nzwani. In oral interviews, long-time town dwellers maintained that Nzwani (also called Anjouans) were the only ones who dared (*mahasaky*) to undertake sanitation work as *m'tzaha maji* (those who take away excrement in Shikomoro) or *mpanary tay* (in Malagasy), cleaning latrines and emptying the moveable steel buckets. As one man in his sixties noted, "Anjouans would come at night, beginning at 10:00 p.m., and empty the barrels of shit" (see figure 6.8 for similar equipment used in Tamatave).[93] Although descendants of Anjouan migrants often cast these descriptions in valuated terms of virtuous work ethic, those of Ajojo backgrounds (from Ngazidja island) tended to frame their commentary around the demeaning aspects of sanitation maintenance. Mama Khalid (whose father was Ajojo) succinctly stated, "Anjouans mostly did this denigrating work. Ajojo refused."[94]

Anjouan sanitation workers apparently relied on Islamic washing practices to return to a neutral, or honorable, status after encountering filth—but some found their integrity questioned in the public eye. Echoing interpretations of capitalism elsewhere, some bystanders (especially those of Ajojo descent, who distinguished themselves from the Anjouan willing to work in sewage) observed a connection between the accrual of wealth through debased work and individual moral corruption.[95] One example involved Ahmed, a Comorian migrant from Nzwani (Anjouan) who was not formally educated, but who nonetheless managed to accrue considerable wealth as commander of Mahajanga's night soil brigade in the 1950s and '60s. Ahmed accumulated enough capital to construct several cement homes in town, in which his descendants now reside, and to send his children overseas to France and Mayotte to study. Known pejoratively as "Madi Tay" (boss of shit), Ahmed was remembered with disdain by those who alluded to the questionable legitimacy of his wealth involving filth. His position as a city

Edition de la Maison P. Ghigiasso, librairie, ameublement, - Tamatave

Tamatave - Le Service des Vidanges.

FIGURE 6.8 Postcard, "Sanitation workers," Tamatave, ca. 1910–20s.
Author's collection.

sanitation worker hovered literally and figuratively between the coveted
position of urban civil servants and the humiliated rank of prison laborer.

Another man of Comorian descent, Madi Sinoa, found political power
through sanitation oversight after retiring from captaining a seafaring vessel that traveled between Mahajanga and France in the 1950s and '60s. His
unusual path to fame began when a Malagasy man from the highlands approached his vessel, which was docked in Mahajanga, and pleaded with the
captain to keep him hidden onboard until the ship arrived in France. Madi
Sinoa agreed, bringing the man safely to France's shores. This man went on
to pursue advanced education in France and later returned to Madagascar,
where he attained a prestigious administrative post in the central government
under President Tsiranana (1960–1972). After Madi Sinoa's retirement from
seafaring, the highlander searched for and found Madi Sinoa, asking him
whether he remembered him. When Madi Sinoa couldn't recall, the man
explained their shared history and his debt of gratitude, and he appointed
Madi Sinoa as director of sanitation, where he was charged with the modernization of the city's sewage system. According to some long-term residents, Madi Sinoa worked energetically to transform the city's sanitation
away from the moveable steel-drum bucket system to one of septic tanks
(*fosse septic*). Although comprehensive success with this changeover was

apparently elusive, Madi Sinoa was named as an important figure in the material cleanliness of the city during the 1970s.[96]

Others entrepreneurs in sanitation work were not Anjouanais. In April 1937, Monsieur Antony Ah-Thon and his brother were, according to officials, "creole" private entrepreneurs granted permission by the city of Mahajanga to "engage in the work of sewage treatment" (*vidange*).[97] Although officials identified the Ah-Thons as "creole," their exact origins are murky—they may have been of Chinese-Malagasy descent or from the nearby Mascarene Islands. City residents recalled that Antony traveled from house to house, using a mechanical extractor designed for emptying pits of sewage. They fondly remembered him as a short guy (*madinika*) who arrived in his green truck, promptly pumped out the sewage, and left latrines clean and empty. After extracting the waste, the Ah-Thon brothers disposed of it in Ambondrona, a settlement on the outskirts of town where the University of Mahajanga currently stands.[98] The Ah-Thon brothers apparently proffered their services well into the 1960s.

There was some temporal overlap among prisoners, Comorians, and the Ah-Thon brothers from the 1940s to the 1960s, but most striking was that the Ah-Thons' work was not cast in the same demoralized terms used to describe the prisoners' and Comorian sanitation workers' labor of emptying latrine barrels. People often commented that Ah-Thon and his brother would work during the daytime because they weren't worried (*tsy vaky loha ireo*) about being watched. Perhaps this was because of the nature of Ah-Thon's infrastructural engagement, relying as it did on mechanical means to extract raw sewage. Although it's not clear whether the mechanical extractor elicited responses of awe or wonder among spectators, it surely altered the sensorial dimensions of sanitation work, with hoses and tanks that masked the revolting appearance and noxious odors of solid waste. In light of prohibitions on direct handling of excrement observed by those of Sakalava descent, the Ah-Thons' mechanical extraction admirably elongated the workers' proximity to filth and minimized bodily contact with abject matter. The use of machinery not only mitigated the moral stakes of sanitation labor, from the perspective many town residents, but also distinguished the Ah-Thons as adept, enterprising outsiders equipped with technologies of concealment. Through the mechanization of their work and abetted by their position as relative newcomers to the town, the Ah-Thon brothers were apparently untouched by the shame historically associated with sewage extraction.

Visibility and Vulnerability

Sometime in the 1970s, the mechanical sewage extractor machine broke. The Ah-Thon brothers left the city. More recent Malagasy migrants increasingly contested Comorians' presence in Mahajanga, notably those from the island's southeast, who, though from different backgrounds, were collectively known in the city as Betsirebaka.. French colonial authorities first recruited Betsirebaka men to work on tobacco and rice plantations in the northwest of Madagascar in the 1920s, and later in factories around Mahajanga.[99] In time they grew to a sizeable portion of the migrant population and worked certain manual-labor niche jobs such as rickshaw drivers, dockers, and guardians, thus occupying a marginalized position in the city's political economy.[100] By the early 1970s, the city began to experience the repercussions of the regional and global economic downturn. Following Madagascar's departure from the French franc zone in 1973, the island nation faced economic recession and decreasing wages.[101] Competition for wage work intensified, and many Betsirebaka found themselves closed out of industrial and manual-labor jobs in factories such as at FITIM (Filature et Tissage de Madagascar), which produced jute twine and sacks. Comorian migrants, who had long provided a steady workforce for companies in Mahajanga, historically held these jobs.[102] It was within this local and regional context of economic austerity that resentment among newer migrants toward those of mixed Comorian-Malagasy descent and those more recently from the archipelago, collectively lumped together as "Comorians," mounted, and eventually Comorians and Comorian-Malagasy were pushed out of these jobs.

During my fieldwork in 2011–2014, migrant laborers, some of whom residents identified as Betsirebaka, worked tirelessly in teams of two and three under the protection of night to empty latrines. In the absence of a mechanical sewage extractor, mpanary tay (those who discard excrement) or *mpangala tay* (those who take away excrement) manually removed the contents of pit toilets and septic tanks, using crowbars, shovels, buckets, and pitchers.[103] To conserve the existing cement or wood standing structure, as well as the septic tank or cesspool, workers sometimes dug a new hole in the household courtyard, where they deposited the retrieved waste. In cases of elevated latrines, they drilled a hole on the side of the sewage vat and filled buckets with sludge that spewed forth. Sometimes they disposed of the sludge in nearby canals or in the sea. Like the Anjouan before them, mpanary tay were drawn to the relatively high wages they could accumulate through waste work. They poured gasoline in and around the sewage pit in an attempt to mask the foul odors, and rubbed their bodies with petrol to prevent odors and sludge from sticking to their skin. Workers labored with little clothing, often just shorts or a *lambahoany* cloth wrapped at the waist, to avoid the permeation of noxious odors in their attire.

Residents who did not perform sanitation work at times criticized the state's failure to provide a system that would avoid such debasement of human beings (*tsy mikarakara ny fanzakana*); at other times they invoked a moral register to differentiate themselves from the migrants who would demean themselves to remove the filth of the city.[104] No one I spoke to directly referenced long-standing histories of distinctions between descendants of enslaved and free peoples in northwest Madagascar, but those histories remained in the background, coloring the hierarchies of labor and class. Many in the city definitely would have perceived cleaning latrines as akin to labors carried out by slaves, or as work that transforms one into a slave (*mampandevo*).[105] Although I met few people who would confess to cleaning their household's latrine, some noted that their landlord conducted the service to conserve funds. Even if a family could afford to pay laborers, finding willing workers could be troublesome. Some explained that workers were more willing if they could perform the work within a courtyard (*lakoro*), but that it would be nearly impossible to find a sanitation worker if the work were publicly visible. The visibility and containment of sanitation work, then, were pivotal criteria by which laborers gauged their willingness to accommodate the request. Being identified as a sanitation worker left one vulnerable to the kind of shame and judgment that could permeate public appraisals of one's character.

That the labor of sanitation repair is highly gendered as masculine work, and that migrants and newcomers have historically performed this disagreeable work, resonates with the labor regimes for sanitation elsewhere on the African continent.[106] In these moments where men engaged with the technologies of filth removal, the "otherness" of certain ethnically defined groups was tacked onto their sanitation labor role, further entrenching perceptions among some that sanitation workers—whether Anjouan or Betsirebaka—had questionable moral character.[107] At the same time, some felt involvement in sanitation infrastructure transformed their sense of their own personhood and human worth. This was particularly evident in households (like Alain's, the man with whom this chapter opened) that could not afford to hire a sanitation worker, which comprise the majority of the island's population in contemporary times.

Conclusion

Water and waste removal systems are bound up in everyday practices in ways that diverge from other infrastructures like dams or roads. They involve embodied habits and corporal intimacies that can transform one's sensory, affective, and social lifeworld. In Mahajanga, control over these infrastructural systems, so essential to basic needs, was also critical to governance practices and to possibilities for remaking different groups' sociopolitical and economic prospects in the city. French colonial authorities sought to shape and constrain the population, not only through selective, disproportionate access to water and waste removal, but also by cultivating a desired urban habitus through water collection and storage, bodily practices of toileting, and porterage of human waste. But in the process of constructing systems that selectively provided water and removed waste, officials failed to anticipate the ecological variations of the region that would transform the outcomes and present unforeseen consequences. Both of these colonial-era systems were inscribed with fundamental assumptions about labor—about the number of laborers needed to sustain these systems and the willingness of imagined workers to perform infrastructural efficacy. City residents' devaluation of sanitation labor challenged colonial efforts to establish a sewage system resembling that of the metropole, stalling it and forcing administrators to alter their designs.

Pivotal to the functionality of Mahajanga's emergent water network, thus, were particular configurations of storage technologies and labor regimes. The system of communal water pumps necessitated a corollary system of storage—one engendered by containers of various sorts—in which households could accumulate enough water for daily cooking and bathing, as well as for extinguishing fires that could otherwise easily spread across the quarter. Looking to comparative historical examples, the importance of containers in colonial Mahajanga's water system mirrors that of emergent urban networks in the late nineteenth century. Throughout European and American cities, water networks were initially constructed with striking disparities in provision between affluent and poor communities. In the absence of indoor plumbing, working-class districts relied on wells, porterage, and containers to supply their household needs.[108] In late nineteenth-century East London, even after the installation of water pipes and a long period of steady, continuous flow, middle-class consumers contended with supply disruptions by placing moveable bathtubs underneath taps running throughout the night.[109] Reformers' efforts to install water pipes in Tianjin, China, between 1904 and 1910 not only "failed to eliminate the traditional water bearers" and their containers, but also gave rise to a new group of middlemen who managed water shops and hydrants throughout the city.[110]

The unfolding of Mahajanga's sanitation system complicates scholarly assumptions about the nature of colonial urban planning. It does not conveniently fit with other accounts of urban policy that suggest colonial-era interventions were driven by the perception that ecological and cultural conditions in the colonies "[were] inherently different [from the metropole] on account of race, climate, and history."[111] Rather, French planners approached sanitation construction in the growing colonial city much as their administrative counterparts in France had done and continued to do. They failed to account for how the city's sandy soil, seasonal rains, and low-lying topography, let alone the existing waste practices and cosmological frameworks of urban dwellers, might profoundly alter the course of the same technologies as those built in the metropole. Mahajanga was not a colonial laboratory for testing new sanitation infrastructure, and French colonial sanitation planners appear to have been quite limited in their capacities to imagine a sanitation system that differed from those commonly found in nineteenth-century France. They carried forth a model of decentralized sanitation from the metropole, configured around parceled latrines, and anticipated an accommodating topographical landscape and compliant colonial citizenry to enact their waste treatment scheme. This was rote city-making, at best.

The process described in this chapter, what I have called the *peopling of infrastructure*, happened through the intersection of specific migratory, economic, and ecological processes. In the case of the water system, junior household members have historically collected and hauled water. With colonial approaches to water provision, this labor shifted toward marginalized groups, namely Makoa men and women, and today newer migrants coming from southeast Madagascar. It also became commodified labor, available for hire by more affluent families, which is today performed exclusively by men (*rano-dahy*, or "water-men") for meager wages, but with little suspicion of their moral character. Waste labor, on the other hand, has historically been deeply stigmatized and far less normalized. Initially carried out by prisoners, and subsequently by waves of newer migrants

(Comorians, the Ah-Thon brothers, and today newer migrants from elsewhere in Madagascar), this labor has also been cast as masculine work. In both cases, more marginal groups to the city were enrolled to perform infrastructural work, but the contrasting valuations of their work arose from the displaced matters: water and waste.

Mahajanga's sanitation story calls for reflecting on the laminated, nuanced forms of violence embedded within and constituted by forms of infrastructure—on technopolitical violence. Encoded in the sewage system's colonial design were acts of exertion (pulling sewage sludge from underground pits, emptying shit-filled pails and buckets) that tore asunder many workers' bodily integrity. For mpanary tay, sewage labor disrupted aspects of personhood that have long been connected to proper emplacement of bodily substances and the dead, through which inclusion in kin and ancestral lineages is affirmed. Infrastructure encompasses space, and this story signals the unevenness of service provision and forms of systemic denial undergirded by racial prejudice throughout the city's history. Infrastructure also envelops vast stretches of time, across which material forms articulate social and economic hierarchies, bringing about repetitive forms of harm. The material design of the early twentieth century's system required human force to function, from its initial construction and across its technological lifespan—enacting recurrent, generational forms of human suffering on marginal groups in the city through maintenance work. Akin to the slowly unfolding violence of toxic contaminations, the earliest work of Mahajanga's sewage engineers gradually gave rise to accumulating streams of human waste that penetrated the soil, sullied the groundwater, and polluted the riverine waterways.[112] With the accretion of more and more human waste came epidemiological violence, in the form of cholera epidemics (most recently in 1999) and widespread diarrheal disease, which persists as the primary cause of mortality across the island.[113] This nexus reveals that infrastructures not only embody and manifest violence in key moments, but also precipitate harm through long-term, intergenerational bodily and material interactions. Those on the margins in African cities contend daily with the aftermath of colonial sanitation systems, what Christina Sharpe calls the violence of "racial calculus and political arithmetic" manifest in the physical forms of waste infrastructure.[114]

In closing, we might ask what can be gained by interrogating the epistemological frameworks of those who have variously rejected and labored in infrastructures mediating their relationship with a colonial state. Studying the logics undergirding water and waste practices helps to reveal the complicated, rich ways in which Malagasy actors in precolonial and colonial times imagined the moral dimensions of their city and the practical norms governing proper and respectable relations with kin and ancestors. Though seemingly imperceptible to French colonial agents, city inhabitants navigated the tenuous demands of the living and the dead, of life and danger, by managing space, harnessing the power of materials, and carefully undertaking laboring acts of care. This is not to nostalgically put forth an imagined past in which nature and humanity were once in harmony, but rather to assert that the seeds for a different kind of urbanity were once there, though they are now long buried.

Epilogue

Unfinished Histories

I am only vestiges, what is still standing of a country that was not, of a country that is not, of a country that perhaps will not be. And I keep the doubt-maybe, because my country, the possible, the imaginable, but which is not yet. . . . I do not know if it will be one day. If in my lifetime. . . . Did it ever exist? Ruins before being built, built on dreams, utopia with storm walls, my columns are erected in the eye of the storm.

— JEAN LUC RAHARIMANANA, *Des ruines*, 2012

The house that this book opened with—Mama Nasra's house—still stands, animated by the chatter of her children and grandchildren, the aromatic scents of braised garlic and ginger, and the melodious call for prayers that envelops the thick air in Mahabibo. The stone walls of Mama Nasra's house stubbornly withstood the passage of time—the relentless downpour of every rainy season, the corrosive salty sea air, and the fierce, feral winds of Cyclone Kamisy in 1984 and Cyclone Gafilo twenty years after. As a living testimony to the devotions of her ancestors, Mama Nasra's hardened home and her relationships to the past embedded in the built environment have been crucial to her claims of being "really" Malagasy. And yet Mama Nasra's story is one with broader significance than the granular particularities of Mahajanga's history. The stories of emplacement offered in this book, taken collectively, signal the active ways built forms and urban spaces can shape people's everyday lives, constituting how urban dwellers understand the stakes of belonging and forge their own ties to the city. They invite us to consider how—in the absence of noisy debates and public memorials—contestations over belonging endure through people's everyday engagements with the material things, buildings, and places of the city. The spatial practices through which people imbue the landscape with their presences are sometimes public and highly visible, for instance, in the elevation of the rova on the Saribengo hilltop or the construction of towering mosques by Comorian-Malagasy Muslim communities. But in many other moments, these practices are quiet and hidden, like the interment of a newborn's placenta in a household's courtyard or the deposition of the dead's bodily fluids in the substratum of the family home. These moments can rarely be found in documentary sources and instead demand an attunement to the oft-unseen, whispered, and nuanced dimensions of everyday life.

Cities are architecturally unruly and never fully contain the excessive affluence or effluence of the earthly substances, ideas, goods, spirits, and bodies that traverse across edges to knit together expanses of time and space. I have endeavored to trace how the Indian Ocean port town of Mahajanga arose through regional, transoceanic, and transgenerational connections that informed ongoing moral debates among inhabitants—over the value of communal and individual lives and the ways in which social collectivities can best flourish. Investigating built forms as historical sources is not only a matter of elasticizing the bounds of the archive or filling empirical gaps to recuperate previously buried voices. Centering everyday dwellers and their architectural forms helps to reframe scholarly views on how cities are made by exposing the multiple moral theories and valuations that undergird material forms—which themselves point to alternative paths for urban life. Tracing building movements in the city using a broad temporal lens revealed not only continuities and changes in the political lives of buildings and valences of materials—the potency of stone, the regenerative capacity of thatch—but also how successive groups appropriated, abandoned, and destroyed left-behind built forms. Central to this narrative are the enmeshed histories of labor and kin-making, and the transformation of emotional attachments into tangible surfaces, through which communities of practice gathered themselves over and again—bringing Mahajanga into being.

Yet despite the seeming solidity of houses like Mama Nasra's, the work of building presence into the city is provisional, unfinished business, ever imperiled by the pregnant silences and absences of memory, by the specters of violence. As in times past, the streets of the city continue to bear witness to the forging of worlds, the making and remaking of lives, and the persistent presences beckoning inhabitants to moments both past and future. But the gravitas of the stakes of urban claims to belonging are most vividly illustrated in a key event to which we now turn, an event that continues to haunt the present-day life of Mahajanga: the rotaka (upheaval, tumult) of 1976–77.

The rotaka, by all accounts, began with a single incident involving filth, soil, and a child.[1] In the last days of December 1976, a small child defecated in the open courtyard of a housing compound inhabited by two families—one broadly identified as "Antesaka" and the other as "Comorian." Enraged, the Comorian owner purportedly smeared the child with the feces. The child immediately ran to his parents, who demanded that the Comorian family make recompense (*fandemenina*) for the grave offense. Some say the Comorian family refused; others say the Antesaka parents lost patience when the Comorian family was slow to make redress. In frustration and protest, the Antesaka parents marched to the police headquarters in Mahabibo.

From there, the details become hazy amid multiple accounts and recollections. Most recall that a crowd gathered in support of the Antesaka family and word spread. Within hours, shocks of violence rippled through the city. Those aligned with the Antesaka family were said to have picked up their machetes, sticks, and stones to drive Comorians out from the city. Comorians were broadly construed to include anybody of Comorian descent, including those from Comorian-Malagasy families who self-identified as zanatany.

In their first-hand accounts of the pogrom, witnesses and survivors conveyed the sheer terror of these moments. They described hiding in latrines, under beds, behind fences, in their own homes. Some recalled the courageous acts of protection and shelter provided by friends and neighbors who offered them safe haven in their closets and toilets. Laced into some narratives were the heroic accounts of parents who had harbored refugees, risking their lives by protecting and hiding Comorians, and of alliances and covert agreements between zanatany and Betsirebaka to offer rescue and refuge.

In desperate attempts to ward away attackers, Malagasy and Comorian-Malagasy families placed a green branch (*famatarana maintso*) outside their homes and scrawled "Malagasy eto" (Malagasy here) in chalk on their doors and walls. Some marked their bodies as Malagasy, wearing green branches in their hair.

But the violence and destruction came. And devastated.

When I asked people now in their late fifties and older what they recalled about the rotaka, many had visceral responses. Covering their eyes. Splaying their hands. Furrowing their brows. Distant gazes. Silence. Gasping. One woman buried her face in her hands and cried, "There was no thought! No meaning!"[2] These gestures were linked to moments of witness, of glimpsing unspeakable atrocities.

Beheadings.

Machetes rising and descending.

Limbs scattered on the street.

Trucks filled with bodies.

Pandemonium.

One woman, who was about twelve at the time, recalled being curious. She wanted to go into the streets and see what had happened. She remembered bodies everywhere, unrecognizable body parts here and there, blood streaming down the roads.

Some recalled houses burning for days and the streets littered with the bodies of dead goats (the beloved livestock of many Comorians and Comorian-Malagasy). Mosques were desecrated with the urine of humans and smashed doors. Feral dogs were running about.

In the aftermath, chaos ensued. Those who could took refuge in the Gendarmes camp and at the French Consulate in Majunga Be. Some recalled that those days were filled with anguish, uncertainty, and chaos. The gendarmes could not accommodate the thousands of people temporarily housed there. Toilets were blocked. Food and water were scarce. Within a matter of days, Belgian Sabena planes and boats transported the refugees to Comoros.

In these narratives, the attribution of blame ranged widely. Many described the defecation incident as a small thing that ignited a fire for those who felt marginalized from the city, because Comorians "had all the houses and all the jobs."[3] Common refrains among some Malagasy blamed Comorians for their tendency to demean (*manambany*) Betsirebaka and other Malagasy, teasing them (*mivazavaza*) and making them suffer (*mampijaly*). Others suggested that Malagasy politicians were bent on expelling Comorians or, alternatively, that politicians in Comoros wished to attract Comorians back to the archipelago to drive postcolonial development. Some invoked the "*côtier*–highlander" distinction, suggesting it was Merina (using the pejorative *bourzany*) who manipulated Betsirebaka for their own interests in gaining Comorian-Malagasy–owned lands and businesses; others cited differences of religion and ethnicity (*entre foko*). Still others contended that this was a misunderstanding of customs and perspectives, in which Comorians failed to understand that matters relating to excrement (*tay*) were provocative and taboo for Betsirebaka. Some drew on stereotypes of Betsirebaka and Comorians as both "hot-hearted" (*mafana fo*). Still others blamed the tumult on the economic decline under Ratsiraka's regime, a time when jobs were scarce, an economic crisis loomed, and competition between groups in town intensified.

Others who were more closely aligned with and attuned to Sakalava royal ancestral practices offered an alternative explanation, tying together the town's moral decline with newcomers' failures to abide by established Sakalava fady that governed the land.[4] One Sakalava spirit medium in his seventies, offered this explanation:

> When I moved here [from Analalava] the land had a master (*mananan-tompo*), and at that time people knew to follow the customs here, and things moved along smoothly. But the royal descendants (*razan'olo*) haven't followed the customs properly at the doany and other sacred sites in town. They have committed "wrongdoings against the land" (*helokon-tany manjary*). At the doany, people just enter the gate, women come in bikinis, nobody stops them! It's being run like a business! People disobey the taboos at the seaside, urinating in the ocean, eating pork. Ndriamisara [an important ancestral spirit] was enraged by these acts. This is why the rotaka happened! And just as these wrongdoings are spread around (*paritaka*), so too is the suffering spread among all who lived here.[5]

His explanation is certainly not embraced by all, but it is intriguing because it intimates the inextricable connections between place, moral rectitude, and subsequent suffering. It reflects a broken cycle of reciprocity, between the living and the dead, to which I will return.

There are strands of truth in these interpretations, all of which reflect local responses to the broader political tumults in the region during the 1970s. Following Madagascar's independence in 1960, President Philibert Tsiranana took the helm, leading the country through the First Republic, a period widely regarded as "neocolonial" due to the government's sustained allegiance to France and the extension of the institutional conditions of French colonial rule, including a highly centralized social democratic system, French as the primary language of educational instruction, and close ties to French concessionaires, diplomats, and financiers.[6] Such arrangements sustained economic growth, which served to further deepen class and regional inequalities. Hailing from northwest Madagascar, Tsiranana originally created his political party (Social Democrat Party [PSD]) in Mahajanga and cultivated strong support among Comorians and Comorian-Malagasy, who as a significant minority sought protection and continued favor from the state in post-independent times. Indeed Tsiranana's government's ties to France were so strong that, with the support of many Comorians across the island, he opposed efforts by the fledging Comorian nationalist movement MOLINACO to establish an autonomous Comorian nation.[7]

By 1972, popular unrest had risen. Mounting frustrations over colonial legacies in the education system and austere economic conditions galvanized student movements and labor unions in Antananarivo and in some coastal cities to unseat the government.[8] In Mahajanga, some student protestors at the Lycée Tsiranana demanded the "Malgachisation" of both the curriculum content and the language of instruction.[9] This movement ousted Tsiranana and unhinged many of the existing French trappings, driving the country into a tumultuous period in which two successive military leaders, General Ramantsoa and Colonel Ratsimandrava, led a series of reforms to disengage from foreign economic interests and revitalize the agrarian sector. In 1975, Admiral Didier Ratsiraka became president. He initiated intensive socialist measures and placed key industries under state control, which alongside global recession, quickly brought about conditions of economic duress across the island.[10] Under Ratsiraka's socialist regime, "Malgachisation" efforts gained momentum. Authorities imposed the highland Merina dialect as the standardized Malagasy language taught in schools and used in official correspondence (thus superseding regional dialect differences), renamed cities to conform to precolonial forms, and reworked the educational system to align to "Malagasy" values, priorities, and histories.[11] It was within these tempestuous conditions—a shrinking labor market, economic decline, persistent tensions between highlanders and coastal inhabitants, and postindependence political uncertainty—that this strikingly rare moment of collective violence toward those of Comorian descent ignited in the city.[12]

Absence and Abstention

As the stories of the rotaka unfolded in my conversations with city residents, I grew ever more aware of the absence of any public marker, site, or event commemorating this historic catastrophe. The only marker of violence of any kind in the city was an aging, decrepit monument to the 1947 anticolonial rebellion, which seemed unnoticed by and unremarkable to most inhabitants.[13] But after some time, I began to see that it was the deserted and ruined places that contained the residues of the horrific violence and through which inhabitants recalled the split moral fibers of the city.

One of these places was Mangatokana ("the lone mango tree"). Since at least the early 1970s, Mangatokana had served as the public cemetery for Malagasy in the city. In earlier times, Antalaotra and Silamo had been buried at the hilltop known as "Plateau des Tombes." In the 1970s, long after the graves had been left to decay, the city seized this land to construct the main administrative offices for the district. When construction workers dug into the land they discovered the remains of Antalaotra, buried with their heads facing toward Mecca.[14] The other ancient cemetery lay at Manjarisoa, now a residential neighborhood known to be populated by highlander migrants; some of the people I spoke to recalled that if you walked there at night, you might be slapped by an angry ghost. Several other cemeteries dotted the town: the "*vazaha* [European] cemetery," in which fallen soldiers from the conquest and colonial settlers were buried, near Mangarivotra; the Bohra cemetery in Majunga Be; and a Muslim cemetery in Antanimisaja.

Yet, the Mangatokana public cemetery was the subject of much talk and consternation for many city inhabitants. Sprawling across several acres, it was notoriously difficult to navigate and find one's kin. Many migrant families buried their kin there temporarily, with the intention of exhuming them and reburying them in their ancestral land (*tanindrazana*) once the families had gathered funds. Others never accumulated the resources and expressed immense guilt that they allowed their kin to languish there. Burial practices have long been a critical way that Malagasy constitute attachments to place, and improper burial amounts to unfulfillment of one's kinship obligations to the living and the dead.[15] But Mangatokana stirred concerns among city residents for another reason. In the early 2010s, the city designated the adjacent terrain as a landfill (figure E.1). Rumors abounded about the origins of this decision. Some claimed a private company began tossing rubbish on the site and that the city only followed suit. At least one city administrator affirmed that the municipality chose the site because the land was abundant. Initially officials planned to clearly demarcate the cemetery from the landfill by building a concrete wall, but as funds failed to materialize, the wall was never built, and in turn the massive garbage heaps gradually spread, encroaching onto the tombs. Some accused local officials of neglect, others claimed city administration was dominated by

FIGURE E.1 Mangatokana landfill, Mahajanga, 2014. Gravestones across the road are not visible in photograph. Photo by author.

rich highlanders who were insensitive to the concerns of local families, while still others blamed the citizenry for not holding the city more accountable. Either way, the close juxtaposition of filth and sanctity remained a widespread point of distress for many city inhabitants.[16]

Mangatokana was also the place reputed to hold the remains of those killed in the 1976–77 rotaka in a mass grave. With this in mind, I visited the Mangatokana cemetery on two occasions, each time asking people who were there tending to graves whether they could direct me to the Comorian grave (*fasana*). But my attempts were unsuccessful. Either people genuinely did not know of the site, or they wanted to avoid delving into this uncomfortable past with an overly inquisitive *vazaha*. In the last weeks of my time in Mahajanga, however, Twawilo offered to accompany me there.[17] Twawilo was a revered leader in the Mosque at Fiofio, the mosque once constructed by Tsepy and his comrades, and the self-appointed caretaker of the Comorian gravesite. As we drove the rocky road ascending to Mangatokana, Twawilo explained that the road had been demarcated in 1972 under Tsiranana. In those days, he continued, the dead of Muslims and non-Muslims were buried separately, but now with so much overcrowding in the city, people claimed any open spaces to farm corn and cassava, and to plant banana trees, and everything was mixed up, "disordered" (*korontana*). We parked the car and walked several hundred feet through cracked tombstones and matted grass dotted with plastic wrappers strewn by the wind. The surrounding landscape seemed to me completely unreadable, and even Twawilo himself seemed uncertain of the precise location of the graves. There were three mass graves in total—one long and narrow, and two circular mounds (one small and one large). We found them loosely marked off with stone, but otherwise unremarkable. As we quietly observed the site, I recalled stories people had told me of bulldozers digging the soil and tumbling the bodies, hastily wrapped in white cloth, into the earthen pits. We stood in silence as the clouds swirled overhead and the wind blew.

After a few minutes, I asked Twawilo whether there had been efforts in the past to create a memorial plaque to mark the site. He responded that there had been some inquiries, and that the city agreed to allow the erection of a small plaque 30 cm (12 inches) in height. Perhaps in a reflection of his own ambivalence, Twawilo then explained that he and his congregants prioritized the construction of a post demarcating the Muslim tombs at Mangatokana, rather than the establishment of a memorial marker at the mass grave of rotaka victims. "Older zanatany don't teach younger people about this history of rotaka," he confessed. "No, no, they don't. They don't want to bring this history up, because it will distinguish and differentiate them from other Malagasy. Long ago we held a memorial service, but that hasn't take place in several years. And the state corroborates this because they fear memorializing this site will incite racial tensions. They are ashamed (*menatra*)." It was those who had escaped from the city and remained in Comoros who pushed for a memorial, he explained. But those in the city abstained from remembering.

This resonated with conversations I had with others in the city indicating that by the 2010s, it was "no longer fashionable to be zanatany," as it had been in the 1950s, 1960s, and early 1970s. By this, they specifically referenced the conception of *zanatany* as Comorian-Malagasy métis people largely regarded as the insiders in town, connected through shared urbanist practices. Zanatany men and women regularly noted dismally that if you had a Muslim name, you should expect government bureaucrats (thought to be mostly highlanders) would discriminate against you. Said Hassan, in his seventies, tied the rise in "racism" to the 1975 coup by General Ramantsoa, followed by the socialist revolution and regime under President Ratsiraka (1976–93): "Under Tsiranana, things were still very good (*mbola tsara be*). But in 1972, there was a force pushing for Malgachisation . . . once the country was led by Merina (*Merina mitondra*), racism began to emerge (*manomboka racisme*) against côtiers." This distancing from "zanatany" markers by those of Comorian-Malagasy mixed descent was further revealed in an ethnographic encounter.

One morning in February 2013, my friend Taoaby introduced me to the head of a *fokontany* (local neighborhood office) in a central quarter said to be historically dominated by Comorians from Ngazidja and mixed Comorian-Malagasy families. In his early thirties with a small child, the fokontany head answered my questions about the historical and contemporary demographics of the neighborhood by way of his own family composition "[Our neighborhood] is very mixed," he explained. "You see, even myself, my mother is Sakalava, and my father is Sihanaka [an ethnic group historically located in central northeastern Madagascar]. And I'm married to a Merina woman."[18] After we conversed a bit more and finished the meeting, I thanked him and left. When I returned to Mama and Papa Taoaby's home, I mentioned his comments about his background. Mama Taoaby exclaimed, "Ha! I knew his parents and his father was actually Comorian-Gasy. I taught him as a student before, and I know he has a Comorian background." Everyone agreed that the fokontany leader had reframed his ancestral background to appear more "Malagasy." Then Papa Taoaby chimed in: "It's ironic. You know, in earlier times, he might've overemphasized his Comorian background, but now in this political moment he tries to appear more Malagasy."

Toward the end of my fieldwork, I found these links between the 1976–77 rotaka, Malgachisation, and the formation of a "Malagasy" national identity more explicit and suggestive. There was little question for most older inhabitants in the city—self-proclaimed zanatany and migrants alike—that the rotaka was a rupture. There was before the rotaka, when life was good, ambiance was lively, and politics were calm (*milamina tsara*). And then there was life after, characterized by economic austerity, ration lines, and rampant filth in the city. For zanatany, the rotaka also signaled an irreparable tear through the urban fabric they had woven for generations. Many noted that once they returned to the city from Comoros, some months or years later, the sense of vibrant community characterized by living together and getting along (*fiaramonina*) was lost; neighborly relations (*jirany*) were ruined (*robaka*); and the moral ethos that had once maintained order had eroded.

The 1976–77 moment, I suggest, can be understood as a crystallization and articulation of a "Malagasy" national identity, afforded by Ratsiraka and the language of Malgachisation, that had hitherto been inconceivable. When I asked informants whether they would agree that the rotaka was a turning point in local articulations of "Malagasy" identity, many agreed. Some noted that in earlier times other kinds of ethnic, residential, or home association affiliations were more pronounced. But during and after the rotaka, the category of "Malagasy" was juxtaposed with "Comorian," "outsider" (vahiny), or "migrant" (mpiavy) in ways shown to be pivotal to the making of nationalist rhetoric and sentiment elsewhere in Africa.[19] One man of Antesaka descent, who recalled his father fighting on the side of Betsirebaka, described how during the rotaka "the Gasy united and became one people" (nitambatra gasy, dia olo iray) in opposition to "arrogant and exploitative Comorians."[20] It was the uniquely disproportionate presence of Comorians in the city, many attested, that gave rise to the zanatany street culture of the 1960s and '70s, and the subsequent eruption of the rotaka. These accounts suggest that the mid-1970s Malgachisation program, manifest in public discourses, as well as in economic, legal, and educational reform, combined with urban tensions over spatial dominance and economic marginality to foster an environment in which people could begin to think of themselves as "Malagasy" in new ways. If the rotaka served to elucidate a "Malagasy" national affiliation—rendering visible the line between "Malagasy" and "other"—it also revealed the fractures hidden underneath official public discourses and the unfinished business of decolonization.

Restless Places

Despite the absence of public markers relating to the rotaka, other places in the city refused to be silenced. Among them were the houses, neighborhoods, and lands once inhabited by Comorians but since abandoned. Some people remarked that if one wanders the streets of Abattoir at night, you can still hear the cries of distress of the Comorians who once lived there and who were violently killed in the pogrom. Papa Taoaby relayed a story emblematic of these wider concerns. "The house next door," he explained, "refuses to let people live in peace." A continuous stream of renters had been haunted by strange happenings, including the sounds of tortured moans and strangulation, as well as some mysterious deaths. The source of these incidents was the house's original owner, a Comorian man, who fled in the midst of the violence. When the man returned to reclaim his house from his Malagasy neighbors several years later, they refused, and he began legal proceedings of reclamation through the town's tribunal. Before the case went to court, however, he was visited by a diviner (*moasy*) who advised him on the Malagasy family's behalf to abandon his legal case. He rebuffed the diviner's warning; on that very night he choked on a fishbone and died. From then on, "the people staying in this house have had many strange things happen to them."[21]

Papa Taoaby's story was one of many I heard about the residual disturbances of the spaces once marked by the violence toward Comorian-Malagasy during the rotaka. Many recalled that Comorians and their Comorian-Malagasy kin hastily pleaded with trusted friends and renters to watch over their homes and their belongings. Others gave a procuration—either quickly before they left, or working through intermediaries once they were in Comoros—to kin or neighbors who remained in the city. One woman whose family rented a home from Comorians in Ambalavola recalled that they hid their landlords until they could usher them to safety. The Comorian family allowed her brother to live on their land free of rent for the years to come.[22] In the aftermath of the rotaka, those left behind seized the then-vacant homes, and many found themselves disturbed by frightening dreams, bad presences, and misfortune. Even those who did not necessarily seize homes once owned by Comorians, but who found themselves renting them, experienced troubles. Mama Rinja, a spirit medium of mixed Vezo-Betsileo background, described how her family rented a home in Ambalavato that had once been owned by Comorians killed during the rotaka.[23] The house was regularly disturbed by ghosts (*lolo*) associated with the previous owners, which terrorized the family. She recalled her mother's attempts to drive out or silence the *lolo* through a powerful act of penetration, reburial, and transformation: "You know, some Comorians had a hole in their home, where they buried the fluids from their dead, after washing them. This house had a hole like that, where the Ajojo used to pour the water from their dead. Well, my mother she wanted to drive out those ghosts (*lolo*). So she opened up the hole, and she heated up pig lard (*menaka kisoa*), turning it into liquid. Very carefully, she poured that fat into the hole. And never again were we bothered by those ghosts." The interment of melted pork fat in a crevice that once held the precious fluids of the Muslim dead was a forceful effort to transform the house through the melding of vital matter—matter thought capable of averting unwanted spirits. It was also an effort to invest the home with a new family's presence, effacing and driving out the harrowing histories that befell the city. Mama Rinja was the only person who described this particular way of suppressing the disturbances of presences, the traces of those who had once lived in the home. Although we do not know how widespread this approach was, it speaks to the ways homes exerted a force on their inhabitants, one which inhabitants were obliged to contend with and mediate through other ritual means.

It was not only occupied homes, however, that caused these odd occurrences. People also linked these incidents to the belongings and objects once owned by Comorians but wrongly seized by Malagasy. In most cases, Comorian and zanatany families fled with little time to collect their belongings, leaving behind their furniture, cooking pots, and even jewelry. Dadilahy Kassim recalled witnessing Betsirebaka carrying away suitcases filled with cloth and gold from Comorian houses, which they dispersed. Malagasy who remained in the city clamored to take over the houses that stood vacant and hastily abandoned.[24] Yet, strange, haunting things befell those who had confiscated Comorian goods and property. One woman exclaimed, "Those things were Comorian things, they were Comorian houses!" Many people became crazy (*lasa adaladala*); many others died of mysterious diseases. One Tsimihety woman who lived through the rotaka recalled, "A good Comorian friend warned us after the rotaka, 'Don't touch a single thing from Comorians, not even a sewing needle!' So we didn't. But those who took things from Comorian houses, they really found themselves troubled, with bad dreams, tormented."[25] Stories abounded of those who appropriated the empty houses or used the belongings of Comorian owners only to be driven to insanity or death. "Looted" objects and houses were saturated with the traces of their former owners, their rightful owners. To be clear, it was primarily older residents (in their forties and older) who narrated these hauntings in the landscape. Younger people sometimes listened quietly to these recollections; others giggled uncomfortably (only to be castigated by their elders), while still others expressed little knowledge of the expulsion of 1976–77, exposing generational tensions in the making of memories. But for those who described these troubles, it seemed clear that vacant houses and left-behind things held a kind of presence that affected those who occupied them.[26]

Scholars working in post-conflict settings elsewhere have documented how difficult pasts that are rarely remembered in explicit verbal accounts instead "reverberate and manifest again" in the objects and spaces left behind.[27] Yael Navaro-Yashin described the experiences of families in Turkish Cyprus who were living with "looted" personal objects and in houses that had been forcefully appropriated from Greek-Cypriots during the war of 1974. These objects exuded "emotive energies," emitting an "affect of melancholy" on the people living with them. At the same time, these objects elicited moral imaginings from the Turkish-Cypriots inhabiting them, obliging them to debate and wrestle with an unresolved past.[28] Like those in Cyprus, many people in Mahajanga described a profound sadness that swept across the city immediately following the expulsion of those of Comorian descent. But many Malagasy interpreted these accounts of ill fortune as retribution for wrongs committed during the rotaka, which they linked to the superior capacities of Comorians—especially Ajojo—to harness supernatural forces through Muslim practices. It was through *badri*, many Malagasy maintained, that Comorians were able to bring divinely ordained justice to bear on Malagasy perpetrators.

Most could not exactly explain the mechanics of *badri*, except that it was constituted through rituals and prayers. What they emphasized was the immense and disproportionate strength of Comorians through *badri*. When I asked one Sakalava ritual specialist about *badri*, he explained, "After the Comorians fled, then the Malagasy took or destroyed all the Ajojo belongings. But afterwards, Ajojo did *badri* and those who had done wrong things were struck. Even if you were Sakalava royalty (*mpanjaka*), if you took something that belonged to the Ajojo, then you would be struck by *badri*. Only *Silamo* could undo the work of *badri*."[29] I asked him, "Does that mean the power of Comorians through *badri* was stronger than the power of royal ancestors?" He replied, "The *mpanjaka* is strong, but if they took something, they would also be the victim of *badri*. They could not avoid it."

These recollections of objects infused with dangerous traces of their rightful owners were both a moral indictment against the wrongs committed by those involved in the rotaka and a warning about the power of unseen forces. Restless places and things expose a severed moral order, where circles of reciprocity are broken and things are taken, never to be returned. If plunder is fundamentally "taking with no obligation to give back," then the appropriation of Comorian belongings and homes were acts of refusal to rebind and recirculate existing ties of neighborhood life.[30] Exchange relations were at the heart of neighborhood life in the quarters of Mahabibo, where acts of giving and receiving sustained neighborly relations for decades before they were destroyed in the rotaka.

During the 1980s and '90s, many Comorians returned to Mahajanga to (re)claim their houses and things, producing new chains of personal and public contestations over space and belonging. Yet, in the absence of public discourses around the painful history of exclusionary violence, people continue to speak about the rotaka through the idioms of place and *presences*.

The surrounding houses, streets, and public spaces also "spoke," and continue to "speak," back to inhabitants, bringing the uncomfortable history of the rotaka into the present, and perhaps even demanding recognition of unresolved histories of loss and appropriation. Residual experiences of loss complicate the notion of the rotaka as a singular event of violence, demarcated neatly in time. Instead, they challenge us to conceptualize violence as stretching across time to include the everyday experiences of place. The past cannot be hermetically sealed, and these disturbed spaces of the city— like the soil on which they stand—are porous, blurring the lines between effacement and ossification, between the slipperiness and solidity of history, and between that which rests and that which rises to punctuate the present.

Introduction

Abbreviations: CPL/EIC (Cleveland Public Library, East India Collection, Cleveland, Ohio, United States); NWL (Rare Books Collection, Melville J. Herskovits Library of African Studies, Northwestern University Library, Evanston, Illinois, United States).

1 While the official spelling of honorific names is Maman'i Nasra, Maman'i Khalil, and so forth, I will use "Mama" throughout to reflect the local verbal usage of these names. All names are fictitious to guarantee anonymity, except in circumstances where interlocutors provided consent. In some cases, individuals selected their own pseudonyms.

2 Stone houses have a long, important history in Indian Ocean architecture, which will be addressed further in chapters 2, 3, and 5. Fieldnotes, September 17, 2012.

3 My approach to biographies of built sites is inspired by Wynne-Jones, "Biographies of Practice," 157–58, with an emphasis on labor as a key practice.

4 Lefebvre made the foundational argument that built space is highly politicized, socially constructed, and deeply intertwined in socioeconomic forces. Lefebvre, *Production of Space*, 33–46. Scholars working across many fields—anthropology, geography, urban studies, architectural history—have built on this insight to unpack the relationship between agency and built environment. This work has been surveyed in Low and Lawrence-Zúñiga, *Anthropology of Space and Place*; Buchli, *Anthropology of Architecture*; Beauregard, *Planning Matter*. On the structuring capacities of buildings, see Foucault, *Discipline and Punish*; Bourdieu, "Kabyle House."

5 A vast literature discusses the symbolic dimensions of houses. See Blier, *Anatomy of Architecture*; Carsten and Hugh-Jones, *About the House*; Waterson, *Living House*. On material arrangements and properties, see Gieryn, "What Buildings Do"; Yaneva, *Five Ways*; Hommels, *Unbuilding Cities*.

6 Trouillot, *Silencing the Past*; Stoler, *Along the Archival Grain*; Zemon Davis, *Fiction in the Archives*; Ginzburg, *Cheese and the Worms*; Cohen, *Combing of History*; Amin, *Event, Metaphor, Memory*.

7   For discussions of post-structuralist influences on historians, see L. Hunt, *Writing History*, 19–23; Eley, *Crooked Line*, 154–60.

8   Fanon, *Black Skin, White Masks*; Anderson and Soto Laveaga, "Decolonizing Histories"; Murphy, "Some Keywords"; Tuck and Yang, "Decolonization Is Not a Metaphor."

9   Meskell, "Introduction," 1–2.

10   Trouillot, *Silencing the Past,* 30.

11   Engelke, "Spirit." African studies scholars have long foregrounded the role of ancestors and spirits in the politics and practice of everyday life. Selected works include Boddy, *Wombs and Alien Spirits*; Feeley-Harnik, *Green Estate*; Graeber, *Lost People*; S. Green, *Sacred Sites*; Johnson, *Spirited Things*; Lambek, *Weight of the Past*; West, *Kupilikula*; R. Shaw, *Memories of Slave Trade*; Mavhunga, *Transient Workspaces*, 58–65; Fontein, *Politics of the Dead*.

12   As archaeologist Zoë Crossland pointed out, in her rich study on the presence of the dead in highland Madagascar, "There is little sense of a separate world of the dead for many people in Madagascar." Crossland, *Ancestral Encounters*, 15.

13   Here, I build on an extensive body of scholarly work that challenges the notion of the colonial (or postcolonial) state as the primary shaper of urban life, and instead reveals the hopes, ideas, tactics, and agentive acts of Africans in the eras leading up to European imperial expansion, including Schoenbrun, *Green Place*; Fields-Black, "Untangling"; Allman and Tashjian, *I Will Not Eat Stone*, xxiii; de Luna, *Collecting Food*.

14   *Madagascar: A World Apart*, released in 1998, is the title of season 2 of the Public Broadcasting Service (PBS) series *The Living Edens*.

15   Beaujard, "First Migrants to Madagascar"; Radimilahy and Crossland, "Situating Madagascar"; Boivin et al., "East Africa and Madagascar."

16   Hooper, *Feeding Globalization*, 5. See also Larson, *History and Memory,* and *Ocean of Letters*; Sanchez, "État marchand et État agraire."

17   Aslanian, *From the Indian Ocean*, 11–15.

18   Literally "people of the sea." Rantoandro, "Une Communauté Mercantile"; Sanchez, "Navigation et gens de mer," 119; also see Middleton, *World of the Swahili*, 20–22. There is some slippage between categories of "Comorian" and "Antalaotra" as many Antalaotra came from Hadramawt to Madagascar in the latter nineteenth century via the Comoros; see Bang, *Islamic Sufi Networks*, 72.

19   Blanchy, *Karana et Banians*.

20   Boyer-Rossol, "De Morima à Morondava."

21   Guyer and Belinga frame this strategy of pulling together people with diverse knowledge and expertise as "composition"; see Guyer and Belinga, "Wealth in People," 110. See also Schoenbrun, "(In)visible Roots"; Stahl, "Africa in the World"; Fleisher and Wynne-Jones, "Authorisation." On Madagascar, see Lombard, *Le Royaume Sakalava*; Feeley-Harnik, *Green Estate*.

22   Bayart, "Africa in the World," 237.

23 Ruud, *Taboo*; Lambek, "Taboo as Cultural Practice"; Walsh, "Responsibility."

24 Guillain, *Documents sur l'histoire*, 34–35.

25 Ghaidan, "Lamu"; H. Wright, "Early Islam"; Blanchy et al., "Guide"; Gensheimer, "Globalization"; Um, *Merchant Houses*; Meier, *Swahili Port Cities*. For overviews, see Horton and Middleton, *The Swahili*; Wynne-Jones and LaViolette, *Swahili World*.

26 *Fanjakana* denotes a culturally and historical mode of governance by "state," "kingdom," or constellation of royal rulers. As early as 1658, French administrator Étienne de Flacourt defined *fanjakana* as "administration, administrator, master, to reign, kingdom" (*Dictionnaire de la langue*, 20). Rich, subsequent scholarship on Madagascar in the nineteenth and twentieth centuries has documented the wide variation of governance approaches associated with fanjakana; see, for instance, Raison-Jourde, *Les souverains*; Feeley-Harnik, *Green Estate*; Larson, *History and Memory*; Ballarin, *Les reliques royales*; Crossland, *Ancestral Encounters*.

27 James Hastie estimated the population in 1824 at 12,000; Hastie, journal, July 2, 1824, CPL/EIC. Guillain writing two decades later estimated 10,000. Guillain, *Documents sur l'histoire*, 213.

28 Noël, "Ile de Madagascar"; Guillain, *Documents sur l'histoire*.

29 Kus and Raharijaona, "House to Palace," 103.

30 Key traits across many Swahili coastal cities are the central location of mosques, concepts of ritual purity, and spatial control and containment of women. On this and fuller explorations of Swahili urban settlements, see Pradines, "Commerce maritime"; Wynne-Jones and Fleisher, "Swahili Urban Spaces," 117; Fleisher et al., "When Did the Swahili Become Maritime?"; Horton, "Islamic Architecture."

31 Rasoamiaramanana, "Pouvoir merina," 323.

32 Rasoamiaramanana, *Aspects économique*; Campbell, *Structure of Slavery*.

33 J. S. Leigh, "Journal of Travels in Eastern Africa, Including Somalia, Mozambique, and Zanzibar, 1836–1840," December 28, 1836, unpublished manuscript, Rare Books Collection, Melville J. Herskovits Library of African Studies, Northwestern University Library (NWL).

34 Campbell, "History of Nineteenth Century," 332–33.

35 Campbell, "Slavery and Fanompoana," 468–72.

36 Grandidier, *Voyage à Madagascar*, 121–22; emphasis added.

37 Ferrand, "Notes sur Madagascar," 232.

38 Alpers, *Ivory and Slaves*; Sheriff, *Slaves, Spices, and Ivory*; Campbell, *Economic History of Imperial Madagascar*.

39 Archaeologist Severin Fowles notes that this defining feature of "absence" stretched across Western understandings of nonwestern histories in "People without Things"; similarly, Trouillot pointed out in "Anthropology and the Savage Slot" that such absences and lacks were critical to constructions used to justify colonization.

40   On "laboratories," see Wright, *Politics of Design*; Hosagrahar, *Indigenous Modernities*; Harris and Myers, "Hybrid Housing."

41   De Raulin, "Majunga," 310.

42   See, for example, de Lanessan, *L'expansion colonial*, 362–65.

43   The ethnonym "Comorians" is problematic because it effaces both the wide range of ethnic and religious affiliations and the varying cultural practices, across the archipelago. It also collapses the complicated history by which the category of "Comorians" was constructed through French census reports and administrative mechanisms. Following local usage in Mahajanga, however, "Comorian" here denotes individuals from the archipelago islands, and primarily from Ngazidja (Grande Comore) and Ndzwani (Anjouan). It refers to first-generation immigrants and those who continued to identify themselves as "Comorians" in oral interviews, yet it is critical to note that identities in contemporary northwest Madagascar are never singular, unilateral, or mutually exclusive. Thompson and Adloff, *Malagasy Republic*, 270. On the 50 percent figure, see Deschamps, *Les migrations intérieures*, 146–47. Importantly, national censuses may have classified zanatany (first-generation descendants of Comorian and Malagasy parentage) as "Malagasy."

44   Gueunier, *Chemins de l'Islam*, 44.

45   Van Onselen, *Studies in the Social*; Cooper, *On the African Waterfront*; Cooper, *Struggle for the City*; Burton, *African Underclass*; Penvenne, *Women, Migration*; Abu-Lughod, "Tale of Two Cities"; Swanson, "Sanitation Syndrome"; Goerg, "From Hill Station"; Wright, *Politics of Design*; Rabinow, *French Modern*; Çelik, *Urban Forms*; Bissell, *Urban Design*. For a synthesis, see Coquery-Vidrovitch, *History of African Cities*, 277–316.

46   White, *Comforts of Home*; P. Martin, *Leisure and Society*; Akyeampong, *Drink, Power*; Fair, *Pastimes and Politics*; Mager, *Beer, Sociability, and Masculinity*; Ivaska, *Cultured States*; Prestholdt, *Domesticating the World*; Plageman, *Highlife Saturday Night*; Quayson, *Oxford Street*; Callaci, *Street Archives*; Fair, *Reel Pleasures*; De Boeck and Baloji, *Suturing the City*.

47   Myers, *Verandahs of Power*; Harris and Myers, "Hybrid Housing"; Brennan, *Taifa*; Makhulu, *Making Freedom*; Melly, *Bottleneck*; Morton, *Age of Concrete*; Gastrow, "DIY Verticality"; Fourchard, "Between World History."

48   Morton, *Age of Concrete*, 14–15.

49   Mitchell, *Rule of Experts*; Nys-Ketels et al., "Planning Belgian Congo's Network"; Miescher, "Building the City," 367–76.

50   Hansen, *Keeping House*; Hoffman, *Monrovia Modern*; Morton, "Shape of Aspiration." Beyond African contexts, see Holston, *Insurgent Citizenship*; Fischer et al., *Cities from Scratch*; Harms, *Saigon's Edge*; Agha and Lambert, "Outrage."

51   See especially Nielson, "Wedge of Time"; Gastrow, "Cement Citizens"; Archambault, "One Beer, One Block." Beyond Africa, see Navaro-Yashin, *Make-Believe Space*; Abourahme, "Assembling and Spilling-Over." On im-

provisational strategies in Africa, see De Boeck and Plissart, *Kinshasa*; Simone, *For the City*.

52 For example, Otter, "Locating Matter"; Bennett and Joyce, *Material Powers*; Mavhunga, *Transient Workspaces*; Saraiva, *Fascist Pigs*; Hecht, "Interscalar Vehicles"; Tsing, *Mushroom at the End*; Raffles, *Insectopedia*; Pilo and Jaffe, "Introduction"; von Schnitzler, *Democracy's Infrastructure*; Fehérváry, *Politics in Color and Concrete*. In East African and Swahili coast contexts, Wynne-Jones, "Thinking Houses through Time," 166–67; Fleisher, "Rituals of Consumption"; Hanson, *Landed Obligation*; Fleisher and Wynne-Jones, "Authorisation and the Process," 189.

53 Siddiqi, "Introduction," 495.

54 Ingold, "Materials against Materiality," 9–10. My approach to "materials and materiality" is especially inspired by the work of Ingold, as well as by other anthropologists and archaeologists, including Miller, *Material Cultures*; Miller et al., *Materiality*; Insoll, *Material Explorations*.

55 Auslander, "Beyond Words," 1018. Over the past two decades, other scholars have made related observations, including LeCain, *Matter of History*; N. R. Hunt, "History as Form"; Findlen, "Objects of History." Didier Nativel makes this point for Madagascar in "À chacun selon ses moyens," 47. For a discussion of the relationship between historical texts and material culture, see Auslander, et al., "AHR Conversation," 1354–1404. Key material-centered histories include N. Thomas, *Entangled Objects*; N. R. Hunt, *Colonial Lexicon*; Mrázek, *Engineers of Happy Land*; Jütte, *Strait Gate*; Hecht, *Being Nuclear*; Halevi, *Modern Things on Trial*.

56 Scholz, "Ghosts and Miracles," 493.

57 See Ballantyne, "Architecture as Evidence," 36–37; Apotsos, *Architecture, Islam, and Identity*, 20–27; see also the special issue "On Evidence," *Journal of the Society of Architectural Historians* 76, no. 4 (2017). For considerations of African architecture, see Prussin, "Introduction"; Blier, *Anatomy of Architecture*; Strother, "Architecture against the State"; Meier, *Swahili Port Cities*; Carey, "Creole Architectural Translation."

58 Trouillot, *Silencing the Past*, 49–53.

59 Feeley-Harnik, *Green Estate*; Lambek, *Weight of the Past*.

60 Hartman, "Venus in Two Acts."

61 Spear, "Neo-traditionalism and the Limits"; Berman and Lonsdale, *Unhappy Valley*; Peterson, "Be Like Firm Soldiers"; Brennan, *Taifa*. John Lonsdale contrasts "moral ethnicity" with "political tribalism," which concerns the ways collective ethnic identities get harnessed in political contestations, in "The Moral Economy of Mau Mau." On the concept of "race" within African studies, see Pierre, *Predicament of Blackness*. Highly relevant for this study, historian Jonathon Glassman has emphasized how racialized discourses animated exchanges between elite intelligentsia (who considered themselves Arab) and "subaltern intellectuals" (linked to African and Shirazi groups) in Zanzibar for whom the rights of citizenship were increas-

ingly allocated based on claims to place and belonging; see Glassman, *War of Words*.

62　For the former, see Geschiere, *Perils of Belonging*; Geschiere and Nyamnjoh, "Capitalism and Autochthony"; Hodgson, "Being Maasai, Becoming Indigenous"; Pelican, "Complexities of Indigeneity and Autochthony"; Meiu, "Panics over Plastics." For the latter, see Schoenbrun, *Green Place*, 96–100, 178–200; Hanson, *Landed Obligation*; Lentz, *Land, Mobility, and Belonging*; Newbury, *Cohesion of Oppression*; Hall, *History of Race in Muslim West Africa*; Lee, *Unreasonable Histories*. Taken collectively, this scholarship has demonstrated several important insights: the distribution of citizenship rights based on territorial claims has been observed in some regions since earliest times; being "local" is reworked by historical actors to accord to their particular circumstances; and the long-standing presence of racial and ethnic difference shaped fervent, exclusionary nationalisms in post-independent times.

63　This study is particularly informed by the work of Prita Meier, who has illuminated how Swahili urban citizens drew on distinctive stone architectural designs of homes and mosques to express their "in between" ties to historical Indian Ocean littoral communities. Meier argues that generations of Swahili coastal dwellers paradoxically summoned the fixity of calcified stone architecture to make overlapping, and at times competing, claims to authentic belonging that hinged on nonterritoriality and transoceanic connections, even if the import of stone structures shifted over time. See Meier, *Swahili Port Cities*, 187. Debates about belonging in Mahajanga diverge from those described in Swahili coastal towns, however, in that they have always unfolded in a more-than-human landscape—one inhabited by ancestral presences, spirits, and associated prohibitions tied to the land—that has shaped not only understandings of who can claim mastery over land, but also moral norms defining ethically responsible land occupation and construction.

64　Mauss, "Les techniques du corps"; Merleau-Ponty, *Phenomenology of Perception*. See also Casey, *Fate of Place*.

65　Pier Larson called for "careful readings of African names of belonging" as a critical way to excavate how and when particular practices of ethnicity gained traction and helped shore up political allegiances. See Larson, "Desperately Seeking 'the Merina,'" 560.

66　Other zana-terms described by Abinal and Malzac include *zanakazo* (young plant or tree), *zanadandy* (chrysalides of silk worms), and *zanabiby* (offspring of an animal). See Abinal and Malzac, *Dictionnaire*, 832.

67　Hull, *Government of Paper*.

68　Cohen, *Combing of History*, 21.

Chapter 1. Casting the Land

Abbreviations: NWL (Rare Books Collection, Melville J. Herskovits Library of African Studies, Northwestern University Library, Evanston, Illinois, United States).

1 Many scholars have called for moving across scales, disciplinary boundaries, and eclectic sources to address enduring humanistic questions, including Shryock and Smail, *Deep History*, 13–15; J. Thomas, "History and Biology," 1600–1607; Schoenbrun, *Green Place*; de Luna et al., "Thinking across the African Past."

2 Myers, "Naming and Placing the Other," 95.

3 Love, "Poetics of Grievance," 423.

4 For critical toponymy scholarship, see Berg and Vuolteenaho, *Critical Toponymies*; Rose-Redwood et al., "Geographies of Toponymic Inscription." On settler-colonial erasures, see Carter, *Road to Botany Bay*; Monmonier, *From Squaw Tit*; DeLucia, *Memory Lands*; O'Brien, *Firsting and Lasting*; Yeoh, "Street-Naming and Nation-Building"; Azaryahu, "Power of Commemorative Street Names." Scholarship on place names in Africa includes Bühnen, "Place Names"; Bigon, "Names, Norms, and Forms"; and Bigon's recent important volume, *Place Names in Africa*.

5 Grunebaum, "Unburying the Dead," 211.

6 Basso, *Wisdom Sits in Places*, 101–3, 120.

7 Wit, "Madagascar," 213.

8 French ethnologist André Dandouau recorded this parable in the early 1900s, published in 1922 as *Contes populaires des Sakalava et des Tsimihety de la region d'Analalava* in 1922. Dandouau, *Contes populaires*, 93.

9 Dandouau translates Moudzangayeh as "terre d'election, lieu de choix." See *Contes populaires*, 93–94.

10 See Rajemisa-Raolison, *Dictionnaire historique*, 213–17; Richardson, *New Malagasy-English Dictionary*, 289. One might note, however, that *janga* also denotes "a licentious person of either sex," promiscuity, or liberated sexual behavior, and more research could reveal a historical relationship to ideas about virility, fertility, and social reproduction.

11 This telling was recorded by French explorers and British missionaries throughout the 1800s; see Grandidier, *Histoire de la géographie*, 123; Pickersgill, "Revision of North-West Place-Names," 493–94; Guillain, *Documents sur l'histoire*, 362; Sibree, *Madagascar before the Conquest*, 134; I. Taylor, *Names and Their Histories*, 184. Note that *angaia* is also the name of a flowering banana plant (*mlali angaia*) present in Comoros, which resonates with Antalaotra origins for the city's toponym.

12 Dandouau, *Contes populaires*, 93.

13 Recent paleo-ecological studies indicate strong support for human presence in Madagascar at least two thousand years ago, with a possibility of human

arrival in the early Holocene period. Douglass et al., "Critical Review," 1; Voarintsoa et al., "Multiple Proxy Analysis," 138.

14 For the colonial-era hypotheses about forests, see Perrier de la Bâthie, "La végétation malgache"; Humbert, "Destruction d'une flore." For recent evidence about Malagasy grass flora, see Vorontsova et al., "Madagascar's Grasses and Grasslands," 1.

15 Proverbs include "[He/She/They] who has no time to grow old, like grass: young, it serves to feed the cattle, old, it serves to feed the hearth" (*Tsy misy hianterana toa bozaka: tanora, sakafon'ny omby; antitra, sakafom-patana*). Houlder, *Ohabolana*, 168. "Life is not like the grass that grows back by the root when the head is withered" (*Ny aina tsy mba bozaka, ka raha maina ny lohant maniry indray ny fakany*). Parrett and Cousins, *Ny Òhabòlan'ny Ntaolo*, 84.

16 *Antalaotra* literally translates as a "people of the sea," deriving from the Malagasy language (*ant* = from, *laut* = sea); see Rantoandro, "Une communauté mercantile"; Gueunier, *Les chemins*.

17 N. Anderson, "Materiality of Islamisation."

18 Key sources for early settlements and the city's founding include Guillain, *Documents sur l'histoire*; Noël, "Ile de Madagascar"; Vérin, *History of Civilisation*, 4–10; Radimilahy, "Mahilaka," 202–4; Radimilahy and Crossland, "Situating Madagascar," 502–4; H. Wright, "Early Islam," 84; H. Wright and Rakotoarisoa, "Rise of Malagasy Societies," 117.

19 Boivin et al., "East Africa and Madagascar," 238–43; Beaujard, "First Migrants"; Kull et al., "Introduced Flora of Madagascar."

20 Wright, "Early Islam," 84; Dewar and Wright, "Culture History of Madagascar," 430, 440, 452–55; Radimilahy, "Ancient Iron-Working in Madagascar"; Vérin and Wright, "Madagascar and Indonesia"; Allibert, "Austronesia Migration," 10, 14; Wright et al., "Early Seafarers," 55–65.

21 Adelaar, "Towards an Integrated Theory"; Dahl, *Migration from Kalimantan*; Beaujard, "First Migrants," 174. Archaeobotanical traces show that rice crops thrived in the alluvial soils of the northwest and sustained a growing population at Mahilaka (north of Mahajanga) well into the fourteenth century; surplus crops might have been funneled into settlers' exchanges with the Indian Ocean trade nexus. Radimilahy, "Mahilaka," 195; Crowther et al., "Ancient Crops," 6637.

22 Hamet Boebachar (a common Islamic name from Abu Bakr, aid to the Prophet), first appears in the 1677 *Voorhout* journal, KA 3990 [VOC 4013] f. 1011v. Email communication with James Armstrong, August 26, 2019; and Armstrong, "Madagascar and the Slave Trade," 214. Armstrong, "De bron van Keulens," 132.

23 On early settlements along the northwest coast, see Wright et al. "Evolution of Settlement Systems," 40; Guillain, *Documents sur l'histoire*; Rantoandro, "Communauté mercantile," 205; Vérin, "Les échelles anciennes," 91. Mariano described Antsoheribory as "the most frequented port" by Portuguese

navigators. Mariano, in Grandidier et al., *Collection des ouvrages anciens*, 3:653, as quoted in Armstrong, "Madagascar and the Slave Trade," 216. On Antsoheribory, see Ellis, "Tom and Toakafo," 443–44; Ellis, "History of Sovereigns," 411. James Armstrong estimated that the volume of slave trade from Massailly (likely Antsoheribory) would have ranged between 40,000 to well over 150,000. Armstrong, "Madagascar and the Slave Trade," 216. The *Voorhoot*'s shipping record indicates the raid on Antsoheribory was a "punitive" mission ordered by Goa's viceroy and was preceded by earlier raids in 1589 and 1635; Armstrong, "De bron van Keulens," 132.

24 For scholarly accounts of the conflicts in Menabe that led to the northern movement of Sakalava, see Lombard, *Le Royaume Sakalava*; Baré, *Sable Rouge*; Chazan-Gillig, *La société Sakalave*; Goedefroit, *A l'ouest de Madagascar*; Ballarin, *Les reliques royales*, 59–60, 323.

25 Drury, *Journal*, 274.

26 On historic ancestral practices, see Feeley-Harnik, *Green Estate*, 159; Ballarin, *Les reliques royales*, 59–60. Sakalava conceptions of nation were grounded on "social and political consensus" rather than on territorial belonging, Ballarin, *Les reliques royales*, 323; Hooper, *Feeding Globalization*, 60–61.

27 Primary sources documenting these events include Drury, *Journal*, 274–75; Johnson, *General History*, 264–65; Noël, "Ile de Madagascar"; Guillain, *Documents sur l'histoire*. For a recent reappraisal of primary sources dealing with these events, see Kneitz, "800 Men." On "massacre of Muslims," see Noël, "Ile de Madagascar," 94.

28 Vérin, *History of Civilisation*, 190–91, 291–98; Wright et al., "Evolution of Settlement Systems," 57–58.

29 Grandidier, *Collection des ouvrages*, 263–67, 327; Vérin, *History of Civilisation*, 190–91, 293.

30 On the presence of trade after invasion, see the visit of Soldaat in 1696, in Armstrong, "Madagascar and the Slave Trade." Archaeologists, however, have found only a few masonry buildings. Wright et al., "Evolution of Settlement Systems," 63–64.

31 On the rise of Muslim traders, see Rasoamiaramanana, "Les motivations et stratégies," 61.

32 See Frappé's account in Westra and Armstrong, *Slave Trade with Madagascar*, 151.

33 Westra and Armstrong, *Slave Trade with Madagascar*, 130.

34 Westra and Armstrong, *Slave Trade with Madagascar*, 130.

35 Burney, "Climate Change," 55; Dransfield and Rakotoarinivo, "Biogeography of Madagascar Palms," 193.

36 On tree species in the northwest, see Moat and Smith, *Atlas of the Vegetation*, 41.

37 Heights are found in Frappé's account in Westra and Armstrong, *Slave Trade*, 130.

38 In Malagasy, "nalefa ho tafon-tranon 'Andriana." Richardson, *New Malagasy–English Dictionary*, 596.

39 Hébert, "L'énumeration des points," 161–72; Feeley-Harnik, "Sakalava House"; Bloch, *Placing the Dead*; Ballarin, *Les reliques royales*. Linguists trace loanwords and terms for Malagasy cardinal orientations to the Malay influences of early settlers; Adelaar, "Austronesians in Madagascar," 82.

40 On burial practices, see Valentin et al., "Les abris sépulcraux."

41 For instance, see "Origine des chiens domestiques," in Dandouau's *Contes populaires*, 138.

42 On Bezavodoany, see Vérin, *History of Civilisation*, 286. Masons would have likely selected limestone for these mortuary structures, commonly found throughout the northwest; see Grubb, "Interpreting Some Outstanding Features," 128.

43 Kus and Raharijaona, "Between Earth and Sky."

44 Crossland, *Ancestral Encounters*, 35, 202.

45 On European traders' visits, see Westra and Armstrong, *Slave Trade with Madagascar*, 109; Hooper, *Feeding Globalization*, 102–3. I am thankful to Kate de Luna for pointing out these multiple explanations for incineration.

46 "Une foule énorme d'habitants"; Hemmy, "Voyage à la baie," 114.

47 Hemmy, "Voyage à la baie," 115–16.

48 Vérin estimates that the shift from Tongay to Marovoay took place under Toakafo's son in the 1730s (*History of Civilization*, 286–87). Based on slaving expedition journals, Westra and Armstrong suggest the move occurred earlier; *Slave Trade with Madagascar*, 151fn52. See also Hemmy, "Voyage à la baie," 117.

49 Hemmy, "Voyage à la baie," 115–16. For more on visibility in Sakalava ritual and architectural practices, see Feeley-Harnik, *Green Estate*, 97; Lambek, *Weight of the Past*, 29.

50 Dumaine, "Idée de la côte," 33; Guillain, *Documents sur l'histoire*, 25–26.

51 Ship's journal of the *Fly*, October 9, 1764, India Office Records, British Library (BL), IOR/L/MAR/B/597A-B.

52 Dumaine, "Idée de la côte," 35–36.

53 The ship's journal of the *Fly* noted of Mahajanga: "Here is easy wooding, and watering"; October 10, 1764, BL, IOR/L/MAR/B/597A-B.

54 In West Africa, for instance, see Koumbi Saleh, Mauritania. Thanks to Kate de Luna for this note.

55 Ship's journal of the *Fly*, October 9, 1764, BL, IOR/L/MAR/B/597A-B.

56 Ship's journal of the *Fly*, October 9, 1764, BL, IOR/L/MAR/B/597A-B.

57 Ship's journal of the *Fly*, October 9, 1764, BL, IOR/L/MAR/B/597A-B.

58 Guillain, *Documents sur l'histoire*, 21–22; Dandouau and Chapus, *Histoire des populations*, 23; Vérin, *History of Civilisation*, 310.

59 On trade activity in the northwest and its connections to the Mascarene Islands, see Campbell, "Structure of Trade," 140; Larson, *History and Mem-*

ory, 53; Hooper, *Feeding Globalization*, 133–34; Allen, "Satisfying the 'Want,'" 53–55; Wright and Rakotoarisoa, "Rise of Malagasy Societies," 118.

60 Guillain, *Documents sur l'histoire*, 34–35.

61 On archaeological evidence in northwest Madagascar see Vérin, *History of Civilisation*; on exclusive use of stone for tombs elsewhere in Madagascar, see Bloch, *Placing the Dead*, 112–15; on royal rituals, see Lambek, *Weight of the Past*, 214–20; Feeley-Harnik, *Green Estate*.

62 Prussin, "Introduction," 205.

63 Zoë Strother discusses similar practices of impermanent building in Central Africa in "Architecture against the State."

64 Bloch, *Placing the Dead*; Raison-Jourde, *Les souverains de Madagascar*; Ottino, "Ancient Malagasy."

65 On the *menaty* service, see Feeley-Harnik, *Green Estate*, 135–36.

66 Guillain, *Documents sur l'histoire*, 34–35.

67 Vérin dates Ravahiny's ascension to the throne to 1785; (*History of Civilisation*, 111). See also Hébert, "Les Francais," 239–40, for a discussion of other historical estimates of the dates of her reign. On the shift to female succession, see Feeley-Harnik, *Green Estate*, 67, 79–88; Ballarin, *Les reliques royales*, 43.

68 In addition to marriages between Antalaotra and Sakalava royals, Antalaotra leaders shared a formidable friendship with Ouza, the eldest son of Ravahiny, who was "elevated among them in the Muslim community and to whom they were devoted." Ouza spoke and wrote Arabic, with the dialect employed by the Muslim traders established in Boeny. Guillain, *Documents sur l'histoire*, 34–35.

69 Thiebaut describes the diminishing role of intermediaries in "Role of 'Brokers.'"

70 Dumaine, "Idée de la côte occidentale," 25.

71 De Lassalle, "Memoires sur Madagascar," 578.

72 Rantoandro, "Une tradition," 58–64.

73 The use of takamaka, especially for the construction of outrigger canoes, was specified later by French explorer Louis Catat, *Voyage à Madagascar*, 201. Vessel styles would shift to dhows and other vessels in the nineteenth century with the rise of Omani power and Zanzibar as the key trading port.

74 Sanchez, "Navigation et gens de mer," 11.

75 Guillain, *Documents sur l'histoire*, 33. "Astonishing trade" is from Dumaine, "Idée de la côte occidentale," 28.

76 Dumaine, "Idée de la côte occidentale," 33

77 Machado, *Ocean of Trade*, 74, 79.

78 Dumaine, "Idée de la côte occidentale," 27. On Indian commercial networks, see Alpers, "Gujarat and the Trade"; Machado, *Ocean of Trade*.

79 Vérin, *History of Civilisation*, 316. Vérin does not, however, provide archaeological evidence for this statement, and it is unclear whether remains have been discovered or whether this assertion is based on oral accounts.

80 Ho, *Graves of Tarim*, 25, 188–90. Oral accounts suggest the presence of the Bohra cemetery near present-day Aranta, both of which were also noted by Rantoandro, "Une tradition," 66.

81 Concerning Makoa (Masombika), see Boyer-Rossol, "De Morima à Morondava"; Catat, *Voyage à Madagascar*, 149; Guillain, *Documents sur l'histoire*, 132; Feeley-Harnik, *Green Estate*, 57–58. On Masombika practices of Islam, see Leigh, "Journal," December 8, 1839, NWL. Among others, Guillain identifies Antalaotra as the builders of stone houses (*Documents sur l'histoire*, 95, 208).

82 Dumaine, "Idée de la côte occidentale," 27–28.

83 For instance, see Lambek and Walsh, "Imagined Community," 308–9.

84 Dumaine emphasizes the point that "not a single Sakalava lived in the city, which was entirely Arab"; Dumaine, "Idée de la côte occidentale," 28. Vérin especially emphasized the town's Islamic character ("Les échelles anciennes du commerce," 457, 482–88).

85 White, *Middle Ground*, 50.

86 Dumaine noted that "when an Indian is accused of disturbing the public order, the chiefs and primary Arabs judge him in the presence of another Indian, [who serves as] the defender and prosecutor *ad hoc* of his compatriots; when justice is exercised for a Seclave [Sakalava] nothing is carried out against him before the Queen has issued her orders concerning the culpable subject." Dumaine, "Idée de la côte occidentale," 28–29.

87 Presumably the "hostilities" were the conflicts that unfolded decades earlier at Antsoheribory. Dumaine, "Idée de la côte occidentale," 30.

88 On the distributed composition of precolonial African polities, see Hanson, "Mapping Conflict," 180–81; McIntosh, "Pathways to Complexity," 11; Monroe, "Power and Agency"; Fleisher and Wynne-Jones, "Authorisation." On Ravahiny and reciprocity, see Hooper, *Feeding Globalization*, 96–100.

89 Hooper, "Pirates and Kings," 239. See also Alpers, "Madagascar and Mozambique," 49.

90 On the Malagasy language as lingua franca, see Larson, *Ocean of Letters*.

91 Richard, *Reluctant Landscapes*, 38–40.

92 Hamilton, *Terrific Majesty*, 26.

93 For instance, in the 1980s the city government wished to build their new administration center on the central hilltop in town (known as Plateau des Tombes; see map 3.2), only to inadvertently discover the land full of Antalaotra graves (which were subsequently excavated). Interview with Ramilisonina, Antananarivo, July 27, 2013.

Chapter 2. Vibrant Matters

Abbreviations: ANRDM (National Archives of the République Démocratique de Madagascar, Antananarivo, Madagascar); BL (British Library, London, United Kingdom); CPL/EIC (Cleveland Public Library, East India Collection, Cleveland, Ohio, United States); CWM/LMS (Council for World Mission—Archives of the London Missionary Society, School of Oriental and African Studies, London, United Kingdom); NWL (Rare Books Collection, Melville J. Herskovits Library of African Studies, Northwestern University Library, Evanston, Illinois, United States).

1 *Doany* refers to a compound, shrine, or sacred place associated with royalty. Feeley-Harnik, *Green Estate*, 592; Lambek, *Weight of the Past*, 21.

2 "Homespun" or "homegrown" historians refer to entrepreneurial African researchers "working outside the university . . . who carried out research, did interviews, collected data and subjected their work to critical review." Peterson and Macola, *Recasting the Past*, 13–15.

3 Fieldnotes, March 12, 2012.

4 Richardson, *New Malagasy-English Dictionary*, 203; Feeley-Harnik, *Green Estate*, 160–62, 442–46n28, 530–39; Feeley-Harnik, "Ravenala Madagascariensis Sonnerat," 34–35.

5 Wickens and Lowe, *Baobabs*, 102–3. On arborescent idioms of national belonging elsewhere in Africa, see Malkki, "National Geographic"; Gautier, "*Ficus.*"

6 Aumeeruddy-Thomas et al., "Sacred Hills of Imerina," 25. In surveys of the Andrantsay region, Zoë Crossland similarly found *Ficus lutea* tracked the historical movement of settlements from Imerina elsewhere in Madagascar. Email, March 27, 2022.

7 Fieldnotes, March 17, 2012. "Tandremo" [Be careful], he warned. "Mila mahay ny tantara tena, tena tantara Sakalava" [You need to learn the veritable history, Sakalava history].

8 Arens and Karp, "Introduction"; Guyer and Belinga, "Wealth in People"; Kriger, *Pride of Men*; Schoenbrun, "(In)visible Roots"; Fleisher and Wynne-Jones, "Authorisation," 178. Scholars differentiate between forms of *instrumental power*, which coercively control people, and *creative (*or what Bourdieu terms *symbolic) power*, through which people create meaning. Bourdieu, *Outline of a Theory*, 74, 163–66.

9 Fleisher "Performance, Monumentality," 273–75; Fleisher and Wynne-Jones, "Authorisation"; Monroe, "Power by Design," 369. On exchange, see Kusimba, *Rise and Fall*; Horton and Middleton, *Swahili.*

10 But see Fleisher, "Gathering of Swahili Religious Practice." Also relevant are Schoenbrun, "Ethnic Formation"; Schoenbrun and Johnson, "Introduction."

11 Fleisher and Wynne-Jones, "Authorisation," 178; Monroe, "Power and Agency," 20; Schoenbrun, "(In)visible Roots."

12 As Jeffrey Fleisher showed for Songo Mnara. See Fleischer, "Gathering of Swahili Religious Practice," 175.

13 See "The Log of the Bark *Palestine*," in Bennett and Brooks, *New England Merchants in Africa*, 188. The log also noted that "poultry was abundant, and vegetation is scarce. There is plenty of wood on the opposite side of the Bay. In short it is a very good place for ships."

14 In 1792, Dumaine estimated the town at "6,000 Arabs and Indians with their families" ("Idée de la côte occidentale," 27). James Hastie estimated the population in 1824 at 12,000; Hastie, journal, July 2, 1824, CPL/EIC. Guillain, writing two decades later, estimated 10,000 (*Documents sur l'histoire*, 213).

15 Boteler, *Narrative of a Voyage*, 113–14.

16 Boteler, *Narrative of a Voyage*, 113–14.

17 Campbell, "History of Nineteenth-Century Madagascar," 333.

18 On the size of the army, see Crossland, *Ancestral Encounters*, 142; on loss of soldiers, see Larson, *History and Memory*, 218–21. The southerly Menabe Kingdom splintered under the external force of Radama's military incursions and internal struggles for succession, but Radama never firmly controlled the territory; see "Journal of James Hastie (1823–1824)," July 1, 1824, and July 4, 1824, CPL/EIC.

19 "Journal of James Hastie (1823–1824)," June 29–30, 1824, CPL/EIC. Scholars have noted the challenges of Hastie's diary as a historical source; see Larson, "Cultural Politics of Bedchamber Construction," 266; Valette, "Reflexions pour une edition." Written in English between 1817 and 1825, the journals are dispersed between Mauritius and the United Kingdom, fragmented, and edited to varying degrees. Herein I rely on journal excerpts found in the Cleveland Library, which I have compared with French translations published by the Académie Malgache when possible. For the latter, see James Hastie, "Le voyage de Tananarive en 1817."

20 The flag was later described as emblazoned with RM in large black letters (for Radama Mpanjaka, or King Radama) on a white background (Osgood, *Notes of Travel*, 4). On the halting of trade, see Campbell, *Economic History*, 58–79; Hooper, "Yankees in Indian Ocean Africa," 36. On taxes, see Grandidier and Grandidier, *Histoire physique*, 604.

21 Hastie, journal, July 3, 1824, CPL/EIC; Guillain, *Documents sur l'histoire*, 94.

22 Hastie, journal, July 4, 1824, CPL/EIC.

23 Hastie, journal, July 5, 1824, CPL/EIC.

24 Isaacs, *Travels and Adventures*, 365.

25 Isaacs, *Travels and Adventures*, 365.

26 Andriantsoly was even permitted to select the site for his exiled home. While Hastie noted that the site the deposed ruler chose possessed "no good quality beyond an exclusive view of swamps, rice grounds, rivers and hills," Andriantsoly explained his rationale as altitudinal power: "that he would then have his feet above the heads of his followers who should build in the low ground, and a constant view of the richest pasturage and best rice groups." This apparently dismayed Radama, who instructed his men to recuperate from Andriantsoly's previous palace in Marovoay with its "sacred door posts and sills, that [were] highly prized in the family," suggesting the sacred power infused in key building materials. Hastie, journal, August 5, 1824, CPL/EIC.

27 Hastie, journal, July 5, 1824, CPL/EIC.

28 Hanson, "Mapping Conflict," 190; Chétima, "You Are Where You Build," 47. For a fascinating counterexample in which lowlands are associated with power, see Malaquais, "Building in the Name of God," 61.

29 Rajaonah, "Modèles européens," 149.

30 Leigh, "Journal," December 28, 1836, NWL. I am grateful to Jane Hooper for sharing this source.

31 Leigh, "Journal," December 28, 1836, NWL.

32 Guillain, *Documents sur l'histoire*, 95–96.

33 This narrative draws from Guillain, *Documents sur l'histoire*, 26, 94–97; Owen, *Narrative of Voyages*, 187–89.

34 Owen describes the events quite similarly to Guillain but adds that "the fragile wooden buildings cracked and fell upon them [the Sakalava warriors]; they were soon obliged to make a precipitate retreat to the sandy jetty ... they fled, panic-stricken, to their vessels." Owen, *Narrative of Voyages*, 188–89.

35 Guillain, *Documents sur l'histoire*, 98–99.

36 Owen, *Narrative of Voyages*, 189.

37 Guillain, *Documents sur l'histoire*, 215.

38 Owen, *Narrative of Voyages*, 189.

39 Hastie estimated the population in 1824 at 12,000; Hastie, journal, July 2, 1824, CPL/EIC. Guillain, writing two decades later, estimated the population at 10,000 (*Documents sur l'histoire*, 213).

40 Guillain, *Documents sur l'histoire*, 213–14. Browne estimated the city's population at 6,000 but did not break down the subgroups (*Etchings*, 239).

41 Accounts of the events leading to the transfer of relics include Guillain, writing in the 1840s, who claimed that when Radama's troops searched Andriantsoly's abandoned doany in Marovoay, they discovered the "irrefutable proof of the chief's royalty, the remains of his ancestors, preciously conserved in a kind of sarcophagus surrounded by layers of white cloth" (*Documents sur l'histoire*, 77). More probable, however, is the account of London Missionary Society (LMS) missionary E. Clayton Pickersgill, written at a later time, which noted a fervent search: "Learning that the sole rallying point [for Sakalava] was neither a living chief, not reigning sovereign, but the relics of an ancient king, Radama conceived the idea of securing [them] as a means of keeping his new subjects from dispersing beyond his reach. For a time his search was fruitless: the fetish had been hidden in the forest. At length, however, a heavy bribe induced a Sakalava to tell of its whereabouts, and a seizure was made by a party of soldiers guided by the informer. For this important service the latter was placed beyond law for the rest of his life, and his family still ranks first in Iboina"; Pickersgill, "North Sakalava-Land," 38–39. Pickersgill's account accords with oral histories about the trajectory and broader significance of the relics.

42 Feeley-Harnik, *Green Estate*, 89 (but compare 505n60); Lambek, *Weight of the Past*, 88; Vérin, *History of Civilisation*, 376.

43 Feeley-Harnik, *Green Estate*, 73–74; Ballarin, "Le 'roi est nu,'" 666–67.

44 Lambek, *Weight of the Past*, 81.

45 Crossland, *Ancestral Encounters*, 142.

46 This account is based on Leigh's diary entry of November 29, 1839, NWL. Leigh referred to the reliquary as a "mitai" (from *mitahy*, meaning "to bless").

47 Leigh, "Journal," November 29, 1839, NWL.

48 Leigh, "Journal," November 29, 1839, NWL.

49 Leigh, "Journal," November 29, 1839, NWL.

50 On fanompoa as care, see Lambek, "Sacrifice and the Problem," 19.

51 Leigh, "Journal," December 30, 1836, NWL.

52 Lambek discusses this extensively in *Weight of the Past*, 45–47, 165–86, 270–75. Feeley-Harnik points out that the "powerfully generative hidden-ness" of the ancestors was foundational to their full recognition and rec-ollection by the living (*Green Estate*, 58). On strategies of concealment in West Africa, see Ferme, *Underneath of Things*, 3.

53 Leigh, "Journal," November 29, 1839, NWL. This was most likely not the famed ritual bathing of relics (fanompoa be, known in the highlands as *fan-droana*), as the group was rather small, the ceremony did not involve the ritual slaughter of cattle, and Leigh did not mention any such washing. Leigh noted that the women were "all Ambolambos" (highlanders).

54 We know this because Leigh was rebuked for pointing his boot soles in the direction of the relics.

55 Leigh, "Journal," November 29, 1839, NWL. The fact that women (presum-ably Sakalava) entreated ancestors through song while Sakalava men were apparently not present suggests that Sakalava women may have enjoyed more mobility into the zomba than Sakalava men did at this time.

56 Guillain, *Documents sur l'histoire*, 215. For similar observations during 1880s, see Pickersgill "North Sakalava-Land," 39.

57 For example, see Leigh, "Journal," June 28, 1839, NWL.

58 Pickersgill, "North Sakalava-Land," 38.

59 W. C. Pickersgill to Foreign Secretary Mullens, London, March 20, 1878, CWM/LMS/13/02/02/054; W. C. Pickersgill to Briggs, Antananarivo, April 20, 1882, CWM/LMS/13/02/02/062; Mbilahy Sahid Aly Andrianamanitra Silamo to Rainilaiarivony, Antananarivo, 5 Alakarabo, 1881, ANRDM/RA/IIIccc /242/3e chemise; 2 sous-chemise.

60 Boteler, *Narrative of a Voyage*, 262; Guillain, *Documents sur l'histoire*, 209; Leigh, "Journal," July 12, 1839, NWL.

61 The precise date of when the gate was constructed in the fashion shown in figure 2.3 is unclear. It is likely that a simpler gate preceded the large stone structure appearing here, and that this was constructed in the mid-century. On enclosures as political processes and artifacts of geographical territori-alization, see Akbari et al., "AHR Conversation," 1519, 1533; Chazkel and Ser-lin, "Editors' Introduction."

62 There is little archival evidence describing the church within the rova. Brit-ish missionary Joseph Mullens noted that the relic shrine "for the moment

seemed to peacefully coexist" with large houses and the garrison church; Mullens, *Twelve Months in Madagascar*, 313. Note that most of Radama's soldiers would have practiced Christianity, owing to the long history of British missionaries in the highlands.

63 Hastie, journal, July 5, 1824, CPL/EIC; Leigh, "Journal," December 28, 1830, NWL; Ferrand, "Notes sur Madagascar," 232; Rakotoarisoa, "Sites et monuments," 97.

64 Rakotoarisoa, "Sites et monuments," 97.

65 Von Jedina, *Voyage de la Frégate*, 171.

66 Von Jedina, *Voyage de la Frégate*, 171.

67 Von Jedina, *Voyage de la Frégate*, 171.

68 Von Jedina, *Voyage de la Frégate*, 167.

69 Osgood, *Notes of Travel*, 5.

70 Osgood, *Notes of Travel*, 4–5.

71 Leigh, "Journal," August 25, 1839, NWL.

72 For instance, Leigh, "Journal," August 28, 1839, NWL.

73 Colomb, *Slave-Catching*, 336–37.

74 Fleisher, "Rituals of Consumption," 200. See also Glassman, *Feasts and Riots*; Monroe and Janzen, "Dahomean Feast."

75 Isaacs, *Travels and Adventures*, 358; Raombana, *Histoires I*, 247; Campbell, *Economic History*, 171–73.

76 Isaacs, *Travels and Adventures*, 358.

77 Hooper notes that American traders' access to these local credit and commodity networks enabled a remarkable transformation toward cattle products as the primary exports in Mahajanga's economy. Hooper, "Yankees in Indian Ocean Africa," 40.

78 Leigh, "Journal," December 13, 1859, NWL; Hooper, "Yankees in Indian Ocean Africa," 46; Vérin, *Les échelles*, 463.

79 Leigh noted that rich Sakalava were commonly accused of a crime and administered the tangena poison penalty: "Once dead, [administrators] divide his property" ("Journal," July 8, 1839, NWL). On one occasion, Leigh observed that five affluent Sakalava, including "one of whom owned 4,000 cattle and hundreds of slaves," were accused by Merina authorities "with the sole object . . . to take possession of [their] property." Merina officials subsequently killed them. ("Journal," November 7, 1839, NWL). When Sakalava were killed, moreover, they were frequently denied a proper burial and instead often "left to rot on the plains" in an act of expulsion and social death. Leigh, "Journal" July 9, 1839, NWL.

80 Rasoamiaramanana, *Aspects économique*, 65–66.

81 According to historian Gwyn Campbell, fanompoana emerged in the highland region as early as the seventeenth century under Andrianjaka (1610–30) to enable labor-intensive rice cultivation and infrastructure projects such as the construction of dykes and walls; "Slavery and Fanompoana," 466–67, 474; Campbell, "History of Nineteenth-Century Madagascar," 353.

82 Rasoamiaramanana, *Aspects économique*, 34.

83 Leigh, "Journal," November 28, 1839, NWL.

84 Leigh, "Journal," December 12, 1839, NWL.

85 As historian Samuel Sanchez points out, the ethnonyms *Masombika* and *Makoa* masked the diverse origins of captives taken from multiple regions in East Africa, though certainly those categorized as such recognized their many linguistic and cultural differences ("Un mouvement antiabolition-niste et anticolonial," 421).

86 Campbell, "Madagascar and the Slave Trade," 203, 214, 226. French colonial authorities subsequently abolished slavery as an institution in 1896.

87 Sheriff, *Slaves, Spices, and Ivory*.

88 In 1874, the Imerina government passed a decree emancipating all those forcibly brought from East Africa to Madagascar since 1865. This decree was amended in 1877 to include all enslaved persons. Mutibwa, *Malagasy and the Europeans*, 335.

89 Leigh, "Journal," December 8, 1839, NWL.

90 Leigh, "Journal," December 15, 1839, NWL.

91 Carey, "How Slaves Indigenized Themselves."

92 The literature on Swahili "stone" architecture is vast. See Donley-Reid, "Structuring Structure"; Myers, "Sticks and Stones"; Wynne-Jones, "Public Life"; Meier, *Swahili Port Cities*.

93 Hastie, journal, July 2, 1845, CPL/EIC.

94 Hastie, journal, July 2, 1845, CPL/EIC.

95 Isaacs, *Travels and Adventures*, 360.

96 Catat similarly remarked on these differences in *Voyage à Madagascar*, 240.

97 Leigh, "Journal," February 5, 1839, NWL.

98 Wright et al., "Evolution of Settlement Systems," 38; Rogers et al., "Stratigraphic Analysis," 289.

99 Leigh, "Journal," June 23, 1839, NWL.

100 Leigh, "Journal," June 23, 1839, NWL.

101 Guillain, *Documents sur l'histoire*, 95, 208. Guillain's account offers a rare historical reference to the ethnicity of the builders of these stone houses. Although it seems likely that Antalaotra typically worked as masons, more research is needed to confirm their role.

102 Rasoamiaramana, *Aspects économique*, 34; Campbell, "Slavery and Fanompoana," 478. Sakalava were evidently conscripted as well, albeit in smaller numbers.

103 Archaeological records show evidence of lime mortar at nearby Antsoheribory from at least the sixteenth century. Wright et al., "Evolution of Settlement Systems," 56–58.

104 Campbell, "History of Nineteenth-Century Madagascar," 332–34.

105 Campbell, "Slavery and Fanompoana," 475; Randrianja and Ellis, *Madagascar*, 136–37.

106 For instance, when officials in Mahajanga learned that Queen Rasoherina

built a house (*trano*) in Antananarivo, they offered silver coins (*volatsivaky*) and five bulls, "as they did with prior kings," while Baoanjoma, leader of the "Arabs" (*komany lehibe' arabo monina*), offered seven ariary as tribute (*ny vola 7a ataoko solompanompoana*). Andrianatoro to Rasoherina Mpanjaka, Antananarivo, 13 Alahasaty 1865, ANRDM/Royal Archive/IIIcc/233/1ère chemise.

107 Andrianatoro to Radama II, Antananarivo, 5 Alohotsy 1863, ANRDM/IIIcc/232; Ramarohanta to Ranavalomanjaka, Antananarivo, 6 Adalo 1860, ANDRM/III/cc/232.

108 Mutibwa, *Malagasy and the Europeans*, 46–52.

109 Randrianatoro to Radama II, Antananarivo, 10 Asorotany 1863 (letter confirming receipt of king's instructions), ANRDM/IIIcc/232.

110 Mutibwa, *Malagasy and the Europeans*, 85.

111 Komandy Rainivoajo to Rasoherimanjaka, Antananarivo, 22 Alakamy, 1863, ANRDM/IIIcc/232.

112 Ramasy to Ranavalomanjaka, Antananarivo, 21 Adimizana 1870, ANRDM/IIIcc /233/2ème chemise; Ramasy to Ranavalomanjaka, Antananarivo, 1 Adalo 1874, ANRDM/IIIcc/233/2ème chemise. Although the causes of these fires were largely undocumented, the fire of 1874 was attributed to an uncontained cooking fire for enslaved men in the rova.

113 Ramasy to Rainilaiarivony Prime Minister Commander in Chief, Antananarivo, 26 Alakoasy 1875, ANRDM/IIIcc/233/2ème chemise.

114 "Arab" likely referred to Antalaotra masons. W. C. Pickersgill to Foreign Secretary Mullens, London, March 20, 1878, cwm/lms/13/02/02/054.

115 Pickersgill, "North-West Madagascar," 328; Imerina District Commission, Madagascar: Minutes of Committee, regular meeting held at Faravohitra, September 9, 1878, and September 10, 1878, cwm/lms/13/02/02/054.

116 W. C. Pickersgill to Foreign Secretary Mullens, London, March 20, 1878, cwm/lms/13/02/02/054.

117 W. C. Pickersgill to B. Briggs, April 20, 1882, cwm/lms/13/02/02/062.

118 Pickersgill to Mullens; Pickersgill to Briggs.

119 Ballarin, *Les reliques royal*, 176–80.

120 Mbilahy Sahid Aly Andrianamanitra Silamo to Rainilaiarivony, Antananarivo, 5 Alakarabo 1881, ANRDM/Royal Archive/IIIccc/242/3e chemise; 2 sous-chemise.

121 "Ka raha lasany tompoka eo io zavatra io 'simba ny fanjakana' refa tsy ny faharatsian'ny fiambenana no anaovako izany, fa ny havitsian'ny." Mbilahy Sahid Aly Andrianamanitra Silamo to Rainilaiarivony. Aly also reported that Pickersgill was thoroughly disgusted with the many Merina soldiers who "honored the devil" in this way.

122 Pickersgill reported that "Makoa" comprised a large proportion of Christian converts; Pickersgill to Briggs, April 20, 1882.

123 Feeley-Harnik, *Green Estate*, 89, 505 n60.

124 Lambek, *Weight of the Past*, 90.

125 Kneitz, "Sakalava Pilgrimage," 260.

126 Kneitz, "Sakalava Pilgrimage," 260–61.

127 Ballarin, "Le 'roi est nu,'" 676–80; Lambek, "Interminable Disputes," 6–9.

128 Bernault, *Colonial Transactions*, 16.

129 Pickersgill noted that though many Sakalava had settled in the hinterlands, away from the purview of imperial officials, they "continued to regard the town as their head-quarters"; Pickersgill, "North Sakalava-Land," 34.

130 Lambek, "On Being Present to History," 322.

131 Lambek, "On Being Present to History," 322.

Chapter 3. Storied Refusals

Abbreviations: ANRDM (National Archives of the République Démocratique de Madagascar, Antananarivo, Madagascar); CAOM (Centre des archives d'Outre-Mer, Aix-en-Provence, France).

1 Mehta, *Dream Half-Expressed*, 17, 53.

2 Desai, "Commerce as Romance,"148.

3 Aiyar, *Indians in Kenya*, 2.

4 This chapter uses *Indian* or *Karana* (the latter is particular to Madagascar) to denote migrants from South Asia. For the foundational history of Indians in Madagascar, see Blanchy, *Karana et Banians*. For additional work addressing how Indians dealt with tensions of belonging in Africa, see Brennan, *Taifa*; Soske, *Internal Frontiers*; Burton, *Africa in the Indian Imagination*.

5 Indian building works are described by Myers, *Verandahs of Power*, 18–32; Soske, *Internal Frontiers*, 50–52; Fair, *Reel Pleasures*.

6 Cooper, "Urban Space, Industrial Time," 27.

7 On urban planning as social engineering, see Mitchell, *Rule of Experts*; Scott, *Seeing Like a State*; Abu-Lughod, "Tale of Two Cities"; Holston, *Modernist City*; Rabinow, *French Modern*; G. Wright, *Politics of Design*.

8 Myers, *Verandahs of Power*; A. D. King, *Colonial Urban Development*.

9 Gallieni, *Neuf ans à Madagascar*, 58–59; Rajaonah, "Modèles européens"; G. Wright, *Politics of Design*. On colonial sublime, see Larkin, *Signal and Noise*.

10 Carse and Kneas, "Unbuilt and Unfinished," 15.

11 On colonial inefficiency, see Bissell, *Urban Design*; Scott, *Weapons of the Weak*.

12 Simpson, *Mohawk Interruptus*; McGranahan, "Theorizing Refusal," 322–23.

13 On "vitality of social relations," see Sobo, "Theorizing (Vaccine) Refusal," 343.

14 Campt, "Visual Frequency," 25.

15 Prasse-Freeman, "Resistance/Refusal," 1.

16 Randrianja and Ellis, *Madagascar*, 138–39. Despite these alliances, the French government continued to officially recognize the highland monarchy as the island's sovereign ruler.

17 Rakotoarisoa, "Sites et monuments," 100. Much of this account comes from the journal of French soldier Antoine Perraud, *Escape from Madagascar*, 13–30. Up to six soldiers were buried per day during Perraud's stay in 1884, but high mortality rates would persist in subsequent military incursions.

18 Gautier, "L'ouest malgache," 315–16.

19 Vasco, "Majunga et son occupation." In 1885, highland troops reoccupied the city and overtook the seaside fort. Rakotoarisoa, "Sites et monuments," 100–102. The highland troops had actually constructed three forts in the area: the principal fort, one at Anorombato, and another at Antsahabingo. According to archaeologist Rakotoarisoa, traces of the latter two no longer exist, but he has documented the primary fort. Wages were "much more on the west coast than on the rest of the island"; the cheapest daily workers in Mahajanga were hired for 30 francs per month, plus food rations. *Revue française de l'étranger et des colonies*, "Notices sur Majunga." Ongoing negotiations between diplomats in Antananarivo, France, and Britain unfolded over the late 1880s. By 1890, Britain and France agreed on their respective spheres of influence, and France laid claim to Madagascar as a protectorate. Campbell, *Economic History*, 4.

20 Landrieu, "Majunga, son importance," 338.

21 Grandidier as cited in Mille, "Une ancienne forteresss merina du XIXe siècle," 150. Troop figures are from Reynaud, *Considérations sanitaires*, 246, 251. Though they must have been important navigators for French troops, porters appear not to have been directly involved in combat; instead, they were tasked primarily with logistical conveyance of military equipment and supplies. Grosclaude commented on "indigene" soldiers (*tirailleurs*) and their families (*Un Parisien à Madagascar*, 35).

22 On seizure, see *Revue française de l'étranger et des colonies*, "Correspondances," 422.

23 *Revue française de l'étranger et des colonies*, "Correspondances," 423; Oliver, "French Operations," 221.

24 *Revue française de l'étranger et des colonies*, "Correspondances," 423.

25 Aubanel, *La France Civilisatrice*, 239–40.

26 Grosclaude, *Un Parisien à Madagascar*, 33.

27 It is not clear whether these Comorian laborers were recruited from the local population in Mahajanga or from Comoros. Those from Somalia were likely *tirailleurs* from the Corps expéditionnaire.

28 Rogers, "Fine-Grained Debris Flows," 300; Abramovich et al., "Age and Paleoenvironment," 29. On navigation and boat technologies, see Sanchez, "Navigation et gens de mer," 105–18.

29 *Revue française de l'étranger et des colonies*, "Correspondances," 422.

30 *Revue française de l'étranger et des colonies*, "Correspondances," 422–23.

31 Reynaud, *Considérations sanitaires*, 2.

32 Aubanel, *La France civilisatrice*, 144, 35.

33 Feeley-Harnik, "Ravenala Madagascariensis Sonnerat," 58: "Le gouver-

nement...rappelle souvent nos droits conquis sur cette île par le sang et l'argent français." Translation by author.

34 Grosclaude, *Un Parisien à Madagascar*, 33–35, 287.

35 Reynaud, *Considérations sanitaires*, 368. Of the dead, barely fifty were killed in battle. Shervinton, *Shervintons*, 222. See Curtin, *Disease and Empire* (188) for a thorough analysis of the statistics pertaining to causes of death during the 1895–96 military campaign. For broader anxieties about the salubrity of Mahajanga in the 1890s, see Vasco, "Madagascar," 80–87; Landrieu, "Majunga," 310–28.

36 Mrázek, *Engineers of Happy Land*, 8.

37 Vasco, "Majunga et son occupation," 76; Catat, *Voyage à Madagascar*, 31.

38 For European descriptions of the town see Grandidier, "Souvenirs"; Ferrand, "Notes sur Madagascar," 232; Bénévent, "Étude sur le Bouéni"; Grainge, "Journal"; Aubanel, *La France civilisatrice*, 100; on narratives of technological lack, see Adas, *Machines as Measure of Men*.

39 Trouillot, *Silencing the Past*, 96.

40 Landrieu, "Majunga," 337. Some of these plans were envisioned almost a decade earlier, see letter from Vice-Residence of Majunga to Resident General Myre de Vilers, relative au commerce à Majunga, November 8, 1886, CAOM/2Z/175.

41 On the "eighteen tribes," see Gallieni, *Neuf ans à Madagascar*, 37–39, 325–27. Also see Raison-Jourde and Randrianja, *La nation malgache; De Majunga à Tananarive*. On Comorians, see Ferrand, "Notes sur Madagascar," 234. On the displacements and divisions of the town, see "Madagascar, la région de Majunga," 282–84. On forcible displacements, see Arrête 1044, October 15, 1897, ANRDM/F40. As in other colonial cities, however, the realization of separate geographies—whether segregated neighborhoods or households—was ever elusive. Mahabibo's spatial and legal boundaries were frequently transgressed. For example, despite official efforts to maintain a certain distance between "natives" and "Europeans," European residents relied on Mahabibo residents as domestic workers, dockworkers, and personal cooks in Majunga Be. For thoughtful discussions of the fixity of colonial segregationist planning and the ambiguity of these geographies, see Cooper, "Conflict and Connection"; Schler, "Ambiguous Spaces"; Bissell, "Between Fixity and Fantasy."

42 Fanon, *Wretched of the Earth*.

43 This dump would later attract copious numbers of rats and serve as an epicenter of bubonic plague in 1907. Le Ray, "Epidémie de peste."

44 Census figures from Rapport Circonscription Majunga, 1902, CAOM/MAD/GGM. Of the 613 South Asian traders, 255 were Baniana, 111 "Sudbi," 144 "Bohras," and 103 "Kodja." Also see Blanchy, *Karana et Banians*, 29.

45 Following Blanchy, I use the term *Karana* broadly to denote the five socioreligious groups of South Asian descent who have resided and traversed through Madagascar; see Blanchy, *Karana et Banians*, 16. Four of these

groups are Muslim and one is Hindu. *Banian* is reserved exclusively for this latter group, but here I sometimes group Banians with the Karana groups when it is appropriate to do so. Missionary Lars Dahle traced the etymology of the word *Karana*, or sometimes *Karany*, to a Kiswahili word meaning "clerk, secretary." Dahle, "Swaheli Element," 106.

46 On Gujarati traders and trading networks, see Dumaine, "Idée de la côte occidentale," 27; Machado, *Ocean of Trade*, 28; Campbell, "Madagascar and Mozambique," 171–72; Campbell, *Economic History*, 292.

47 McDow, *Buying Time*, 8–11.

48 Mehta, *Dream Half-Expressed*, 53.

49 On mobility and rootedness, see Bang, *Sufis and Scholars*; Ho, *Graves of Tarim*; Aslanian, *From the Indian Ocean*; Prange, *Monsoon Islam*.

50 On Daosa's contributions, see Ramasy to Ranavalona, Antananrivo, 8 Alakarabo 1871, ANRDM/IIIcc/233/2ème chemise; Andrianatoro to Radama II, 15 Alahamady 1863, ANRDM/IIIcc/232, which states: "Famboarany ladoany rahamisy tokony ho simba" (He will rebuild the customhouse when it is in disrepair.") Ramasy also noted that Daosa donated a barrel of vinegar to treat patients suffering from smallpox and that "Abidine," another Karana, invited the military and commoners to retrieve rice from his storehouse during a rice shortage in town.

51 Blanchy, *Karana et Banians*, 88. There is also an ancient Bohra cemetery that contains tombs possibly dating from 1769, with stone stele grave markers clearly dated to the mid-nineteenth century; Vérin,"Les échelles anciennes," 501.

52 On the mosques, see Blanchy, *Karana et Banians*, 85–88; Delval, "Les musulmans," 21.

53 Green, *Bombay Islam*, 208–34.

54 Letter from Aide-Marie (AM) Majunga A. Carron to Gov. General, Tananarive, April 30, 1912, ANRDM/F161.

55 Letter from AM Majunga A. Carron to Gov. General, April 30, 1912.

56 Meier, *Swahili Port Cities*, 2.

57 Grainge, "Journal"; Mullens, *Twelve Months*, 315.

58 Mullens, *Twelve Months*, 315.

59 Mullens, *Twelve Months*, 315.

60 Mullens, *Twelve Months*, 315.

61 The presence of carved wooden doors marked Indian Ocean towns as important trade centers. See Myers, "Eurocentrism and African Urbanization," 205; Ballarin, "Portes sculptées"; Nooter, "Zanzibar Doors," 35. For general descriptions of Old Majunga, see Grainge, "Journal"; Mullens, *Twelve Months*, 315.

62 Colomb, *Slave-Catching*, 324.

63 Colomb, *Slave-Catching*, 324–25.

64 Meier, *Swahili Port Cities*, 140; see also Prestholdt, *Domesticating the World*.

65 On alignment plans, Procés-Verbaux, June 22, 1902, ANRDM/F41; Arrete, June 9, 1902, Fixant les limites de la Commune de Majunga, ANRDM/F48; Rapport du Chef de Bataillon to Chef du Service Travaux Publics, Tananarive, January 30, 1903, ANRDM/VIIJ/347.

66 Personnel, Voirie, Divers, Photo (1898–1940), September 25, 1912, Arrete no. 99, ANRDM/F51.

67 Bernard, "Le main-d'oeuvre aux colonies," 11.

68 Jacquier, "La main-d'oeuvre locale à Madagascar." See also Feeley-Harnik's discussion of Jacquier and others on securing labor in "Political Economy of Death."

69 Jacquier, "La main-d'oeuvre locale à Madagascar."

70 Chang and King, "Towards a Genealogy"; Harrison, *Climates and Constitutions*.

71 On prestations and fleeing in Madagascar, see Fremigacci, "Autocratie administrative," 403; Rijke-Epstein, "Neglect as Effacement," 360.

72 "La Main d'Oeuvre à Madagascar," *La Depeche de Majunga*, May 4, 1902; on equating wage work with servitude in northwest Madagascar, see Feeley-Harnik, "Political Economy of Death," 12–13.

73 For instance, *Notes, Reconnaissance and Exploration*, "Bulletin Mensuel," (2e semestre, 1898): 1099–1110. Jacquier, "La main-d'oeuvre locale à Madagascar," 1.

74 Rapports Mensuel sur les travaux executes dans la subdivision de Majunga, April 1898, ANRDM/DTP 28.

75 Rapports Mensuel sur les travaux.

76 McGranahan, "Theorizing Refusal," 323.

77 On roadbuilding in colonial Africa, see Freed, "Networks of (Colonial) Power" On roadbuilding in Madagascar, see Sharp, "Laboring for the Colony," 79–84; Sodikoff, "Land and Languor," 369–80; Rijke-Epstein, "Neglect as Effacement," 358–60.

78 "La Main d'Oeuvre à Madagascar," *La Depeche de Majunga*, May 4, 1902; Decision no. 73 from Admin. en Chef de la Province et Maire de Majunga, June 24, 1902, ANRDM/DTP 29.

79 French colonial officials' decision to employ Chinese indentured workers in Madagascar derived from earlier precedents in Senegal, where they built the Dakar–Saint Louis railway between 1883 and 1885 and the Kankan-Conakry railway between 1899 and 1904. Anshan, *History of Chinese Overseas*, 60–75.

80 Following the French abolition of slavery in 1897, French authorities in Madagascar were even more desperate for laborers and stepped up recruitment efforts for Chinese laborers, especially coming from the Guangzhou region. Li Anshan estimates that between 1850 and 1910, 7,500 Chinese indentured workers were brought to Madagascar; Anshan, *History of Chinese Overseas*, 92–93.

81 On Chinese laborers as "inherently docile," see Martinez, "'Unwanted

Scraps,'" 79. On the need for "energetic discipline," see Travaux Public Rapport Annual, 1901, ANRDM/DTP 28.

82 Letter from Chef Moriceau to Gov. General, August 23, 1901, CAOM 6(5)D1.

83 Letter from Chef Moriceau to Gov. General, September 3, 1903, ANRDM/F48; "La Main d'Oeuvre à Madagascar," *La Depeche de Majunga*, May 4, 1902; Decision no. 73 from Adm. in Chef de la Province et Maire de Majunga; *Guide Annuaire de Madagascar* (1902), 502.

84 Letter from Chef de Colonies to Gov. General, March 10, 1902, CAOM 6(5) D1.

85 Letter from Chef de Colonies to Gov. General, March 10, 1902.

86 Notices of the arrangement with Codja and Premjee were published in *La Depeche de Majunga*, May 4, 1902.

87 *Livret d'engagé Indien*, 1900, CAOM 6(5)D1. They were provided a daily ration of 900 grams (2 pounds) of rice, 40 grams (1½ ounces) of salt, and 6 grams (less than ¼ ounce) of tea, as well as 1 kilogram (2¼ pounds) of Indian butter per month, and 20 centimes to buy meat, fish, and other incidentals. At the termination of their contract, workers were given the option of remaining in the colony or returning to Porbandar; French records suggest that most opted to return to India., Note from Administration Gov. General to Chef de 3ème bureau, June 22, 1902, CAOM 6(5)D1.

88 Telegram, October 13, 1902, CAOM, 6(5)D1; letter from Chef de Colonies to Gov. General, March 10, 1902.

89 On the origins of workers, Blanchy, *Karana et Banian*, 84.

90 Letter from Chef de Colonies to Gov. General, March 10, 1902.

91 *La Depeche de Majunga*, May 4, 1902.

92 Colonial authorities anticipated a large number of Indians would establish themselves permanently in the region, where they could "contribute powerfully to the general prosperity." *Guide Annuaire de Madagascar* (1902), 502.

93 Letter from Chef de Colonies to Gov. General, March 10, 1902.

94 On housing, see Letter from Admin. en Chef Moriceau to Gouverneur General, May 1, 1903, ANRDM/DTP28. On plagues, see Harrison, *Contagion*, 174–76. Origins of the plague are discussed in Rapport Politique et Administratif, 1903, CAOM/MAD/GGM/2D/133; Dispatch from Majunga, June 15, 1902, CAOM/BIB/SOM/ePOM/603; Le Ray, "Epidémie de peste." The Indian migrants' boat departed from Porbandar in January 1902, and by February 1902 the city of Porbandar was under duress with an extreme epidemic of the plague. This origin was later debated among medical researchers, because the boat captain reported no passengers were ill during the journey, and the craft and baggage were quarantined for five days upon arriving at the Mahajanga port. The time lapse between February and May weakened the case for medical researchers that the disease traveled on these particular boats, and some contended that the bacteria had been latent in the soil and erupted infectiously with coincidental timing. Clarac, "Epidémie de peste," 28–46; "Peste."

95　On expropriation, see Rapport Politique et Administratif, 1903. Authorities planned to clear Karana-owned homes to construct broad streets and to convert Old Majunga into a commercial district, with some housing for Europeans. The sum for expropriation of the said area was estimated at some seven million to eight million francs. *La Depeche de Majunga*, May 4, 1902.

96　Clarac, "Epidémie de peste," 43. Although little evidence existed that targeted incineration would prevent the spread of the bubonic plague, experts perceived that the *Yersinia pestis* bacteria could hide in the crevices of wood planks, in clothing and furniture, and behind walls, so they believed that burning them would destroy these residual threats. Compare with Mohr, *Plague and Fire*, 89–96.

97　It is unclear whether Karana were expected to build these homes at their expense or with government funding. "Commission municipale (Séance du 12 Juin)," *La Depeche de Majunga*, June 15, 1902; Proces-Verbaux de la séance de la Commission Municipale, June 12, 1902, ANRDM/F41.

98　Letter from petitioners to Gouverneur Général Gallieni, June 15, 1902, ANRDM/F52.

99　Annique Hommels, in another context, cogently signaled the technopolitics of obduracy in cities; Hommels, *Unbuilding Cities*, 11, 20.

100　Letter from Chef des Colonies Moriceau to Gouverneur Général Gallieni, June 17, 1902, ANRDM/F52. For more biographical background on colonial adminstrator Moriceau and his extensive ethnological and paleontological collections as part of the colonial enterprise in New Caledonia and Madagascar, see Bounoure, "Éléments," 226–28.

101　Le Ray "Epidémie de peste," 216.

102　Le Ray "Epidémie de peste," 216.

103　Le Ray "Epidémie de peste," 216; Mavhunga, "Vermin Beings," 151–52.

104　"Tribune Publique," *La Depeche de Majunga*, June 8, 1902.

105　Massey, "Travelling Thoughts," 229.

106　Jacquier, *La Main-d'Oeuvre locale à Madagascar*, 16.

107　On conditions of labor and the shifting labor market, see Thompson and Adloff, *Malagasy Republic*, 449; Feeley-Harnik, "Political Economy of Death"; Ellis, *Rising of the Red Shawls*, 126; Campbell, "Unfree Labour," 76–77; Rabearimanana, "Les descendants d'Andevo," 522–24.

108　On the rise of Karana commerce, see Blanchy, *Karana et Banians*, 170. See also Bardonnet, "Les Minorités asiatiques à Madagascar."

Chapter 4. Sedimentary Bonds

Abbreviations: ANRDM (National Archives of the République Démocratique de Madagascar, Antananarivo, Madagascar); BNF (Bibliothèque nationale de France, Paris, France); CAOM (Centre des archives d'Outre-Mer,

Aix-en-Provence, France); MAD/GGM (Gouvernement général de Madagascar); PM (Province de Majunga).

1   The precise cause of the fire was unclear. City officials did, however, praise the courageous efforts of "the Senegalais Boubou" who entered a burning house to retrieve three kilograms of gunpowder that would have exploded and caused great damage. To reward him for his valiant efforts, he was permitted to freely exploit the nearby stone mine. Extrait du registre des déliberations de la Comission Municipale de Majunga, séance September 27, 1912, ANRDM/F52: Urbanisme. Colonial officials debated about post-fire aid; letter from Maire Carron to Gouverneur Général, February 14, 1912, ANRDM/F52.

2   Up to this point, colonial authorities surveyed and worked to retroactively to codify land holding permits for those who already occupied land in Mahabibo.

3   Quote is from letter from M. Raulet to Gouverneur Général, October 12, 1912, ANRDM/F52; This letter explains that residents could rent homes at eight francs per month (below the market rate of 10 francs/month) and become owners after ten years of continuous, timely payment. Officials claimed the rate of eight francs was "below the price paid by the indigene renter to the indigene owner to live in a foliage house, in which the least hygenic prescriptions are far from observed." On deliberations about this proposal, see letter from Maire Carron to Gouverneur Général, October 24, 1912, ANRDM/F52; letter from Mayor Carron to Gouverneur Général, February 14, 1912, ANRDM/F41; extrait du registre des délibérations, séance September 27, 1912, ANRDM/F52.

4   Letter to Gov. Général de Madagascar, November 9, 1912, ANRDM/F51. Translation by author.

5   See note 28 for more detailed statistics over the first several decades of the 1900s.

6   On building activities as political mediums elsewhere in Africa, see Malaquais, "Building in the Name of God"; Elleh, *Architecture and Power in Africa*. Science and technology studies scholars have documented how lay people have entered techno-scientific circles, questioned experts' credibility and claims, and redrawn the boundaries of experts and publics; see, for instance, B. Wynne, "Misunderstood Misunderstandings"; Epstein, "Construction of Lay Expertise." On epistemic effacement, see Trouillot, *Silencing the Past*; Spivak, "Can the Subaltern Speak?"

7   Rabinow, *French Modern*; G. Wright, *Politics of Design*.

8   Byrd, *Transit of Empire*, 53.

9   On colonialism as epistemic processes of "making sense of new people, things and places based in material practices," see R. King, "Living on Edge," 533; Stoler, "Epistemic Politics."

10 Key works on histories of emotion include Reddy, *Navigation of Feeling*; Rosenwein, *Emotional Communities*; Plamper, "History of Emotions,"

252–53. Lynn Thomas and Jennifer Cole have cogently asserted the lack of attention to emotion, especially love, in African studies; see Thomas and Cole, "Introduction," 2–4.

11 S. Ahmed, *Cultural Politics of Emotion*, 11; de Luna, "Affect and Society." On affect and architecture, see Rajagopalan, *Building Histories*. On the affective properties of buildings, see Archambault, "'One Beer, One Block'"; Navaro-Yashin, *Make-Believe Space*. See also Harris and Sørensen, "Rethinking Emotion and Material Culture," 149.

12 "Global racial capitalism" refers to the ways capitalism works through and reproduces constructed racial, gender, and geographical categories; see Robinson, *Black Marxism*; Lowe, *Intimacies of Four Continents*; Du Bois, *World and Africa*.

13 Interview with D. H., Mahabibo, April 26, 2013.

14 The Malagasy language contains a considerable number of loanwords from Shikomoro, though Comorian dialects show fewer Malagasy loanwords. see Dahl, "Bantu Substratum"; Adelaar, "Loanwords in Malagasy," 726–27; Gueunier, *Les chemins*, 42–43.

15 On multiple factors for urban migration in African pasts, see L. White, *Comforts of Home*; Harries, *Work, Culture, and Identity*.

16 Cooper, "From Enslavement to Precarity?," 142.

17 Manchuelle, *Willing Migrants*, 59–65.

18 This section necessarily condenses much historical complexity and follows from Walker, *Islands in a Cosmopolitan Sea*; Alpers, "Slavery, Antislavery"; Newitt, *Comoro Islands*; J. Martin, *Comores*; Isnard, "L'archipel des Comores," 188. For more on the history of the Comoros and its involvement in trading networks during the seventeenth to nineteenth centuries, see Alpers, "French Slave Trade." Migration dynamics played out quite differently on the two islands; see Mohamed, "Entre Anjouanais et Grands-Comoriens," 458. On the historical fluctuations of global sugar production, see Deerr, *History of Sugar*; Bosma, *Sugar Plantation*, 164–210.

19 Consider that following the Governor General of Madagascar's request to send workers to Mahajanga in 1904, resident Renè Perrè sent only twenty-five Mohelians. Perrè apologized profusely for his inability to recruit more men and explained that nearly half of the 1,440 men in Moheli were already "engaged" in projects. Letter from Resident de France à Moheli, Renè Perrè, August 22, 1904, ANRDM/DTP 29.

20 Lafont, "Géographie médicale, L'Île d'Anjouan," 161. Like other medical geographers of the time, Lafont was a medical doctor and an officer in the French colonial army, and early French medical geography was tightly knit with colonial conquest. Medical geographers were informed by military priorities of assuring sanitary conditions for troop deployment, imperatives to map and chart peoples, and assessment of environmental issues relevant to military expansion, and they generated theories on racial difference, degeneration, and environmental considerations critical to European terri-

torial expansion. See Valenčius "Histories of Medical Geography," 15–16; Osborne, *Emergence of Tropical Medicine.*

21 Lafont, "Géographie médicale, L'Île d'Anjouan," 161.

22 Lafont, "Géographie médicale, L'Île d'Anjouan," 161.

23 Saïd, "Contribution a l'étude," 105.

24 Gueunier, *Les chemins*; Bang, *Islamic Sufi Networks.* See also Dandouau, *Contes populaires*; Charles-Roux et al., *Les colonies françaises*, 230.

25 Prud'Homme surmised that "his official elevation to such a position would of itself constitute a guarantee for the loyalty of the Arabs, so great is the well-merited prestige that he enjoys" ("Observations," 430). Concerns about potential Islamic threats and official efforts to cultivate loyalty of Muslim subjects stretched across the French empire; see Robinson, *Paths of Accommodation*; Seesemann and Soares, "Being as Good Muslims," 93–95; Maussen et al., *Colonial and Post-colonial Governance of Islam.*

26 N. Green, *Bombay Islam*, 6.

27 On Sufi expansion in the Indian Ocean, see Bang, *Islamic Sufi Networks*, 75–84; Alpers, "Complex Relationship," 84–86; Bonate, "Advent and Schisms," 484–86; C. Ahmed, "Networks of the Shadhiliyya," 317–24. For the spread of Shadhiliyya to Madagascar, see Gueunier, *Les chemins*, 55–56, 74–75.

28 Population statistics for this time are fraught. In order of dates provided: Rapport Circonscription Annual, 1902, caom/mad/ggm, recorded a total population in Mahajanga of 4,703, of which 266 were "Anjounais," 152 "Comoriens" [from Grande Comore], and 108 "Matsores" [Moheli]. By 1913, the number was 12,616 (of which 2,415 were "Comorian"); caom/d/6(1)/12. By 1921, there were 6,300 "Comorians," and by 1936 that number grew to 15,000; Delval, "Les migrations comoriennes," 97. In the 1950s, French administrator Hubert Deschamps gauged the "Comorian" population to be "50 percent" of the town's overall count of around 16,500; Deschamps, *Les migrations intérieures*, 90, 188–89.

29 Annexation of the Comoros to Madagascar, decree of April 9, 1908, Article 2, bnf. See Ibrahime, *État français*, 29–31.

30 I conducted most of these oral interviews in Mahajanga between 2011 and 2014.

31 Letter from Chef de l'Arrondissement Travaux Publics to Chef de la Subdivision des Travaux Publiques de Majunga Ville, December 1, 1932, anrdm/vIIj/391; Nativel, "Les migrants comorians," 120.

32 Saïd, "Contribution a l'étude," 107; Radifison, "Conflits ethniques," 135; Amigues, "Variole et Vaccine," 492; Lafont, "Géographie médicale, Mohéli," 508.

33 The shift to working in colonial administration was not inevitable. In the 1900s and 1910s, French administrators in the northwest region wielded an "anti-Muslim campaign" organized around economic arguments in which (among other contentions) Comorian traders were accused of pushing Sakalava to steal cattle. Fremigacci, "Autocratie," 407–10.

34 Interview with H. A., Abattoir, June 19, 2013; fieldnotes, October 14, 2013. Note that Mama Beatrice's recollections of her father were bound up with her own unrealized childhood aspirations to obtain institutionalized learning. Comorian parents in the 1930s and '40s customarily sent both male and female children to Qu'ranic schools but not to secular French colonial schools. Many older women of mixed Comorian and Malagasy descent described their deep desire and occasional good fortune if able to pursue formal secular schooling. On Comorian complicity in colonial rule, see Rajaonah, "La communauté comorienne," 102–15.

35 Rajaonah, "La communauté comorienne," 100–110. In 1921, one city council member noted that migrants from Ngazidja and Nwani comprised the great majority of the city's police force, because they were "undaunted by night rounds and long hours." Procés-Verbal (PV) séance, May 3, 1921, ANRDM/F42.

36 Interview with Hasandrama, Tsaramandroso, February 2, 2014.

37 Walker elaborates historical marriage practices and "cycles of indebtedness" across the Comoros; *Islands*, 118–20.

38 Oral accounts referenced reputations in the Comoros obliquely, and more research could help historicize these dynamics. On fame, mobility, and work, see de Luna, "Tracing the Itineraries," 24; "Marksmen and the Bush."

39 Bourdieu, *Outline of a Theory of Practice*, 6–7.

40 Interview with M. N., Manga, October 18, 2013. *Fondi* (or *fondry*), related to Swahili *fundi*, denotes a teacher, specialist, or skilled person. See Richardson, *New Malagasy-English Dictionary*, 201.

41 Bonate, "Islam in Northern Mozambique," 583. On Shadhiliyya, see "Shadhiliyya Tariqah," *Oxford Dictionary of Islam*; "Shādhiliyya," *Encyclopaedia of Islam*, 2nd ed. On Sufi brotherhoods more generally, see B. Martin, *Muslim Brotherhoods*. Bang is among several historians who have attributed the spread and relative strength of Shadhiliyya in the Comoros and northern Madagascar to the charismatic leadership of Muhammaed Ma'ruf (1853–1905), a noble of Hadramawt descent and disciple of Abdallah bin Said bin Darwish. See Martin, *Muslim Brotherhoods*, 152–55; Walker, *Islands in a Cosmopolitan Sea*, 121–55. On the spread of Shadhiliyya to northern Mozambique, see Alpers, "Complex Relationship"; Bonate, "Advent and Schisms," 484–88; to South Africa, see Kaarsholm, "Zanzibaris or Amakhuwa," 198; to Tanzania, see C. Ahmed, "Networks of the Shadhiliyya."

42 Bang, *Islamic Sufi Networks*, 76–80.

43 Gueunier, *Les chemins*, 74–76; Walker, *Islands in a Cosmopolitan Sea*, 120–22. Interview with Maître Youssef, Mahajanga, July 16, 2013.

44 Interview with D. H., Mahabibo, April 26, 2013. The interpretation of Mahajanga as the "birthplace" of Islam in Madagascar conflicts with accounts among Ankaranana Muslim communities in northern Madagascar, or even southeast Madagascar, who believe that Islam first arrived on their shores. Interview with D. P., Abattoir, February 16, 2014.

45 Interview with H. A., Abattoir, July 9, 2013.

46 See Gueunier, *Les chemins*; Bang, *Islamic Sufi Networks*. On language imprints, see Gueunier, *Les chemins*, 42–43; he points out that Comorian and Swahili languages are so close that it is difficult to distinguish the origins of imprints in Malagasy.

47 Letter from AM Majunga A. Carron to Gov. General, April 30, 1912, ANRDM/F161.

48 Letter from AM Majunga A. Carron to Gov. General, April 30, 1912. Blanchy, *Karana et Banians*, 63–67, 84–88.

49 Dumaine, "Idée de la côte occidentale." Archaeological evidence suggests that mosques and Muslim tombs were constructed near Mahajanga in the late seventeenth and eighteenth centuries and even earlier in areas of northern Madagascar. See Vérin, *Les échelles anciennes*; letter from AM Majunga A. Carron to Gov. General, April 30, 1912; Blanchy, *Karana et Banians*, 63–67, 84–88. Sectarian separation remained the case in the 2010s and was a source of contention and resentment for many Malagasy who maintained that although Karana were welcome in their mosques, the hospitality was never reciprocated. Malagasy and mixed Comorian-Malagasy experienced this as racist exclusion on the part of Karana.

50 Meier, *Swahili Port Cities*, 67.

51 Vahed, "Unhappily Torn," 45.

52 On early Islamic conceptions of mosques, see "Masdjid," *Encyclopaedia of Islam*, 2nd ed. See also Delval, "Les musulmans," 28. The literature on mosques in East Africa is vast but primarily concentrates on early periods. For an overview, see Horton, "Islamic Architecture." For nineteenth- and twentieth-century mosques in particular, see Meier, *Swahili Port Cities*; Sheriff, "Mosques, Merchants."

53 Other means of acquiring land were purchase or accessing land through inlaws, though this was reportedly uncommon. Note that *mamaky* also means "to break" and "to read"; Richardson defines this as "to range or go through the land; to divide out a piece of land; to refuse to join with others in any business" (*A New Malagasy–English Dictionary*, 728). This is also the name of a Sakalava ceremony for preparing the land for burial of the dead, as described by Goedefroit, *A l'ouest de Madagascar*, 53; Feeley-Harnik, *Green Estate*, 373.

54 These surveys present challenges as sources; French authorities may have undercounted, and perhaps guessed, at these figures.

55 Letter from AM Majunga A. Carron to Gov. General, April 30, 1912; See also Rapport Politique et Administrative, 1911, CAOM/2D.

56 Letter from AM Majunga A. Carron to Gov. General, April 30, 1912.

57 Letter from AM Majunga A. Carron to Gov. General. Lambek has described how those of Islamic and Sakalava descent in Mahajanga "juggle conflicting or incommensurable identities and obligations" (*Weight of the Past*, 81).

58 For permits on religious edifices in the city, see government-issued procla-
mations and authorizations found in ANRDM/F119; ANRDM/F125; and AN-
RDM/F161. Christian London Missionary Society (LMS) missionaries were
frustrated by the building permit process, which they interpreted as evidence of French colonial agents' hostility to their religious propagation and
their British presence. See, for example, Kendall Gale, Report of a Journey
to the Marofotsy, the Sihanaka and the Bezanozano, November 30, 1918,
CWM/LMS, Madagascar Reports 1918–1927, Box 10.

59 Letter from AM Majunga A. Carron to Gov. General, April 30, 1912.

60 PV séance, February 12, 1926, ANRDM/F42.

61 In 1902, the city's population was 4,703; by 1927, the population had grown
to 21,172. For the former, see Rapport circonscription Majunga, 1902,
CAOM/MAD/GGM. For the latter, see Documentation relative à la Munici-
palité de Majunga, 1931, ANRDM/Serié F/F40; PV séance, February 12, 1926.

62 Walker, "Islam in Madagascar," 395. Walker mentioned, "Isma'ils have endeavored to extend Islamic missionary influence in the island, but the only
place where the Mohammedan faith is not moribund is on the west coast."

63 PV séance, June 22, 1936, ANRDM/F44; PV séance, November 21, 1944,
ANRDM/F45.

64 On different durations of stay, see Chappelet, Le problème démographique,
cited in Mohamed, "Entre Anjouanais et Grands-Comoriens," 458–59.
The predominance of migrants from Ngazidja was true in Antananarivo,
though similar statistics for Mahajanga are difficult to locate. Rajaonah, "La
communauté comorienne," 104.

65 This account is largely based on an interview with Tsepy's son, El Had, Ambalavola, March 26, 2014; interview with Papa Taoaby, Abattoir, April 12,
2013, and October 29, 2013; interview with Twawilo, Mangatokana, December 18, 2013.

66 Mohamed, "Entre Anjounaais et Grands-Comoriens," 460.

67 "Renseignements concernant des paroles prononcées par les nommés Allaoui et Rakotoharitsifa," August 1, 1941, Administrateur Supérieur de la Région en tournée, CAOM PM/0152.

68 On Ralaimongo's movement, see Domenichini, "Jean Ralaimongo"; Randrianja, "Élites malgaches."

69 City Mayor Carron lamented that "Muslims, especially Anjouan, take refuge in the Mosque des Anjouanais. . . . They only rarely stay in the sectors
(in neighborhoods) without a domicile." Letter from AM Majunga A. Carron to Gouverneur Général, April 30, 1912.

70 Meier, Swahili Port Cities, 73; for West African contexts, see Robinson,
Paths of Accommodation; Seesemann and Soares, "Being as Good Muslims,"
93–95.

71 Gueunier, Les chemins, 44.

72 Resume de la enquete relative a l'incident de la Mosque Anjouanis, July 22,
1941, CAOM PM/0152.

73 Rapport sur l'Affair Said Allaoui prevenue de propos susceptibles de porter atteinte au moral de la nation, August 1, 1941, CAOM PM/0152.

74 Blanchy, "Mosquées du Vendredi," 22.

75 For conflicts and reformist debates in the Indian Ocean, see C. Ahmed, *Islam et politique*; Mohamed, *La transmission de l'Islam*; Bang, *Sufis and Scholars*, 93–125; Loimeier, *Islamic Reform*; Vahed, "Unhappily Torn"; Bonate, "Advent and Schisms," 496; Mathews, "Imagining Arab Communities."

76 Guyer, *Marginal Gains*, 120–22, 165; Adebayo, "Money, Credit and Banking"; Bascom, "The Esusu."

77 Islamic solidarity became especially important in the 1970s, following the expulsion of Comorians and mixed Comorian-Malagasy from the city, which was blamed by President Ratsiraka and others on internal "quarrels among Comorians." Mohamed, "Entre Anjouanais et Grands-Comoriens," 464. In the Comoros' Shikomori language groups *shikoa* is often transliterated as *shunggu*. On *shunggu*, see Blanchy, *La vie quotidienne à Mayotte*; Lambek, "Exchange, Time, and Person." Anthropologists and historians have described *shikao* (phonetically close to *shikoa*) as a masculine age-system that was linked to Islamic generational groups, but interlocutors consistently specified the economizing groups as *shikoa*, which they noted were made up of (and led by) both men and women. On Comorian age-sets, see Blanchy, "Matrilocalite et systeme d'age," 9–10.

78 Common refrains among the mixed Comorian-Malagasy people whom I interviewed were expressed in Malagasy: "Manao plaisir, manangy, misotra toaka ny Malagasy" (Malagasy seek pleasure in women and alcohol). For instance, interview with P. R., Manga, November 12, 2013.

79 Michael Lambek noted that in Mayotte, *shikoa* were mainly carried out by women (email to author, May 16, 2017). On Sufi norms, see "Tarīkah," *Encyclopaedia of Islam*, 2nd ed.

80 Apotsos, *Architecture, Islam, and Identity*, 10.

81 Interview with Maître Youssef, Mahajanga, July 16, 2013.

82 Interview with Papa Taoaby, Abattoir, April 12, 2013. See Rosenwein, *Emotional Communities*, 2.

83 Interview with Maître Youssef, Mahajanga, July 16, 2013.

84 Interview with Maître Youssef, Mahajanga, July 16, 2013. Sufi notions of mosque-building as expressions of love have been described elsewhere; see, for instance, Werbner, *Pilgrims of Love*.

85 S. Ahmed, "Happy Objects," 29.

86 The concept of "everyday expert" is inspired by science and technology scholars' conception of "lay experts," Antonio Gramsci's "organic intellectual" and Steven Feierman's work on subordinate groups who "create their own counter-discourse" (*Peasant Intellectuals*, 19). Science and technology studies scholar Harry Collins is usually credited with this distinction between "tacit" and "explicit" knowledge (*Tacit and Explicit Knowledge*). Inter-

view with Maître Youssef who explained, "Tsy olona mianatra, fa olo tsotra, olo zatra manamboatra!" (It wasn't the educated people, but ordinary people, people who were accustomed to building). Translation by author. Interview with El Had, Ambalavola, March 26, 2014.

87 Da Rosa, "Adobe as an Islamic Standard," 19. See also Cantone, "Historiography of Sub-Saharan African Mosques," 66; Pradines, *Earthen Architecture*.

88 On mosques in the Comoros, see Walker, *Islands in a Cosmopolitan Sea*, 44–46. See also H. Wright, "Early Islam," 117–22; Horton, "Islamic Architecture," 488.

89 Rabbat, "Islamic Architecture," 20–21.

90 Interview with D. H., Mahabibo, April 26, 2013.

91 PV séance, June 22, 1936, ANRDM/F44.

92 Cantone, "Historiography of Sub-Saharan African Mosques," 73.

93 Meier, *Swahili Port Cities*, 86–96, 100. See also Sheriff, "Mosques, Merchants," 6.

94 Blanchy et al., *Guide des monuments historiques*, 10–12.

95 Letter from AM Majunga A. Carron to Gov. General, April 30, 1912; Rapport Politique et Administratif, 1911, CAOM/2D/134.

96 For West African mosque designs, see Apotsos, *Architecture, Islam, and Identity*; Cantone, "Historiography of Sub-Saharan African Mosques," 69–71.

97 Malkki, "National Geographic," 24.

98 Interview with D. H., Abattoir, April 26, 2013.

99 Zahra, "Imagined Noncommunities."

100 Rizvi, *Transnational Mosque*, 22.

101 Green, *Sufism*, 3.

102 M. Jackson, *At Home in the World*.

103 Fremigacci, "Autocratie administrative," 407.

Chapter 5. Garnered Presences

Abbreviations: ACM (Archives Commune de Mahajanga, Madagascar); ANRDM (National Archives of the République Démocratique de Madagascar, Antananarivo, Madagascar); CAOM (Centre des archives d'Outre-Mer, Aix-en-Provence, France); MAD/GGM (Gouvernement général de Madagascar); PM (Province de Majunga).

1 "Silamos" denoted Muslims of Comorian, Antalaotra, and Malagasy descent. Letter from Chef de la Province Analalava to Gov. General Picquié, August 24, 1913, ANRDM/Serié D/755.

2 On Sakalava "vagabondage," for instance, see Rapport Politique, 1908, CAOM/MAD/GGM/2/D/134; Rapport Annual, 1941, CAOM/D/755. The latter noted that "more than any other city or region, Mahajanga and its native quarter of Mahabibo are affected" by Comorians. Officials claimed that

aimless Comorian migrants were "generally lazy and draw most of their resources by exploiting the local population."

3   Rapport Annual, 1941.
4   Elyachar, "Phatic Labor," 457.
5   "Affective circuits" is from Cole and Groes, "Introduction," 2.
6   Bachelard, *Poetics of Space*, xxxvi.
7   African studies scholars have extensively documented how improvisational practices are central to urban life. See Degani, "Shock Humor"; Quayson, *Oxford Street*; Pype, "(Not) Talking Like a Motorola"; Newell, *Modernity Bluff*; Fair, *Pastimes and Politics*; Fair, *Reel Pleasures*; Apter, *Pan-African Nation*; Ivaska, *Cultured States*; Callaci, *Street Archives*. With regard to building practices, see Gastrow, "Cement Citizens"; Morton, *Age of Concrete*; Myers, "Sticks and Stones"; Nativel, *Maisons royales*.
8   This work is voluminous, and key works have addressed how "ethnic patriots" and political entrepreneurs have taken up categorizations of difference to advance competing descent-based imaginaries for social collectivities. See Klieman, *"Pygmies Were Our Compass"*; Lentz and Nugent, *Ethnicity in Ghana*; Hamilton, *Terrific Majesty*; Lonsdale, "Moral Economy"; Peterson, *Ethnic Patriotism*. Jonathan Glassman's argument is crucial for decentering the colonial encounter as *the* defining moment in categories of difference, grappling with multiple genealogies of, and the wide-ranging roles of, African thinkers in producing collective ethnic, racial, and nationalist ideologies. See Glassman, *War of Words*; Glassman, "Slower Than a Masssacre"; and, most recently, Glassman, "Ethnicity and Race."
9   In this move, I build on Schoenbrun and Johnson's recent intervention arguing for historians of ethnicity and difference to account for the role of multispecies ecologies in "thinking and making groups"; see Schoenbrun and Johnson, "Introduction." I suggest we extend this to vital, material substances and architectural forms as well.
10 Here I am influenced by Merleau-Ponty's conception of sedimentation as "realization" of thought as well as by anthropologists who have considered how diverse communities have understood and harnessed the capacities of the material world to navigate their prospects in uncertain futures. See Merleau-Ponty, *Phenomenology of Perception*; Navaro-Yashin, *Make-Believe Space*; Abourahme, "Assembling and Spilling-Over"; Gordillo, *Rubble*; Nielson, "Wedge of Time"; Allerton, *Potent Landscapes*. In particular, Julie Archambault has signaled that once emplaced, certain building materials are "charged with transformative potential," offering possibilities for remaking one's social standing, kin network, and future prospects; see Archambault, "'One Beer, one Block,'" 694.
11 Delval, "Les migrations comoriennes," 97.
12 For 1912, see Census, October 1912, ANRDM/F41. For 1936, see Rapport Annual, 1941. For the 1950s, see Deschamps, *Les migrations*, 146–47; 188–89. The figure given by Deschamps represents the population of the district of

Mahajanga. By comparison, other sources put the total population of the city in 1955 at 44,229; see, for example, Poirier, "Aspects de l'urbanisation," 81. Since some sources account for Majunga (Mahajanga) district and others for Majunga (Mahajanga) ville, comparisons are not clear. There is, furthermore, some discrepancy between accounts of the Comorian population in Mahajanga owing to the problems inherent to classification of people along ethnic lines. Poirier (82) states that in 1965, 26 percent of the city's population were "Comorians." Moreover, national censuses may have classified zanatany (first-generation descendants of Comorian and Malagasy parentage) as "Malagasy."

13 Delval, "Les migrations comoriennes," 98.

14 Chappelet, who conducted an inquiry in two villages in Ngazidja (Grande Comore), suggests the dominance of men within the migrant population from Comoros to Madagascar and elsewhere, as cited in Nativel, "Les migrants comorians," 121. Census records from Nzwani (Anjouan) and Ngazidja in 1931, moreover, indicate a marked majority of women in the adult population of Comoros, providing further evidence that men dominated emigration from the archipelago (Lavau, "Les Comores," 127). In early-twentieth-century Ngazidja, Europeans noted that women comprised two-thirds of the island's population; Voeltzkow, as cited in Walker, *Islands in a Cosmopolitan Sea*, 118n8. Some of my interviewees explained this gender imbalance in terms of inheritance customs in the archipelago: daughters would inherit land and houses from their fathers and uncles. Enjoying the fruits of their family wealth and obliged by cultural norms to remain close to home, daughters rarely left the archipelago, but sons might. Others, like Mama Beatrice, suggested that men migrated because they were more pressed to earn wages so that they could support their kin in Comoros and could return home and establish their own households.

15 In 1936, for instance, there were 3,585 women and 3,229 men (as well as 1,660 children) from the Comorian archipelago recorded in Mahajanga's overall population (Arrondissement de Majunga, Rapport Politique, 1936, CAOM/MAD/PM/0436/0831). See also Nativel, "Les migrants comorians," for very similar statistics from 1932.

16 In interviews, Comorian-Malagasy individuals described their fathers' contribution to the family lineage as stronger and more powerful (*mahery*). Sophie Blanchy recently pointed out that Comorian fathers' contributions over their children's lifespan enable them to establish their status and carve out a morally distinct role in a matrilineal and matrilocal society. Blanchy, "Matrilineal and Matrilocal Muslim Society in Flux."

17 See, for instance, the figures cited by Rajaonah, "La communauté comorienne," 110.

18 Deschamps, *Les migrations*, 27–43.

19 Deschamps, *Les migrations*, 45, 31.

20 Frère, *Madagascar*, 131.

21 So sizable was the Comorian staff at the jute-cord factory, FITIM (Filature et Tissage de Majunga), for instance, that the company constructed a prayer room. "They are the slowest to adapt to the work," one company representative noted, "but thereafter they accomplish it with the utmost regularity." They were joined by other migrants from the highlands and "locals" (likely Sakalava or longer-standing migrants from elsewhere). Rapport de Tournee, July 23 to August 19, 1933, Region de Majunga, Inspection du Travail, no. 137, ANRDM/Serié D/366.

22 PV séance May 3, 1921, ANRDM/F42.

23 Colonial administrators sought to recruit laborers from newer migrant groups, even journeying to distant places (as far as Farafaganana in the southeast) to bring back workers. Arrondissement de Majunga, Rapport Annuels Travaux Publics, 1925, ANRDM/Ij/2214.

24 On forced labor schemes in Madagascar, see Sharp, "Laboring for the Colony"; Sodikoff, "Forced and Forest Labor Regimes."

25 According to historian Eric Jennings, forced labor ramped up in 1940 when the colonial authority fell under the authority of the Vichy regime. Crucially, all of the factories in the northwest region were heavily reliant on forced labor, and industrialists feared that the end of coercion would lead to massive economic decline. Jennings, "Madagascar under Vichy," 63.

26 Interview with B. P., Amborovy, February 8, 2013.

27 Fieldnotes, April 29, 2013.

28 Interview with Attoumani Mohamed, Village Touristique, April 18, 2013; interview with Papa Taoaby, Abattoir, April 12, 2013. On the grand marriage (*ndola nkuu*) and the related customary exchange of goods (*āda*), see Blanchy, "Matrilineal and Matrilocal Muslim Society," 24–26.

29 This resonates with, and may derive partly from, the stereotype of Malagasy women as sexually free and promiscuous, which was projected from colonial times onward. For example, see Stoebenau, "'Côtier' sexual identity."

30 Interview with El Had, Ambalavola, April 18, 2014.

31 Throop, "Moral Sentiments," 151. On moral sensibilities, see Bateson, *Naven*; Mauss, *Gift*; Das, "Ordinary Ethics."

32 Here and throughout, I use "Sakalava" as a political identifier to indicate a degree of "loyalty or subservience to members of a royal clan and the historical kingdoms they founded," following Lambek, "Ritual as a Social Diagnostic," 65.

33 Interview with Hasandrama, Tsaramandroso, February 2, 2014.

34 Also important were the shared burial practices. Whereas many Malagasy groups practice ritual exhumation and reburial, Comorians and Sakalava do not.

35 McClenahan, "Notes on Current Topics," 85.

36 Ferrand, *Les musulmans*, 70.

37 Lambek notes that approaches to multiple traditions in northwest Madagascar and Mayotte are generally "mutually incorporative," rather than

"mutually exclusive" ("Ritual as a Social Diagnostic," 66–67). Elsewhere, he describes how Muslim (Silamo) identity in Madagascar could "be interpreted as a descent-based category rather than an exclusivity religious faith"; see Lambek, *Weight of the Past*, 195. See also Gueunier, *Les chemins*.

38 Lambek describes these tensions and differences in great detail; see *Weight of the Past*, 202–4, 194. See also Feeley-Harnik, *Green Estate,* 264–65, 437–38.

39 I am indebted to Leor Halevi for this point.

40 Lambek noted the importance of funerals in Mahajanga as "acts of completion." Lambek, "Ritual as a Social Diagnostic," 75.

41 Maître Youssef noted, "The faith was developed by taking Malagasy (*mangala gasy*)." Interview with Maître Youssef, Mahajanga, July 16, 2013.

42 By contrast, Malagasy newcomers to the city could access kin relations, as well as those from *fatidra* (blood siblings) and *ziva* (joking allies). Mzé Mohamed notes that Comorian migrants to Mahajanga formed blood-sibling ties (*fwareida*) with other Comorian men who were already established in the city, relationships that became important economic and kinship networks. See Mohamed, "Les 'Sabena' de la grande Comore," 19.

43 Fieldnotes, April 24, 2014.

44 On matrilineality in Comoros, see Blanchy, *Maisons des femmes*; Blanchy, "Matrilineal and Matrilocal Muslim Society." Bonate describes the endurance of matriliny in Mozambique; "Matriliny, Islam, and Gender."

45 Blanchy, "Beyond 'Great Marriage,'" 572.

46 On Mozambique, see Bonate, "Advent and Schisms," 487.

47 Interview with M. A., Manga, October 16, 2013.

48 Interview with Dadilahy Kassim, Tsaramandroso, October 6, 2013.

49 Thompson and Adloff, *Malagasy Republic*, 329; Müller and Evers, "Case Studies of Land Access."

50 Interview, El Had, Ambovoalanana, April 18, 2014. He described this as "the family doesn't extend/go far, it keeps the family together" (*tsy mandeha lavitra, garder famille*).

51 Fieldnotes, April 26, 2014

52 Fieldnotes, April 14, 2014.

53 Interview with H. A., Abattoir, July 9, 2013; interview with M. N., Manga, October 1, 2013.

54 Fieldnotes, February 14, 2013; April 29, 2013; May 7, 2013; September 16, 2013.

55 Fieldnotes, Abattoir, May 7, 2013.

56 The emphasis on "nobility" could have been an implicit reference to histories of enslavement, but none of the people with whom I spoke directly referenced slavery. Interview with D. H., Mahabibo, July 11, 2013; interview with M. K., Abattoir, June 28, 2013.

57 Interview with Dadilahy Kassim, Tsaramandroso, October 11, 2013.

58 Abinal and Malzac, *Dictionnaire malgache-francais*, 832.

59 J. Freeman, *Dictionary*, 263.

60 J. Freeman, *Dictionary*, 246; Grandidier and Grandidier, *Ethnographie de Madagascar*, 1:219, 229, 273.

61 Feeley-Harnik, *Green Estate*, 159; Ballarin, *Les reliques royales*, 59–60. Feeley-Harnik notes that the related transitive verb *manompo* (to serve) was employed to describe how "people make ampanjaka [royal leaders] masters over themselves by their very service" in northwest Madagascar; in other words, mastery was granted by royal followers; *Green Estate*, 348–50.

62 This follows from Berger and Branchu, "L'Islam à l'épreuve de l'ancestralité," 4. See also Lombard, *La royauté Sakalava*, 97; Berger, "Les voix des ancêtres," 132.

63 Richardson, *New Malagasy–English Dictionary*, 689; Feeley-Harnik, *Green Estate*, 348. On "acting responsibly," see Walsh, "Responsibility, Taboos," 457; Goedefroit, *A l'ouest de Madagascar*, 164–65; Evers, *Constructing History*, 28; Fuglestad, "Tompon-tany," 61–62; Bloch, *Placing the Dead*, 105–37; Evers, "Lex Loci Meets Lex Fori," 127–28.

64 Sharp, *Possessed and Dispossessed*, 297fn6.

65 Abinal and Malzac, *Dictionnaire malgache-français*, 803; Marre, *Vocabulaire français-malgache*, 9, 160, 212; Malzac, *Dictionnaire français-malgache*, 128–29, 436, 547.

66 For instance, state officials proclaimed Madagascar "Zanatany Frantsay" in a legal ruling published as "Ny Résident Général-ny Madagascar, Noho ny didy navoaka tamy ny 11 Décembre 1895, Noho ny lalàna navoaka tamy ny 6 Août 1896 milaza any Madagascar sy ny Nosy rehetra momba azy ho Colonie Française (Zanatany Frantsay)," *Journel Officiel de Madagascar et Dépendances Madagascar*, October 9, 1896, 51.

67 This continues today. Interview with Michel Ducaud, Majunga Be, October 8, 2013; Rajaonah defines *zanatany* as "a European born and established in Madagascar"; *Cultures citadines*, 7–9, 91. See also Cantier and Jennings, *L'empire colonial sous Vichy*, 396.

68 Anthropologist Gillian Feeley-Harnik signaled similar understandings of *zanatany* in Analalava in the 1970s; *Green Estate*, 253.

69 In 1959, French colonial administrators described zanatany as "those which were born in Madagascar, and specifically among them are found those métis from Antalaotra or Sakalava mothers." ACM/Monographie 267: District Majunga (1959).

70 "Projet des Status" and "Note: Formation d'une amicale Comorienne à Majunga," July 13, 1957, CAOM/PM/0266/32. Five men and one woman made up the founding members: Ali Alimassi, Cassim Ahmed, Aboudou M'Drahoma, Binti, Cassim Ali, and Mansour. Men and women were both permitted to join, but it is difficult to gauge the gender dynamics or demographic composition of the group.

71 Each member received a membership card emblazoned with "AZAM" and the iconic Islamic symbol of a star-topped crescent. Note, September 24, 1957, CAOM/PM/0266/32.

72 Note, January 16, 1958; Note, August 13, 1957, CAOM/PM/266/32.

73 Gueunier, *Les chemins d'Islam*, 50.

74 Glassman, "Ethnicity and Race in African Thought," 207. Here it is important to note that within Madagascar, the conception of *zanatany* as a nativist, generational, and ethnic identification seems to have been historically unique to Mahajanga.

75 Interview with P., Manga, December 13, 2013. Also, interview with S., Mahvoky Avaratra, April 2, 2013.

76 Interview with Pastor Toky, Mahabibokely, March 29, 2013.

77 This can also be found in journalistic accounts. See, for example, "Mahajanga—Les autorites sur le qui-vive!," AllAfrica.com, March 25, 2014, https://fr.allafrica.com/stories/201403251312.html.

78 Although official census data collected by *fokontany* (neighborhood offices) no longer include ethnic background, several fokontany leaders affirmed that Comorian-Malagasy families still constituted a critical landholding mass in these areas during my research from 2011 to 2014. Interview with F. P., Manga, November 21, 2013; interview with F. P., Mahajanga, February 19, 2013; interview with F. P., Ambovoalana, November 7, 2013.

79 The quotation is from interview with M. A., Manga, October 16, 2013. Further information provided in interview with M. A., Mahajanga, February 7, 2013.

80 Interview with P. K., Ambalavola, October 29, 2012; interview with M. N., Manga, October 18, 2013; interview with M. K., Abattoir, June 28, 2013; interview with M. A., Manga, October 31, 2013; interview with Mama N., Morafeno, February 18, 2013.

81 Interview with Attoumani Mohamed, Village Touristique, April 18, 2013.

82 Interview with Said Hassan, Majunga Be, May 7, 2013. There may have been similar economizing practices among Malagasy, but interlocutors repeatedly stressed the Comorian origin of this institution in Mahajanga.

83 Although Mama Mariam didn't discuss her siblings and their wealth, it was widely known that several of her brothers and sisters lived in France, where they accrued funds to purchase more properties in town.

84 The idea of a "living" house is inspired by Waterson, *Living House*.

85 Lonsdale, "Moral and Political Argument," 76.

86 Interview with H. A., Abattoir, July 9, 2013.

87 Interview with P. R., Mahajanga, November 12, 2013; interview with C., Manga, October 25, 2013.

88 Interview with M. A., Manga, October 16, 2013.

89 "Tamin'ny taloha, nahazo karama, kibo voky, dia anefa zanaka-lany!" Interview with D. S., Mahavoky Atsimo, October 19, 2013.

90 Interview with I. A., Tsaramandroso, September 28, 2013; interview with M. A., Manga, September 26, 2013.

91 Interview with Said Hassan, Majunga Be, May 7, 2013. Original Malagasy:

"Zanaka'malagasy valeura an'azy sitrana gonin'ny vary." A gunnysack equals 50 kilograms (110 pounds) of rice.

92   Interview with P. R., Manga, November 12, 2013.

93   Interview with I. A. Tsaramandroso, September 28, 2013. See also Brennan, *Taifa*.

94   Gautier, "Mission," 363; Feeley-Harnik, "Sakalava House," 564.

95   Feeley-Harnik, "Sakalava House"; Bloch, "Resurrection of the House"; Kus and Raharijaona, "House to Palace."

96   On adobe construction knowledge elsewhere in Madagascar, see Esoavelo-mandroso, "Aménagement et occupation," 352; Poirier, "Aspects de l'urban-isation," 90. On practices of followers of Sakalava polity, see Feeley-Harnik, "Sakalava House," 570; Decary, "Les emplois du bamboo," 66.

97   Myers, "Sticks and Stones"; Carey, "Creole Architectural Translation," 84.

98   Feeley-Harnik, "Sakalava House," 571, 575; Hébert, "L'enumeration des points cardinaux," 165; Esoavelomandroso, "Aménagement et occupation," 342; Kus and Raharijaona, "House to Palace."

99   Cited in Hébert, "L'enumeration des points cardinaux," 152. Another prov-erb linked spiritual agency to the north corner of the house: "No one prays towards the west, but all pray towards the north; yet wealth needs luck (or destiny), and if it isn't your lot, it doesn't come." Houlder, *Ohabo-lana*, 14.

100   Raibmon, "Living on Display," 290.

101   Decary, "L'habitation," as cited in Feeley-Harnik, "Sakalava House." See also Jully, "L'habitation à Madagascar"; Decary, *Contribution à l'étude de l'habitation*.

102   Feeley-Harnik, "Sakalava House," 580.

103   Dandouau, "Coutumes funéraires," 157–58.

104   Dandouau, "Coutumes funéraires," 164.

105   Interview with I. A., Mahajanga, September 21, 2013.

106   Dandouau, "Coutumes funéraires," 158.

107   Interview with Dadilahy Kassim, Tsaramandroso Ambony, October 11, 2013.

108   Gevrey describes how the walls were constructed by horizontal and vertical juxtaposition of raffia ribs "so as to form small square panels"; see Gevrey, *Essai sur les îles Comores*, 94.

109   Walker et al., "Un explorateur," 360.

110   Gevrey, *Essai sur les îles Comores*, 94.

111   Interview with M. A., Manga, October 16, 2013; interview with El Had, Am-balavola, March 26, 2014.

112   Petit, "La vie sur les côtes," 150. Although these observations referred to Comorians living north of Mahajanga, all evidence indicates they applied to those living in the city as well.

113   Original text: "L'habitation du Comorien est toute différente. . . . L'extérieur

en est presque élégant, les feuilles de rofia, au lieu d'être simplement juxta-poses, s'entremêlent symétriquement et forment un dessin assez gracieux à l'œil. La portee n est toujours hermétiquement fermée comme celle de toute maison musulman; mais, à travers les fentes ou les jours des feuilles qui ser-vent de cloture, le vazaha (Européen) qui passe peut apercevoir, comme derrière les moucharabiés du Caire, les yeux des habitants de la case qui le suivent tant qu'il semble ne pas se douter de la curiosité don't il est l'objet." Ferrand, "Notes sur Madagascar," 233. Translation by author. *Moucharabiés* (or *mashrabiya*) is the French transliteration of the Arabic term for lattice-work windows, common across the Islamic world and connected to con-ceptions of privacy.

114   These attributes also aroused conflicts and suspicion. Feeley-Harnik de-scribed in the 1970s how Sakalava families found their Silamo neighbors' fences suspicious and disruptive to the equalizing flows of reciprocity in ru-ral areas of northwest Madagascar; see Feeley-Harnik, "Sakalava House," 581.

115   Blanchy, *La vie quotidienne*, 35.

116   Isnard, "L'archipel," 11.

117   For French descriptions, see Gevrey, *Essai sur les îles Comores*, 94–95.

118   "Flow of sociality" is from Helliwell, "Space and Sociality," 144.

119   De Vere Allen, "Swahili House"; Donley-Reid, "Structuring Structure." But also see Fleisher, "Situating the Swahili House"; Wynne-Jones, "Public Life of the Swahili Stone House."

120   Edgerton, *Shock of the Old*, 41–42.

121   Herbert, *Pioneers of Prefabrication*.

122   Mrázek, *Engineers of Happy Land*, 8–9.

123   The popularity of tôly may also be attributed to the scarcity of cement in the 1910s–1950s. Although limestone could be easily found among the coastal coral banks, colonial authorities found it difficult and costly to mine and transport to the city as city dwellers had done in precolonial times. Laurent, *Les produits coloniaux*, 202–5.

124   On "cosmopolitan technologies," see Rijke-Epstein, "On Humble Technolo-gies," 296.

125   Letter from Admin. en Chef Moriceau to Gov. Gen. Gallieni, May 1, 1903, ANRDM/DTP 28.

126   Letter from Mayor Carron to Gov. Gen., February 14, 1913, ANRDM/F45. It is difficult to pinpoint where the tôly was produced, but some older residents recalled that there was a factory in Antsirabe, a town in the highlands. In-terview with I. A., Mahajanga, September 21, 2013; interview with P. R. and C., Mahajanga, October 25, 2013; interview with Maître Youssef, Maha-janga, July 16, 2013.

127   Interview with H. A, Abattoir, July 9, 2013.

128   "Trano olobelona sarobidy." Interview with D. H., Abattoir, July 11, 2013.

129 "Tsisy trano, tsisy valeur, tsisy trano, tsisy tresor." Interview with I. A., Tsaramandroso, September 21, 2013.

130 Interview with Mama Amelie, Manga, October 16, 2013.

131 Interview with M. A., Mahajanga, September 26, 2013.

132 "Tsy mandrava ny trano. Raotra, raha misy automobile, dia amaray misy accident, mandrava jiaby. Fa raha mahavit trano tsara, trano matanjaka, dia tsy mandrava, matanjaka jusqu'a matoy. Ny voaloahany zavatra, tokony manomboatra trano. Fa amin'ny trano fonenana, dia tena misy valeur, mandova trano." Interview with Dadilahy Kassim, Tsaramandroso Ambony, October 6, 2013.

133 Interview with I. A., Tsaramandroso, September 28, 2013; interview with Maître Youssef, Manga, July 16, 2013.

134 In some instances, migrants had to negotiate these attachments with tensions and demands from kin in Comoros who vied for their material investment in social reproduction.

135 Fieldnotes, April 11, 2013.

136 Walter Benjamin also made the observation that "to live is to leave traces"; Benjamin, "Paris," 155–56.

137 Thomas describes very similar processes of placenta burial and rooting in southeastern Madagascar; P. Thomas, "River," 371.

138 Some residents noted that in situations where the family rented a home, complications emerged, and sometimes arrangements had to be negotiated. One woman said that some landlords—particularly if they were of other "kinds" (*karazana*)—feared that burying the fluids of the dead would entrap or attract the dead's spirit or ghost (*lolo*).

139 Interview with I. A., Tsaramandroso, September 28, 2013.

140 House societies literature is vast. See, for example, Bourdieu, "Kabyle House"; Waterson, *Living House*; Carsten and Hugh-Jones, *About the House*; Bahloul, "Memory House"; Birdwell-Pheasant and Lawrence-Zúniga, *House Life*; Joyce and Gillespie, *Beyond Kinship*; Fehérváry, "American Kitchens." On houses as a living body, see also Blier, *Anatomy of Architecture*; Jütte, "Living Stones."

141 Other definitions include "to range over or go through the land; to divide out a piece of land." Richardson, *New Malagasy–English Dictionary*, 728.

142 Decary, *Contribution à l'étude*, 46–70 (on Sakalava house-construction practices); Testa, "Habitat traditionnel ancien"; Kus, "Role of the Mpanadro"; Kus and Raharijaona, "Where to Begin."

143 Interview with M. N., Manga, October 1, 2013.

144 Geschiere, *Perils of Belonging*; Pelican, "Complexities of Indigeneity and Autochthony"; Ceuppens and Geschiere, "Autochthony"; Mbembe, "Afropolitan," 28. See also the special issue of *Africa* on "The Politics of Inclusion and Exclusion in Africa" (vol. 85, no. 1, 2015). Note that *autochthon* derives

from the Greek *auto* (the same) and *chthon* (land), meaning "to live in the same place for a long time."

145 Lentz, *Land, Mobility, and Belonging*; Prestholdt, "Politics of the Soil"; Brennan, *Taifa*; Glassman, *War of Words*.

146 Mararo, "Land, Power," 508; Lentz, *Land, Mobility, and Belonging*, 4.

147 Leonhardt, "Baka and the Magic of the State," 70.

148 See Peterson, "Be Like Firm Soldiers," 72; Gautier et al., "Woodcutting and Territorial Claims in Mali"; Lonsdale, "Soil, Work," 306, 309.

149 Geschiere and Lentz assert the "emptiness" of autochthonous discourses, which make blanket assertions without reference to the textures and tumult of history. See Geschiere, *Perils of Belonging*, 12, 28, 103; Lentz, *Land, Mobility, and Belonging*, 19.

150 One older woman also insisted that Makoa were, together with Sakalava, the true *tompony* of the city; interview with M. M., Morafeno, November 14, 2013.

151 "Tsy miady, manaja tena . . . dia nilefa ireo." Interview with P. K., Ambalavato, October 29, 2012. One state worker of Tsimihety-Sakalava background and in his late forties explained, "Sakalava were the masters of the land here before (*tompony eto tamin'ny taloha*). But during the time of the French and into the First Republic under Tsiranana, the Sakalava began to recede (*mihembotra*), to move out of the city, because they are very strict with their lifestyle, and they don't like to socialize with many people (*sarotony fiainanana, tsy tia mifanerasera*). The French liked to use/enslave people, but Sakalava didn't like this, so they fled (*mampiasa olo ny Frantsay, fa ny Sakalava tsy tia, dia nilefa*)." Interview with J. R. S., Plateau des Tombes, October 22, 2013. Additional information provided in interview with Pastor Toky, Mahabibokely, March 29, 2013.

152 Interview with Said Hassan, Mahajanga, May 7, 2013.

153 Fontein, "Graves, Ruins, and Belonging"; James, *Gaining Ground?*; Mujere, "Land, Graves and Belonging."

154 Ballarin, *Les reliques royales*; Lambek, *Weight of the Past*.

155 Interview with B. P., Amborovy, February 8, 2013.

156 Bakhtin, *Dialogic Imagination*, 84. Here I am inspired by other scholars of Madagascar who have fruitfully drawn on Bakhtin's concept to grapple with the making of Sakalava sacred royal domains (Feeley-Harnik, *Green Estate*, 327–29); Sakalava ritual practice and historical consciousness (Lambek, *Weight of the Past*, 27–29); and the significance of homes (Evers and Seagle, "Stealing the Sacred," 103).

157 Casey, "How to Get from Space," 46.

158 Basso, *Wisdom Sits in Places*, 34.

159 Interview with H., Manga, December 11, 2013.

160 This is inspired by Rothberg's argument against "competitive memory" and formulation of "multidirectional memory"; see Rothberg, *Multidirectional Memory*, 2–6.

161 To be clear, *zanatany* did not indicate that their Comorian fathers negotiated directly with Sakalava spirits to enable their presence on the land.
Many zanatany, however, have linkages to Sakalava royal ancestral spirits
and practices—or are themselves spirit mediums. Most claimed that Comorian ancestors refused these practices, seeing them as counter to Islam, but
many Sakalava spouses and zanatany children in past and contemporary
times maintain linkages with spirit mediums and spirit possession. Indeed,
among the members of the Manga *fikambanana* to which I belonged, at least
one-third of the zanatany women were active in spirit possession gatherings.

162 Hilgers, "Autochthony as Capital."

Chapter 6. Violent Remnants

Sections of this chapter appeared in slightly altered form as "The Politics of Filth: Sanitation and Competing Moralities in Urban Madagascar
1890s–1972," *Journal of African History* 62 no. 2 (2019): 229–56, reprinted
with the permission of Cambridge University Press; and "On Humble Technologies: Containers, Care, and Water Infrastructure in Northwest Madagascar, 1750s–1960s," *History and Technology* 37, no. 3 (2021): 1–36, reprinted
with permission of Routledge, Taylor and Francis Group.

Abbreviations: BNF (Bibliothèque nationale de France, Paris, France);
CAOM (Centre des archives d'Outre-Mer, Aix-en-Provence, France); MAD/
GGM (Gouvernement général de Madagascar); NWL (Rare Books Collection, Melville J. Herskovits Library of African Studies, Northwestern University Library, Evanston, Illinois, United States).

1 *Vazaha* is a historical term used here to reference European foreigners.

2 Interview with Allain, Amborovy, October 25, 2013.

3 Puig de la Bellacasa, "Matters of Care in Technoscience," 90.

4 This literature is vast, but some foundational and recent works include Lefebvre, *Le droit à la ville*; Cooper, *Struggle for the City*; Graham and Marvin,
Splintering Urbanism; Holston, *Cities and Citizenship*.

5 Simone, "People as Infrastructure"; see also de Boeck, "Infrastructure."

6 As Kenny Cupers and Prita Meier recently observed, this literature has left
"intact what it writes against—namely, the power of infrastructure and the
state." Cupers and Meier, "Infrastructure between Statehood and Selfhood,"
62.

7 Work that has illuminated the labor dimensions of infrastructure include
Fredericks, *Garbage Citizenship*; Millar, *Reclaiming the Discarded*; Reno,
Waste Away; Chalfin, "Public Things." Achille Mbembe discusses the *in-
strumental labor* so critical to Johannesburg's historical political economy.
Mbembe, "Aesthetics of Superfluity."

8 Akrich, "De-scription of Technological Objects."

9 Hecht, "Residue."

10 Boudia et al., "Residues," 166.

11 I am borrowing here from Boudia et al., who described these dynamics for chemical residues ("Residues," 166).

12 Many others have signaled the indeterminacy and processual nature of infrastructures in contemporary settings; see Anand et al., *Promise of Infrastructure*, 17; Larkin, "Politics and Poetics of Infrastructure."

13 For instance, see the ship journal of the *Fly*, October 10, 1764, IOR/L/MAR /B/597A-B, BL.

14 James Hastie, journal, July 2, 1823, CL.

15 Osgood, *Notes of Travel*, 3.

16 *De Majunga à Tananarive*, 7.

17 Guillain, *Documents sur l'histoire*, 209.

18 Ingold, *Making*. For an exploration of "nature as infrastructure" in contemporary times, see Carse, "Nature as Infrastructure," 540.

19 Guillain, *Documents sur l'histoire*, 209. See also J. S. Leigh, journal, February 1, 1837, NWL.

20 Guillain, *Documents sur l'histoire*, 209.

21 Guillain, *Documents sur l'histoire*, 210.

22 de Bocage, *Madagascar possession française depuis 1642*, 152. In many observations, de Bocage appears to have drawn largely from earlier accounts by Charles Guillain.

23 Guillain, *Documents sur l'histoire*, 216.

24 P. Thomas, "River," 371; Graeber, "Dancing with Corpses Reconsidered," 268.

25 On the bathing of royal relics, see Molet, *Le bain royal*; Decary, "Les eaux douces," 243; Hébert (1960) as cited in Ballarin, *Les reliques royales*, 118. On funerary sculptures, see Camboué, "Aperçu sur les Malgaches," 7.

26 Haile, "Malagasy Village Life," 16; Decary, "Les eaux douces," 236.

27 Delord, "Le site touristique," 30.

28 Decary, "Les eaux douces," 237.

29 For further discussion of the role of containers, including the multiple sources of technical knowledge of potters in Mahajanga's precolonial and colonial water system, see Rijke-Epstein, "On Humble Technologies," 300–310; Hocquard, *L'expedition de Madagascar*, 40. On the use of containers in the highlands, see G. Shaw, *Madagascar and France*, 35.

30 It is difficult to accurately appraise the material composition, form, and quality of household wells during this time, though this image suggests they were fortified of stone.

31 Hocquard, *L'expedition de Madagascar*, 38.

32 Guillain, *Documents sur l'histoire*, 210.

33 Brockway, "Visit to Ambohimanga," 61.

34 Pickersgill, "North Sakalava-Land," 34.

35 Hocquard, *L'expedition de Madagascar*, 49.

36 Hocquard, *L'expedition de Madagascar*, 49.

37 This transformation is elaborated in Rijke-Epstein, "On Humble Technologies."

38 Interview with B. B., Mahajanga, June 24, 2019.

39 Sara Pritchard has signaled the centrality of "hydroimperialism"—the mapping and management of water—in French colonial conquest and its foundational role in "hydrocapitalism," rendered visible through the spread of development expertise in postcolonial times; see Pritchard, "From Hydroimperialism to Hydrocapitalism," 599.

40 One possible translation for *Betsiboka* is "ample freshwater" (*be-*, much; *tsy boka*, "not brackish "). *Boka* can mean "spoiled" or "false," "counterfeit," and "dethroned"; see Feeley-Harnik, "Political Economy of Death," 9. It also can refer to the connection between water and legitimate royal power.

41 Gautier, "Mission," 363. See also Adas, *Machines as the Measure of Men*, 60.

42 "Regimes of perceptibility" denotes the "regular and sedimented contours of perception and imperception produced within a disciplinary or epistemological tradition"; Murphy, *Sick Building Syndrome*, 24.

43 Among these hydrographic missions were Favé and Cauvet, 1887–89; Mion and Fichot, 1889; Rollet de l'Isle, Driencourt, and Laporte, 1891–95; and Colin and Roblet, 1891, noted in de Martonne and described in several French-led hydrographical missions between 1904 and 1907; see Roussilhe, "Mission hydrographique de Madagascar," as well as similarly titled reports by Lesage and Courtier, *Annales Hydrographies*, 141–278; Delville, *Partage de l'Afrique*, 39.

44 Duchesne, *L'expedition de Madagascar*, 65.

45 *Journel Officiel de Madagascar et Dépendances*, October 17, 1900, 489, BNF.

46 *Rapport Circonscription*, 1902, 8, CAOM/MAD/GGM/2/D/134.

47 *Rapport Circonscription*, 8.

48 "Les projets de conduite d'eau," *La Dépeche de Majunga*, June 22, 1902, BNF.

49 The literature on discriminatory and unequal provision of infrastructure in colonial cities is vast. See Graham and Marvin, *Splintering Urbanism*; Njoh, "Urban Planning"; Hungerford and Smiley, "Comparing Colonial Water Provision." *Assimilées* ("assimilated") was a term designated for colonial subjects who adopted aspects of French civilization—including language, dress, and education.

50 *Rapport Politique et Administratif*, 1903, CAOM MAD/GGM/2/D/133.

51 For a corollary study of Tamatave, see Rajaonah, "Usages et usagers."

52 *Rapport Politique et Administratif* (1896–1904), CAOM MAD/GGM/2/D/133.

53 *Rapport Politique et Administratif* (1896–1904).

54 Extrait du register des deliberations de la Commission municipale de Majunga, Séance, September 27, 1912, ANRDM/F52.

55 Letter from Aide-Maire Carron of Majunga to Gov. General, October 24, 1912, ANRDM/F52.

56 Proces-Verbaux, January 10, 1939, ANRDM/F45.

57 Proces-Verbaux January 10, 1939.

58 Grundlingh, "Municipal Modernity," 771–74.

59 "Conseil Municipal de Majunga," *Le Phare de Majunga*, February 28, 1934.
    Le Phare was a French-language weekly newspaper published in Mahajanga.

60 Quichotte, "Chateau en Espagne."

61 Residents described the original seawater pool, built into the rocky coast, as
    having a beautiful aesthetic: "entirely metallic," constructed of "iron posts
    planted in the sand every three metres and joined to each other by sheets of
    expanded metal, all painted with a shimmering glaze." The pool measured
    more than 100 meters (330 feet) by 40 meters (131 feet). "La Piscine est ou-
    verte," *Le Réveil de la Côte Ouest*, October 6, 1932, BNF.

62 Prochaska, "Fantasia of the Photothèque," 42.

63 The newly reconstructed pool, which apparently sat just above the exist-
    ing seawater pool, measured 50 meters (164 feet) by 25 meters (82 feet). Lit-
    tle else is known about the pool in Mahajanga, but it is most probable that
    any sports competitions or other activities were limited to Europeans only,
    as elsewhere in Madagascar and other French colonies. See Combeau-Mari,
    "Sport in the French Colonies," 35.

64 Today, the pool contains salt water from the ocean. It is not clear whether it
    was originally constructed as such or converted later, owing to freshwater
    shortages.

65 Letter from Aide-Maire to Secretaire Général, Bureau des Affaires Munici-
    pals, November 22, 1941, ANRDM/F51.

66 Renseignements from 4ème Brigade Mobile to Adm. Superieur de la region
    de Majunga, October 27, 1941, ANRDM/F51.

67 "Imagined hygienic modernity" is a concept borrowed from Rogaski, *Hy-
    gienic Modernity*, 226. Letter from Admin. en Chef Moriceau to Gouverneur
    Gallieni, May 1, 1903, ANRDM/DTP28. Alain Corbin narrates the genealogy
    of ideas about paving roads and pathways as a means to hermetically "seal
    off the filth of the soil or the noisomeness of underground water"; Corbin,
    Foul and the Fragrant, 89–95.

68 For a lengthier discussion of this, see Rijke-Epstein, "Politics of Filth."

69 For more on precolonial waste practices, see Rijke-Epstein, "Politics of
    Filth," 234–40.

70 Wright, *Politics of Design*, 3.

71 Tarr, "Separate vs. Combined Sewer Problem," 309; Gaillard, *Paris, La Ville*.

72 Barnes, *Great Stink*, 54–55; Jacquemet, "Urbanisme parisien," 543.

73 Rajaonah, 'Modèles européens.'

74 Kermorgant, *Hygiène coloniale*, 37–38.

75 Arrondissement de Majunga, Rapport Annuels Travaux Publics: Commune
    de Majunga, 1915, ANRDM/Ij/2083–4; letter 14-V from Chef du Service
    de la Voirie to the Administrateur-Maire de Majunga, January 29, 1917,
    ANRDM/vIIj 391–061. For lengthier discussion of problems associated with
    latrines, see Rijke-Epstein, "Politics of Filth," 243–44.

76 Arrondissement de Majunga, Rapport Annuels Travaux Publics, 1915; letter

14-V from Chef du Service de la Voirie. The presence of stones could have been linked to Islamic practices of purification after defecation, observed by the many Muslim inhabitants of the city. Historian Leor Halevi describes prophetic norms around using "three stones" and water to cleanse oneself, ongoing debates about the use of toilet paper among Islamic jurists, and British concepts of hygiene in colonial-era Sudan; Halevi, *Modern Things on Trial*, 31–32, 39–44.

77 Charles-Roux, *Compte rendu*, 167. Roux was a colonial campaigner and subsequent colonial administrator for Madagascar.

78 Arrete no. 30 fixant les conditions d'installation des cabinets d'aisances dans la Commune de Majunga, signed April 24, 1913, ANRDM/vIIj 391; Arret no. 257, approved September 10, 1926, ANRDM/vIIj 391.

79 For more on cosmological valences and ancestral prohibitions around waste, see Rijke-Epstein, "Politics of Filth," 231, 237–39.

80 Interview with Tsiavono, Antanimisaja, January 25, 2014.

81 Interview with Tsiavono, Antanimisaja, January 25, 2014. "Hafahafa" also has the sense of something "different, unseemingly, improper . . . peculiar," depending on the context. Richardson, *New Malagasy-English Dictionary*, 217.

82 Proces-Verbaux, May 11, 1937, ANRDM/F45.

83 Tarr, "Separate vs. Combined Sewer Problem," 309; Tarr and McMichael, "Evolution of Wastewater Technology," 166–67.

84 Anand, "Pressure"; Chalfin, "Public Things"; Jensen, "Pipe Dreams."

85 Larkin, "Politics and Poetics of Infrastructure," 329.

86 Jackson, "Rethinking Repair," 222.

87 Feeley-Harnik, "Political Economy of Death," 12–13.

88 Rapport Mensuel sur les travaux executes dans la subdivision de Majunga pendant le mois d'Avril 1898, ANRDM/DTP 28; letter from Resident de France in Moheli, Renè Perrè to Gouverneur Général of Madagascar, August 22, 1904, ANRDM/DTP/29; *La Dépeche de Majunga*, April 27, 1902, and May 4, 1902.

89 Arrondissement de Majunga, Rapport Annuels Travaux Publics: Commune de Majunga, 1915.

90 Interview with J. R. S., Mangarivotra, October 28, 2013; interview with Tsiavono, Antanimisaja, January 25, 2014; interview with Papa Taoaby, Abattoir, December 9, 2013.

91 Interview with Papa Taoaby, Abattoir, December 9, 2013.

92 Interview with Papa Taoaby, Abbatoir, December 9, 2013. *Folaka razana* literally means "broken ancestors," signaling a rupture in ancestral well-being.

93 Interview with D. H., Mahabibo, April 26, 2013.

94 Mama Khalid is a pseudonym. Interview with M. N., Manga, October 18, 2013.

95 For comparative contemporary studies of moral tensions around polluted wealth in Madagascar, see Walsh, "'Hot Money.'" For studies beyond Madagascar, see De Boeck, "Domesticating Diamonds and Dollars"; Taussig, *Devil and Commodity Fetishism*.

96 Interview with P. K., Mahajanga, February 14, 2013.

97 Arretes et Decision Municipaux (1937–47), Arrete Municipal 111.16, April 3, 1937, signed April 26, 1937, ANRDM/F47.

98 Interview with Tsiavono, Antanimisaja, January 25, 2014.

99 Arrondissement de Majunga, Rapport Annuel Travaux Publics, 1925, ANRDM/Ik 2214; Deschamps, *Les migrations intérieures*, 45.

100 Deschamps, *Les migrations intérieures*; Gueunier, *Les Chemins*, 45–46.

101 Mohamed, "'Les 'Sabena,'" 48; Radifison, "Conflits ethniques," 151.

102 Radifison, "Conflits ethniques," 151.

103 A research report conducted in 2010 by the multinational development organization Institut Régional de Coopération Développement (IRCOD) as part of a larger sanitation initiative suggested that the sanitation workers were primarily male, in their thirties and forties, and from a wide range of ethnic and religious backgrounds. See Larvido and Dodane, *Assainissement des matières fécales*, 27.

104 For more on the perceptions of mpanary tay, see Rijke-Epstein, "Politics of Filth."

105 This was also true in eastern Madagascar. Genese Sodikoff, email message to author, June 21, 2016.

106 Van Der Geest, "Night-soil Collector," 203.

107 Rijke-Epstein, "Politics of Filth," 254–56.

108 Melosi, *Sanitary City*, 20–25.

109 Taylor and Trentmann, "Liquid Politics," 199.

110 Rogaski, *Hygienic Modernity*, 217.

111 Chattopadhyay, *Unlearning the City*, 77.

112 Nixon, *Slow Violence*; Hecht, "Residue."

113 Troeger et al., "Estimates."

114 Sharpe, "Black Studies," 60.

Epilogue

1 Other turbulent political events in Mahajanga have also been referred to as *rotaka*—for instance, the standoff between Ratsiraka and Ravalomanana in 2002.

2 *Tsisy hevitra!* Interview with N., Ambondrona, October 31, 2012.

3 "Zavatra kely lasa nampiretra afo . . . nahazo asa sy trano jiabyjiaby Comorien, dia lasa mialona Betsirebaka." Interview with D. P., Abattoir, February 16, 2014.

4 Relatedly, others attributed the destruction of several buildings by rising tides to the egregious dismissal of fady by a group of Catholic nuns and highlanders (*bourzany*) who consumed pork (*kisoa*) there in the 1940s. In 1999, the encroachment of the sea destroyed one of the two existing hotels there, the Greek-owned Hotel Sakanyes. The Hotel Karon was left remain-

ing (*tavela*) because the owners and patrons were said to observe the appropriate customs, especially the prohibition on consumption of pork on the seaside.

5 He added, "When people know how to follow the customs here, then things are calm" (*Mahay manaraka ny fomba ety, dia milamina tsara*). Interview with Dadilahy Kassim, Tsaramandroso, January 18, 2013.

6 Rabearimanana, "Madagascar 1975," 353–56.

7 George Roberts recently described how, despite the Comorian nationalist movement MOLINACO gaining momentum elsewhere in the southwestern Indian Ocean region, Comorians in northwest Madagascar (especially those from Anjouan, because the movement derived from Ngazidja) "saw little to gain from unsettling the status quo." Roberts, "MOLINACO," 15–18.

8 Blum, "Madagascar 1972"; Raison-Jourde and Roy, *Paysans, intellectuels et populisme*.

9 Rabearimanana, "Madagascar 1975," 362–63.

10 Randrianja and Ellis, *Madagascar*.

11 Malgachisation was the official policy and approach under General Gabriel Ramanantsoa (1972–75) and Ratsiraka. It included nationalizing the economy, reforming education to provide instruction exclusively in Malagasy, and fostering a new, unified national identity.

12 Francophone scholars have explored these factors elsewhere; see Gueunier, *Les chemins*; Radifison, "Conflit ethniques"; Mohamed, "Les 'Sabena'"; Abdallah, "Hostilities Anti-Comoriennes."

13 This resonates with studies of memory of the 1947 rebellion in other Malagasy contexts. See, for instance, Cole, *Forget Colonialism?*; Tronchon, *L'insurrection malgache*.

14 Construction was halted and archaeologists were called to the site to excavate the area.

15 Bloch, *Placing the Dead*; Graeber, *Lost People*; Cole and Middleton, "Rethinking Ancestors"; Feeley-Harnik, *Green Estate*.

16 This was relayed in oral accounts. Some newspaper accounts reveal these concerns as well as debates to halt the trash dumping at Mangatokana. Zafimahova, "Fahadiovana."

17 Fieldnotes, December 18, 2013.

18 Interview with F. P., Mahajanga, February 19, 2013.

19 Glassman, *War of Words*; Weitzberg, *We Do Not Have Borders*; Brennan, *Taifa*.

20 Interview with D., Amborovy, March 21, 2014.

21 Fieldnotes, November 6, 2012.

22 Interview with A. A., Ambovoalanana, November 13, 2013.

23 Interview with M. R., Ambohidamina, February 14, 2014.

24 Interview with Dadilahy Kassim, Tsaramandroso Ambony, October 11, 2013.

25 "Tsy milamina saina, lasa adaladala." Interview with D. L., Tsararano Avaratra, April 4, 2014.

26 See also Munn, "Excluded Spaces," 451.
27 Navaro et al., *Reverberations*, 3.
28 Navaro-Yashin, *Make-Believe Space.*
29 "Rehefa alefa ny Comorians, dia manjary lasa gasy tompony. Nandrava fa-
    nanana Ajojo [They destroyed all the belongings of the Ajojo] . . . but the
    Ajojo nanao badri, apres the rotaka, dia ny olona nanao ratsy mamango."
    Interview with Dadilahy Kassim, Tsaramandroso Ambony, October 11,
    2013.
30 Bryant, "History's Remainders," 685.

Archives

Archives Commune de Mahajanga, Madagascar (ACM)

Bibliothèque de Musée d'Art et Archeologie, Antananarivo, Madagascar (BMA)

Bibliothèque et Archives Universitaires, Université d'Antananarivo, Madagascar (BUA)

Bibliothèque nationale de France, Paris, France (BNF)

Bibliothèque nationale de Madagascar, Antananarivo, Madagascar (BNA)

British Library, London, United Kingdom (BL)

Centre des archives d'Outre-Mer, Aix-en-Provence, France (CAOM)

Cleveland Public Library, East India Collection, Cleveland, Ohio, United States (CPL/EIC)

Council for World Mission—Archives of the London Missionary Society, School of Oriental and African Studies, London, United Kingdom (CWM/LMS)

East India Company Records, British Library, London, United Kingdom (IOR)

Foiben-Taosarintanin'I Madagasikara (Geographical and Hydrographic Institute of Madagascar), Antananarivo, Madagascar (FTM)

Institut National de la Statistique, Antananarivo, Madagascar (INSTAT)

National Archives of the République Démocratique de Madagascar, Antananarivo, Madagascar (ANRDM)

Northwestern University Library, Evanston, Illinois, United States (NWL)

Interviews

Malagasy was the primary language of my field research, and all interviews were conducted in Malagasy. After studying standard Malagasy (as used in the highlands and commonly taught in schools across the island) with language instructor Vololona Rasolofoson in Ann Arbor, with Olga Ramilisonina in Antananarivo, and with Ben Taoaby in Mahajanga, I eventually became proficient in the northern dialect of Malagasy spoken in Mahajanga (what some linguists have called "Northern Sakalava") during my fieldwork in the city (2011–14). Although early on in the fieldwork I worked closely with Ben Taoaby as a research assistant during interviews, as my proficiency increased I conducted interviews on my own. Throughout the interviews many residents selectively incorporated French words, and those with closer ties to the Comoros used some Shikomoro words; friends and kin who joined us helped to interpret and translate these latter terms. Many interviews emerged organically during long afternoon visits or over meals; these were informal and diverse in content, ranging from memories of times past to political debates to didactic lessons on cooking, moral comportment, and proper gender relations. After several attempts to record these conversations were met with reticence, I resolved to rely entirely on handwritten notes. In addition, my partner, David Epstein, and I photographed, with the permission of those present, gatherings of spirit mediums and spirit possession (*tromba*) and life-cycle events such as marriages, funerals, and circumcisions. I also worked with a group of high school and university students to document their experiences in the city through photography and journals, which we collectively compiled into a photo novella that we used to facilitate discussion about belonging and urban life.

Because many of the oral accounts wove references to the highly sensitive events of the 1976–77 expulsion into broader discussions of the city's past, and given the tensions around this history today, I have chosen to maintain most interviewees' anonymity and to identify them only with initials, except in cases where people explicitly expressed a preference for recognition. Some residents asked to be identified by name, and others chose their own pseudonyms; I have honored these requests throughout. Interviews were all conducted in Mahajanga and its surrounding areas and are listed chronologically.

Hadj Soudjay Bachir Adehame, La Corniche, February 14, 2012.
Hadj Soudjay Bachir Adehame, La Corniche, February 16, 2012.
Hadj Soudjay Bachir Adehame, La Corniche, February 21, 2012.
Hadj Soudjay Bachir Adehame, La Corniche, February 27, 2012.
Hadj Soudjay Bachir Adehame, La Corniche, February 29, 2012.
Hadj Soudjay Bachir Adehame, La Corniche, March 12, 2012.
Hadj Soudjay Bachir Adehame, La Corniche, March 15, 2012.
G., Mahajanga, July 18, 2012.
M., Fiofio, October 28, 2012.
P. K., Ambalavola, October 29, 2012.
N., Ambondrona, October 31, 2012.
Papa Taoaby, Abattoir, November 6, 2012.
Dadilahy Kassim, Tsaramandroso, January 18, 2013.
Volasoa, Amborovy, January 21, 2013.
B. P., Amborovy, February 8, 2013.
Dadilahy Kassim, Tsaramandroso, February 9, 2013.
J., Manga, February 12, 2013.

J., Manga, February 13, 2013.

Mama and Papa Taoaby, Abattoir, February 14, 2013.

Mama N., Morafeno, February 18, 2013.

F. P., Mahajanga, February 19, 2013.

Albert Ranaivamanana, Antanimalandy, March 21, 2013.

Francoeur Razafiarison, Antanimalandy, March 28, 2013.

Pastor Toky, Mahabibo Kely, March 29, 2013.

S., Mahavoky Avaratra, April 2, 2013.

Papa Taoaby, Abattoir, April 12, 2013.

Papa Taoaby, Abattoir, April 16, 2013.

Attoumani Mohamed, Village Touristique, April 18, 2013.

I. A., Tsaramandroso, April 19, 2013.

P. M., Mahavoky, April 24, 2013.

D. H., Mahabibo, April 26, 2013.

Mama Taoaby, Abattoir, April 29, 2013.

Mama Taoaby, Abattoir, May 7, 2013.

Said Hassan, Majunga Be, May 7, 2013.

Sheik Mamodrazy and Sheik Moustapha Nasser, Mahabibo, May 7, 2013.

H. A., Abattoir, June 19, 2013.

M. K., Abattoir, June 28, 2013.

P. T., Majunga Be, July 3, 2013.

Tourabaly, Majunga Be. July 4, 2013.

H. A., Abattoir, July 9, 2013.

Yakoubaly Abdoulhoussen, Majunga Be, July 11, 2013.

D. H., Mahabibo, July 11, 2013.

R., Abattoir, July 13, 2013.

M. J., Majunga Be., July 15, 2013.

Maître Youssef, Mahajanga, July 16, 2013.

Ramilisonina, Antananarivo, July 27, 2013.

M. Theophile, Analakely, August 12, 2013.

M. Theophile, Analakely, August 14, 2013

M. G., Marolaka, August 16, 2013.

Mama Taoaby, Abattoir, September 16, 2013.

I. A., Tsaramandroso, September 21, 2013.

M. A.. Manga, September 26, 2013.

I. A., Tsaramandroso, September 28, 2013.

M. N., Manga, October 1, 2013.

J. C., Antanimalandy, October 2, 2013.

Dadilahy Kassim, Tsaramandroso, October 6, 2013.

M. S., Amborovy, October 6, 2013.

M. R., Manga, October 7, 2013.

Michel Ducaud, Majunga Be, October 8, 2013.

Dadilahy Kassim, Tsaramandroso, October 11, 2013.

R. D., Mangarivotra, October 11, 2013.

M. A., Manga, October 16, 2013.

M. S., Amborovy, October 16, 2013.

M. N., Manga, October 18, 2013.

D. S., Mahavoky Atsimo, October 19, 2013.

M. C., Amborovy, October 19, 2013.

J. R. S., Mangarivotra, October 22, 2013.

Allain, Ambondrona, October 23, 2013.

C., Manga, October 25, 2013.

Allain, Amborovy, October 25, 2013.

J. R. S., Mangarivotra, October 28, 2013.

M. B., Manga, October 30, 2013.

M. A., Manga, October 31, 2013.

M. Z., Manga, November 4, 2013.

Allain, Amborovy, November 5, 2013.

F. P., Ambovoalanana, November 7, 2013.

M. G., Abattoir, November 11, 2013.

P. R., Manga, November 12, 2013.

A. A., Ambovoalanana, November 13, 2013.

M. M., Morafeno, November 14, 2013.

F. P., Manga, November 21, 2013.

Tsiavono, Antanimisaja, December 2, 2013.

Papa Taoaby, Abattoir, December 9, 2013.

H., Manga, December 11, 2013.

I., Mahabibo, December 11, 2013.

P., Manga, December 13, 2013.

Tsiavono, Antanimisaja, December 14, 2013.

M. M., Morafeno, December 15, 2013.

M. C., Village Touristique, December 18, 2013.

Twawilo, Mangatokana, December 18, 2013.

J.-F. Rabedimby, Ambondrona, December 19, 2013.

C., Mahajanga, January 7, 2014.

J. R., Mahajanga, January 15, 2014.

L. H., Mahajanga, January 15, 2014.

E., Mahajanga, January 20, 2014.

G. J., Mahajanga, January 20, 2014.

Tsiavono, Antanimisaja, January 25, 2014.

S., Mahajanga, January 27, 2014.

P., Mahajanga, January 27, 2014.

F., Mahajanga, January 29, 2014.

C., Mahajanga, January 31, 2014.

E. Mahajanga, January 31, 2014.

T., Mahajanga, January 31, 2014.

Hasandrama, Tsaramandroso, February 2, 2014.

T., Mahajanga, February 3, 2014.

P., Mahajanga, February 3, 2014.

F., Mahajanga, February 3, 2014.

Hasandrama, Tsaramandroso, February 5, 2014.

Valentin Razafindrakoto, SOTEMA, February 7, 2014.

M. S., Ambohidamina, February 8, 2014.

M. R., Ambohidamina, February 14, 2014.

D. P., Abattoir, February 16, 2014.

R., Manga, February 17, 2014.

W. H., Abattoir, February 22, 2014.

D., Amborovy, March 21, 2014.

El Had, Ambalavola, March 26, 2014.

M. F., Manga, March 28, 2014.

D. L. Tsararano Anosykely, April 4, 2014.

M. Z., Manga, April 7, 2014.

Hasandrama, Tsaramandroso, April 10, 2014.

M. N., Manga, April 11, 2014.

Bachir, La Corniche, April 14, 2014.

D. L. Tsararano Anosykely, April 18, 2014.

El Had, Ambalavola, April 18, 2014.

Periodicals

Antananarivo Annual and Madagascar Magazine
La Dépeche de Majunga
Inona no Vaovao
Journal Officiel de Madagascar et Dépendances
Notes, Reconnaissances et Explorations
Le Phare de Majunga
Le Réveil de la Côte Ouest

Published Primary and Secondary Sources

Abdallah, Elamine. "Hostilites Anti-Comoriennes de Majunga du 20 au 23 Decembre 1976." Master's thesis, University of Toamasina, Madagascar, 2005.

Abinal, Antoine, and Victor Malzac. *Dictionnaire malgache-français par Abinal et (V.) Malzac de la Comp. de Jesus*. Tananarive, Madagascar: Imprimerie de la mission catholique, 1888.

Abourahme, Nasser. "Assembling and Spilling-Over: Towards an 'Ethnography of Cement' in a Palestinian Refugee Camp." *International Journal of Urban and Regional Research* 39 (2014): 200–217.

Abramovich, S., G. Keller, T. Adatte, W. Stinnesbeck, L. Hottinger, D. Stueben, Z. Berner, B. Ramanivosoa, and A. Randriamanantenasoa. "Age and Paleoenvironment of the Maastrichtian to Paleocene of the Mahajanga Basin, Madagascar: A Multidisciplinary Approach." *Marine Micropaleontology* 47 (2002): 17–70.

Abu-Lughod, Janet. "Tale of Two Cities: The Origins of Modern Cairo." *Comparative Studies in Society and History* 7, no. 4 (1965): 429–57.

Adas, Michael. *Machines as the Measure of Men: Science, Technology, and Ideologies of Western Dominance*. Ithaca, NY: Cornell University Press, 1989.

Adebayo, A. G. "Money, Credit and Banking in Precolonial Africa: The Yoruba Experience." *Anthropos* 89, no. 4 (1994): 379–400.

Adelaar, Alexander. "Austronesians in Madagascar: A Critical Assessment of the Works of Paul Ottino and Philippe Beaujard." In *Early Exchange between Africa and the Wider Indian Ocean World*, edited by Gwyn Campbell, 77–112. Switzerland: Palgrave Cham, 2016.

Adelaar, Alexander. "Loanwords in Malagasy." In *Loanwords in the World's Languages: A Comparative Handbook*, edited by Martin Haspelmath and Uri Tadmor, 717–46. Berlin: De Gruyter Mouton, 2009.

Adelaar, Alexander. "Towards an Integrated Theory about the Indonesian Migrations to Madagascar." In *Ancient Human Migrations: Integrative Approaches to Complex Processes*, edited by I. Peiros, P. Peregrine, and M. Feldman, 149–72. Salt Lake City: University of Utah Press, 2009.

Agha, Menna, and Léopold Lambert. "Outrage: Informality Is a Fallacy." *Architectural Review*, December 16, 2020.

Ahmed, Chanfi. "Networks of the Shādhiliyya Yashrutiyya Sufi Order in East Africa." In *The Global Worlds of the Swahili: Interfaces of Islam, Identity and Space in 19th- and 20th-Century East Africa*, edited by Roman Loimeier and Rüdiger Seesemann, 317–52. Berlin: Lit Verlag, 2006.

Ahmed, Chanfi. *Islam et politique aux Comores: Évolution de l'autorité spirituelle depuis le protectorat français (1886) jusqu'à nos jours*. Paris: Harmattan, 1999.

Ahmed, Sara. *The Cultural Politics of Emotion*. New York: Routledge, 2013.

Ahmed, Sara. "Happy Objects." In *The Affect Theory Reader*, edited by Melissa Gregg and Gregory Seigworth, 29–51. Durham, NC: Duke University Press, 2010.

Aiyar, Sana. *Indians in Kenya: The Politics of Diaspora*. Cambridge, MA: Harvard University Press, 2015.

Akbari, Suzanne Conklin, Tamar Herzog, Daniel Jütte, Carl Nightingale, William Rankin, and Keren Weitzberg. "AHR Conversation: Walls, Borders, and Boundaries in World History." *American Historical Review* 122, no. 5 (2017): 1501–53.

Akrich, Madeline. "The De-scription of Technological Objects." In *Shaping Technology/Building Society: Studies in Sociotechnical Change*, edited by Wiebe Bijker and John Law, 205–24. Cambridge, MA: MIT Press, 1992.

Akyeampong, Emmanuel. *Drink, Power and Cultural Change: A Social History of Alcohol in Ghana, c. 1800 to Recent Times*. Portsmouth, NH: James Currey, 1996.

Allen, Richard. "Satisfying the 'Want for Labouring People': European Slave Trading in the Indian Ocean, 1500–1850." *Journal of World History* 21, no. 1 (2010): 53–55

Allerton, Catherine. *Potent Landscapes: Place and Mobility in Eastern Indonesia*. Honolulu: University of Hawai'i Press, 2013.

Allibert, Claude. "Austronesian Migration and the Establishment of the Malagasy Civilization: Contrasted Readings in Linguistics, Archaeology, Genetics and Cultural Anthropology." *Diogenes* 55, no. 2 (2008): 7–16.

Allman, Jean Marie, and Victoria B. Tashjian. *"I Will Not Eat Stone": A Women's History of Colonial Asante*. Portsmouth, NH: Heinemann, 2000.

Alpers, Edward. "A Complex Relationship: Mozambique and the Comoro Islands in the 19th and 20th Centuries." *Cahiers d'études africaines* 161 (2001): 73–95.

Alpers, Edward. "The French Slave Trade in East Africa (1721–1810)." *Cahiers d'études africaines* 10, no. 37 (1970): 80–124.

Alpers, Edward. "Gujarat and the Trade of East Africa, c. 1500–1800." *International Journal of African Historical Studies* 9, no. 1 (1976): 22–44.

Alpers, Edward. *Ivory and Slaves in East Central Africa: Changing Pattern of International Trade in East Central Africa to the Later Nineteenth Century*. Berkeley: University of California Press, 1975.

Alpers, Edward. "Madagascar and Mozambique in the Nineteenth Century: The Era of the Sakalava Raids." *Omaly sy Anio* 5–6 (1977): 337–53.

Alpers, Edward. "Slavery, Antislavery, Political Rivalry and Regional Networks in East African Waters, 1877–1883." *Afriques: Débats, méthodes et terrains d'histoire*, no. 6. https://doi.org/10.4000/afriques.1744.

Amigues, M. "Variole et vaccine à Anjouan pendant les années 1901–1902." *Annales d'hygiène et de médecine colonials* (1903): 490–97.

Amin, Shahid. *Event, Metaphor, Memory: Chauri Chaura, 1922–1992*. Berkeley: University of California Press, 1995.

Anand, Nikhil. "Pressure: The PoliTechnics of Water Supply in Mumbai." *Cultural Anthropology* 26, no. 4 (2011): 542–64.

Anand, Nikhil, Akhil Gupta, and Hannah Appel. *The Promise of Infrastructure*. Durham, NC: Duke University Press, 2018.

Anderson, Nathan. "The Materiality of Islamisation as Observed in Archaeological Remains in the Mozambique Channel." PhD diss. University of Exeter, 2021.

Anderson, Warwick, and Gabriela Soto Laveaga, eds. "Decolonizing Histories in Theory and Practice." Special issue, *History and Theory* 59, no. 4 (2020).

Anshan, Li. *A History of Chinese Overseas in Africa to 1911*. Beijing: Chinese Overseas Publishing House, 2000.

Apotsos, Michelle. *Architecture, Islam, and Identity in West Africa: Lessons from Larabanga*. New York: Routledge, 2016.

Apter, Andrew. *The Pan-African Nation: Oil and the Spectacle of Culture in Nigeria*. Chicago: University of Chicago Press, 2008.

Archambault, Julie. "'One Beer, One Block': Concrete Aspiration and the Stuff of Transformation in a Mozambican Suburb." *Journal of the Royal Anthropological Institute* 24, no. 4 (2018): 692–708.

Arens, William, and Ivan Karp. "Introduction." In *Creativity of Power*, edited by William Arens and Ivan Karp, xi–xxvii. Washington, DC: Smithsonian Institution Press, 1989.

Armstrong, James. "De bron van Keulens gedrukte kaart van Nieuw Matheleage." *Caert Thresoor* 33, no. 4 (2014): 129–35.

Armstrong, James. "Madagascar and the Slave Trade in the Seventeenth Century." *Omaly sy Anio* 17 (1983–84): 211–33.

Aslanian, Sebouh David. *From the Indian Ocean to the Mediterranean: The Global Trade Networks of Armenian Merchants from New Julfa*. Berkeley: University of California Press, 2011.

Aubanel, Napoléon. *La France civilisatrice: Madagascar*. Paris: Decombejean, 1895.

Aumeeruddy-Thomas, Yildiz, Verohanitra Miarivelomalala Radifison, Finn Kjellberg, and Martine Hossaert-McKey. "Sacred Hills of Imerina and the Voyage of *Ficus lutea* Vahl (Amontana) in Madagascar." *Acta Oecologica* 90 (2018), 18–27.

Auslander, Leora. "Beyond Words." *American Historical Review* 110, no. 4 (2005): 1015–45.

Auslander, Leora, Amy Bentley, Leor Halevi, H. Otto Sibum, and Christopher Witmore. "AHR Conversation: Historians and the Study of Material Culture." *American Historical Review* 114, no. 5 (2009): 1355–1404.

Azaryahu, Maoz. "The Power of Commemorative Street Names." *Environment and Planning D: Society and Space* 14, no. 3 (1996): 311–30.

Bachelard, Gaston. *The Poetics of Space*. 1958. Boston: Beacon Press, 1994.

Bahloul, Joëlle. "The Memory House: Time and Place in Jewish Immigrant Culture in France." In *House Life*, edited by Donna Birdwell-Pheasant and Denise Lawrence-Zúñiga, 239–49. New York: Routledge, 1999.

Bakhtin, Mikhail. *The Dialogic Imagination: Four Essays by M. M. Bakhtin*. Edited by Michael Holquist. Translated by Caryl Emerson and Michael Holquist. Austin: University of Texas Press, 1981.

Ballantyne, Andrew. "Architecture as Evidence." In *Rethinking Architectural Historiography*, edited by Dana Arnold, Elvan Altan Ergut, and Belgin Turan Özkaya, 36–49. London: Routledge, 2006.

Ballarin, Marie-Pierre. *Les reliques royales à Madagascar: Source de legitimation et enjeu de pouvoir (XVIII–XX siècles)*. Paris: Karthala, 2000.

Ballarin, Marie Pierre. "Le 'roi est nu': Les imaginaires du sacré dans la tourmente judiciaire: Procès autour des 'regalia' de la royauté sakalava du Boina, nord-ouest de Madagascar, 1957–2006." *Cahiers d'études africaines* 48, no. 192 (2008), 665–85.

Ballarin, Marie-Pierre. " Portes sculptées swahilies et indo-arabes des villes du Sud-Ouest de l'océan Indien." In *Cultures citadines dans l'océan Indien occidental (XVIIIe–XXIe siècles)*, edited by Faranirina Rajaonah, 87–101. Paris: Karthala, 2011.

Bang, Anne. *Islamic Sufi Networks in the Western Indian Ocean (c. 1880–1940)*. Leiden, Netherlands: Brill, 2014.

Bang, Anne K. *Sufis and Scholars of the Sea: Family Networks in East Africa, 1860–1925*. London: Routledge Curzon, 2003.

Bardonnet, Daniel. "Les minorités asiatiques à Madagascar." *Annuaire français de droit international* 10 no. 1 (1964): 127–224.

Baré, Jean-François. *Sable rouge: Une monarchie du nord-ouest malgache dans l'histoire*. Paris: Harmattan, 1980.

Barnes, David. *The Great Stink of Paris and the Nineteenth-Century Struggle against Filth and Germs*. Baltimore: Johns Hopkins University Press, 2006.

Bascom, William. "The Esusu: A Credit institution of the Yoruba." *Journal of the Royal Anthropological Institute of Great Britain and Ireland* 82, no. 1 (1952): 63–69.

Basso, Keith H. *Wisdom Sits in Places: Landscape and Language among the Western Apache*. Albuquerque: University of New Mexico Press, 1996.

Bateson, Gregory. *Naven: A Survey of the Problems Suggested by a Composite Picture of the Culture of a New Guinea Tribe Drawn from Three Points of View*. Stanford, CA: Stanford University Press, 1958 [1936].

Bayart, Jean-François. "Africa in the World: A History of Extraversion." *African Affairs* 99, no. 395 (2000): 217–67.

Beaujard, Philippe. "The First Migrants to Madagascar and Their Introduction of Plants: Linguistic and Ethnological Evidence." *Azania: Archaeological Research in Africa* 46, no. 2 (2011): 169–89.

Beauregard, Robert. *Planning Matter: Acting with Things*. Chicago: University of Chicago Press, 2015.

Bénévent, Charles. "Étude sur le Bouéni." *Notes, reconnaissances, et explorations* 1 (1897): 355–79.

Benjamin, Walter. "Paris, Capital of the Nineteenth Century," In *Reflections: Essays, Aphorisms, Autobiographical Writings*, translated by Edmund Jephcott, 155–72. New York: Schocken Books, 1986.

Bennett, Norman R., and George E. Brooks. *New England Merchants in Africa: A History through Documents, 1802 to 1865*. Boston: Boston University Press, 1965.

Bennett, Tony, and Patrick Joyce, eds. *Material Powers: Cultural Studies, History and the Material Turn*. New York: Routledge, 2013.

Berg, Lawrence, and Jani Vuolteenaho, eds. *Critical Toponymies: The Contested Politics of Place Naming.* Surrey, UK: Ashgate, 2009.

Berger, Laurent. "Les voix des ancêtres et les voies du développement: Les populations de l'Ankaraña en butte à la mondialisation." *Études rurales* 178 (2006): 129–60.

Berger, Laurent, and Olivier Branchu. "L'Islam à l'épreuve de l'ancestralité dans les villes et campagnes du nord de Madagascar." In *L'Islam politique au sud du Sahara: Identités, discours, et enjeux,* edited by Muriel Gomez-Perez, 69–118. Paris, Karthala, 2005.

Berman, Bruce, and John Lonsdale. *Unhappy Valley: Conflict in Kenya and Africa. Book 2: Violence and Ethnicity.* London: James Currey, 2002.

Bernard, Augustin. "Le main-d'oeuvre aux colonies." *Congrès international colonial: Rapport, mémoires and procès-verbaux,* 11–41. Paris: Challemel, 1900.

Bernault, Florence. *Colonial Transactions: Imaginaries, Bodies and Histories in Gabon.* Durham, NC: Duke University Press, 2019.

Bigon, Liora. "Names, Norms, and Forms: French and Indigenous Toponyms in Early Colonial Dakar, Senegal." *Planning Perspectives* 23, no. 4 (2008): 479–501.

Bigon, Liora. *Place Names in Africa: Colonial Urban Legacies, Entangled Histories.* Cham, Switzerland: Springer, 2016.

Birdwell-Pheasant, Donna, and Denise Lawrence-Zúniga, eds. *House Life: Space, Place and Family Life in Europe.* New York: Routledge, 1999.

Bissell, William Cunningham. "Between Fixity and Fantasy: Assessing the Spatial Impact of Colonial Urban Dualism." *Journal of Urban History* 37, no. 2 (2011): 208–29.

Bissell, William. *Urban Design, Chaos, and Colonial Power in Zanzibar.* Indianapolis: Indiana University Press, 2011.

Blanchy, Sophie. "Beyond 'Great Marriage': Collective Involvement, Personal Achievement and Social Change in Ngazidja (Comoros)." *Journal of Eastern African Studies* 7, no. 4 (2013): 569–87.

Blanchy, Sophie. *Karana et Banians: Les communautés commerçantes d'origine Indienne à Madagascar.* Paris: Harmattan, 1995.

Blanchy, Sophie. *La vie quotidienne à Mayotte, archipel des Comores.* Paris: Harmattan, 1990.

Blanchy, Sophie. *Maisons des femmes, cités des hommes: Filiation, âge et pouvoir à Ngazidja, Comores.* Nanterre, France: Société d'ethnologie, 2010.

Blanchy, Sophie. "A Matrilineal and Matrilocal Muslim Society in Flux: Negotiating Gender and Family Relations in the Comoros." *Africa* 89, no. 1 (2019): 30–32.

Blanchy, Sophie. "Matrilocalite et systeme d'age à Mayotte." *Taarifa: Revue des Archives départementales de Mayotte* 3 (2012): 9–21.

Blanchy, Sophie. "Mosquées du Vendredi, pouvoir et différenciation sociale à Ngazidja (Comores)." *Tarehi* 10 (2004): 16–24.

Blanchy, Sophie, Ben Ali Damir, and Saïd Moussa. *Guide des monuments historiques de la Grande Comore (Moroni, Ikoni, Itsandra-mdjini, Ntsudjini).* Moroni, Comoros: Éditions du Centre National de Documentation et de Recherche Scientifique (CNDRS), 1989.

Blanchy, Sophie, A. Pal, and T. Chakrabarti. "Indians in Madagascar: Religion, Ethnicity and Nationality." In *Critiquing Nationalism, Transnationalism and Indian Diaspora*, edited by Adesh Pal and Tapas Chakraborty, 92–105. New Delhi: Creative Books, 2005.

Blier, Suzanne Preston. *The Anatomy of Architecture: Ontology and Metaphor in Batammaliba Architectural Expression*. Chicago: University of Chicago Press, 1994.

Bloch, Maurice. *Placing the Dead: Tombs, Ancestral Villages and Kinship Organization in Madagascar*. New York: Seminar Press, 1971.

Bloch, Maurice. "The Resurrection of the House amongst the Zafimaniry of Madagascar." In *About the House: Levi-Strauss and Beyond*, edited by Janet Carsten and Stephen Hugh-Jones, 69–83. Cambridge: Cambridge University Press, 1995.

Blum, Françoise. "Madagascar 1972: L'autre independence." *Le mouvement social* 3, no. 236 (2011): 61–87.

Boddy, Janice. *Wombs and Alien Spirits: Women, Men, and the Zar Cult in Northern Sudan*. Madison: University of Wisconsin Press, 1989.

Boivin, Nicole, Alison Crowther, Richard Helm, and Dorian Fuller. "East Africa and Madagascar in the Indian Ocean World." *Journal of World Prehistory* 26 (2013): 213–81.

Bonate, Liazzat. "The Advent and Schisms of Sufi Orders in Mozambique, 1896–1964." *Islam and Christian–Muslim Relations* 26, no. 4 (2015): 483–501.

Bonate, Liazzat. "Islam in Northern Mozambique: A Historical Overview." *History Compass* 8, no. 7 (2010): 573–93.

Bonate, Liazzat. "Matriliny, Islam and Gender in Northern Mozambique." *Journal of Religion in Africa* 36, no. 2 (2006): 139–66.

Bosma, Ulbe. *The Sugar Plantation in India and Indonesia: Industrial Production, 1770–2010*. Cambridge: Cambridge University Press, 2013.

Boteler, Thomas. *Narrative of a Voyage of Discovery to Africa and Arabia: Performed in His Majesty's Ships, Leven and Baracouta from 1821 to 1826, under the Command of Capt. F. W. Owen*. Vol. 2. London: Richard Bentley, 1835.

Boudia, Soraya, Angela Creager, Scott Frickel, Emmanuel Henry, Nathalie Jas, Carsten Reinhardt, and Jody Roberts. "Residues: Rethinking Chemical Environments." *Engaging Science, Technology, and Society* 4 (2018): 165–78.

Bounoure, Gilles, "Éléments sur la collection Moriceau." *Journal de la Société des Océanistes* 138–39 (2014): 225–32.

Bourdieu, Pierre. "The Kabyle House or the World Inversed." In *Algeria 1960: The Disenchantment of the World; the Sense of Honor; the Kabyle House or the World Reversed: Essays*, translated by Richard Nice, 133–53. Cambridge: Cambridge University Press, 1979.

Bourdieu, Pierre. *Outline of a Theory of Practice*. Translated by Richard Nice. Cambridge: Cambridge University Press, 1977.

Boyer-Rossol, Klara. "De Morima à Morondava: Contribution à l'étude des Makoa de l'ouest de Madagascar au XIXe siècle." In *Madagascar et l'Afrique: Entre identité insulaire et appartenances historiques*, edited by Didier Nativel and Fara Rajaonah, 183–217. Paris: Harmattan, 2007.

Brennan, James R. *Taifa: Making Nation and Race in Urban Tanzania*. Athens: Ohio University Press, 2012.

Brockway, T. "A Visit to Ambohimanga in the Tanala Country." *Antanarivo Annual* 1 (1876): 178–84.

Browne, J. Ross. *Etchings of a Whaling Cruise, with Notes of a Sojourn on the Island of Zanzibar. To Which Is Appended a Brief History of the Whale Fishery*. New York: Harper, 1846.

Bryant, Rebecca. "History's Remainders: On Time and Objects after Conflict in Cyprus." *American Ethnologist* 41, no. 4 (2014): 681–97.

Buchli, Victor. *An Anthropology of Architecture*. New York: Routledge, 2020.

Bühnen, Stephan. "Place Names as an Historical Source: An Introduction with Examples from Southern Senegambia and Germany." *History in Africa* 19 (1992): 45–101.

Burney, David. "Climate Change and Fire Ecology as Factors in the Quaternary Biogeography of Madagascar." In *Biogéographie de Madagascar*, edited by Wilson R. Lourenço, 49–58. Paris: ORSTOM, 1996.

Burton, Andrew. *African Underclass: Urbanization, Crime, and Colonial Order in Dar es Salaam, 1916–1991*. Athens: Ohio University Press, 2005.

Burton, Antoinette. *Africa in the Indian Imagination: Race and the Politics of Postcolonial Citation*. Durham, NC: Duke University Press, 2016.

Byrd, Jodi. *The Transit of Empire: Indigenous Critiques of Colonialism*. Minneapolis: University of Minnesota Press, 2011.

Callaci, Emily. *Street Archives and City Life: Popular Intellectuals in Postcolonial Tanzania*. Durham, NC: Duke University Press, 2017.

Camboué, P. Paul. "Aperçu sur les Malgaches et leurs conceptions d'art sculptural." *Anthropos* 1/2 (1928): 1–18.

Campbell, Gwyn. *An Economic History of Imperial Madagascar 1750–1895: The Rise and Fall of an Island Empire*. New York: Cambridge University Press, 2005.

Campbell, Gwyn. "The History of Nineteenth-Century Madagascar: 'Le Royaume' or 'L'Empire'?" *Omaly sy Anio*, 33–36 (1994): 331–79.

Campbell, Gwyn. "Labour and the Transport Problem in Imperial Madagascar, 1810–1895." *Journal of African History* 21, no. 3 (1980): 341–56.

Campbell, Gwyn. "Madagascar and Mozambique in the Slave Trade of the Western Indian Ocean, 1800–1861." *Slavery and Abolition* 9, no. 3 (1988): 166–93.

Campbell, Gwyn. "Madagascar and the Slave Trade, 1810–1895." *Journal of African History* 22, no. 2 (1981): 203–27.

Campbell, Gwyn. "Slavery and Fanompoana: The Structure of Forced Labour in Imerina (Madagascar), 1790–1861." *Journal of African History* 29, no. 3 (1988): 463–86.

Campbell, Gwyn. "The Structure of Trade in Madagascar, 1750–1810." *International Journal of African Historical Studies* 26, no. 1 (1993): 111–48.

Campbell, Gwyn, ed. *Structure of Slavery in Indian Ocean Africa and Asia*. London: Frank Cass, 2004.

Campbell, Gwyn. "Unfree Labour and the Significance of Abolition in Madagascar, c. 1825–97." In *Abolition and Its Aftermath in the Indian Ocean Africa and Asia*, edited by Gwyn Campbell, 76–92. London: Routledge, 2013.

Campt, Tina M. "The Visual Frequency of Black Life: Love, Labor, and the Practice of Refusal." *Social Text* 37, no. 3 (2019): 25–46.

Cantier, Jacques, and Eric Jennings, eds. *L'empire colonial sous Vichy*. Paris: Odile Jacob, 2004.

Cantone, Cleo. "A Historiography of Sub-Saharan African Mosques: From Colonialism to Modernity." In *Routledge Handbook of Islam in Africa*, edited by Terje Østebø, 65–78. London: Routledge, 2021.

Carey, Dwight. "Creole Architectural Translation: Processes of Exchange in Eighteenth-Century Mauritius." *Art in Translation* 10, no. 1 (2018): 71–90.

Carey, Dwight. "How Slaves Indigenized Themselves: The Architectural Cost Logs of French Colonial Mauritius." *Grey Room* 71 (2018): 68–87.

Carse, Ashley. "Nature as Infrastructure: Making and Managing the Panama Canal Watershed." *Social Studies of Science* 42, no. 4 (2012): 539–63.

Carse, Ashley, and David Kneas. "Unbuilt and Unfinished: The Temporalities of Infrastructure." *Environment and Society: Advances in Research* 10 (2019): 9–28.

Carsten, Janet, and Stephen Hugh-Jones, eds. *About the House: Lévi-Strauss and Beyond*. Cambridge: Cambridge University Press, 1995.

Carter, Paul. *The Road to Botany Bay: An Exploration of Landscape and History*. New York: Knopf, 1988.

Casey, Edward S. *The Fate of Place: A Philosophical History*. Berkeley: University of California Press, 1997.

Casey, Edward. "How to Get from Space to Place in a Fairly Short Stretch of Time." In *Senses of Place*, edited by Steven Feld and Keith Basso, 14–51. Santa Fe, NM: School of American Research Press, 1996.

Catat, Louis. *Voyage à Madagascar (1889–1890)*. Paris: Hachette, 1895.

Çelik, Zeynep. *Urban Forms and Colonial Confrontations: Algiers under French Rule*. Berkeley: University of California Press, 1997.

Ceuppens, Bambi, and Peter Geschiere. "Autochthony: Local or Global? New Modes in the Struggle over Citizenship and Belonging in Africa and Europe." *Annual Review of Anthropology* 34 (2005): 385–407.

Chalfin, Brenda. "Public Things, Excremental Politics, and the Infrastructure of Bare Life in Ghana's City of Tema." *American Ethnologist* 41, no. 1 (2014): 92–109.

Chang, Jiat-Hwee, and Anthony D. King. "Towards a Genealogy of Tropical Architecture: Historical Fragments of Power-Knowledge, Built Environment and Climate in the British Colonial Territories." *Singapore Journal of Tropical Geography* 32, no. 3 (2011): 283–300.

Chappelet, F. "Le problème démographique et l'émancipation à la Grande-Comore." Mémoire. L'École nationale de la France d'outre-mer (ENFOM), 1958.

Charles-Roux, Jules. *Compte rendu des travaux du Congrès colonial de Marseille.* Vols. 3 and 4. Paris: A. Challamel, 1907.

Charles-Roux, Jules, Marcel Dubois, Auguste Terrier, Ambroise Cecile Arnaud, Camille Guy, Hugues Maurice André Méray, Henri Froidevaux et al. *Les colonies françaises.* Paris: A. Challamel, 1900.

Chattopadhyay, Swati. *Unlearning the City: Infrastructure in a New Optical Field.* Minneapolis: University of Minnesota Press, 2012.

Chazan-Gillig, Suzanne. *La société sakalave: Le Menabe dans la construction nationale malgache, 1947–1972.* Paris: Karthala, 1991.

Chazkel, Amy, and David Serlin. "Editors' Introduction" to "Enclosures: Fences, Walls, and Contested Spaces." Special issue, *Radical History Review* 108 (2010): 1–10.

Chétima, Melchisedek. "You Are Where You Build: Hierarchy, Inequality, and Equalitarianism in Mandara Highland Architecture." *African Studies Review* 62, no. 3 (2019): 40–64.

Clarac, A. Mainguy. "Epidémie de peste de Majunga en 1902." *Annales d'hygiène et de médecine colonials* 7 (1904): 28–46.

Cohen, David William. *The Combing of History.* Chicago: University of Chicago Press, 1994.

Cole, Jennifer. *Forget Colonialism? Sacrifice and the Art of Memory in Madagascar.* Berkeley: University of California Press, 2001.

Cole, Jennifer, and Christian Groes, eds. *Affective Circuits: African Migrations to Europe and the Pursuit of Social Regeneration.* Chicago: University of Chicago Press, 2016.

Cole, Jennifer, and Karen Middleton. "Rethinking Ancestors and Colonial Power in Madagascar." *Africa* 71, no. 1 (2001): 1–37.

Collins, Harry. *Tacit and Explicit Knowledge.* Chicago: University of Chicago Press, 2010.

Colomb, P. H. *Slave-Catching in the Indian Ocean: A Record of Naval Experiences.* London: Longmans, Green and Co., 1873.

Comaroff, John, and Jean Comaroff. *Of Revelation and Revolution.* Vol. 2, *The Dialectics of Modernity on a South African Frontier.* Chicago: University of Chicago Press, 2009.

Combeau-Mari, Evelyne. "Sport in the French Colonies (1880–1962): A Case Study." *Journal of Sport History* 33, no. 1 (2006): 27–57.

Cooper, Frederick. "Conflict and Connection: Rethinking Colonial African History." *American Historical Review* 99, no. 5 (1994): 1516–45.

Cooper, Frederick. "From Enslavement to Precarity? The Labour Question in African History." In *The Political Economy of Everyday Life in Africa: Beyond the Margins,* edited by Wale Adebanwi, 45–76. Suffolk: James Currey, 2017.

Cooper, Frederick. *On the African Waterfront: Urban Disorder and the Transformation of Work in Colonial Mombasa.* New Haven, CT: Yale University Press, 1987.

Cooper, Frederick. "Urban Space, Industrial Time, and Wage Labor in Africa." In

Struggle for the City: Migrant Labor, Capital, and the State in Urban Africa, edited by Frederick Cooper, 7–50. Beverly Hills, CA: Sage, 1983.

Cooper, Frederick, ed. *Struggle for the City: Migrant Labor, Capital, and the State in Urban Africa.* Beverly Hills, CA: Sage, 1983.

Coquery-Vidrovitch, Catherine. *The History of African Cities South of the Sahara: From the Origins to Colonization.* Translated by Mary Baker. Princeton, NJ: Markus Wiener, 2005.

Corbin, Alain. *The Foul and the Fragrant: Odor and the French Social Imagination.* Leamington Spa: Berg, 1986.

"Correspondances: La vie à Majunga; L'encombrement." *Revue francaise de l'etranger et des colonies* 20 (1895): 421–24.

Courtier, M. "Mission hydrographique de Madagascar." *Annales hydrographiques: Recueil de documents et mémoires relatifs à l'hydrographie et à la navigation* 30, no. 2 (1908–1909–1910): 207–78.

Crossland, Zoë. *Ancestral Encounters in Highland Madagascar: Material Signs and Traces of the Dead.* New York: Cambridge University Press, 2014.

Crowther, Alison, Leilani Lucas, Richard Helm, Mark Horton, Ceri Shipton, Henry T. Wright, Sarah Walshaw, et al. "Ancient Crops Provide First Archaeological Signature of the Westward Austronesian Expansion." *Proceedings of the National Academy of Sciences* 113, no. 24 (2016): 6635–40.

Cupers, Kenny, and Prita Meier. "Infrastructure between Statehood and Selfhood." *Journal of the Society of Architectural Historians* 79, no. 1 (2020): 61–81.

Curtin, Philip D. *Disease and Empire: The Health of European Troops in the Conquest of Africa.* Cambridge: Cambridge University Press, 1998.

Dahl, Otto Christian. "Bantu Substratum in Malagasy." *Études Océan Indien* 9 (1988): 91–132.

Dahl, Otto Christian. *Migration from Kalimantan to Madagascar.* Oslo: Norwegian University Press, 1991.

Dahl, Øyvind. *Meanings in Madagascar: Cases of Intercultural Communication.* Westport, CT: Bergin and Garvey, 1999.

Dahle, Lars. "The Swaheli Element in the New Malagasy-English Dictionary." *Antananarivo Annual and Madagascar Magazine* 9 (1885): 99–115.

Dandouau, André. *Contes populaires des Sakalava et des Tsimihety de la région d'Analalava.* Alger: Jules Carbonel, 1922.

Dandouau, Andre. "Coutumes funéraires dans le Nord-Ouest de Madagascar." *Bulletin de l'Academie malgache* 9 (1911): 157–72.

Dandouau, André, and Georges Chapus. *Histoire des populations de Madagascar.* Paris: Larose, 1952.

da Rosa, Rolando Melo. "Adobe as an Islamic Standard: Vernacular Cosmopolitics." In *Earthen Architecture in Muslim Cultures,* edited by Stéphane Pradines, 11–21. Leiden: Brill, 2018

Das, Veena. "Ordinary Ethics." In *A Companion to Moral Anthropology,* edited by Didier Fassin, 133–49. Malden, MA: John Wiley and Sons, 2012.

de Bocage, Victor Amédée Barbié. *Madagascar possession française depuis 1642:*

Ouvrage accompagné d'une grande carte dressée par V.A. Malte-Brun. Paris: A. Bertrand, 1859.

De Boeck, Filip. "Domesticating Diamonds and Dollars: Identity, Expenditure and Sharing in Southwestern Zaire (1984–1997)." *Development and Change* 29, no. 4 (1998): 777–810.

de Boeck, Filip. "Infrastructure: Commentary from Filip De Boeck." Curated Collections. *Cultural Anthropology Online,* November 26, 2012. https://journal .culanth.org/index.php/ca/infrastructure-filip-de-boeck.

de Boeck, Filip, and Sammy Baloji. *Suturing the City: Living Together in Congo's Urban Worlds.* London: Autograph ABP, 2016.

De Boeck, Filip, and Marie-Françoise Plissart. *Kinshasa: Tales of the Invisible City.* Leuven, Belgium: Leuven University Press, 2014.

Decary, Raymond. *Contribution à l'étude de l'habitation à Madagascar.* Paris: Imprimerie Marrimpouey jeune, 1958.

Decary, Raymond. "Les eaux douces et leurs habitants dans les traditions et les industries malgaches." *Mémoires de l'Institut scientifique de Madagascar, Série C: Sciences Humaines* 5 (1959): 233–66.

Decary, Raymond. "Les emplois du bamboo à Madagascar." *Journal d'agriculture traditionelle et de botanique appliquée* 9, no. 1 (1962): 65–70.

Deerr, Noël. *The History of Sugar.* London: Chapman and Hall, 1949.

de Flacourt, Étienne. *Dictionnaire de la language de Madagascar d'après l'édition de 1658 et l'histoire de la grande isle Madagascar de 1661.* Paris: E. Leroux, 1905.

Degani, Michael. "Shock Humor: Zaniness and the Freedom of Permanent Improvisation in Urban Tanzania." *Cultural Anthropology* 33, no. 3 (2018): 473–98.

de Lanessan, Jean-Louis. *L'expansion colonial de la France: Étude économique, politique, et géographique sur les établissements français d'outre-mer.* Paris: F. Alcan, 1886.

de Lassalle, Jacques. "Memoires sur Madagascar" (1797). Translated by Antoine Jully. *Notes, reconnaissances et explorations* 3, nos. 17–18 (1898): 556–95.

Delord, Raymond. "Le site touristique et mystique d'Ampijoroa." *Bulletin de l'Académie malgache* 39 (1961): 29–31.

DeLucia, Christine M. *Memory Lands: King Philip's War and the Place of Violence in the Northeast.* New Haven, CT: Yale University Press, 2018.

de Luna, Kathryn. "Affect and Society in Precolonial Africa." *International Journal of African Historical Studies* 46, no. 1 (2013): 123–50.

de Luna, Kathryn. "Marksmen and the Bush: The Affective Micro-politics of Landscape, Sex and Technology in Precolonial South-Central Africa." *Kronos* 41, no. 1 (2015): 37–60.

de Luna, Kathryn. "Tracing the Itineraries of Working Concepts across African History." *African Economic History* 44 (2016): 235–57.

de Luna, Kathryn. *Collecting Food, Cultivating People: Subsistence and Society in Central Africa.* New Haven, CT: Yale University Press, 2017.

de Luna, Kathryn, Jeffrey Fleischer, and Susan Keech McIntosh. "Thinking across the African Past: Interdisciplinarity and Early History." *African Archaeological Review* 29 (2012): 75–94.

Delval, Raymond. "Les musulmans à Madagascar en 1977." *L'Afrique et l'Asie modernes* 115 (1977): 28–46.

Delval, Raymond. "Les migrations comoriennes à Madagascar, flux et reflux." In *Migrations, minorités et échanges en ocean Indien XIXe–XXe siècle: Table ronde 1978, IHPOM, CHEAM, ACOI*. Aix-en-Provence: Institute d'histoire des pays d'outre-mer, 1978.

Delville, Victor. *Partage de l'Afrique: Exploration, colonization, état politique*. Paris: Joseph André, 1898.

De Majunga à Tananarive: Renseignements et impression de voyage. Tananarive, Madagascar: Imprimerie Officielle, 1900.

De Martonne, Édouard-Guillaume. "La Cartographie de Madagascar." *Annales de géographie* 103 (1910): 49–69.

De Raulin, Gustav [Landrieu]. "Majunga, son importance et son avenir." *Revue maritime et coloniale* (1894): 310–28.

Desai, Gaurav. "Commerce as Romance: Nanji Kalidas Mehta's Dream Half-Expressed." *Research in African Literatures* 42, no. 3 (2011): 147–65.

Deschamps, Hubert. *Les migrations intérieures passées et présentes à Madagascar*. Paris: Berger-Levrault, 1959.

de Vere Allen, James. "The Swahili House: Cultural and Ritual Concepts Underlying Its Plan and Structure." In *Swahili Houses and Tombs of the Coast of Kenya*, edited by James de Vere Allen and Thomas Wilson, 1–32. London: Art and Archaeology Research Papers, 1979.

Dewar, Robert, and Henry Wright. "The Culture History of Madagascar." *Journal of World Prehistory* 7 (1993): 417–66.

Domenichini, Jean-Pierre. "Jean Ralaimongo (1884–1943) ou Madagascar au seuil du nationalism." *Outre-Mers: Revue d'histoire* 56, no. 204 (1969): 236–87. https://www.persee.fr/doc/outre_0300-9513_1969_num_56_204_1488.

Donley-Reid, Linda. "A Structuring Structure: The Swahili House." In *Domestic Architecture and the Use of Space*, edited by Susan Kent, 114–26. New York: Cambridge University Press, 1990.

Douglass, Kristina, Sean Hixon, Henry T. Wright, Laurie R. Godfrey, Brooke E. Crowley, Barthélémy Manjakahery, Tanambelo Rasolondrainy, Zoë Crossland, and Chantal Radimilahy. "A Critical Review of Radiocarbon Dates Clarifies the Human Settlement of Madagascar." *Quaternary Science Reviews* 221 (2019): 1–11.

Dransfield, John, and Mijoro Rakotoarinivo. "The Biogeography of Madagascar Palms." In *The Biology of Island Floras*, edited by David Branwell and Juli Caujapé-Castells, 179–96. Cambridge: Cambridge University Press, 2011.

Drury, Robert. *Madagascar, or, Robert Drury's Journal during Fifteen Years' Captivity on that Island, and a Further Description of Madagascar by Abbé Alexis Rochen*. Edited by Samuel Pasfield Oliver. 1729, 1890. Reprint, New York: Negro Universities Press, 1969.

Du Bois, W. E. B. *The World and Africa; Color and Democracy*. New York: Oxford University Press, 2007.

Duchesne, Jacques. *L'expedition de Madagascar: Rapport d'ensemble fait au ministre de la guerre le 25 avril 1896*. Paris: Charles-Lavauzelle, 1896.

Dumaine, Julien-Pierre. "Idée de la côte occidentale de Madagascar depuis Ancouala au nord jusqu'à Moroundava en 1792." *Annales des voyages*, no. 11 (1810): 20–52.

Edgerton, David. *The Shock of the Old: Technology and Global History Since 1900*. Oxford: Oxford University Press, 2007.

Eley, Geoff. *A Crooked Line: From Cultural History to the History of Society*. Ann Arbor: University of Michigan Press, 2005.

Elleh, Nnamdi. *Architecture and Power in Africa*. Westport, CT: Praeger, 2002.

Ellis, Stephen. "The History of Sovereigns in Madagascar: New Light from Old Sources." In *Madagascar revisitée: En voyage avec Françoise Raison-Jourde*, edited by Françoise Raison-Jourde, 405–31. Paris: Karthala, 2009.

Ellis, Stephen. *The Rising of the Red Shawls: A Revolt in Madagascar, 1895–1899*. Cambridge: Cambridge University Press, 1985.

Ellis, Stephen. "Tom and Toakafo: The Betsimisaraka Kingdom and State Formation in Madagascar, 1715–1750." *Journal of African History* 48, no. 3 (2007): 439–55.

Elyachar, Julia. "Phatic Labor, Infrastructure, and the Question of Empowerment in Cairo." *American Ethnologist* 37, no. 3 (2018): 452–64.

Encyclopaedia of Islam. 2nd ed. Edited by P. Bearman, Th. Bianquis, C. E. Bosworth, E. van Donzel, and W. P. Heinrichs. https://referenceworks-brillonline-com.proxy.library.vanderbilt.edu/browse/encyclopaedia-of-islam-2. Accessed December 6, 2021.

Engelke, Matthew. "Spirit." In *Critical Terms for the Study of Africa*, edited by Gaurav Desai and Adeline Masquelier, 288–301. Chicago: University of Chicago Press, 2018.

Epstein, Steven. "The Construction of Lay Expertise: AIDS Activism and the Forging of Credibility in the Reform of Clinical Trials." *Science, Technology, and Human Values* 20, no. 4 (1995): 408–37.

Esoavelomandroso, Faranirina [Faranirina Rajaonah]. "Aménagement et occupation de l'espace dans la ville moyenne d'Antananarivo pendant la colonization." *Cahiers d'études africaines* 25, no. 99 (1985): 337–61.

Esoavelomandroso, Faranirina. "Les 14 Juillet à Antananarivo au temps de la colonization." In *Ravao ny "La Bastille": Regards sur Madagascar et la Révolution Française*. Actes du colloque d'Antananarivo, June 5–6, 1989, edited by Guy Jacob. Antananarivo, Madagascar: CNAPMAD.

Esposito, John L., ed. *The Oxford Dictionary of Islam*. New York: Oxford University Press, 2003.

Evers, Sandra. *Constructing History, Culture, and Inequality: The Betsileo in the Extreme Southern Highlands of Madagascar*. Leiden: Brill, 2021.

Evers, Sandra. "Lex Loci Meets Lex Fori: Merging Customary Law and National

Land Legislation in Madagascar." In *Contest for Land in Madagascar: Environment, Ancestors and Development*, edited by Sandra Evers, Gwyn Campbell, and Michael Lambek, 119–40. Boston: Brill, 2013.

Evers, Sandra, and Caroline Seagle. "Stealing the Sacred: Why 'Global Heritage' Discourse Is Perceived as a Frontal Attack on Local Heritage-Making in Madagascar." *Madagascar Conservation and Development* 7, no. 2S (2012): 97–106.

Fair, Laura. *Pastimes and Politics: Culture, Community, and Identity in Post-abolition Urban Zanzibar, 1890–1945*. Athens: Ohio University Press, 2001.

Fair, Laura. *Reel Pleasures: Cinema Audiences and Entrepreneurs in Twentieth-Century Urban Tanzania*. Athens: Ohio University Press, 2018.

Fanon, Frantz. *Black Skin, White Masks*. Translated by Richard Philcox. 1952. New York: Grove, 2008.

Fanon, Frantz. *The Wretched of the Earth*. Translated by Richard Philcox. 1963. New York: Grove, 2004.

Feeley-Harnik, Gillian. *A Green Estate: Restoring Independence in Madagascar*. Washington, DC: Smithsonian, 1991.

Feeley-Harnik, Gillian. "The Political Economy of Death: Communication and Change in Malagasy Colonial History." *American Ethnologist* 11, no. 1 (1984): 1–19.

Feeley-Harnik, Gillian. "Ravenala Madagascariensis Sonnerat: The Historical Ecology of a 'Flagship Species' in Madagascar." *Ethnohistory* 48, no. 1–2 (2001): 31–86.

Feeley-Harnik, Gillian. "Sakalava." *The Encyclopedia of Vernacular Architecture*. Cambridge: Cambridge University Press, 1997.

Feeley-Harnik, Gillian. "The Sakalava House (Madagascar)." *Anthropos* 75, nos. 3–4 (1980): 559–85.

Fehérváry, Krisztina. "American Kitchens, Luxury Bathrooms, and the Search for a 'Normal' Life in Postsocialist Hungary." *ethnos* 67, no. 3 (2002): 369–400.

Fehérváry, Krisztina. *Politics in Color and Concrete: Socialist Materialities and the Middle Class in Hungary*. Bloomington: Indiana University Press, 2013.

Feierman, Steven. *Peasant Intellectuals: Anthropology and History in Tanzania*. Madison: University of Wisconsin Press, 1990.

Ferme, Mariane C. *The Underneath of Things: Violence, History, and the Everyday in Sierra Leone*. Berkeley: University of California Press, 2001.

Ferrand, Gabriel. *Les Musulmans à Madagascar at aux îles Comores*. Paris: Ernest Leroux, 1891–1902.

Ferrand, Gabriel. "Notes sur Madagascar." *Bulletin de la Société de géographie de l'est* 12 (1887): 577–80.

Fields-Black, Edda. "Untangling the Many Roots of West African Mangrove Rice Farming: Rice Technology in the Rio Nunez Region, Earliest Times to c. 1800." *Journal of African History* 49, no. 1 (2008): 1–21.

Findlen, Paula. "Objects of History: The Past Materialized." *History and Theory* 59, no. 2 (2020): 270–82.

Fischer, Brodwyn, Bryan McCann, and Javier Auyero, eds. *Cities from Scratch: Poverty and Informality in Urban Latin America.* Durham, NC: Duke University Press, 2014.

Fleisher, Jeffrey. "The Gathering of Swahili Religious Practice: Mosques-as-Assemblages at 1000 CE." In *New Materialisms, Ancient Cities,* edited by Timothy Pauketat and Susan Alt, 158–83. London: Routledge, 2019.

Fleisher, Jeffrey. "Performance, Monumentality and the 'Built Exterior' on the Eastern African Swahili Coast." *Azania: Archaeological Research in Africa* 48, no. 2 (2013): 263–81.

Fleisher, Jeffrey. "Rituals of Consumption and the Politics of Feasting on the Eastern African Coast, AD 700–1500." *Journal of World Prehistory* 23, no. 4 (2010): 195–217.

Fleisher, Jeffrey B. "Situating the Swahili House." In *Theory in Africa, Africa in Theory,* edited by Stephanie Wynne-Jones and Jeffrey Fleisher, 72–89. London: Routledge, 2015.

Fleisher, Jeffrey, Paul Lane, Adria LaViolette, Mark Horton, Edward Pollard, Eréndrina Quintana Morales, Thomas Vernet, Annalisa Christie, and Stephanie Wynne-Jones. "When Did the Swahili Become Maritime?" *American Anthropologist* 117, no. 1 (2015): 100–115.

Fleisher, Jeffrey, and Stephanie Wynne-Jones. "Authorisation and the Process of Power: The View from African Archaeology." *Journal of World Prehistory* 23, no. 4 (2010): 177–93.

Fontein, Joost. *The Politics of the Dead in Zimbabwe 2000–2020: Bones, Rumours and Spirits.* United Kingdom: James Currey, 2022.

Fontein, Joost. "Graves, Ruins, and Belonging: Towards an Anthropology of Proximity." *Journal of the Royal Anthropological Institute* 17, no. 4 (2011): 706–27.

Foucault, Michel. *Discipline and Punish.* Translated by Anthony Sheridan. Paris: Gallimard, 1975.

Fourchard, Laurent. "Between World History and State Formation: New Perspectives on Africa's Cities." *Journal of African History* 52, no. 2 (2011): 223–48.

Fowles, Severin. "People without Things." In *An Anthropology of Absence: Materializations of Transcendence and Loss,* edited by Mikkel Bille, Frida Hastrup, Tim Flohr Soerensen, 23–41. New York: Springer-Verlag, 2010.

Fredericks, Rosalind. *Garbage Citizenship: Vital Infrastructures of Labor in Dakar, Senegal.* Durham, NC: Duke University Press, 2018.

Freed, Libbie. "Networks of (Colonial) Power: Roads in French Central Africa after World War I." *History and Technology* 26, no. 3 (2010): 203–23.

Freeman, Joseph John. *A Dictionary of the Malagasy Language in Two Parts.* Tananarive, Madagascar: LMS Press, 1835.

Freeman, Luke. "Separation, Connection and the Ambiguous Nature of Émigré Houses in Rural Highland Madagascar." *Home Cultures* 10, no. 2 (2013): 93–100.

Fremigacci, Jean. "Autocratie administrative et société coloniale dans la région de

Majunga (1900–1940). Les dominants: Appareil administratif, colons français et minorités indigènes." *Omaly sy Anio* 16 (1983): 383–432.

Frère, Suzanne. *Madagascar: Panorama de l'Androy.* Paris: Aframpe, 1958.

Fuglestad, Finn. "The Tompon-tany and the Tompon-drano in the History of Central and Western Madagascar." *History in Africa* 9 (1982): 61–76.

Gaillard, Jeanne. *Paris, La Ville (1852–1870).* Lille-Paris: Honoré Champion, 1976.

Gallieni, Joseph-Simon. *Neuf ans à Madagascar.* Paris: Librairie Hachette, 1908.

Garbit, Hubert. "Introduction." In *Madagascar: Étude économique*, edited by Xavier Loisy, 1–20. Paris: Augustin Challamel, 1914.

Gastrow, Claudia. "Cement Citizens: Housing, Demolition and Political Belonging in Luanda, Angola." *Citizenship Studies* 21, no. 2 (2017): 224–39.

Gastrow, Claudia. "DIY Verticality: The Politics of Materiality in Luanda." *City and Society* 32, no. 1 (2020): 93–117.

Gautier, Denis. "*Ficus* (Moraceae) as Part of Agrarian Systems in the Bamileke Region (Cameroon)." *Economic Botany* 50, no. 3 (1996): 318–26.

Gautier, Denis, Baptiste Hautdidier, and Laurent Gazuli. "Woodcutting and Territorial Claims in Mali." *Geoforum* 42, no. 1 (2011): 28–39.

Gautier, Émile-Félix. "L'ouest malgache." *Annales de géographie* 4, no. 16 (1895): 310–24.

Gautier, Émile-Félix. "Mission Émile Gautier à Madagascar." *Annales de Géographie* 1, no. 7 (1893): 355–64.

Gensheimer, Thomas. "Globalization and the Medieval Swahili City." In *Globalization and Urbanization in Africa*, edited by Toyin Falola and Steven Salm, 171–86. Trenton, NJ: Africa World Press, 2004.

Geschiere, Peter. *The Perils of Belonging: Autochthony, Citizenship, and Exclusion in Africa and Europe.* Chicago: University of Chicago Press, 2009.

Geschiere, Peter, and Francis Nyamnjoh. "Capitalism and Autochthony: The Seesaw of Mobility and Belonging." In *Millennial Capitalism and the Culture of Neoliberalism*, edited by John Comaroff, Jean Comaroff, and Robert Weller, 159–90. Durham, NC: Duke University Press, 2001.

Geurts, Kathryn. *Culture and the Senses: Bodily Ways of Knowing in an African Community.* Berkeley: University of California Press, 2002.

Gevrey, Alfred. *Essai sur les îles Comores.* Paris: A. Saligny, 1870.

Ghaidan, Usam. "Lamu: A Case Study of the Swahili Town." *Town Planning Review* 45, no. 1 (1974): 84–90.

Gieryn, Thomas. "What Buildings Do." *Theory and Society* 31, no. 1 (2002): 35–74.

Ginzburg, Carlo. *The Cheese and the Worms: The Cosmos of a Sixteenth-Century Miller.* Baltimore: Johns Hopkins University Press, 2013.

Glassman, Jonathon. "Ethnicity and Race in African Thought." In *A Companion to African History*, edited by William Worger, Charles C. Ambler, and Nwando Achebe, 199–223. Newark, NJ: John Wiley, 2019.

Glassman, Jonathon. *Feasts and Riot: Revelry, Rebellion, and Popular Consciousness on the Swahili Coast, 1856–1888.* Portsmouth, NH: Heinemann, 1995.

Glassman, Jonathon. "'Slower Than a Massacre': The Multiple Sources of Racial Thought in Colonial Africa." *American Historical Review* 109, no. 3 (2004): 720–54.

Glassman, Jonathon. *War of Words, War of Stones: Racial Thought and Violence in Colonial Zanzibar.* Bloomington: Indiana University Press, 2011.

Gobbers, Erik. "Ethnic Associations in Katanga Province, the Democratic Republic of Congo: Multi-tier System, Shifting identities and the Relativity of Autochthony." *Journal of Modern African Studies* 54, no. 2 (2016): 211–36.

Goedefroit, Sophie. *A l'ouest de Madagascar: Les Sakalava du Menabe.* Paris: ORSTOM-Karthala, 1998.

Goerg, Odile. "From Hill Station (Freetown) to Downtown Conakry: Comparing French and British Approaches to Segregation in Colonial Cities at the Beginning of the Twentieth Century." *Canadian Journal of African Studies* 32, no. 1 (1998): 1–31.

Gordillo, Gastón. *Rubble: The Afterlife of Destruction.* Durham, NC: Duke University Press, 2014.

Graeber, David. "Dancing with Corpses Reconsidered: An Interpretation of 'Famadihana' (in Arivonimamo, Madagascar)." *American Ethnologist* 22, no. 2 (1995): 258–78.

Graeber, David. *Lost People: Magic and the Legacy of Slavery in Madagascar.* Bloomington: Indiana University Press, 2007.

Graham, Stephen, and Simon Marvin. *Splintering Urbanism: Networked Infrastructures, Technological Mobilities and the Urban Condition.* London: Routledge, 2001.

Grainge, Herbert. "Journal of a Visit to Mojanga and the North-West Coast." *Antananarivo Annual and Madagascar Magazine* 1 (January 1, 1875): 11–38.

Gramsci, Antonio. *Selections from Prison Notebooks.* Edited and translated by Quintin Hoare and Geoffrey Nowell Smith. New York: International Press, 1971.

Grandidier, Alfred. *Collection des ouvrages anciens concernant Madagascar.* Vol. 2. Paris: Comité de Madagascar, 1904.

Grandidier, Alfred. *Histoire de la géographie.* Vol. 1. Paris: Imprimerie nationale, 1885.

Grandidier, Alfred. "Souvenirs de voyages (1885–1870) d'après son manuscrit inédit de 1916." *Documents anciens sur Madagascar, no. 6.* Tananarive, Madagascar: Association Malgache d'Archéologie, 1971.

Grandidier, Alfred. *Voyage à Madagascar: Notes et souvenirs.* Tananarive, Madagascar: ORSTOM, 1869.

Grandidier, Alfred, and Guillaume Grandidier. *Histoire physique, naturelle et politique de Madagascar.* Tananarive, Madagascar: Imprimerie officielle, 1892.

Grandidier, Alfred, and Guillaume Grandidier. *Ethnographie de Madagascar.* Vols. 1–4. Paris: Imprimerie Nationale, 1908–1928.

Grandidier, Alfred, Guillaume Grandidier, Henri Froidevaux, and Jules Charles-Roux, eds. *Collection des ouvrages anciens concernant Madagascar.* 10 vols. Paris: Comité de Madagascar, 1903.

Green, Nile. *Bombay Islam: The Religious Economy of the West Indian Ocean, 1840–1915.* New York: Cambridge University Press, 2011.

Green, Nile. *Sufism: A Global History.* Malden, MA: Wiley-Blackwell, 2012.

Green, Sandra. *Sacred Sites and the Colonial Encounter: A History of Memory and Meaning in Ghana.* Bloomington: Indiana University Press, 2002.

Grosclaude, Etienne. *Un Parisien à Madagascar: Aventures et impressions de voyage.* Paris: Hachette, 1898.

Grubb, Peter. "Interpreting Some Outstanding Features of the Flora and Vegetation of Madagascar." *Perspectives in Plant Ecology, Evolution and Systematics* 6, nos. 1–2 (2003): 125–46.

Grundlingh, Louis. "Municipal Modernity: The Politics of Leisure and Johannesburg's Swimming Baths, 1920s to 1930s." *Urban History* 49, no 4 (2021): 771–90. https://doi.org/10.1017/S096392682100047X.

Grunebaum, Heidi. "Unburying the Dead in the 'Mother City': Urban Topographies of Erasure." PMLA 122, no. 1 (2007): 210–19.

Gueunier, Noel. *Les chemins de l'Islam à Madagascar.* Paris: Harmattan, 1994.

Guide-annuaire de Madagascar et dépendances. Tananarive, Madagascar: Imprimerie Officielle, 1902.

Guillain, Charles. *Documents sur l'histoire, la géographie et le commerce de la partie occidentale de Madagascar.* Paris: Imprimerie Royale, 1845.

Guyer, Jane. *Marginal Gains: Monetary Transactions in Atlantic Africa.* Chicago: University of Chicago Press, 2004.

Guyer, Jane, and Samuel M. Eno Belinga. "Wealth in People as Wealth in Knowledge: Accumulation and Composition in Equatorial Africa." *Journal of African History* 36, no. 1 (1995): 91–120.

Haile, John. "Malagasy Village Life: Pen and Ink Sketches of the People of Western Imerina." *Antananarivo Annual and Madagascar Magazine* 18 (1893): 1–20.

Halevi, Leor. *Modern Things on Trial: Islam's Global and Material Reformation in the Age of Rida, 1865–1935.* New York: Columbia University Press, 2019.

Hall, Bruce. *A History of Race in Muslim West Africa, 1600–1960.* Cambridge: Cambridge University Press, 2011.

Hamilton, Carolyn. *Terrific Majesty: The Powers of Shaka Zulu and Limits of Historical Invention.* Cambridge, MA: Harvard, 1998.

Hansen, Karen Tranberg. *Keeping House in Lusaka.* New York: Columbia University Press, 1997.

Hanson, Holly. *Landed Obligation: The Practice of Power in Buganda.* Portsmouth, NH: Heinemann, 2003.

Hanson, Holly. "Mapping Conflict: Heterarchy and Accountability in the Ancient Capital of Buganda." *Journal of African History* 50, no. 2 (2009): 179–202.

Harms, Erik. *Saigon's Edge: On the Margins of Ho Chi Minh City.* Minneapolis: University of Minnesota Press, 2011.

Harries, Patrick. *Work, Culture, and Identity: Migrant Laborers in Mozambique and South Africa, c. 1860–1910.* Portsmouth, NH: Heinemann, 1994.

Harris, Oliver, and Tim Flohr Sørensen. "Rethinking Emotion and Material Culture." *Archaeological Dialogues* 17, no. 2 (2010): 145–63.

Harris, Richard, and Garth Myers. "Hybrid Housing: Improvement and Control in Late Colonial Zanzibar." *Journal of the Society of Architectural Historians* 66, no. 4 (2007): 476–93.

Harrison, Mark. *Climates and Constitutions: Health, Race, Environment and British Imperialism in India, 1600–1850.* Oxford: Oxford University Press, 1999.

Harrison, Mark. *Contagion: How Commerce Has Spread Disease.* New Haven, CT: Yale University Press, 2012.

Harter, Jim. *World Railways of the Nineteenth Century: A Pictorial History in Victorian Engravings.* Baltimore: Johns Hopkins University Press, 2005.

Hartman, Saidiya. "Venus in Two Acts." *Small Axe: A Caribbean Journal of Criticism* 12, no. 2 (2008): 1–14.

Hastie, James. "Le voyage de Tananarive en 1817: Manuscrit de James Hastie." *Bulletin de l'Academie malgache* 2, no. 3 (1903): 173–78.

Hébert, Jean-Claude. "La cosmographie ancienne malgache suivie de l'énumération des points cardinaux et l'importance du nord-est." *Taloha* 1 (1965): 83–149.

Hébert, Jean-Claude. "L'énumeration des points cardinaux et l'importance du nord-est." *Taloha* 1 (1965): 150–95.

Hébert, Jean-Claude. "Les Français sur la cote oust de Madagascar au temps de Ravahiny (1780–1812?)." *Omaly sy Anio* 17–20 (1983–84): 235–77.

Hecht, Gabrielle. *Being Nuclear: Africans and the Global Uranium Trade.* Cambridge, MA: MIT Press, 2012.

Hecht, Gabrielle. "Interscalar Vehicles for an African Anthropocene: On Waste, Temporality, and Violence." *Cultural Anthropology* 33, no. 1 (2018): 109–41.

Hecht, Gabrielle. "Residue." *Somatosphere,* January 8, 2018. http://somatosphere .net/2018/residue.html/.

Helliwell, Christine. "Space and Sociality in a Dayak Longhouse." In *Things As They Are: New Directions in Phenomenological Anthropology,* edited by Michael Jackson, 128–48. Bloomington: Indiana University Press, 1996.

Hemmy, Otto Luder. "Voyage à la baie de Masselage ou de Bombetoke." In *Collections des ouvrages anciennes concernant Madagascar.* Vols. 5–6. Paris: Comité de Madagascar, 1907.

Herbert, Gilbert. *Pioneers of Prefabrication: The British Contribution in the Nineteenth Century.* Baltimore: Johns Hopkins University Press, 1978.

Hilgers, Mathieu. "Autochthony as Capital in a Global Age." *Theory, Culture and Society* 28, no. 1 (2011): 34–54.

Ho, Engseng. *The Graves of Tarim: Genealogy and Mobility across the Indian Ocean.* Berkeley: University of California Press, 2006.

Hocquard, Charles-Édouard. *L'expedition de Madagascar: Journal de compagne.* Paris: Imprimerie Lahure, Hachette, 1897.

Hodgson, Dorothy. "Being Maasai, Becoming Indigenous: Modernity and the Production of Maasai Masculinities." In *Men and Masculinities in Modern*

Africa, edited by Lisa Lindsay and Stephen Miescher, 211–29. Portsmouth, NH: Heinemann, 2003.

Hoffman, Danny. *Monrovia Modern: Urban Form and Political Imagination in Liberia*. Durham, NC: Duke University Press, 2017.

Holston, James. *Insurgent Citizenship: Disjunctions of Democracy and Modernity in Brazil*. Princeton, NJ: Princeton University Press, 2007.

Holston, James. *Cities and Citizenship*. Durham, NC: Duke University Press, 1999.

Holston, James. *The Modernist City: An Anthropological Critique of Brasília*. Chicago: University of Chicago Press, 1989.

Hommels, Anique. *Unbuilding Cities: Obduracy in Urban Socio-Technical Change*. Cambridge, MA: MIT Press, 2005.

Hooper, Jane. *Feeding Globalization: Madagascar and the Provisioning Trade, 1600–1800*. Athens: Ohio University Press, 2017.

Hooper, Jane. "Pirates and Kings: Power on the Shores of Early Modern Madagascar and the Indian Ocean." *Journal of World History* 22, no. 2 (2011): 215–42.

Hooper, Jane. "Yankees in Indian Ocean Africa: Madagascar and Nineteenth-Century American Commerce." *African Economic History* 46, no. 2 (2018): 30–62.

Horton, Mark. "Islamic Architecture of the Swahili Coast." In *The Swahili World*, edited by Stephanie Wynne-Jones and Adria LaViolette, 487–99. New York: Routledge, 2017.

Horton, Mark Chatwin, and John Middleton. *The Swahili: The Social Landscape of a Mercantile Society*. Oxford: Blackwell Publishers, 2001.

Hosagrahar, Jyoti. *Indigenous Modernities: Negotiating Architecture and Urbanism*. London: Routledge, 2012.

Houlder, John Alden. *Ohabolana, or, Malagasy Proverbs: Illustrating the Wit and Wisdom of the Hova of Madagascar*. Tananarive, Madagascar: Imprimerie FFMA, 1915.

Hull, Matthew. *Government of Paper: The Materiality of Bureaucracy in Urban Pakistan*. Berkeley: University of California Press, 2012.

Humbert, Henri. *Destruction d'une flore insulaire par le feu*. Tananarive, Madagascar: Imprimerie Moderne de l'Emyrne, 1927.

Hungerford, Hilary, and Sarah L. Smiley. "Comparing Colonial Water Provision in British and French Africa." *Journal of Historical Geography* 52 (2016): 74–83.

Hunt, Lynn. *Writing History in the Global Era*. New York: W. W. Norton, 2014.

Hunt, Nancy Rose. *A Colonial Lexicon of Birth Ritual, Medicalization, and Mobility in the Congo*. Durham, NC: Duke University Press, 1999.

Hunt, Nancy Rose. "History as Form, with Simmel in Tow." *History and Theory* 57, no. 4 (2018): 126–44.

Hurd, Duane Hamilton. *A History of Essex County Massachusetts with Biographical Sketches of the Many of Its Pioneers and Prominent Men*. Vol 1. Philadelphia: J. W. Lewis and Co., 1887.

Ibrahime, Mahmoud. *État français et colons aux Comores (1912–1946)*. Paris: Ceroi-Inalco, 1997.

Ingold, Tim. *Making: Anthropology, Archaeology, Art and Architecture*. London: Routledge, 2013.

Ingold, Tim. "Materials against Materiality." *Archaeological Dialogues* 14, no. 1 (2007): 1–16.

Insoll, Timothy. *Material Explorations in African Archaeology*. Oxford: Oxford University Press, 2015.

Isaacs, Nathaniel. *Travels and Adventures in Eastern Africa, Descriptive of the Zoolus, Their Manners, Customs, Etc. Etc. with a Sketch of Natal*. 2 vols. London: E. Churton, 1836.

Isnard, Hildebert. "L'archipel des Comores." *Les cahiers d'outre-mer* 21, no. 6 (1953): 5–22. https://doi.org/10.3406/caoum.1953.1831.

Ivaska, Andrew. *Cultured States: Youth, Gender, and Modern Style in 1960s Dar es Salaam*. Durham, NC: Duke University Press, 2011.

Jackson, Michael. *At Home in the World*. Durham, NC: Duke University Press, 1995.

Jackson, Steven. "Rethinking Repair." In *Media Technologies: Essays on Communication, Materiality, and Society*, edited by Tarleton Gillespie, Pablo J. Boczkowski, and Kristen A. Foot, 221–40. Cambridge, MA: MIT Press, 2014.

Jacquemet, Gérard. "Urbanisme parisien: La bataille du tout-al'égout a la fin du XIXe siècle." *Revue d'histoire moderne et contemporaine (1954–)* 26, no. 4 (1979): 505–48.

Jacquier, Léonce. *La main-d'oeuvre locale à Madagascar*. Paris: Imprimerie H. Jouve, 1904. https://archive.org/details/lamaindoeuvrelo00jacqgoog/page/n8/mode/2up.

James, Deborah. *Gaining Ground? Rights and Property in South African Land Reform*. New York: Routledge, 2007.

Jennings, Eric. "Madagascar under Vichy, 1940–42: Autarky, Forced Labour and Resistance on the 'Red Island.'" In *Resisting Bondage in Indian Ocean Africa and Asia*, edited by Edward Alpers, Gwyn Campbell, and Michael Salman, 60–68. New York: Routledge, 2007.

Jennings, Eric T. *Vichy in the Tropics: Petain's National Revolution in Madagascar, Guadeloupe, and Indochina, 1940–44*. Stanford, CA: Stanford University Press, 2004.

Jensen, Casper Bruun. "Pipe Dreams: Sewage Infrastructure and Activity Trails in Phnom Penh." *Ethnos* 82, no. 4 (2016): 627–47.

Johnson, Charles. *A General History of the Pyrates*. Vol. 2, *The History of Pyrates, Containing the Lives of Captain Misson, Captain Bowen, Captain Kidd . . .* London: Woodward, 1728.

Johnson, Paul Christopher, ed. *Spirited Things: The Work of "Possession" in Afro-Atlantic Religions*. Chicago: University of Chicago Press, 2014.

Joyce, Rosemary, and Susan Gillespie. *Beyond Kinship: Social and Material Reproduction in House Societies*. Philadelphia: University of Pennsylvania Press, 2000.

Jully, Antoine. "L'habitation à Madagascar." *Notes, reconnaissances et explorations* 4 (1898): 899–934.

Jütte, Daniel. "Living Stones: The House as Actor in Early Modern Europe." *Journal of Urban History* 42, no. 4 (2016): 659–87.

Jütte, Daniel. *The Strait Gate: Thresholds and Power in Western History.* New Haven, CT: Yale University Press, 2015.

Kaarsholm, Preben. "Zanzibaris or Amakhuwa? Sufi Networks in South Africa, Mozambique, and the Indian Ocean." *Journal of African History* 55, no. 2 (2014): 191–210.

Kermorgant, Alexandre Marie. *Hygiène coloniale.* Paris: Masson, 1911.

King, Anthony D. *Colonial Urban Development: Culture, Social Power, and Environment.* London: Routledge and Kegan Paul, 1976.

King, Rachel. "Living on Edge: New Perspectives on Anxiety, Refuge and Colonialism in Southern Africa." *Cambridge Archaeological Journal* 27, no. 3 (2017): 533–51.

Klieman, Kairn. *"The Pygmies Were Our Compass": Bantu and Batwa in the History of West Central Africa. Early Times to c. 1900.* Portsmouth, NH: Heinemann, 2003.

Kneitz, Peter. "The Sakalava Pilgrimage as a Royal Service (Western Madagascar)." In *Approaching the Sacred: Pilgrimage in Historical and Intercultural Perspective,* edited by Ute Luig, 239–74. Berlin: Edition Topoi, 2018.

Kneitz, Peter. "'With 800 Men . . .'—The Foundation of the Boeny Kingdom (ca. 1683–1686). A Critical Reconstruction of a Major Event in Political History." *Anthropos* 109 (2014): 81–102.

Kriger, Colleen. *Pride of Men: Iron Working in 19th Century West Central Africa.* Portsmouth, NH: Heinemann, 1999.

Kull, Christian A., Jacques Tassin, Sophie Moreau, Hervé Rakoto Ramiarantsoa, Chantal Blanc-Pamard, and Stéphanie M. Carrière. "The Introduced Flora of Madagascar." *Biological Invasions* 14, no. 4 (2012): 875–88.

Kus, Susan. "The Role of the Mpanadro in the Preservation of Betsileo Traditions." *Bulletin de l'Académie malgache* 65, no. 1–2 (1987): 105–10.

Kus, Susan, and Victor Raharijaona. "Between Earth and Sky There Are Only a Few Large Boulders: Sovereignty and Monumentality in Central Madagascar." *Journal of Anthropological Archaeology* 17, no. 1 (1998): 53–79.

Kus, Susan, and Victor Raharijaona. "House to Palace, Village to State: Scaling Up Architecture and Ideology." *American Anthropologist* 102, no. 1 (2000): 98–113.

Kus, Susan, and Victor Raharijaona. "Where to Begin a House Foundation: Betsileo 'Mpanandro' and the Creation of Tradition." In *L'extraordinaire et le quotidien: Variations anthropologues,* edited by Claude Allibert and Narivelo Rajaonarimanana, 135–44. Paris: Harmattan, 2000.

Kusimba, Chapurukha. *The Rise and Fall of Swahili States.* Walnut Creek, CA: Altamira, 1999.

Lafont, M. "Géographie médicale, L'Île d'Anjouan." *Annales d'hygiène et de médecine colonials* 4, no. 11 (1901): 157–92.

Lafont, M. "Géographie médicale, Mohéli." *Annales d'hygiène et de médecine colonials* 4 (1905): 497–501.

Lambek, Michael. "Exchange, Time, and Person in Mayotte: The Structure and Destructuring of a Cultural System." *American Anthropologist* 92, no. 3 (1990): 647–61.

Lambek, Michael. "Interminable Disputes in Northwest Madagascar." In *Religion in Disputes*, edited by Franz von Benda-Beckmann, Keebet von Benda-Beckmann, Martin Ramstedt, and Bertram Turner, 1–18. New York: Palgrave Macmillan, 2013.

Lambek, Michael. "On Being Present to History: Historicity and Brigand Spirits in Madagascar." *HAU: Journal of Ethnographic Theory* 6, no. 1 (2016): 317–41.

Lambek, Michael. "Ritual as a Social Diagnostic and Lens of Comparison in Mayotte and Its Neighbours." *Études rurales* 194 (2014): 63–77.

Lambek, Michael. "Sacrifice and the Problem of Beginning: Meditations from Sakalava Mythopraxis." *Journal of the Royal Anthropological Institute* 13, no. 1 (2007): 19–38.

Lambek, Michael. "Taboo as Cultural Practice among Malagasy Speakers." *Man* (1992): 245–66.

Lambek, Michael. *The Weight of the Past: Living with History in Mahajanga, Madagascar.* New York: Palgrave Macmillan, 2002.

Lambek, Michael, and Andrew Walsh. "The Imagined Community of the Antankaraña: Identity, History, and Ritual in Northern Madagascar." *Journal of Religion in Africa* 27, no. 3 (1997): 308–33.

Larkin, Brian. "The Politics and Poetics of Infrastructure." *Annual Review of Anthropology* 42 (2013): 327–43.

Larkin, Brian. *Signal and Noise: Media, Infrastructure, and Urban Culture in Nigeria.* Durham, NC: Duke University Press, 2008.

Larson, Pier Martin. "Desperately Seeking 'the Merina' (Central Madagascar): Reading Ethnonyms and Their Semantic Fields in African Identity Histories." *Journal of Southern African Studies* 22, no. 4 (1996): 541–60.

Larson, Pier Martin. "A Cultural Politis of Bedchamber Construction and Progressive Dining in Antananarivo: Ritual Inversions during the Fandroana of 1817." *Journal of Religion in Africa* 27, no. 3 (1997): 239–69.

Larson, Pier Martin. *History and Memory in the Age of Enslavement: Becoming Merina in Highland Madagascar, 1770–1822.* Portsmouth, NH: Heinemann, 2000.

Larson, Pier Martin. *Ocean of Letters: Language and Creolization in an Indian Ocean Diaspora.* Critical Perspectives on Empire. Cambridge: Cambridge University Press, 2009.

Larvido, Alix, and Pierre-Henri Dodane. *Assainissement des matières fécales de la ville de Mahajanga: Caracterisation du secteur informel de la vidange des latrines dans la ville.* Mahajanga, Madagascar: Institut Régional de Coopération Développement (IRCOD), 2011.

Laurent, Louis. *Les produits coloniaux d'origine minérale.* Paris: J. B. Baillière et Fils, 1903.

Lavau, Georges. "Les Comores." *La revue de Madagascar* 6 (1934): 105–32.

LeCain, Timothy. *The Matter of History: How Things Create the Past.* New York: Cambridge University Press, 2017.

Lee, Christopher J. *Unreasonable Histories: Nativism, Multiracial Lives, and the Genealogical Imagination in British Africa.* Durham, NC: Duke University Press, 2014.

Lefebvre, Henri. *Le droit à la ville: Suivi de espace et politique.* Collection Points. Paris: Anthropos, 1968.

Lefebvre, Henri. *The Production of Space.* Translated by Donald Nicholson-Smith. Oxford: Blackwell, 1991.

Lentz, Carola. *Land, Mobility, and Belonging in West Africa.* Bloomington: Indiana University Press, 2013.

Lentz, Carola, and Paul Nugent, eds. *Ethnicity in Ghana: The Limits of Invention.* London: Macmillan, 2000.

Leonhardt, Alec. "Baka and the Magic of the State: Between Autochthony and Citizenship." *African Studies Review* 49, no. 2 (2006): 69–94.

Lesage, M. "Mission hydragraphique de Madagascar." *Annales hydrographiques: Recueil de documents et mémoires relatifs à l'hydrographie et à la navigation* 30, no. 2 (1908–1909–1910): 199–206.

Le Ray, P. "Epidémie de peste à Majunga en 1907." *Annales d'hygiene et de pharmacologue coloniale* 11 (1908): 212–41, 393–408.

Loimeier, Roman. *Islamic Reform in Twentieth-Century Africa.* Edinburgh: Edinburgh University Press, 2016.

Lombard, Jacques. "La royauté Sakalava: Formation, développement, effondrement du 17e au 20e siècle; Essai d'analyse d'un système politique." Working paper, Office of Scientific and Technical Research Overseas (ORSTOM), Tananarive, Madagascar, January 1973.

Lombard, Jacques. *Le royaume sakalava du Menabe: Essai d'analyse d'un système politique à Madagascar, XVIIe–XXe siècle.* Travaux et Documents, no 214. Paris: ORSTOM, 1988.

Lonsdale, John. "The Moral Economy of Mau: Wealth, Poverty and Civic Virtue in Kikuyu Political Thought." In Berman and Lonsdale, *Unhappy Valley*, Bk. 2, 315–467.

Lonsdale, John. "Moral and Political Argument in Kenya." In *Ethnicity and Democracy in Africa*, edited by Bruce Berman, Dickson Eyoh, and Will Kymlicka, 73–95. Oxford: James Currey, 2004.

Lonsdale, John. "Soil, Work, Civilisation and Citizenship in Kenya." *Journal of Eastern African Studies* 2, no. 2 (2008): 305–14.

Love, Stephanie. "The Poetics of Grievance: Taxi Drivers, Vernacular Placenames, and the Paradoxes of Post-coloniality in Oran, Algeria." *City and Society* 33, no. 3 (2021): 422–43.

Low, Setha, and Denise Lawrence-Zúñiga. *The Anthropology of Space and Place: Locating Culture.* Oxford, MA: Blackwell Publishing, 2003.

Lowe, Lisa. *The Intimacies of Four Continents.* Durham, NC: Duke University Press, 2015.

Machado, Pedro. *Ocean of Trade: South Asian Merchants, Africa and the Indian Ocean, c. 1750-1850.* New York: Cambridge University Press, 2014.

"Madagascar, la région de Majunga." *Revue française de l'étranger et des colonies* 24 (1899): 281–86.

Mager, Anne Kelk. *Beer, Sociability, and Masculinity in South Africa.* Bloomington: Indiana University Press, 2010.

Makhulu, Anna-Maria. *Making Freedom: Apartheid, Squatter Politics, and the Struggle for Home.* Durham, NC: Duke University Press, 2015.

Malaquais, Dominique. "Building in the Name of God: Architecture, Resistance, and the Christian Faith in the Bamileke Highlands of Western Cameroon." *African Studies Review* 42, no. 1 (1999): 49–78.

Malkki, Liisa. "National Geographic: The Rooting of Peoples and the Territorialization of National Identity among Scholars and Refugees." *Cultural Anthropology* 7, no. 1 (1992): 24–44.

Malzac, Victorin. *Dictionnaire français-malgache.* Tananarive, Madagascar: Imprimerie de la mission catholique, 1893.

Manchuelle, François. *Willing Migrants: Soninke Labor Diasporas, 1848–1960.* Athens: Ohio University Press, 1997.

Mararo, Bucyalimwe. "Land, Power, and Ethnic Conflict in Masisi (Congo-Kinshasa), 1940s–1994." *International Journal of African Historical Studies* 30, no. 3 (1997): 503–38.

Marre, Aristide. *Vocabulaire français-malgache.* Paris: E. Leroux, 1895.

Martin, Bradford G. *Muslim Brotherhoods in Nineteenth Century Africa.* Cambridge: Cambridge University Press, 1976.

Martin, Jean. *Comores: Quatre îles entre pirates et planteurs.* Paris: Harmattan, 1983.

Martin, Phyllis. *Leisure and Society in Colonial Brazzaville.* Cambridge: Cambridge University Press, 1995.

Martinez, Julia. "'Unwanted Scraps' or 'An Alert, Resolute, Resentful People'? Chinese Railroad Workers in French Congo." *International Labor and Working-Class History* 91 (2017): 79–98.

Massey, Doreen. "Globalisation: What Does It Mean for Geography?" *Geography* 87, no. 4 (2002): 293–96.

Massey, Doreen. "Travelling Thoughts." In *Without Guarantees: In Honour of Stuart Hall*, edited by Paul Gilroy, Lawrence Grossberg, and Angela McRobbie. 225–44. London: Verso, 2000.

Mathews, Nathaniel. "Imagining Arab Communities: Colonialism, Islamic Reform, and Arab Identity in Mombasa, Kenya, 1897–1933." *Islamic Africa* 4, no. 2 (2013): 135–63.

Mattingly, Cheryl, and Jason Throop. "The Anthropology of Ethics and Morality." *Annual Review of Anthropology* 47 (2018): 475–92.

Mauss, Marcel. *The Gift: The Form and Reason for Exchange in Archaic Societies.* Translated by W. D. Halls. London: Routledge, 1990 [1954].

Mauss, Marcel. "Les techniques du corps." *Journal de psychologie* 32, nos. 3–4 (1936– 1934): 4–23.

Maussen, Marcel, Veit Bader, and Annelies Moors. *Colonial and Post-colonial Governance of Islam: Continuities and Ruptures.* Amsterdam: Amsterdam University Press, 2011.

Mavhunga, Clapperton Chakanetsa. *Transient Workspaces: Technologies of Everyday Innovation in Zimbabwe.* Cambridge, MA: MIT Press, 2014.

Mavhunga, Clapperton Chakanetsa. "Vermin Beings: On Pestiferous Animals and Human Game." *Social Text* 29, no. 1 (2011): 151–76.

Mbembe, Achille. "Aesthetics of Superfluity." *Public Culture* 16, no. 3 (2004): 373–405.

Mbembe, Achille. "Afropolitan." In *Africa Remix: Contemporary Art of a Continent,* edited by Simon Njami, 26–30. Johannesburg: Jacana, 2007.

Mbembe, Achille. *On the Postcolony.* Berkeley: University of California Press, 2001.

McClenahan, W. L. "Notes on Current Topics: Islam in Madagascar." *Muslim World* 4, no. 1 (1914): 85–98.

McDow, Thomas F. *Buying Time: Debt and Mobility in the Western Indian Ocean.* Athens: Ohio University Press, 2018.

McGranahan, Carole. "Theorizing Refusal: An Introduction." *Cultural Anthropology* 31, no. 3 (2016): 319–25.

McIntosh, Susan Keech. "Pathways to Complexity: An African Perspective." In *Beyond Chiefdoms: Pathways to Complexity in Africa,* edited by Susan McIntosh, 1–30. Cambridge: Cambridge University Press, 1999.

Mehta, Nanji Kalidas. *Dream Half-Expressed: An Autobiography.* Bombay: Vakils, Feffer, and Simons, 1996.

Meier, Prita. *Swahili Port Cities: The Architecture of Elsewhere.* Bloomington: Indiana University Press, 2016.

Meiu, George Paul. "Panics over Plastics: A Matter of Belonging in Kenya." *American Anthropologist* 122, no. 2 (2020): 222–35.

Melly, Caroline. "Inside-Out Houses: Urban Belonging and Imagined Futures in Dakar, Senegal." *Comparative Studies in Society and History* 52, no. 1 (2010): 37–65.

Melly, Caroline. *Bottleneck: Moving, Building, and Belonging in an African City.* Chicago: University of Chicago Press, 2016.

Melosi, Martin. *The Sanitary City: Environmental Services in Urban America from Colonial Times to the Present.* Pittsburgh, PA: University of Pittsburgh Press, 2008.

Merleau-Ponty, Maurice. *Phenomenology of Perception.* Translated by Donald Landes. 1945. New York: Routledge, 2012.

Meskell, Lynn. "Introduction: Globalizing Heritage." In *Global Heritage: A Reader,* edited by Lynn Meskell, 1–21. Chichester, UK: Wiley-Blackwell, 2015.

Middleton, John. *The World of the Swahili: An African Mercantile Civilization.* New Haven, CT: Yale University Press, 1992.

Miescher, Stephan F. "Building the City of the Future: Visions and Experiences of Modernity in Ghana's Akosombo Township." *Journal of African History* 53, no. 3 (2012): 367–90.

Millar, Kathleen. *Reclaiming the Discarded: Life and Labor on Rio's Garbage Dump.* Durham, NC: Duke University Press, 2018.

Mille, Adrien. "Une ancienne forteresse merina du XIXe siècle: Ambohitrombikely." *Annales de l'Université de Madagascar* 7 (1968): 143–51.

Miller, Daniel, ed. *Material Cultures: Why Some Things Matter.* Chicago: University of Chicago Press, 1998.

Miller, Daniel, Lynn Meskell, Michael Rowlands, Fred R. Myers, and Matthew Engelke. *Materiality.* Durham, NC: Duke University Press, 2005.

Mitchell, Timothy. *Rule of Experts: Egypt, Techno-Politics, Modernity.* Berkeley: University of California Press, 2002.

Moat, Justin, and Paul Smith. *Atlas of the Vegetation of Madagascar.* Kew: Key, 2007.

Mohamed, Mzé. "Les 'Sabena' de la grande Comore: Étude d'une migration." *Études océan Indien*, nos. 38–39 (2007): 11–112.

Mohamed, Toibibou Ali. "Entre Anjouanais et Grands-Comoriens à Majunga (1908–1960)." In *Cultures citadines dans l'océan Indien occidental (XVIIIe–XXIe siècles),* edited by Faranirina Rajaonah, 457–66. Paris: Karthala, 2011.

Mohamed, Toibibou Ali. *La transmission de l'islam aux Comores, 1933–2000: Le cas de la ville de Mbéni (Grande-Comore).* Paris: Harmattan, 2008.

Mohr, James. *Plague and Fire: Battling Black Death and the 1900 Burning of Honolulu's Chinatown.* Oxford: Oxford University Press, 2005.

Molet, Louis. *Le bain royal à Madagascar: Explication de la fête malgache du Fandroana par la coutume disparue de la manducation des morts.* Tananarive, Madagascar: Imprimerie luthérienne, 1956.

Monmonier, Mark. *From Squaw Tit to Whorehouse Meadow.* Chicago: University of Chicago Press, 2008.

Monroe, J. Cameron. "Power and Agency in Precolonial African States." *Annual Review of Anthropology* 42 (2013): 17–35.

Monroe, J. Cameron. "Power by Design: Architecture and Politics in Precolonial Dahomey." *Journal of Social Archaeology* 10, no. 3 (2010): 367–97.

Monroe, J. Cameron, and Anneke Janzen. "The Dahomean Feast: Royal Women, Private Politics, and Culinary Practices in Atlantic West Africa." *African Archaeological Review* 31, no. 2 (2014): 299–337.

Morton, David. *Age of Concrete: Housing and the Shape of Aspiration in the Capital of Mozambique.* Athens: Ohio University Press, 2019.

Morton, David. "The Shape of Aspiration: Clandestine Masonry House Construction in Lourenço Marques, Mozambique (1960–75)." *Journal of African History* 59, no. 2 (2018): 283–304.

Mrázek, Rudolf. *Engineers of Happy Land: Technology and Nationalism in a Colony.* Princeton, NJ: Princeton University Press, 2002.

Mujere, Joseph. "Land, Graves and Belonging: Land Reform and the Politics of

Belonging in Newly Resettled Farms in Gutu, 2000–2009." *Journal of Peasant Studies* 38, no. 5 (2011): 1123–44.

Mullens, Joseph. *Twelve Months in Madagascar.* New York: R. Carter, 1875.

Müller, Daniëlle, and Sandra J. T. M. Evers. "Case Studies of Land Access Practices in Fianarantsoa Province, Madagascar." *Taloha* 43, no. 18 (2007).

Munn, Nancy. "Excluded Spaces: The Figure in Australian Aboriginal Landscape." *Critical Inquiry* 22, no. 3 (1996): 446–65.

Murphy, Michelle. *Sick Building Syndrome and the Problem of Uncertainty.* Durham, NC: Duke University Press, 2006.

Murphy, Michelle. "Some Keywords toward Decolonial Methods: Studying Settler Colonial Histories and Environmental Violence from Tkaronto." *History and Theory* 59, no. 3 (2020): 376–84.

Mutibwa, Phares. *The Malagasy and the Europeans: Madagascar's Foreign Relations 1861–1895.* London: Longman, 1974.

Myers, Garth Andrew. "Eurocentrism and African Urbanization: The Case of Zanzibar's Other Side." *Antipode* 26, no. 3 (1994): 195–215.

Myers, Garth. "Naming and Placing the Other: Power and Urban Landscape in Zanzibar." In *Critical Toponymies: The Contested Politics of Place Naming*, edited by Lawrence Berg and Jan Vuolteenaho, 85–100. London: Routledge, 2016 [2009].

Myers, Garth Andrew. "Sticks and Stones: Colonialism and Zanzibari Housing." *Africa* 67, no. 2 (1997): 252–72.

Myers, Garth. *Verandahs of Power: Colonialism and Space in Urban Africa.* Syracuse, NY: Syracuse University Press, 2003.

Nativel, Didier. "À chacun selon ses moyens: Pratiques d'appropriation et construction de modes de vie citadins à Tananarive au XIXe siècle." *Afrique et Histoire* 5, no. 1 (2006): 47–64.

Nativel, Didier. "Les migrants comorians à Majunga et Diego-Suarez durant l'époque coloniale (1895–1960)." In *Etre étranger et migrant en Afrique au XXe diècle: Enjeux identitaires et modes d'insertion*, edited by Catherine Coquery-Vidrovitch, Odile Goerg, I. Mande, and F. Rajaonah, 117–32. Paris: Harmattan, 2003.

Nativel, Didier. *Maisons royales, demeures des grands à Madagascar: L'inscription de la réussite sociale dans l'espace urbain de Tananarive au XIXe siècle.* Paris: Karthala, 2005.

Navaro-Yashin, Yael. *The Make-Believe Space: Affective Geography in a Postwar Polity.* Durham, NC: Duke University Press, 2012.

Navaro, Yael, Zerrin Özlem Biner, Alice von Bieberstein, and Seda Altug, eds. *Reverberations: Violence across Time and Space.* Philadelphia: University of Pennsylvania Press, 2021.

Newbury, Catharine. *The Cohesion of Oppression: Clientship and Ethnicity in Rwanda 1860–1960.* New York: Columbia University Press, 1988.

Newell, Sasha. *The Modernity Bluff: Crime, Consumption, and Citizenship in Cote d'Ivoire.* Chicago: University of Chicago Press, 2012.

Newitt, Malyn. *The Comoro Islands: Struggle against Dependency in the Indian Ocean*. Boulder, CO: Westview Press, 1984.

Nielson, Morten. "A Wedge of Time: Futures in the Present and Presents without Futures in Maputo, Mozambique." *Journal of Royal Anthropological Institute* 20, no. 1 (2014): 166–82.

Nixon, Rob. *Slow Violence and the Environmentalism of the Poor*. Cambridge, MA: Harvard University Press, 2011.

Njoh, Ambe J. "Urban Planning as a Tool of Power and Social Control in Colonial Africa." *Planning Perspectives* 24, no. 3 (2009): 301–317.

Noël, Vincent. *Ile de Madagascar: Recherches sur les Sakkalava*. Paris: Imprimerie de Bourgogne et Martinet, 1843.

Nooter, Nancy Ingram. "Zanzibar Doors." *African Arts* 17, no. 4 (1984): 34–96.

"Notices sur Majunga." *Revue française de l'étranger et des colonies* 22, no. 227 (1897): 542–45.

Nys-Ketels, Simon de, Laurence Heindryckx, Johan Lagae, and Luce Beeckmans. "Planning Belgian Congo's Network of Medical Infrastructure: Type-Plans as Tools to Construct a Medical Model-Colony, 1949–59." *Planning Perspectives* 34, no. 5 (2019): 757–78.

O'Brien, Jean M. *Firsting and Lasting: Writing Indians Out of Existence in New England*. Minneapolis: University of Minnesota Press, 2010.

Oliver, Samuel Pasfield. "French Operations in Madagascar, 1883–1885." *Royal United Services Institution Journal* 30, no. 137 (1886): 1071–1132.

Oliver, Samuel Pasfield. *The True Story of the French Dispute in Madagascar*. London: T. Fisher Unwin, 1885.

Osborne, Michael. *The Emergence of Tropical Medicine in France*. Chicago: University of Chicago Press, 2014.

Osgood, Joseph B. F. *Notes of Travel, Or, Recollections of Majunga, Zanzibar, Muscat, Aden, Mocha, and Other Eastern Ports*. Salem, MA: G. Creamer, 1854.

Otter, Chris. "Locating Matter: The Place of Materiality in Urban History." In *Material Powers: Cultural Studies, History and the Material Turn*, edited by Tony Bennett and Patrick Joyce, 48–69. New York: Routledge, 2013.

Ottino, Paul. "Ancient Malagasy Dynastic Succession: The Merina Example." *History in Africa* 10 (1983): 247–92.

Owen, W. F. W. *Narrative of Voyages to Explore the Shores of Africa, Arabia, and Madagascar, Performed in H.M. Ships Leven and Barracouta under the Direction of Captain W. F. W. Owen, R.N.* 2 vols. New York: J. and J. Harper, 1833.

Parrett, John, and William Edward Cousins. *Ny Òhabòlan'ny Ntaolo: Nangònina sy Nalahatry*. Imarivolanitra, Madagascar: Ny London Missionary Society, 1885.

Pelican, Michaela. "Complexities of Indigeneity and Autochthony: An African Example." *American Ethnologist* 36, no. 1 (2009): 52–65.

Penvenne, Jeanne. *Women, Migration, and the Cashew Economy in Southern Mozambique 1945–1975*. Woodbridge, Suffolk: James Currey, 2015.

Perraud, Antoine. *Escape from Madagascar: Journals of a French Marine, 1884–1887*. Translated by Marilyn O'Day. Renton, WA: Marilyn O'Day, 2002.

Perrier de la Bathie, Henri. "La végétation malgache." *Annales du Musée colonial de Marseille* 3 (1921): 1–268.

"Peste." *Bulletin de l'Académie de Médicine* (1904): 166–67.

Peterson, Derek R. "'Be like firm soldiers to develop the country': Political Imagination and the Geography of Gikuyuland." *International Journal of African Historical Studies* 37, no. 1 (2004): 71–101.

Peterson, Derek. *Ethnic Patriotism and the East African Revival: A History of Dissent, c. 1935–1972*. Cambridge: Cambridge University Press, 2012.

Peterson, Derek R., and Giacomo Macola. *Recasting the Past: History Writing and Political Work in Modern Africa*. Athens: Ohio University Press, 2009.

Petit, Georges. "La vie sur les côtes de Madagascar et l'industrie indigene de la pêche." *Annales de géographie* 32, no. 176 (1923): 142–64.

Pickersgill, W. Clayton. "North Sakalava-Land." *Antananarivo Annual and Madagascar Magazine* 17 (1893): 29–43.

Pickersgill, W. Clayton. "Revision of North-West Place-Names: Some Curiosities of Topographical Nomenclature." *Antananarivo Annual and Madagascar Magazine* 12 (1888): 488–94.

Pickersgill, W. Clayton. "North-West Madagascar—Mojanga." *Evangelical Magazine and Chronicle of the London Missionary Society*, October 1882, 323–28.

Pierre, Jemima. *The Predicament of Blackness: Postcolonial Ghana and the Politics of Race*. Chicago: University of Chicago Press, 2012.

Pilo, Francesca, and Rivke Jaffe. "Introduction: The Political Materiality of Cities." *City and Society* 32, no. 1 (2020): 8–22.

Plageman, Nate. *Highlife Saturday Night: Popular Music and Social Change in Urban Ghana*. Bloomington: Indiana University Press, 2013.

Plamper, Jan. "The History of Emotions: An Interview with William Reddy, Barbara Rosenwein, and Peter Stearns." *History and Theory* 49, no. 2 (2010): 237–65.

Poirier, Jean. "Aspects de l'urbanisation à Madagascar: Les villes malgaches et la population urbaine." *Civilisations* 18, no. 1 (1968): 80–112.

Pradines, Stéphane. "Commerce maritime et islamisation dans l'océan Indien: Les premières mosquées swahilies (XIe–XIIIe siècles)." *Revue des mondes musulmans et de la Méditerranée* 130 (2012): 131–49.

Pradines, Stéphane, ed. *Earthen Architecture in Muslim Cultures: Historical and Anthropological Perspectives*. Leiden: Brill, 2018.

Prange, Sebastian R. *Monsoon Islam: Trade and Faith on the Medieval Malabar Coast*. New York: Cambridge University Press, 2018.

Prasse-Freeman, Elliott. "Resistance/Refusal: Politics of Manoeuvre under Diffuse Regimes of Governmentality." *Anthropological Theory* 22, no. 1 (2022): 102–27.

Prestholdt, Jeremy. *Domesticating the World: African Consumerism and the Genealogies of Globalization*. Berkeley: University of California Press, 2008.

Prestholdt, Jeremy. "Politics of the Soil: Separatism, Autochthony, and Decolonization at the Kenyan Coast." *Journal of African History* 55, no. 2 (2014): 249–70.

Pritchard, Sara. "From Hydroimperialism to Hydrocapitalism: 'French' Hydraulics in France, North Africa, and Beyond." *Social Studies of Science* 42, no. 4 (2012): 591–615.

Prochaska, David. "Fantasia of the Photothèque: French Postcard Views of Colonial Senegal." *African Arts* 24, no. 4 (1991): 40–47.

Prud'Homme, Breveté. "Observations on the Sakalava." *Antananarivo Annual and Madagascar Magazine* 24 (1900): 408–36.

Prussin, Labelle. "An Introduction to Indigenous African Architecture." *Journal of the Society of Architectural Historians* 33, no. 3 (1974): 183–205.

Puig de la Bellacasa, Maria. "Matters of Care in Technoscience: Assembling Neglected Things." *Social Studies of Science* 41, no. 1 (2011): 85–106.

Pype, Katrien. "'[Not] Talking Like a Motorola': Mobile Phone Practices and Politics of Masking and Unmasking in Postcolonial Kinshasa." *Journal of the Royal Anthropological Institute* 22, no. 3 (2016): 633–52.

Quayson, Ato. *Oxford Street, Accra: City Life and Itineraries of Transnationalism.* Durham, NC: Duke University Press, 2014.

Rabbat, Nasser. "Islamic Architecture as a Field of Historical Enquiry." *Architectural Design* 6 (2004): 18–23.

Rabearimanana, Lucile. "Les descendants d'Andevo dans la vie économique et sociale au XXe siècle: Le cas de la Plaine d'Ambohibary Sambaina." In *Fanandevozana ou Esclavage: Colloque international sur l'esclavage à Madagascar,* edited by François Rajason and Ignace Rakoto, 519–32. Antananarivo, Madagascar: Musée d'Art et d'Archéologie de l'Université d'Antananarivo, 1996.

Rabearimanana, Lucile. "Madagascar 1975: De néocolonisme au socialism à la malgache." *Revue historique de l'océan Indien* (2009): 353–64.

Rabinow, Paul. *French Modern: Norms and Forms of the Social Environment.* Chicago: University of Chicago Press, 1989.

Radifison, Nathalie. "Conflits ethniques et leur résolution à Majunga, de 1740 à aujourd'hui." *Études océan Indien,* no. 38–39 (2007): 113–68.

Radimilahy, Chantal. "Ancient Iron-Working in Madagascar." In *The Archaeology of Africa: Food, Metals and Towns,* edited by Bassey Andah, Alex Okpoko, Thurstan Shaw, and Paul Sinclair, 478–93. London: Routledge, 1993.

Radimilahy, Chantal. "Mahilaka: An Archaeological Investigation of an Early Town in Northwestern Madagascar." PhD diss., Uppsala University, 1998.

Radimilahy, Chantal M., and Zoë Crossland. "Situating Madagascar: Indian Ocean Dynamics and Archaeological Histories." *Azania: Archaeological Research in Africa* 50, no. 4 (2015): 495–518.

Raffles, Hugh. *Insectopedia.* New York: Pantheon, 2010.

Raharimanana, Jean Luc. *Des ruines.* Paris: Vents d'ailleurs, 2012.

Raibmon, Paige. "Living on Display: Colonial Visions of Aboriginal Domestic Spaces." *BC Studies: The British Columbian Quarterly* 140 (2003/2004): 69–89

Raison-Jourde, Françoise. *Les souverains de Madagascar: L'histoire royale et ses résurgences contemporaines.* Paris: Karthala, 1983.

Raison-Jourde, Françoise, and Solofo Randrianja, eds. *La nation malgache au défi de l'ethnicité*. Paris: Karthala Editions, 2002.

Raison-Jourde, Françoise, and Gérard Roy. *Paysans, intellectuels et populisme à Madagascar: De Monja Joana à Ratsimandrava (1960–1975)*. Paris: Karthala, 2010.

Rajagopalan, Mrinalini. *Building Histories: The Archival and Affective Lives of Five Monuments in Modern Delhi*. Chicago: University of Chicago Press, 2017.

Rajaonah, Faranirina, ed. *Cultures citadines dans l'océan Indien occidental (XIXe–XXIe siècles): Pluralisme, échanges, inventivité*. Paris: Karthala, 2011.

Rajaonah, Faranirina. "La communauté comorienne d'Antananarivo pendant la colonization: Entre intrégation et marginalisation." In *Être étranger et migrant en Afrique au XXe siècle: Enjeux identitaire et modes d'insertion*, edited by Catherine Coquery-Vidrovitch, Odile Goerg, Issiaka Mandé, and Faranirina Rajanoah, 97–115. Paris: Harmattan, 2003.

Rajaonah, Faranirina. "Modèles européens pour une ville malgache: Antananarivo XIXe–XXe siècle." In *La Ville européene outre-mers: Un modèle conquérant?*, edited by Catherine Coquery-Vidrovitch and Odile Goerg, 149–62. Paris: Harmattan, 1996.

Rajaonah, Faranirina. "Usages et usagers de l'eau à Tamatave pendant la periode coloniale (1896–1960)." In *Politiques d'équipement et services urbaines dans les villes du sud*, edited by Chantal Chanson-Jabeur, Catherine Coquery-Vidrovitch, and Odile Goerg, 171–95. Paris: Harmattan, 2004.

Rajemisa-Raolison, Régis. *Dictionnaire historique et géoraphique de Madagascar*. Fianarantsoa, Madagascar: Librairie Ambozontany, 1966.

Rakotoarisoa, Jean-Aimé. "Sites et monuments de Madagascar: Le Fort Merina de Majunga." *Bulletin de Madagascar* 308 (1971): 95–102.

Randrianja, Solofo. "Élites malgaches: Politique et idéologie (1913–47)." *Omaly sy Anio: Revue d'études historiques* 29–32 (1989): 367–79.

Randrianja, Solofo, and Stephen Ellis. *Madagascar: A Short History*. London: Hurst, 2009.

Rantoandro, Gabriel. "Une communauté mercantile du nord-ouest, les Antalaotra." *Omaly sy Anio* 17–20 (1983–1984): 195–210.

Rantoandro, Gabriel. "Une tradition de construction navale: Les boutres de Majunga." *Omaly sy Anio* 27 (1988): 57–75.

Raombana. *Histoires I*. Fianarantsoa, Madagascar: Librairie Ambozontany, 1980.

Rasoamiaramanana, Micheline. *Aspects économique et sociaux de la vie à Majunga entre 1862–1881*. PhD diss., University of Madagascar, 1981.

Rasoamiaramanana, Micheline. "Les motivations et stratégies d'occupation du nord-ouest de Madagascar jusqu'au XIXe siècle." *Cahiers du CRA* [Centre de Recherches Africaines] 7 (1989): 57–70.

Rasoamiaramanana, Micheline. "Pouvoir merina et esclavage dans le Boina dans la seconde moitie du XIXe diecle (1862–1883)." *Omaly sy Anio* 17–20 (1983–1984): 323–35.

Reddy, William M. *The Navigation of Feeling: A Framework for the History of Emotions.* Cambridge: Cambridge University Press, 2001.

Reno, Josh. *Waste Away: Working and Living with a North American Landfill.* Berkeley: University of California Press, 2016.

Reynaud, Gustave Adolphe. *Considérations sanitaires sur l'expédition de Madagascar et quelques autres expéditions coloniales Françaises et Anglaises, avec une préface de M. de Mahy.* Paris: L. Henry May, 1898.

Richard, François G. *Reluctant Landscapes: Historical Anthropologies of Political Experience in Siin, Senegal.* Chicago: University of Chicago Press, 2018.

Richardson, James. *A New Malagasy–English Dictionary.* Antananarivo, Madagascar: London Missionary Society, 1885.

Rijke-Epstein, Tasha. "Neglect as Effacement: The Multiple Lives of the Jardin Ralaimongo, Mahajanga, Madagascar." *Africa* 88, no. 2 (2018): 352–84.

Rijke-Epstein, Tasha. "On Humble Technologies: Containers, Care, and Water Infrastructure in Northwest Madagascar, 1750s–1960s." *History and Technology* 37, no. 3 (2021): 293–328.

Rijke-Epstein, Tasha. "The Politics of Filth: Sanitation and Competing Moralities in Urban Madagascar 1890s–1972." *Journal of African History* 60, no. 2 (2019): 229–56.

Rizvi, Kishwar. *The Transnational Mosque: Architecture and Historical Memory in the Contemporary Middle East.* Chapel Hill: University of North Carolina Press, 2015.

Roberts, George. "MOLINACO, the Comorian Diaspora, and Decolonisation in East Africa's Indian Ocean." *Journal of African History* (2021): 1–19.

Robinson, David. *Paths of Accommodation: Muslim Societies and French Colonial Authorities in Senegal and Mauritania, 1880–1920.* Athens: Ohio University Press, 2001.

Robinson, Cedric J. *Black Marxism: The Making of the Black Radical Tradition.* Rev. and updated 3rd ed. Chapel Hill: University of North Carolina Press Books, 2020.

Rogaski, Ruth. *Hygienic Modernity: Meanings of Health and Disease in Treaty-Port China.* Berkeley: University of California Press, 2004.

Rogers, Raymond R. "Fine-Grained Debris Flows and Extraordinary Vertebrate Burials in the Late Cretaceous of Madagascar." *Geology* 33, no. 4 (2005): 297–300.

Rogers, Raymond R., Joseph H. Hartman, and David W. Krause. "Stratigraphic Analysis of Upper Cretaceous Rocks in the Mahajanga Basin, Northwestern Madagascar: Implications for Ancient and Modern Faunas." *Journal of Geology* 108, no. 3 (2000): 275–301.

Rose-Redwood, Reuben, Derek Alderman, and Maoz Azaryahu. "Geographies of Toponymic Inscription: New Directions in Critical Place-Name Studies." *Progress in Human Geography* 34, no. 4 (2010): 453–70.

Rosenwein, Barbara H. *Emotional Communities in the Early Middle Ages.* Ithaca, NY: Cornell University Press, 2006.

Rothberg, Michael. *Multidirectional Memory: Remembering the Holocaust in the Age of Decolonization.* Stanford, CA: Stanford University Press, 2009.

Roussilhe, M. "Mission hydrgraphique de Madagascar." *Annales hydrographiques: Recueil de documents et mémoires relatifs à l'hydrographie et à la navigation* 30, no. 2 (1908–1909–1910): 141–98.

Ruud, Jörgen. *Taboo: A Study of the Malagasy Fady.* Oslo: Oslo University Press, Humanities Press, 1960.

Saïd, Mariata Moussa. "Contribution a l'étude des minorites étrangères a Madagascar: Les Comoriens de Majunga 1947–1960." *Identity, Culture and Politics* 1–2 (2007): 101–30.

Sanchez, Samuel. "État marchand et État agraire dans l'océan Indien occidental: Le sultanat de Zanzibar et le royaume de Madagascar (1817–1874)" *Cahiers d'histoire: Revue d'histoire critique* 128 (2015): 37–57. https://doi.org/10.4000/chrhc.4535.

Sanchez, Samuel. "Navigation et gens de mer dans le canal du Mozambique." In *Madagascar et l'Afrique: Entre identité insulaire et appartenances historiques,* edited by Didier Nativel and Faranirina Rajaonah, 103–33. Paris: Karthala, 2007.

Sanchez, Samuel "Un mouvement antiabolitionniste et anticolonial: La révolte sakalava de 1849 dans le Nord-Ouest de Madagascar." In *Traite et esclavage en Afrique Orientale et dans l'océan Indien,* edited by Henri Médard, Marie-Laure Derat, Thomas Vernet, and Marie-Pierre Ballarin, 413–39. Paris: Karthala, 2013.

Saraiva, Tiago. *Fascist Pigs: Technoscientific Organisms and the History of Fascism.* Cambridge, MA: MIT Press, 2018.

Schler, Lynn. "Ambiguous Spaces: The Struggle over African Identities and Urban Communities in Colonial Douala, 1914–45." *Journal of African History* 44, no. 1 (2003): 51–72.

Schoenbrun, David. *A Green Place, a Good Place: Agrarian Change, Gender, and Social Identity in the Great Lakes Region to the 15th Century.* Portsmouth, NH: Heinemann, 1998.

Schoenbrun, David L. "The (In)visible Roots of Bunyoro-Kitara and Buganda in the Lakes Region: 800–1300." In *Beyond Chiefdoms: Pathways to Complexity in Africa,* edited by Susan Keech McIntosh, 136–50. New York: Cambridge University Press, 1999.

Schoenbrun, David L. "Ethnic Formation with Other-Than-Human Beings: Island Shrine Practice in Uganda's Long Eighteenth Century." *History in Africa* 45 (2018): 397–443.

Schoenbrun, David L., and Jennifer L. Johnson. "Introduction: Ethnic Formation with Other-Than-Human Beings." *History in Africa* 45 (2018): 307–45.

Scholz, Natalie. "Ghosts and Miracles: The Volkswagen as Imperial Debris in Postwar West Germany." *Comparative Studies in Society and History* 62, no. 3 (2020): 487–519.

Scott, James C. *Seeing Like a State: How Certain Schemes to Improve the Human Condition Have Failed.* New Haven, CT: Yale University Press, 1998.

Scott, James C. *Weapons of the Weak: Everyday Forms of Peasant Resistance.* New Haven, CT: Yale University Press, 2008.

Seed, Patricia. *Ceremonies of Possession in Europe's Conquest of the New World 1492–1640.* Cambridge: Cambridge University Press, 1995.

Seesemann, Rüdiger, and Benjamin F. Soares. "'Being as Good Muslims as Frenchmen': On Islam and Colonial Modernity in West Africa." *Journal of Religion in Africa* (2009): 91–120.

Sharp, Lesley. "Laboring for the Colony and Nation: The Historicized Political Consciousness of Youth in Madagascar." *Critique of Anthropology* 23, no. 1 (2003): 75–91.

Sharp, Lesley. *The Possessed and the Dispossessed: Spirits, Identity, and Power in a Madagascar Migrant Town.* Berkeley: University of California Press, 1993.

Sharpe, Christina. "Black Studies: In the Wake." *Black Scholar* 44, no. 2 (2014): 59–69.

Shaw, George. *Madagascar and France: With Some Account of the Island, Its People, Its Resources and Development.* London: William Clowes, 1885.

Shaw, Rosalind. *Memories of the Slave Trade: Ritual and the Historical Imagination in Sierra Leone.* Chicago: University of Chicago Press, 2002.

Sheriff, Abdul. "Mosques, Merchants and Landowners in Zanzibar Stone Town." *Azania: Journal of the British Institute in Eastern Africa* 27, no. 1 (1992): 1–20.

Sheriff, Abdul. *Slaves, Spices, and Ivory in Zanzibar: Integration of an East African Commercial Empire into the World Economy, 1770–1873.* Athens: Ohio University Press, 1987.

Shervinton, Kathleen. *The Shervintons: Soldiers of Fortune, Shervinton of Madagascar, Shervinton of Salvador, and Tom Shervinton, NNC.* London: T. Fisher Unwin, 1899.

Shryock, Andrew, and Daniel Lord Smail. *Deep History: The Architecture of Past and Present.* Berkeley: University of California Press, 2011.

Sibree, James. *Madagascar before the Conquest: The Island, the Country, and the People, with Chapters on Travel and Topography, Folk-lore, Strange Customs and Superstitions, the Animal Life of the Island, and Mission Work and Progress among the Inhabitants.* New York: Macmillan, 1896.

Siddiqi, Anooradha Iyer. "Introduction: Architecture as a Form of Knowledge." *Comparative Studies of South Asia, Africa and the Middle East* 40, no. 3 (2020): 495–506.

Simone, AbdouMaliq. *For the City Yet to Come: Changing African Life in Four Cities.* Durham, NC: Duke University Press, 2004.

Simone, AbdouMaliq. "People as Infrastructure: Intersecting Fragments in Johannesburg." *Public Culture* 16, no. 3 (2004): 407–29.

Simpson, Audra. *Mohawk Interruptus: Political Life Across the Borders of Settler States.* Durham, NC: Duke University Press, 2014.

Sobo, Elisa J. "Theorizing (Vaccine) Refusal: Through the Looking Glass." *Cultural Anthropology* 31, no. 3 (2016): 342–50.

Sodikoff, Genese. "Forced and Forest Labor Regimes in Colonial Madagascar, 1926–1936." *Ethnohistory* 52, no. 2 (2005): 407–35.

Sodikoff, Genese. "Land and Languor: Ethical Imaginations of Work and Forest in Northeast Madagascar." *History and Anthropology* 15, no. 4 (2004): 367–98.

Soske, Jon. *Internal Frontiers: African Nationalism and the Indian Diaspora in Twentieth-Century South Africa.* Athens: Ohio University Press, 2017.

Spear, Thomas. "Neo-traditionalism and the Limits of Invention in British Colonial Africa." *Journal of African History* 44, no. 1 (2003): 3–27.

Spivak, Gayatri Chakravorty. "Can the Subaltern Speak?" In *Marxism and the Interpretation of Culture,* edited by Cary Nelson and Larry Grossberg, 271–313. Urbana: University of Illinois Press, 1988.

Stahl, Ann B. "Africa in the World: (Re)centering African History through Archaeology." *Journal of Anthropological Research* 70, no. 1 (2014): 5–33.

Stoebenau, Kirsten, "'Côtier' Sexual Identity as Constructed by the Urban Merina of Antananarivo, Madagascar." *Études océan Indien* 45 (2010): 93–115.

Stoler, Ann Laura. *Along the Archival Grain: Epistemic Anxieties and Colonial Common Sense.* Princeton, NJ: Princeton University Press, 2010.

Stoler, Ann Laura. "Epistemic Politics: Ontologies of Colonial Common Sense." *Philosophical Forum* 39, no. 3 (2008): 349–61.

Strother, Zoë. "Architecture against the State: The Virtues of Impermanence in the Kibulu of Eastern Pende Chiefs in Central Africa." *Journal of the Society of Architectural Historians* 63, no. 3 (2004): 272–95.

Swanson, Maynard. "The Sanitation Syndrome: Bubonic Plague and Urban Native Policy in the Cape Colony, 1900–1909." *Journal of African History* 18, no. 3 (1977): 387–410.

Tarr, Joel. "The Separate vs. Combined Sewer Problem: A Case Study in Urban Technology Design Choice." *Journal of Urban History* 5, no. 3 (1979): 308–39.

Tarr, Joel, and Francis Clay McMichael. "The Evolution of Wastewater Technology and the Development of State Regulation: A Retrospective Analysis." In *Retrospective Technology Assessment,* 165–90. San Francisco, CA: San Francisco Press, 1977.

Taussig, Michael. *The Devil and Commodity Fetishism in South America.* 1980. Chapel Hill: University of North Carolina Press, 2010.

Taylor, Isaac. *Names and Their Histories: A Handbook of Historical Geography and Topographical Nomenclature.* London: Rivingtons, 1898.

Taylor, Vanessa, and Frank Trentmann. "Liquid Politics: Water and the Politics of Everyday Life in the Modern City." *Past and Present* 211, no. 1 (2011): 199–241.

Testa, Jean-Pierre. "Habitat traditionnel ancien." *Revue de Madagascar* (1972): 73–110.

Thiebaut, Rafael. "The Role of 'Brokers' in Securing the Dutch Slave Trade on Madagascar during the Eighteenth Century." In *Fluid Networks and Hegemonic Powers in the Western Indian Ocean,* edited by Iain Walker, Manuel João Ramos, and Preben Kaarsholm, 37–64. Lisbon: CEI-IUL, 2017.

Thomas, Julia Adeney. "History and Biology in the Anthropocene: Problems of Scale, Problems of Value." *American Historical Review* 119, no. 5 (2014): 1587–1607.

Thomas, Lynn M., and Jennifer Cole. "Introduction: Thinking through Love in Africa." In *Love in Africa*, edited by Jennifer Cole and Lynn Thomas, 1–30. Chicago: University of Chicago Press, 2009.

Thomas, Nicholas. *Entangled Objects: Exchange, Material Culture, and Colonialism in the Pacific*. Cambridge, MA: Harvard University Press, 2009.

Thomas, Philip. "The River, the Road, and the Rural-Urban Divide: A Postcolonial Moral Geography from Southeast Madagascar." *American Ethnology* 29, no. 2 (2002): 366–91.

Thompson, Virginia, and Richard Adloff. *Malagasy Republic: Madagascar Today*. Stanford, CA: Stanford University Press, 1965.

Throop, C. Jason. "Moral Sentiments." In *A Companion to Moral Anthropology*, edited by Didier Fassin, 150–68. Malden, MA: John Wiley and Sons, 2012.

Tisseau, Violaine. "Madagascar: Une île métisse sans métis?—La catégorie 'métis' et son contournement dans les Hautes Terres centrales de Madagascar pendant la période coloniale (1896–1960)." *Anthropologie et sociétés* 38, no. 2 (2014): 27–44.

Troeger, Christopher, Brigette F. Blacker, Ibrahim A. Khalil, Puja C. Rao, Shujin Cao, and S. R. Zimsen. "Estimates of the Global, Regional, and National Morbidity, Mortality, and Aetiologies of Diarrhoea in 195 Countries: A Systematic Analysis for the Global Burden of Disease Study 2016." *Lancet Infectious Diseases* 18, no. 11 (2018): 1211–28.

Tronchon, Jacques. *L'insurrection malgache de 1947*. Paris: Karthala, 1986.

Trouillot, Michel-Rolph. *Silencing the Past: Power and the Production of History*. Boston: Beacon Press, 2015.

Trouillot, Michel-Rolph. "Anthropology and the Savage Slot: The Poetics and Politics of Otherness." In *Recapturing Anthropology: Working in the Present*, edited by Richard G. Fox, 17–44. Santa Fe, NM: School of American Research Press, 1991.

Tsing, Anna. *The Mushroom at the End of the World: On the Possibility of Life in Capitalist Ruins*. Princeton, NJ: Princeton University Press, 2015.

Tuck, Eve, and Wayne Yang. "Decolonization Is Not a Metaphor." *Education and Society* 1, no. 1 (2012): 1–40.

Um, Nancy. *The Merchant Houses of Mocha: Trade and Architecture in an Indian Ocean Port*. Seattle: University of Washington Press, 2011.

Vahed, Goolam. "'Unhappily Torn by Dissensions and Litigations': Durban's 'Memon' Mosque, 1880–1930." *Journal of Religion in Africa* 36, no. 1 (2006): 23–49.

Valenčius, Conevery Bolton. "Histories of Medical Geography." In *Medical Geography in Historical Perspective*, edited by Nicolaas A. Rupke, 3–30. London: Wellcome Trust Centre for the History of Medicine, 2001.

Valentin, Frédérique, Beby Ramanivosoa, Dominique Gommery, and Sabine Tombomiadana-Raveloson. "Les abris sépulcraux de la presqu'île de Narinda (Province de Mahajanga, Madagascar)." *Afrique: Archéologie Arts* 4 (2006): 7–22.

Valette, Jean. "Réflexions pour une edition des journaux d'Hastie." *Bulletin de Madagascar* 264 (1968): 472–74.

Van Der Geest, Sjaak. "The Night-Soil Collector: Bucket Latrines in Ghana." *Postcolonial Studies: Culture, Politics, Economy* 5, no. 2 (2002): 197–206.

Van Onselen, Charles. *Studies in the Social and Economic History of the Witwatersrand, 1886–1914*. Johannesburg: Ravan Press, 1982.

Vasco, Gabriel. "Majunga et son occupation." *Revue française de l'étranger et des colonies et Exploration Gazette Géographique* (1895): 75–80.

Vasco, Gabriel. "Madagascar." *Revue française de l'étranger et des colonies et Exploration Gazette Géographique* (1895): 75–87.

Vérin, Pierre. "Les échelles anciennes du commerce sur les côtes nord de Madagascar." PhD diss., Université de Lille, 1975.

Vérin, Pierre. *The History of Civilisation in North Madagascar*. Boston: A. A. Balkema, 1986.

Vérin, Pierre, and Henry Wright. "Madagascar and Indonesia: New Evidence from Archaeology and Linguistics." *Bulletin of the Indo-Pacific Prehistory Association* 18 (1999): 35–42.

Veyrières, Paul de, and Guy de Méritens. *Le livre de la sagesse malgache*. Paris: Éditions maritimes et d'outre-mer, 1967.

Voarintsoa, Ny Raivo, Lixin Wang, L. Bruce Railsback, George Brook, Fuyuan Liang, Hai Cheng, and R. Lawrence Edwards. "Multiple Proxy Analyses of a U/Th-dated Stalagmite to Reconstruct Paleoenvironmental Changes in Northwestern Madagascar between 370 CE and 1300 CE." *Palaeogeography, Palaeoclimatology, Palaeocecology* 469 (2017): 138–55.

Von Jedina, L. *Voyage de la frégate autrichienne Helgoland autour de l'Afrique, par Leopold de Jedina, Lieutenant de Vaisseau autrichien*. Translated by M. Vallee. Paris: M. Dreyfus, 1878.

von Schnitzler, Antina. *Democracy's Infrastructure: Techno-Politics and Protest after Apartheid*. Princeton, NJ: Princeton University Press, 2016.

Vorontsova, Maria S., Guillaume Besnard, Félix Forest, Panagiota Malakasi, Justin Moat, W. Derek Clayton, Paweł Ficinski, et al. "Madagascar's Grasses and Grasslands: Anthropogenic or Natural?" *Proceedings of the Royal Society B: Biological Sciences* 283, no. 1823 (2016): 1–8.

Walker, Iain. *Islands in a Cosmopolitan Sea: A History of the Comoros*. New York: Oxford University Press, 2019.

Walker, Iain, Marie-Aude Fouéré, and Nadine Beckmann. "Un explorateur allemande à Ngazidja en 1864, Otto Kersten." *Etudes océan Indien* 53/54 (2018): 349–93.

Walker, John. "Islam in Madagascar." *Muslim World* 22, no. 4 (1932): 383–97.

Walsh, Andrew. "'Hot Money' and Daring Consumption in a Northern Malagasy Sapphire-Mining Town." *American Ethnologist* 30, no. 2 (2003): 290–305.

Walsh, Andrew. "Responsibility, Taboos and 'the Freedom to Do Otherwise' in Ankarana, Northern Madagascar." *Journal of the Royal Anthropological Institute* 8, no. 3 (2002): 451–68.

Waterson, Roxana. *The Living House: An Anthropology of Architecture in South-East Asia.* New York: Oxford University Press, 1990.

Weitzberg, Keren. *We Do Not Have Borders: Greater Somalia and the Predicaments of Belonging in Kenya.* Athens: Ohio University Press, 2017.

Werbner, Pnina. *Pilgrims of Love: The Anthropology of a Global Sufi Cult.* Bloomington: Indiana University Press, 2003.

West, Harry G. *Kupilikula: Governance and the Invisible Realm in Mozambique.* Chicago: University of Chicago Press, 2005.

Westra, P. E, and James C Armstrong. *Slave Trade with Madagascar: The Journals of the Cape Slaver Leijdsman, 1715 = Slawehandel Met Madagaskar : Die Joernale van Die Kaapse Slaweskip Leijdsman, 1715.* Kaapstad [Cape Town]: Africana Uitgewers, 2006.

White, Richard. *The Middle Ground: Indians, Empires, and Republics in the Great Lakes Region, 1650–1815.* 1991. New York: Cambridge University Press, 2011.

White, Luise. *The Comforts of Home: Prostitution in Colonial Nairobi.* Chicago: University of Chicago Press, 1990.

Wickens, Gerald Ernest, and Pat Lowe, *The Baobabs: Pachycauls of Africa, Madagascar and Australia.* Dordrecht, Netherlands: Kluwer, 2008.

Wit, Maarten J. de. "Madagascar: Heads It's a Continent, Tails It's an Island." *Annual Review of Earth and Planetary Sciences* 31, no. 1 (2003): 213–48.

Wright, Gwendolyn. *The Politics of Design in French Colonial Urbanism.* Chicago: University of Chicago Press, 1991.

Wright, Henry T. "Early Islam, Oceanic Trade and Town Development on Nzwani: The Comorian Archipelago in the XIth–XVth Centuries AD." *Azania: Journal of the British Institute in Eastern Africa* 27, no. 1 (1992): 81–128.

Wright, Henry, and Jean-Aimé Rakotoarisoa. "The Rise of Malagasy Societies." In *The Natural History of Madagascar,* edited by Steven Goodman and Jonathan Benstead, 112–19. Chicago: University of Chicago Press, 2003.

Wright, Henry T., Carla Sinopoli, Laura Wojnaroski, Ellen S. Hoffman, Susan L. Scott, Richard W. Redding, and Steven M. Goodman. "Early Seafarers of the Comoro Islands: The Dembeni Phase of the IXth–Xth Centuries AD." *Azania: Journal of the British Institute in Eastern Africa* 19, no. 1 (1984): 13–59.

Wright, Henry T., Pierre Vérin, Ramilisonina, David Burney, Lida Pigott Burney, and Katsumi Matsumoto. "The Evolution of Settlement Systems in the Bay of Boeny and the Mahavavy River Valley, North-Western Madagascar." *Azania: Journal of the British Institute in Eastern Africa* 31, no. 1 (1996): 37–73.

Wynne, Brian. "Misunderstood Misunderstandings: Social Identities and the Public Uptake of Science." In *Misunderstanding Science? The Public Reconstruction of Science and Technology,* edited by Alan Irwin and Brian Wynne, 19–46. Cambridge: Cambridge University Press, 1996.

Wynne-Jones, Stephanie. "Biographies of Practice and the Negotiation of Swahili at Nineteenth-century Vumba." In *Medical Geography in Historical Perspective,* edited by François G. Richard, 155–75. New York: Springer, 2015.

Wynne-Jones, Stephanie. "The Public Life of the Swahili Stone House, 14th–15th Centuries AD." *Journal of Anthropological Archaeology* 32, no. 4 (2013): 759–73.

Wynne-Jones, Stephanie. "Thinking Houses through Time." *Norwegian Archaeological Review* 51, no. 1–2 (2018): 166–69.

Wynne-Jones, Stephanie, and Jeffrey Fleisher, "Swahili Urban Spaces of the Eastern African Coast." In *Making Ancient Cities: Space and Place in Early Urban Societies*, edited by Andrew Creekmore III and Kevin D. Fisher, 111–44. Cambridge: Cambridge University Press, 2014.

Wynne-Jones, Stephanie, and Adria Jean LaViolette, eds. *The Swahili World*. New York: Routledge, 2018.

Yaneva, Albena. *Five Ways to Make Architecture Political: An Introduction to the Politics of Design Practice*. London: Bloomsbury Publishing, 2017.

Yeoh, Brenda. "Street-Naming and Nation-Building: Toponymic Inscriptions of Nationhood in Singapore." *Area* (1996): 298–307.

Zafimahova, Vanessa. "Fahadiovana: Tsy azo anariana fako intsony ao Manapatanana fa eny Mangatokana indray." *Inona no Vaovao*, June 24, 2011.

Zahra, Tara. "Imagined Noncommunities: National Indifference as a Category of Analysis." *Slavic Review* 69, no. 1 (2010): 93–119.

Zemon Davis, Natalie. *Fiction in the Archives: Pardon Tales and Their Tellers in Sixteenth-Century France*. Stanford, CA: Stanford University Press, 1987.

Note: page numbers followed by *f* refer to figures.

imaginaries, 163; collective, 3; around colonial infrastructures, 209; descent-based, 275n8; durability and, 2; French, 206; liberatory, 13; political, 14; unscripted, 4; utopian, 91

Imerina, 60–62, 74, 253n6; government of, 258n88; imperial rule of, 106; monarchy, 67, 78, 81

imperialism: French, 128; hydroimperialism, 204, 287n39

indebtedness, 40, 135, 175, 270n37

Indian communities, 48, 89, 106; mosque construction and, 138; Shi'ite, 128

Indian Ocean, 2; circulating knowledge, 127; Madagascar and 7, 10, 26, 29; migrants, 88, 105, 1273–1; Muslim communities, 67–, 108, 1313–6, 147, 155; sixteen towns and cities, 29, 60, 73; trade routes, 32, 343–5, 464–7; 505–2

Indians, 6, 12, 48, 50, 254n14, 260n4, 265n92; African historiography and, 88; labor and, 121; limestone homes of, 108; Muslim, 105, 142–43; oceanic connections of, 110; plague and, 87, 117, 119; racial hierarchy and, 167; as rentier class, 178; urbanism and, 89. *See also* Karana

indigeneity, 6, 14, 17–18, 164, 171–72

indigenes, 96–97, 123, 207, 210, 261n21, 267n3

Indonesia, 7; colonial, 183

infrastructure, 11, 89, 91, 101, 198–99, 211, 214, 221, 223, 286n12; colonial-era, 6, 121, 196, 209; labor dimensions of, 285n7; nature as, 286n18; people as, 197; peopling of, 196, 222; power of, 285n6; projects, 72, 115, 121, 215, 257n81; provision of, 287n49; rats and, 120; sanitation, 212, 220, 222; water, 206–7

intermarriage, 49, 142, 156

Islam, 128, 136–38, 140, 168, 270n44, 285n61; Masombika practices of, 252n81; Sunni, 21

Islamic communities, 12, 131, 142, 148

Islamic traders, 9, 17, 55–56, 91. *See also* Antalaotra

Islamic world, 34, 136, 139, 147, 150, 281–82n113

Karana, 73–74, 82, 112, 262–63n45, 266n97, 271n49; commerce, 266n108; families, 106–7, 110, 117, 121–22; traders, 121. *See also* Indians

Katsepy, 30, 63

kinship, 48, 128–29, 142, 163, 169, 200, 231

knowledge, 5, 8, 13, 28–29; commercial, 44, 115; ecological, 47, 115, 206; planning and design, 125–27; regimes of, 11, 42, 58; ritual, 66, 82, 136, 146, 155, 193, 242n21; technical, 7, 34, 49, 51, 74, 76–77, 94, 113, 149, 179

labor, 3, 14, 29, 47; access to, 60; architectural, 18, 1484–9; care, 1565–7, 202; and colonial conquest, 969–9; conditions of, 266n107; costs, 107; forced, 10, 72–73, 78, 92, 112, 128, 277nn24–25; hierarchies of, 220; household, 201; infrastructural, 196–97, 285n7; Makoa, 94; markets, 121, 230, 266n107; migrant, 126; migrants, 184, 192–93; migration, 125, 131, 177; movements, 13; networks, 108; norms, 71; political communities and, 8; power, 82; regimes, 11, 45, 58–59, 72, 198, 205, 221, 264n68, 277n24; relations of, 171; reservoir, 165; rice fields and, 35; sanitation, 218, 220–21; scarcity of, 113, 115, 120, 166; sewage, 216, 226; shortages, 12, 111; wage, 818–3, 128–29, 135–36, 162, 178, 215; waste, 203, 222–23; of water provision, 222

laborers, 12, 74, 92, 112, 114–15, 129, 131, 216, 220–21, 277n23; Chinese, 115, 264nn80–81; coerced, 16; Comorian, 261n27; Comorian-Malagasy, 6; conscripted, 79, 82; demand for, 44, 142; emancipated, 202; enslaved, 62, 78; indentured, 8, 114–15, 264nn79–80; local, 58, 97–98; Makoa, 9; migrant, 12, 90, 114, 117, 215, 219; prison, 112, 114, 215; refusal of, 91; sanitation, 212, 215; sewage, 198; water, 205

Ranavalona I, 63, 66, 78

Rasoamiaramanana, Micheline, 73, 249n31

Rasoherina, 79, 258n106

Ratsiraka, Didier, 229–30, 233–34, 273n77, 290n1, 291n11

Ravahiny, 46, 49–51, 251n67, 252n88; fady and, 9

reciprocity, 45–46, 50, 126, 157, 282n114; between living and dead, 19; broken cycle of, 229, 238; Islamic ethos of, 167; logic of, 175; networks of, 193; Ravahiny and, 252n88. *See also* shikoa (communal sharing and economizing)

refusal, 91–92, 95, 97, 111, 121, 193, 238; architectural, 9, 15, 18, 46, 53, 91; collective, 73; of colonial logic, 135; of laborers, 16, 58, 91, 112–14, 120; politics of, 65

relics, 256nn53–54, 286n25; ancestral, 71, 200; Sakalava royal, 10, 41, 58, 64–67, 79–82, 84, 255n41

repair, 10, 16, 18, 24, 215; infrastructure, 198; sanitation, 220; ship, 52–53

resistance, 91, 193; anticolonial, 89; buildings and, 15; everyday, 90; to French military conquest, 97; Malagasy, 135; to obligatory labor, 92

rice, 1, 7, 29, 35, 44, 47, 70–71, 103, 117, 177, 248n21; cultivation, 257n81; plantations, 219; provision of, 107, 265n87

Rifā'īyah, 136, 140, 143, 151. *See also* Maskiriny Rifa'i

ritual experts, 127, 180; Merina, 82; Sakalava, 17, 58, 65, 68, 79

roadbuilding, 113–15, 264n77

rootedness, 105, 190, 263n49

rotaka (upheaval of 1976–77), 7, 165, 227–39, 290n1

sacred spaces, 146, 156; Sakalava, 55

sajoa (water jugs), 200, 202, 203f

sand, 7, 27, 73, 97, 288n61; as building material, 49, 74, 102, 120, 127, 149

sanitation, 211–17, 222–23, 290n103; facilities, 117; infrastructural design, 198;

rapid, 207; work, 196–97, 218, 220–21. *See also* latrines; Mahajanga: sewage system; mpanary tay

Saribengo hilltop, 9–10, 56–59, 81–82, 105; rova (royal palace and fort), 5, 42, 55, 58, 62, 64, 66, 94, 96, 103, 199, 226

satrana palm, 14, 58, 82; as building/construction material, 43, 65, 69–70, 75, 94, 179, 181; fences, 189

self-determination, 13, 53, 184

Shadhiliyya, 131–32, 136–37, 140, 144, 147, 169, 269n27, 270n41. *See also* Maskiriny Shadhiliyya

shame, 79, 185, 196, 216, 218, 220

shikoa (communal sharing and economizing), 147–48, 175–76, 178, 273n77, 273n79

Silamo, 79, 161, 167, 231, 238, 274n1, 278n37, 282n114

silence, 4; rotaka (upheaval of 1976–77) and, 228; sewage laborers and, 198

slavery, 44–45, 258n86; enslaved people (andevo) 10, 40–41, 44, 46, 48, 73–74, 105, 220, 257n79; former, 129–30; royal, 49; slave trade, 38, 48, 60, 204, 249n23; Indian Ocean, 10; trans-Mozambican channel, 8

socialist period 230; revolution, 233

sociality, 13, 62, 109, 142, 198, 210; of Comorians, 162; flows of, 182, 282n118; fraternal, 6, 126; networks of, 193; spontaneous, 161; of street life, 169

solidarity, 18, 126, 135, 142, 154, 167; collective, 155, 193; Islamic, 147, 273n77; social, 175

spirit realm, 33, 59

spirits, 66, 8–84, 226, 242n11; Sakalava, 285n161; troubled, 180; unwanted, 236; vazimba, 200. *See also* ancestral spirits

stone houses, 2, 9–10, 38, 41, 74, 106, 110, 186f, 241n2; builders of, 252n81

stone structures, 6, 38, 91, 107, 150; import of, 246n63

subalterns, 68; emotions of, 127; homes of, 120

Sufi communities, 128, 149, 154
Surat, 29, 43, 47–48, 52, 105
Swahili coast, 7, 10, 29, 74, 146, 182, 245n52; cities, 243n30; distinctive features of mosques along, 151; interior aesthetic of homes along, 110; merchants, 34; mosque construction along, 138; stone construction along, 49, 246n63
Swahili world, 139, 150; Sufi ties between diasporic Muslims in, 152

tactics, 16, 46; agentive, 91, 242n13; architectural, 5, 29, 53; of architectural governance, 8; trading, 87
takamaka tree (*Calophyllum inophyllum*), 47, 251n73
Tandroy, 177, 186, 195
temporalities, 15, 155–56; of architectural forms, 4; of Mahajanga's material composition, 215; overlapping, 7
thatch, 7, 15, 27, 29, 38, 71, 77f, 123, 179, 184–85; regenerative capacity of, 226; satrana, 94, 181
tombs, 38, 66, 99, 107–8, 213, 231, 263n51; ancestral, 14, 55, 103; family, 21; Muslim, 233, 271n49; Sakalava, 40–41, 45, 179; stone, 48, 251n61
tompontany (masters of the land), 37, 172–73, 190
Tongay, 39, 41, 250n48
topographies, 4, 83–84, 89, 222; of intimate being, 163; material, 178; moral, 2; urban, 52
toponyms, 27–29, 34, 47, 247n4, 247n11. *See also* naming
Trouillot, Michel-Rolph, 4, 102, 243n39, 267n6
Tsirinana, Philibert, 137, 217, 229–30, 232–33, 284n151

urban designers, 125, 212
urban designs, 4, 13

urbanism, 18, 22, 90, 125, 135; colonial, 5; performed, 89; zanatany, 6
urban life, 14, 111, 121, 164; alternative paths for, 226; colonial, 126; improvisational practices and, 275n7; Islam and, 156; state and, 242n13
urban planning, 14, 90–91, 125; colonial, 89, 180, 222; as social engineering, 260n7

vagabondage, 161–62, 169, 274n2
vahiny, 6, 163, 171–73, 187, 192, 235
veneration, 15; ancestral, 38; of relics, 66
violence, 16, 38, 92, 172, 196, 198, 223, 226–27, 231, 235–36, 239; cartographic, 103; collective, 204, 230; exclusionary, 238; performances of, 61; settler-colonial, 28

waste, 23, 196–99, 211–15, 223, 288n69, 289n79; disposal, 179; labor, 203, 220, 222; removal, 197, 199, 218–19, 221; systems, 6, 197, 213, 221. *See also* cesspools; latrines; Mahajanga: sewage system
water, 27, 33, 149, 198–211, 213–14, 228, 288n67, 289n76; fresh, 43, 94; healing properties of, 32; salt, 288n64; spirits, 4; systems, 6, 101, 196–97, 200, 205, 209, 211, 215, 221–23, 286n29. *See also* Betsiboka
wind, 27, 150

zanatany, 2, 6–7, 13, 17–20, 146, 163–64, 171–76, 186, 189–90, 192–94, 244n43, 276n12, 279nn67–69, 280n74; discourses of, 126; families, 170, 184–85, 188; homes, 165, 182, 188; rotaka (upheaval of 1976–77) and, 227, 233–34, 237; spirits and, 285n161; street culture, 235; way of life, 135
Zanzibar, 11, 47, 63, 104, 136, 179, 251n73; subaltern intellectuals in, 245n61